D1187658

TX   Bennett,
335   1001 ways to stretch a
.B42   dollar

JUN 1

DATE DUE			
MAY 24 '78	APR 0 7 1986		
JAN 23 '80	APR 2 9 1986		
FEB 1 '82	APR 1 8 1995		
MAY 3 '82			
AUG 9 '82	JUN 2 7 '82		
JUL 14 '83			
SEP 22 '83			
May 23-84			
NOV 20 '84			
FEB 13 '85			
AUG 04 1994			

1001 Ways to Stretch a Dollar

Also by Vivo Bennett and Cricket Clagett / **1001 Ways to Be Your Own Boss**

Vivo Bennett
and Cricket
Clagett

1001 Ways to Stretch a Dollar

PRENTICE-HALL, INC., Englewood Cliffs, New Jersey

1001 Ways to Stretch a Dollar
by Vivo Bennett and Cricket Clagett
Copyright © 1977 by Vivo Bennett and Alice Clagett
All rights reserved. No part of this book may be
reproduced in any form or by any means, except
for the inclusion of brief quotations in a review,
without permission in writing from the publisher.
Printed in the United States of America
Prentice-Hall International, Inc., London
Prentice-Hall of Australia, Pty. Ltd., Sydney
Prentice-Hall of Canada, Ltd., Toronto
Prentice-Hall of India Private Ltd., New Delhi
Prentice-Hall of Japan, Inc., Tokyo
Prentice-Hall of Southeast Asia Pte. Ltd., Singapore
Whitehall Books Limited, Wellington, New Zealand

10 9 8 7 6 5 4 3 2 1

Library of Congress Cataloging in Publication Data
Bennett, Vivo.
    1001 ways to stretch a dollar.
    Includes bibliographical references.
    1. Consumer education.   I. Clagett, Cricket,
joint author.   II. Title.
TX335.B42   640.73   77-2817
ISBN 0-13-636688-0
ISBN 0-13-636670-8   pbk.

This book is dedicated to Hugh Clagett of Mills, Clagett
& Wening, Architects-Engineers-Planners;
to Katherine Clagett, who came up with the original idea;
and to Sylvia Bayer, who diligently and artfully
employs many of the suggestions contained herein.
In addition, we would like to pay special tribute to the
loving memory of Leon Bayer.

ACKNOWLEDGMENT

To John Douglas Clagett (DKSTUJ),
in appreciation for comments and assistance!

CONTENTS

1001 Ways to Stretch a Dollar

HOW TO STRETCH A DOLLAR

As a hurricane descends on a ship at sea, the whirlwind of inflation has swooped down and engulfed all of us, rich and poor alike. More so than ever before, it seems as if yesterday's affluence is today's poverty. For one out of ten, the paychecks have stopped completely; with monthly income perhaps amounting to a less-than-adequate unemployment or public assistance check.

What is the answer to this drastic dollar dilemma? The best solution is to start your own business—to write your own generous paycheck. In our book *1001 Ways to Be Your Own Boss*, we told you how to do just that. But the book you're about to read concerns *conserving* the funds you now have. You'll learn how to stretch your dollars two, four, even ten times as far. You can enjoy steak every day of the week, if that is your whim. You can buy that new home, or even a vacation home by the sea. Your children can go to the finest colleges. You can travel in style and still have money in the bank! You can live like a prince on a pauper's paycheck!

Let us begin with the following list of twenty-four general, but excellent, source ideas for making your dollars stretch to the utmost.

1

- *Buy direct from the manufacturer or the wholesaler.* See your Yellow Pages. For factory outlets, read Jean Bird's *Factory Outlet Shopping Guides*, P.O. Box 95, Oradell, New Jersey 07649, 1975 (eastern United States); *S.O.S. Save on Shopping: Thirty-Five Hundred Factory Outlets*, Iris Ellis, *S.O.S. Directory*, Inc., P.O. Box 10482, Jacksonville, Florida 32207, 1974; or *The Factory Outlet Bargain Book*, Judith Bonnesen and Janet Burkley, New York, Tower (orders to Belmont-Tower); 1972.
- *Become a member of* Consumer Digest, 6316 North Lincoln Avenue, Chicago, Illinois 60659. Membership entitles you to discounts of up to 30 percent on products advertised in Consumer Digest's *Annual Price-Buying Directory*. Subscribe to *Consumer Reports, Consumers' Research Magazine, Consumer Life*, and *Consumer Gazette* for up-to-date tips on bargain buying and product quality.
- *Shop discount department stores*—which now exist in every major marketing area of the country. Bulk buying and label removing allow such stores to offer top brands at surprisingly low prices.
- *Introduce yourself to auctions* where you'll find everything from autos to xylophones. For details, get Michael De Forrest's *How to Buy at Auction*, New York, Cornerstone Library (orders to Simon & Schuster), 1974.
- *Patronize thrift shops*, your "secondhand department stores." Check out Goodwill, Purple Heart, St. Vincent de Paul Center Stores, Volunteers of America, and the Salvation Army. See your Yellow Pages under "Thrift shops" for small dealers. Also check under "Product [whatever]—used." For more information on thrift shop clothes buying, get *Cheap Chic*, Caterine Milinaire and Carol Troy, New York, Harmony (orders to Crown), 1976.
- *Claim the unclaimed!* A myriad of low-priced, unclaimed merchandise awaits you at such places as photo stores, small appliance repair shops, power tool repair facilities, dry cleaning and laundry plants, pawn shops, and moving and storage companies. At one of the latter, we once found a beautiful unclaimed Duncan Phyfe bed for $10, not to mention a sturdy dinette set for $7. See your Yellow Pages under the appropriate product name. Also read *Consumer Guide to Used and Surplus Home Appliances and Furnishings*, Patricia Wilson, Boston, Houghton Mifflin, 1973.
- *Search bulletin boards* at supermarkets, laundromats, health food stores, colleges, and community centers.
- *Garage sales* (alias porch, patio, tag, or yard sales) can get you fantastic bargains on all types of merchandise. For fine points of this art, get *The Garage Sale Shopper: A Complete Illustrated Guide for Buyers and Sellers*, Sunny Wicka, Dafran House, 185 Bethpage Sweet Hollow Road, Old Bethpage, New York 11804, 1973.
- *Church charity bazaars* can yield handmade pocketbooks for $2; pillows for a quarter. See your Yellow Pages under "Religious organizations."
- *Check classified ads* in straight and underground newspapers. Don't overlook swap sheet, pennysaver, or flea market newspapers such as the Atlanta *Advertiser*, New York *Buy-Lines*, *Customart Press* (New York, New Jersey, Con-

necticut, California, Florida), the Denver *Rocky Mountain Trader*, the Nashville *Trader's Post*, and the Seattle *Little Nickel*. See your Yellow Pages under "Publishers—periodical."

● *Shop by mail*. For addresses of mail-order firms, get the *World-Wide Mail Order Shoppers' Guide: How to Shop at Home and Abroad by Mail*, Eugene Moller, Staten Island, New York, E. V. Moller (orders to C & M Enterprises), 1973; *Mail Order USA: A Consumer's Guide to Over 1500 Top Mail Order Catalogs in the United States and Canada*, Dorothy O'Callaghan, ed., Mail Order USA, P.O. Box 19083, Washington, D.C. 20036; or *The New Catalogue of Catalogues*, Maria de la Iglesia, New York, Random House, 1975.

● *Find special sales* in newspaper display ads—seasonal merchandise specials and supermarket loss leaders.

● *Do-it-yourself*. For the most savings, do it from scratch with plans from *Mechanix Illustrated* Plans Service, Fawcett Building, Greenwich, Connecticut 06830 (*Home Workshop Handbook and Plans Catalog*, $1.35). Plans are also available through *Family Handyman* and *Popular Science*, or specialty catalogs such as *Heathkit* (electronics) and *Herter's* (sports).

● *Kits*. These require less effort but a little more cash than from-scratch work, yet they are still 50 percent less than retail. Get the *Catalog of Kits*, Jeffrey Fernman, ed., West Caldwell, New Jersey, William Morrow & Company, 1975. Check display and classified ads of the specialty catalog in which you're interested—autos, for example, or sports—for kit offers.

● *Watch the Public Broadcasting System's "Consumer Survival Kit" series* on television. Or, request booklets summarizing weekly shows from Consumer Survival Kit, P.O. Box 1975, Owings Mills, Maryland 21117 ($1 each). See your *TV Guide*, or check the Yellow Pages under "Television stations and broadcasting companies." Get a copy of John Darfman's *The Consumer Survival Kit*, New York, Praeger, 1975.

● *Purchase in quantity*, for 10 percent or more off, such items as wine, beer, soft drinks, and toilet paper, even in your supermarket. Ask the manager for a case discount. You can stockpile the surplus for your family, or form a co-op among several families for wholesale discounts on everything from typewriters to trucks. For more information, get *OURS: How to Organize a Consumer Co-op*, Art Danforth, Chicago, Cooperative League of the USA, 1971.

● *Freebies* are all around you. Did you just move to a new area? Contact Welcome Wagon for free gifts.Professional people and specialists will find free sample offers through ads in professional magazines. There's a fifty-fifty chance that enthusiastic fan letters to manufacturers (see product label for address) will get you free samples. For more freebies, read Mort Weisinger's *1001 Valuable Things You Can Get Free*, New York, Bantam, 1974; and Mark Weiss' *Encyclopedia of Valuable Free Things for the Bride and Young Marrieds*, *501 Free Cookbooks* (1973), *501 Valuable Tips and Free Materials for Motorists* (1973), *The Handbook for Free Materials on Organic Foods*, and *1001 Free Things to Help You Keep Your Mate in Love with You*, all by Books for Better Living, Chatsworth, California. See also, *1001 Free Things for Your Family's Health*, Mark Weiss and Blanche Weiss, New York, Universal Publishing and Distributing (orders to Award), 1971.

• *Bargaining*. In our country, the age-old practice of haggling for goods (except at the auto dealer and real estate broker) is frowned upon. Exception: Bargaining will save you money when you deal with independent merchants, who are normally after any sale they can get.

• *House-wrecking contractors* are your secondhand home improvement centers. From them you can purchase cut-rate lumber, fixtures, architectural ornaments, hardware, plants, even sculptures. See your Yellow Pages under "Wrecking contractors."

• *Barter*, not to be confused with bargaining, allows you to trade your talents or unwanted goods for something you need, such as painting someone's house in exchange for their repairing your car. Check newspaper classifieds for barter opportunities, or arrange them through personal contact. Also, check the "swaps" column of *The Mother Earth News*, P.O. Box 70, Hendersonville, North Carolina 28739 ($2 per issue).

For work-trades, such as pick-your-own-strawberries, cut-your-own-Christmas tree, even catch-your-own-fish and pan-your-own-gold, write to the State Development Commission, in care of the capital city of the state in which you're interested.

• *Flea markets and swap meets*. For the lowdown, get the *Flea Market Shopper: Buying, Selling, and Trading Guide for Antiques and the New Collectables*, Ralph De Vincenzo, Dafran House, 185 Bethpage Sweet Hollow Road, Old Bethpage, New York 11804, 1972.

Traveling? Get *Europe's Hidden Flea Markets and Budget Antique Shops*, John Byrns, New York, Hastings House, 1968.

• *The city dump*. Furniture, large and small appliances, bicycles, clothing and more can be yours for the taking at the local "sanitary landfill." Be sure, however, to get there before the professional scavengers and before these goodies are all bulldozed under.

• *Street picking* can be a fine-honed art. Find out when the trash is collected in your city's poshest residential neighborhoods. Arrive at dawn on T-Day, and pick up a plush sofa here, a floor lamp there. Also, check outside of student dormitories at semester's end. For further information, read *The "Steal Yourself Rich" Book*, Abbie Hoffman, Insider's Mailbox, Inc., 595 Madison Avenue, 29th Floor, New York, New York 10022.

• *Free goods and services* are everywhere. Call your community hotline, guideline, switchboard, or United Way office (see your Yellow Pages under "Social service and welfare organizations," or write for the *Directory of Hotlines, Switchboards, and Related Services*, The Communication Company, 1826 Fell Street, San Francisco, California 94117), and they will put you onto free food, clothes, shelter, medical care, legal aid, educational opportunities, and other goodies.

Or, get a local edition of the *People's Yellow Pages* genre: *Resource Tie Line* (Los Angeles); *Davis Mello Pages* (Davis, California); *Colorado Express; Contact*

(Connecticut); *Compost* (Iowa); *Human Resources Directory* (San Diego); *Living: A Guide to the Other St. Louis*; *Whole City Catalogue, Synapse* (Philadelphia); or *Red Pages* (Washington, D.C.). The states of Massachusetts and Missouri, and the cities of San Francisco, San Jose, Denver, and San Diego, all have local editions of the *People's Yellow Pages*.

Happy hunting!

CRICKET CLAGETT
VIVO BENNETT

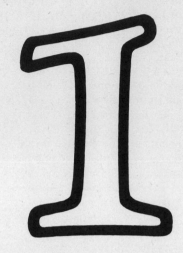

A SEA OF
SHELTER SAVINGS

The average family or individual spends more money every month on housing than on any other single item. Fully one quarter of every paycheck goes to the landlord, bank, or mortgage company. But although shelter is a basic necessity, masochistically throttling oneself with a gargantuan monthly rent or mortgage payment is not. Naturally, if you're able to forsake the usual amenities and make your home in a cave, yurt, tepee, or tree —which constitutes the life-style of more people around the world than we'd care to realize—you're sure to unburden yourself of such a ponderous obligation.

In reality, though, one needn't go to such Spartan extremes in order to stretch the shelter dollar. There are places in the world where the cost of a roof over one's head is truly negligible. A few years back, on the idyllic Balearic island of Ibiza, we rented a house in the country for a paltry $15 per month. Of course, the structure was devoid of everything except roof, walls, and doors. But a cozy fireplace, the use of candles at night, and water from a nearby well made living bearable—even comfortable at times.

Even in this country, you'll soon see, one can buy a modern, completely built two-bedroom home for under $13,000. Or, cheaper yet, a house can be purchased in kit form, then assembled, thus saving additional thousands of dollars.

So join us now in exploring the many possible ways in which you can shave your shelter costs to the bone—and still have your home as your castle.

Buying, Building, Remodeling, and Selling a Home

THE $1 HOUSE

If you would like to buy a house in New York City; Jersey City, New Jersey; or Islip, New York; can afford to fix it up, and are willing to live in it for three years, the federal government will sell it to you *for $1!*

These are houses that the government has foreclosed upon in its various home-loan programs. Some need extensive repairs, while others need only light work in order to fix them up.

For further information: .

U.S. Department of Housing and Urban Development, 451 Seventh Street, S.W., Washington, D.C. 20024.

MOD POD

You can knock $10,000 off the cost of a three-bedroom house by purchasing a modular home rather than one built on the site. These are factory built, and shipped in halves or large sections which are then easily assembled at the homesite. Once in place, a well-designed modular home is indistinguishable from its conventionally built counterpart.

For a list of 250 modular manufacturers, send $2 to *House & Home*, 1221 Avenue of the Americas, New York, New York 10020, for their *Directory of Modular Housing Producers*.

For further information:

"Mobiles, Modulars: Two Ways to Low-Cost Housing 1. The Case for the Modular Home," David Lampe, *Popular Mechanics*, June 1975, pages 88–89, 132–133.

PARADISE FOR PENNIES

If your income does not depend on your location, if you enjoy the year-round vacation atmosphere of secluded hamlets or the slower pace of small town living, why not buy a house for under $15,000 in one of America's bargain hideaways?

In modern Grass Valley, in the heart of California's gold-rush country, two-bedroom homes can be found for $13,000. In Truth or Consequences, New Mexico, you can get a two-bedroom for under $10,000. And in Weslaco, on the tip of Texas, older two-bedrooms go for as low as $8,500!

For further information:

Off the Beaten Path: America's Own Bargain Paradises, Norman Ford. Greenlawn, New York, Harian, 1973.

RETIREMENT RETREATS

U.S. Bureau of Labor Statistics figures show that among principal American cities, the cheapest cost of living for the retired couple is in Baton Rouge, Louisiana. Next, in order of increasingly higher living costs are: Austin, Texas; Atlanta; Dallas; Durham, North Carolina; Orlando, Florida; Houston; Nashville; Cincinnati; and Baltimore. The most expensive retirement traps for the retired couple are Honolulu; Hartford; Seattle; New York City; Boston; Buffalo; San Francisco; Indianapolis; Cleveland; and Milwaukee.

For further information:

Where to Retire on a Small Income, Norman Ford. Greenlawn, New York, Harian (orders to Grosset & Dunlap), 1975.

SCHOOLHOUSE HOUSE

For a unique, inexpensive home, buy a used schoolhouse. At $100 to $3,500, these are indeed bargains, even considering the several thousand dollars you will have to invest in remodeling the structure. Most have well, furnace, and plumbing already installed and are sold by sealed bid through regional school administrators' offices.

Write the Department of Education for the state in which you're interested and ask for a list of school administrators' addresses. You may, like Mr. and Mrs. Archie Barney of Wisconsin, parlay a $4,000 investment into a $15,000 home.

For further information:

"How to Have a House for Pennies," *The Mother Earth News Almanac*, *The Mother Earth News* Staff. New York, Bantam, 1973, pages 13–16.

OF MANSIONS AND MUD HUTS

What's best economically? A mansion in a run-down neighborhood; or a shack in one of the better areas of town? The latter, by far!

By purchasing that fine house in a run-down neighborhood at a bargain price, you're letting yourself in for possible declining property values in the future. Instead, look for an improvable home in the better section of town. Then you'll find the value of your property increasing over the years.

For further information:

Buying Your House: A Complete Guide to Inspection and Evaluation, Joseph Davis and Clayton Walker. Buchanan, New York, Emerson, 1975.

Home Buyer's Guide, Jack Wren. Scranton, Pennsylvania, Barnes & Noble (orders to Harper & Row), 1970.

CURBING WALK WORRIES

If sidewalks and curbs outside your intended residence are in need of repair, chances are that sooner or later the local street maintenance department will decide to make the repairs and send *you* the bill. Before signing the purchase agreement, demand that the seller either make the necessary repairs himself or compensate you now for any future outlay you may have to make.

For further information:

The Housebuying Checklist, Don Smith and Jo-An Smith. New York, Avon, 1975.

FRILL FACTS

Buying a house in a brand-new development? Since developers charge handsomely for such extras as fancy shutters, planters, and interior frills, make a deal with the developer *before* he builds to buy the basic house and add these extras yourself. Same goes for refrigerator, range, washer, dryer, and other "built-in" appliances. If their cost is included in your mortgage, you will be paying interest on them for twenty or thirty years. Far better to pay cash for them, or arrange your own purchase for less at a discount house or secondhand appliance dealer.

One exception to the no-frills rule is the model house in a development—the fully landscaped, interior-decorated showpiece, often with furniture thrown in, that is left after all the other houses are sold. Since the developer is anxious at this point to clear out, his impatience will often get you a good deal here.

For further information:

House Construction and Purchase: A Guide to Buying, Building, and Living in Your Own House, Eric Kelsey. North Pomfret, Utah, David & Charles, 1973.

LOOK UP!

Before buying a house, always—but always—thoroughly inspect the ceiling of every room on the top floor of the house for signs of water stains. If the ceilings have a suspiciously fresh coat of paint, or if they are covered with tiles or panels, demand to use the garden hose to simulate rain on the roof of the house.

The broker or owner may think you're a trifle weird, but believe us, testing roof leakage *before* buying has saved countless home buyers hundreds of thousands of dollars in roof repair costs.

For further information:

So You Want to Buy a House, Al Griffin. Chicago, Henry Regnery, 1970.

Home Buyer's Guide, Jack Wren. Scranton, Pennsylvania, Barnes & Noble (orders to Harper & Row), 1970.

EMINENT DOMAIN

Ever heard of eminent domain? This is the right of a governmental agency to take private property for public use.

Every year thousands of families are ungraciously evicted from their homes by federal, state, county, and municipal agencies so that this property can be turned into freeways, schools, and parks. Although compensation paid to the property owner in these cases legally must be equal to or exceed the going market value, payments are invariably on the low side—not to mention the inconvenience to the property owner.

Before buying, check with appropriate governmental agencies on *all* levels to make sure foreseeable plans are not contemplated for your intended place of residence.

WATCH THAT WATER PRESSURE!

One of the most common faults found in older dwellings is low water pressure due to buildup, over the years, of rust and mineral deposits in the pipes. Correcting the problem, which entails tearing out and replacing all water pipes, is extremely costly. Living with the problem can be even worse! If you've ever been ten minutes into a twenty-minute hot, relaxing shower and had the water suddenly slow to a dribble because somebody's flushed the toilet, you know what we mean.

Before buying an older home; check the pipes by turning on all the faucets in the house. Then flush all the toilets. If the faucets continue to run at full blast, the pipes are okay. If the faucets slow to a drizzle, the pipes are clogged.

For further information:

"Ins and Outs of Inspecting a House," Avery Comarow, *Money*, July 1973, pages 20–27.

HIGH CEILINGS

Although spacious and elegant old Victorian homes can be a joy to live in, their nine- and ten-foot-high ceilings can make your winter heat bills a nightmare. If you're concerned about heating costs, buy a home with lower ceilings.

For further information:

Buying Your House: A Complete Guide to Inspection and Evaluation, Joseph Davis and Clayton Walker. Buchanan, New York, Emerson, 1975.

COUNTRY CUNNING

There is nothing as discouraging as buying a country house with its own well and septic tank, only to find that your neighbors have just decided to put in community water and sewer lines. While it is true that payments of the assessment for these improvements —often costing thousands of dollars—can sometimes be spread out over several years, the fact is that, any way you slice it, you've been had.

Check with the appropriate agency at your city hall or county courthouse and talk to the residents in the community to see if such plans are afoot. One of our friends had the foresight to do this and then discovered that water and sewer lines were indeed planned for his intended community. With this knowledge, he was able to induce the seller to lower his price by $1,000, covering nearly all of the future assessment.

For further information:

Finding and Buying Your Place in the Country, Les Scher. Riverside, New Jersey, Macmillan, 1974.

SOIL SENSE

Okay, so you've inspected your intended home thoroughly: foundation, walls, roof, plumbing, and heating system—the works. But before you sign on the dotted line, better conduct a soil survey to determine whether or not the land on which your dream home is situated is subject to erosion, shifting, or worse yet, floods. Otherwise, you may find you've bought a worthless "houseboat" rather than a liveable home.

For further information:

Homebuyers . . . Soil Surveys Can Help You, PA 1050. Information Division, Conservation Service, U.S. Department of Agriculture, Washington, D.C. 20250 (free).

CANADIAN LAND

Although homesteading days are virtually over in the United States, much lush and fertile land can be had in Canada. For a list of land available, write to the Department of Land and Forests, Parliament Building, Quebec City, Canada. Other sources of information include: Geographical Branch,

Department of Mines and Technical Surveys, Parliament Building, Quebec City, Canada; and Communications Group, 2630 Point Grey Road, Vancouver 8, British Columbia, Canada.

VERMONT VENTURE

Write to Earth People's Park, P.O. Box 313, San Francisco, California 94133, for information on the 600 acres of northern Vermont land they handle. They will allow good people to settle there free. These folks act as a clearing house between landowners and settlers.

LAND HO!

Check through county records for land that the county holds for nonpayment of taxes. Have the land assessed, then negotiate with the county appraiser for a fair price.

When the deal goes through, you will have an unwarranted deed for the land. If, when you go to court to obtain title to the land, the owner emerges from the woodwork with his back taxes in hand, you must return the land to him, but you will still get back your investment from the county plus interest from the owner. If the owner doesn't show, title is yours, free and clear.

In some parts of the country, laws preclude buying land in this manner. If this is the case in your area, you can still save on a land purchase by contacting the owner of land for which taxes are due. One of Vivo's California acquaintances was able to purchase five acres from a tax-delinquent owner for $1,200 in back taxes. Although the land was worth $1,500 *an acre*, the owner was only too happy to make a quick sale on the parcel in order to pay off his debt and keep the rest of his land.

For further information:

Locating Low Cost Land, John and Dore Cuddy, Sunflower Farm, Rural Route 2, Shevlin, Minnesota 56676 ($1).

Information Bureau, Norval 62, Ontario, Canada (information on purchase of Canadian tax-arrears property, $2).

TAX SALE SAVINGS

Many counties hold annual tax-sale public auctions in order to sell tax-delinquent rural land. The opening bid is the amount of back taxes outstanding. Always have the property appraised beforehand to avoid overbidding.

When buying property in this manner, however, you can't be in a hurry to build. You must normally wait a few years in order to give the previous owners the opportunity to pay their back taxes. If they don't, you may then take court action to gain title. If the previous owners come up with the back taxes during the grace period, you get your investment back, plus interest. Not a bad deal!

To find these auctions, check your newspaper classifieds or call your county property tax office.

For further information:

Tax Land Guide, Box 122, New Castle, Delaware 19720 ($4.99).

HOME ON THE RANGE

There's an old saying: Show me a home where the buffalo roam and I'll show you a *very* dirty house! You can buy a site for a home on the plains or in an isolated mountain area at a rock-bottom price. How? Government lands like this are sold at public auction, the opening bids being the government's appraisal of the land values. The appraisals run from a few dollars an acre up into three or four figures. Tracts are two to five acres and may be used for a vacation, business, or permanent home.

Your local Bureau of Land Management Land Office will advise you of lands up for auction.

For further information:

Circulars Numbers 1895 and 1939, Bureau of Land Management, U.S. Department of the Interior, C Street between 18th and 19th, N.W., Washington, D.C. 20240.

Our Public Lands, Bureau of Land Management, U.S. Government Printing Office, Washington, D.C. 20402 (quarterly magazine).

TOGETHERNESS

If you're in the process of selecting house plans, consider this. A plan with the kitchen back-to-back with the bathroom will allow the same waste water and fresh water main lines to be used for both. What's it to you? More than $100 in your pocket.

For further information:

The Owner-Built Home and Preliminary House Design, Ken Kern. P.O. Box 550, Oakhurst, California 93644, Owner-Built Publications, 1961.

BUDGET BLUEPRINTS

No need to pay $300 or so for a set of custom-made blueprints! Check with lumberyards, building materials firms, and in your local library's building books for free plans. If you're building in a rural area, you can cheaply purchase building plans developed for your particular area from the extension agricultural engineer at a nearby agricultural college, or from your county agent.

Or, write the U.S. Department of Agriculture, Agricultural Research Service, Cooperative Farm Building Plan Exchange and Rural Housing, Beltsville, Maryland 20705, for a "List of Current Farmhouse Plans" and the address of the plan-distributing agency nearest you. The cost of the plans averages less than $3!

For further information:

Low-Cost Wood Homes for Rural America —Construction Manual, L. O. Anderson. Superintendent of Documents, U.S. Government Printing Office, Washington, D.C. 20402, 1969.

BUILDING SHILLINGS

Some local building codes insist on 16-inch spacing for floor-, wall-, and roof-frame members. However, the Federal Housing Administration has determined that 24-inch spacing is perfectly safe.

Check with the county building inspection office, and determine whether your local building code allows 24-inch spacing. If so, use it and save several hundred dollars on lumber.

For further information:

How to Build a Wood-Frame House, L. O. Anderson. New York, Dover, 1973.

PLANNING POINTERS

Your selection of an economical house plan can shave thousands of dollars off construction costs for your new home.

To decrease cost-per-square-foot, select a rectangular floor plan rather than the more difficult to build U- or L-shaped plan. Choosing a two-story house will cut roof costs in half. If your building site allows for it, choose a plan including a basement, which can double your living space for a fraction of normal dollars per foot.

For further information:

650 Ways to Save Money. Goodhart, 178 Ann Street, Valley Stream, New York 11580, 1975.

FANTASTIC PLASTIC

Planning on paving the crawl space under your new home with concrete as you build? You can save over $100 on the average, and still keep that crawl space dry and clean, by covering it with plastic sheeting instead.

For further information:

All Your Home Building and Remodeling Questions Answered, Stanley Schuler. Riverside, New Jersey, Macmillan, 1971.

A PLAUSIBLE CLAUSE

While you and a builder are writing up a contract for the construction of your dream home, be sure to have a clause inserted whereby the builder agrees to compensate you at so much per day if construction is not completed by a certain date. Then, should there be delays in construction, you'll be reimbursed for the inconvenience and ex-

pense of an unexpected wait between residences.

For further information:

Do-It-Yourself Contracting to Build Your Own Home, Richard Stillman. Radnor, Pennsylvania, Chilton, 1974.

Your Home: Building, Buying, Financing, L. Donald Meyers and Richard Demske. Englewood Cliffs, New Jersey, Reston (orders to Prentice-Hall), 1975.

TRUE GRIT

Once you've purchased the land for your dwelling, more than half the construction problems are licked—for the walls of your home can be constructed free by using the very dirt on which they stand. The dirt is rammed into lumber forms, which can later be knocked down and sold or reused.

For further information:

Earth for Homes: Ideas and Methods Exchange PB 188918 ($3) and *Handbook for Building Homes of Earth PB 179 327* ($3), Superintendent of Documents, U.S. Government Printing Office, Washington, D.C. 20402. The last-named publication is out of print, but is available at large libraries.

STONEWALL IT!

Is your homesite located on very stony ground? The material is at hand for attractive, low-cost walls. While building mortarless stone walls is an art requiring practice and skill, the technique outlined below allows even an amateur to build straight stone walls with a minimum of effort.

Set wooden forms ten inches apart. Place your stones in the space between them, filling any empty spaces with concrete. After the concrete sets, the form is removed and set up for another pouring.

For further information:

Our House of Stone, Lewis and Sharon Watson. Sweet, Idaho, Stonehouse Publications, 1974.

BRICK SHTICK

If you were to build a 2,800-square-foot brick home, the bricks alone would cost $2,000. After buying a Cisva-Ram brick press for $175 (F.O.B. Akron, Ohio) from Bellows-Valvair, 200 West Exchange Street, Akron, Ohio 44309, you can make as many bricks as you need—absolutely free. The bricks can be made from dirt, using manure—or, for a slight cost, using lime or cement—as a binder.

For further information:

Soil Cement—Its Use in Building. United Nations, Sales Section, New York, New York 10017, 1964.

IN THE BAG

More expensive than adobe brick, but cheaper than formed concrete walls, this wall-building technique requires no wood forms and the bare minimum of skill. Costs about half as much as wooden walls.

Cut a zillion old gunny sacks in half lengthwise and sew up the cut sides to form a long narrow sack. Fill with a mixture of sand and concrete. Stack the sacks to form a wall, pounding reinforcing bars down through the middle of the stacks and around corners to form doorways and windows. Next, wet down the sacks with a hose. The rustic results can be plastered with concrete for a smooth wall or left as is.

For further information:

Dicker Stack Sack International, 2600 Fairmont Street, Dallas, Texas 75201. (These folks can supply you with pre-filled sacks. Just stack and wet . . .)

WOODEN NICKELS

Would you believe $9,000 worth of first-quality lumber—for just $900? Here's the plan: Find a National Forest area where a lumber mill has recently operated. Such areas are littered with "cull," logs up to eight inches in diameter which are too small for lumber mills to bother with. You can get a permit to haul out huge amounts of cull for $15. Your own small but effective lumber mill can be built for $600, and county inspection of the resulting lumber for soundness may cost $50–$300. For details, read "We Built Our Own Sawmill for $600!" David Hayes and Raymond Hege, *The Mother Earth News*, No. 37, January 1976, pages 122–124.

LUMBER LUCRE

The budget-conscious home-builder can shave a sizeable amount off lumber costs in several ways. Odds and ends of unplaned lumber can be obtained at a local sawmill for as low as half the price of the stuff at your lumberyard.

Or you can arrange with the owner of a temporary dwelling or sagging shed to cart off the lumber from the structure in exchange for clearing his property of an eyesore. Make sure, however, that the lumber is still sound before you make the deal. Molding, doors, even wood paneling, can be had from the owner of a house that is about to be demolished or from the wrecking company for free or next to nothing. Why, we know of one couple who saved $20,000 in lumber costs for their home by using old railroad ties with a mortar binding.

For further information:

"All the Good Wood You Want—Free (or Very Cheap)," C. Wayne Close, *Family Handyman*, April 1975, pages 50–51.

"Build Yourself a Recycled House . . . and Save a Bundle!" *The Mother Earth News Almanac, The Mother Earth News* Staff. New York, Bantam, 1973, pages 102–105.

DOUBLE DEALING

Double-insulating the walls of a new home or addition is now being widely used by multitudes of cost-conscious homeowners. This technique involves placing tongue-in-groove Styrofoam sheets instead of sheathing under exterior siding, then filling the space between sheathing and interior wall with the conventional full-thick fiber glass batt.

While initially the fiber glass costs $135 more for the average house, after two and a half years this cost will be recouped and you will begin saving as much as $60 a year on heat in the northern United States.

For further information:

"New Answer for Home Heat Loss: Double-insulated Walls," Al Lees, *Popular Science*, February 1975, page 39.

Amspec Incorporated, 1880 Mackenzie Drive, Columbus, Ohio 43220.

ON THE SIDE

If you're just now deciding on an exterior finish for your home, or are faced with a major stripping and repainting job on a weatherworn exterior, choose one of the new vinyl, aluminum, galvanized steel, hardboard, particle board, or asbestos board sidings.

Due to low maintenance, these sidings save you *half* the cost of painting and repainting your home over the years. Other siding pluses: Increased insulating efficiency saves you money on heating and cooling bills. Moreover, such siding is rot-, vermin-, fire-, warp-, and split-resistant, easy to obtain, and prepainted with up to a 30-year guarantee.

For further information:

"PS Homeowner's Guide to Siding," Jackson Hand, *Popular Science*, March 1974, pages 98–100, 139.

SHINGLE THING

A do-it-yourself clapboard or roof shingle at one-fortieth of conventional prices can be made by dipping gunny sacks in a wet concrete-sand mixture, and then simply attaching these to the wall frame.

For roof shingles, hang them to dry before nailing in place.

ROOFING ROUNDELAY

For a unique roof—both in price and in looks—purchase odds and ends of asphalt shingles from roofing contractors. Mix the various colors and the results will be an eyecatching roof at a mere *tenth* of retail prices.

THATCH CASH

Imagine a roof that lasts 10 to 20 years, the materials for which are free for the taking. Such is the thatched roof, which is covered with dry reeds or grass, straw, bracken ferns, or palm leaves. For details on using this oft-overlooked technique, get *Book Two, Huts and Thatching*, The Ten Bushcraft Books, Richard Graves, New York, Schocken Books. Then call the local city hall to make sure you are permitted to use this unusual roofing.

FINISH FINAGLING

You can save close to $4,000 on the construction cost of an average-size house by doing your own finishing work—installing wallboard, plumbing, electrical wiring, and interior doors, locks, and trim. Lack of experience need not be a deterrent, provided you have sufficient fortitude and local zoning laws allow you to do your own finishing.

Purveyors of finish-it-yourself homes include: Jim Walter Corp., P.O. Box 22601, Tampa, Florida 33622 (mostly southern United States, prices $5,000 to $15,000); Evans Products Co., 1121 Southwest Salmon Street, Portland, Oregon 97208 (all United States except the southeast and Hawaii, $15,000 to $30,000); and Kaufman and Broad Custom Homes, Inc., Highway 101, Shakopee, Minnesota 55379 ($9,000 to $32,800).

BUILDING BUCKS

If you're about to embark on a major building or remodeling project, do as the pros do. Purchase your material from a wholesale building supply house. You'll get your goods at a healthy 20 percent discount this way.

For less ambitious projects, get your goods from a cash-and-carry house, with 10 percent discounts for do-it-yourself delivery. If there are none of these in your area, ask your local building supply store for a similar discount if you pay cash and pick up the materials yourself instead of having them delivered.

For further information:

Discount Home Building: How to Save Thousands of Dollars When Building Your Own Home, Ray Tassin. New York, Drake, 1974.

$100 ROOM

Add a room for one-twentieth the usual $2,000 building contractor's fee by assembling your own free-standing redwood dome! Domes come in kit form and cost $100 to $270 for models ranging from super-economy 10-foot diameter to fully equipped 20-foot diameter. They can be assembled in your backyard, using only a hammer, screwdriver, and wrench.

For further information:

Redwood Domes, Aptos, California 95003.

Dome East, 325 Duffy Avenue, Hicksville, New York 11801.

CUTTING CORNERS

Cricket's father saved $500 in remodeling the family dining and living rooms simply by renovating old floors and walls instead of putting out money for new floorboards and plaster. Looks great!

Rent a floor sander for a day and sand down those floors. Vacuum carefully, then apply a few coats of penetrating sealant. Holes in wall plaster—even large ones—are easily patched with plaster patch, obtainable at any hardware store. For a new look, and to hide worn plaster, add an inexpensive wainscot. Run a piece of wooden framing around the wall at waist level and apply wallpaper below it. Hundreds of additional money-saving ideas are contained in:

Repairing and Remodeling Guide for Home Interiors: Planning, Materials, Methods, Ralph Dalzell, New York, McGraw-Hill, 1973; *Popular Mechanics Complete Manual of Home Repair and Improvements*, Richard Nunn, New York, Avon, 1975; and *The Building a New, Buying an Old, Remodeling a Used, Comprehensive Home and Shelter How to Do It Book*, Gary Paulsen, Englewood Cliffs, New Jersey, Prentice-Hall, 1976.

TOILET TROUBLES?

Nothing is more irritating or harder on your water bill than a noisy toilet that leaks and groans even after refilling. You can eliminate this problem without paying a $20 plumber bill by using the Flusher Fixer kit. At less than $5, the kit includes a noise-proof, leak-proof tank ball, a flapper, and a stainless steel seat. Available from Fluidmaster, Inc., 1800 Via Burton, Anaheim, California 92707.

BATHROOM BLUES

Does the thought of how much it will cost to remodel your bathroom give you that sinking sensation? Be aware that you can save 20 percent—that's nigh onto $100 these days —on the cost of bathroom sink, tub, and toilet by purchasing white rather than colored fixtures.

If you *must* have color and you're a bit of an artist, hop down to your local paint dealer and pick up a quart of epoxy paint. First, however, you must sand the slickness off the surface to be painted so that the epoxy will stick to it. Then create your *own* colorful commode, beautiful bathtub, and stunning sink—at a fraction of the cost!

For further information:

Complete Book of Home Painting, John Scherer. Blue Ridge Summit, Pennsylvania, TAB Books, 1975.

BEAM DREAM

At $2 a foot, who can afford the rustic effect created by those easy-to-install simulated-wood (plastic) ceiling beams? Fashion your own beams at less than 25¢ a foot by cutting Styrofoam insulation board in strips, simulating a rough wood grain with wire brush marks, and finishing with an oil stain.

For further information:

"Make Your Own Fake Beams," Tom Ziegler, *Mechanix Illustrated*, January 1974, pages 68–69, 124–125.

BRICKS AND STONES

It may interest you to discover that, just as you can remodel a house, you can do likewise with any internal or external wall. These can be easily and inexpensively covered with brick or stone using Thin-Brik or Thin-Stone. Fire-proof and handsome, these materials are the real thing but only a half inch thick.

For information contact Ridgerock Industries, Thin-Brik/Stone Division, Sebring, Ohio 44672. Other manufacturers of similar items are Z-Brick Co., 2834 Northwest Market Street, Seattle, Washington 98107; and Flexi-Bricks (thirty bricks to cover five square feet, $5.50), available at home improvement centers.

PREFAB FIREPLACES

A fashionable fireplace which the amateur carpenter can easily add in only a weekend, half the installed cost of the conventional all-masonry type? Yes! Prefab fireplaces are available for as little as $300, including the basic metal firebox, metal chimney, and firescreen (but not including interior facing or trim). To top it off, you get the increase of $1,000 or so in home resale value that is usual in the installation of a fireplace.

Prefab fireplaces may be ordered from Majestic Co., Huntington, Indiana 46750; Martin Industries, Box 1527, Huntsville, Alabama 35807; Preway, Inc., Wisconsin Rapids, Wisconsin 54494; or Superior Fireplace Co., 4325 Artesia Avenue, Fullerton, California 92633.

For further information:

"Prefab Metal Liners and Chimneys: The Fast, Easy Way to a Built-in Fireplace," Darrell Huff and Al Lees, *Popular Science*, December 1975, pages 86–92, 127.

HOUSE HUCKSTER

If you feel that your tongue is at least as glib as the average real estate salesman's, save those heavy commission charges and sell your home yourself.

You'll have to hire your own appraiser, write and circulate your own advertising material, and retain a lawyer to handle the legal aspects of the transaction. But, in return for your trouble, you'll save about $1,700 in commission for the average $35,000 house.

For further information:

For Sale by Owner: How to Sell Your Own Home Without a Broker and Save Thousands of Dollars, Louis Gilmore. New York, Simon & Schuster, 1973.

Rent Reducers and Removers

SUBSIDY FROM HUD

Is your income less than 80 percent of the average for your area? If so, you may qualify, under the U.S. Department of Housing and Urban Developments' Section 8, Housing Assistance Payments Program, for a rent subsidy. Under this program, you need to contribute only one fourth of your income to the rent—HUD will pay the rest.

Here's an example. Let's suppose that $15,000 is the median income for your area. If you earn $12,000 annually and pay $350 a month rent, HUD will pay $100 of your rent for you.

This program is such a big giveaway that some tenants of $700-a-month apartments in New York City are being subsidized under this plan by HUD.

For further information:

U.S. Department of Housing and Urban Development, 451 Seventh Street, S.W., Washington, D.C. 20024. Ask for Section 8 information.

AN UNDERPRICED UTOPIA

If your source of income is independent of your physical location, there are many places in the world you can live for a fraction of your current living expenses—with a housekeeper and maid thrown in! Where? In Turkey, where lovely furnished villas go for $100 a month. In Greece, where quaint fishermen's cottages rent for the same, and cooks or maids earn $30 a month, plus board. In Spain, where a pension with a sea view will cost you $1,750 a year, all meals included. Or, in Mexico, Costa Rica, Ireland, Portugal, South Africa—to name just a few places.

For further information:

Bargain Paradises of the World, Norman Ford. Greenlawn, New York, Harian, 1974.

COMMUNAL LIVING

Whether you simply share an urban apartment with another individual, or live on a farm commune with fifty or more, communal or shared living is a sure way to cut down drastically on your rent. It's also an excellent way to meet people and make friends.

How to find a shared living situation? Register with a roommate service. Check out, or advertise in, the city or underground newspaper classifieds. Put up notices on supermarket, laundromat, and college bulletin boards.

For further information:

Communes: Creating and Managing the Collective Life, Rosabeth Kanter. Scranton, Pennsylvania, Harper & Row, 1973.

A RADICAL DEPARTURE

Our landlord recently found himself in a crunch between his income and his outgo, and simply could not meet his mortgage payments when his union went on strike. What to do, short of having the bank foreclose on the property? He rented his house to us, and used the difference between our rent and his mortgage payments to live rent-free in a modest apartment.

If you've owned your home long enough for rental rates to exceed your mortgage payments, you can do the same.

For further information:

How to Outsmart Your Landlord (If You're a Tenant) or How to Outsmart your Tenant (If You're a Landlord), Stuart Faber. Hollywood, California, Good Life Press, 1975.

FOOD AND FRIENDS

If you're fortunate enough to live in a city such as San Francisco, which abounds in residence clubs or hotels, check out these inexpensive alternatives to apartment living. For a modest monthly fee, you receive room and board, the companionship of many other people, and the use of a get-together room such as a group TV or game-playing room.

Some residence clubs cater to the young, some to the elderly, and some to both. Although some clubs exist exclusively for men or for women, the vast majority cater to both sexes and, in addition to being inexpensive, are a superb way to make friends.

See your Yellow Pages under "Residence clubs" or "Residence hotels."

STATE YOUR BENEFICIARY!

Does a fixed income make it increasingly difficult for you to meet expenses, even though you own your own home? Many state governments, and colleges as well, have plans in effect whereby you'll live tax-free—possibly with some of your living expenses thrown in as well—in your own home for the rest of your life, in exchange for willing them your home. Contact your state or college treasurer.

An appealing alternative is to arrange to have your children pay your living expenses and reimburse them for this in your will. This removes the burden of guilt from both parties and alleviates your financial worries for good. For details, see your local Legal Aid Society or your family lawyer.

SHELTER FOR SENIORS

Senior citizens looking for homes should contact their local Lions Club, Volunteers of America, or Salvation Army chapter. Each of these organizations has programs to assist the elderly with low-cost housing.

If you can't get the information locally, write to Lions International, 22nd Street, Oak Brook, Illinois 60521; Volunteers of America, 340 West 85th Street, New York, New York 10024; or The Salvation Army, National Headquarters, 120 West 14th Street, New York, New York 10011.

A RETIREMENT RESIDENCE

If a fixed retirement income has you worried that inflation will deprive you of basic needs or force you to rely on the charity of family and friends, consider buying into a retirement home. Such homes as Kingsley Manor in Los Angeles and Pohai Nani Retirement Residence in Oahu offer meals, medical and nursing care, housekeeping, linens, and social and recreational activities in exchange for your signing over to them all assets —investment income, life insurance, and savings. Or, if your pocketbook allows it, you can pay them a lump sum for the privilege of living there until your death.

Even if you outlive your assets, you'll always have a place to call home.

For further information:

Guide to Retirement Living, Paul Holter. New York, Rand McNally, 1973.

APARTMENTS FOR THE AGED

While retirement residences and hotels are often quite expensive, apartment houses whose construction has been funded with the assistance of the Federal Housing Administration, the Community Facilities Administration, or the Public Housing Administration often offer quarters for senior citizens in lower income brackets at prices that are quite moderate. In San Diego, for example, one-bedroom apartments on this program run as low as $90 per month, including utilities. A two-bedroom apartment goes for $110 a month, including utilities.

For information on low-cost housing in your area, contact local offices of the agencies mentioned above (see "U.S. Government" listings in your phone book).

For further information:

Guide to Elderly Housing and Related Facilities, U.S. Department of Housing and Urban Development. Superintendent of Documents, U.S. Government Printing Office, Washington, D.C. 20402, 1971.

Alternate Housing

FOAM HOME??

Homes built entirely of urethane foam have two distinct advantages over homes constructed with more conventional building materials: Their initial cost is low (about $1,500 for a dome foam home 30 feet in diameter) and their excellent insulating abilities allow heat bills to be slashed to $1/18$ of the cost for average houses with $3\frac{1}{2}$-inch fiber glass insulation.

The major drawback of foam homes— their flammability—can be dealt with by using flame-resistant CPR #421 foam by Upjohn, by painting with such flame-retardant paints as United Paints Manufacturer's (Spokane) Thermogard, or by plastering the interior of the home.

Suppliers of foam include: Upjohn Co. % Atlas Insulation, Ayer, Massachusetts 01432; Stepan Chemical Co., Nopco Division, 175 Shuyler Avenue, North Arlington, New Jersey 07032; and Witco Chemical Co., Isocyanate Products Division, P.O. Box 1681, Wilmington, Delaware 19899.

For further information:

"Urethane Foam," Gary Allen, *Alternative Sources of Energy*, No. 12, October–November, 1973, pages 14–15.

A YURT'S WORTH

The yurt, a modern version of the portable round homes used by Gobi Desert nomads

for centuries, is worth far more to you in living space than the $350 it costs to build it. For that price, you get a truly distinctive home 17 feet in diameter. Or, for $4,000, just one-seventh the cost of conventional housing, you can build a full-size yurt home 32 feet in diameter. Construction requires only the most basic knowledge of carpentry.

The plans are available from Dr. William Coperthwaite, The Yurt Foundation, Bucks Harbor, Maine 04618 ($3.50, small yurt; $8.50, large concentric yurt).

For further information:

"Convert to a 'Yurt,' the Incredible $350 House," R. Clifford Webster, *Moneysworth*, 20 January 1975, page 6.

CAVE SAVINGS

To save 25 percent on building costs and up to half on heating and cooling your home, with practically maintenance-free design and attention to ecological integrity thrown into the bargain, make your home a cave! The underground dwelling of architect John Barnard does all these things. A central, sunken atrium provides light and greenery. Additional fresh air is pumped in by an electric cooling-heating unit.

For further information:

"Underground Living in the Ecology House Saves Energy, Cuts Building Costs, Preserves the Environment," V. Elaine Smay, *Popular Science*, June 1974, pages 88–89, 132.

DOME DOMAIN

If you own land, but have little money with which to build on it, consider a fully equipped geodesic dome, tailored to fit suburban zoning codes. Prices start as low as $2,000 for 485 square feet of living space. For 2,800 square feet, you pay $12,950—about half the cost of conventional housing.

Manufacturers include Geodesic Structures, Inc., P.O. Box 176, Hightstown, New Jersey 08520 (free info); Dome East, 325 Duffy Avenue, Hicksville, New York 11801 (free info); Dyna Dome, 22226 North 23rd Avenue,

Phoenix, Arizona 85027; and Hide-a-way Domes—Circle Systems, 571 East Fourth Street, Winona, Minnesota 55987.

For dome blueprints: *Popular Science* Plans, 380 Madison Avenue, New York, New York 10017 (Plan Number 5519—$5).

For further information:

The Dome Builders Handbook, John Prenis. Philadelphia, Running Press, 1973.

DIG-A-DOME

For a grand total of $65, you can easily construct a dome home of concrete. Start halfway down the side of a hill and dig out a huge V-shaped section, piling the excised dirt up just below the V to form a large mound of earth. Cover with 4 to 6 inches of concrete, using reinforcing bars and wire mesh to strengthen the structure. Leave spaces for windows and doors, through which the dirt will be excavated after the concrete sets. Tools needed: shovel, wire pliers, concrete mixing box, and hoe.

For further information:

"How to Dig a Dome," Virgil Byxbe, *The Updated Last Whole Earth Catalog: Access to Tools*, Pam Cokeley, ed. *The Whole Earth Catalog*, Box 428, Sausalito, California 94965.

TENT HOME

A summer home, including bed, kitchen, and toilet, for $500? This can be built by using a combination tent-cabin design which folds up into a secure 4 by 7 by 8 foot box for convenient storage. The tent cabin is $2,800 cheaper than a recreational vehicle of similar size, and it includes a 96-square-foot floor area.

For plans, write to *Popular Science* Plans, 380 Madison Avenue, New York, New York 10017, for Plan Number 5489: Tent Cabin ($5).

For further information:

"A Leisure Home for This Season: Build a Tent Cabin," Al Lees and Jeff Milstein, *Popular Science*, June 1975, pages 86–88.

TEPEE TIP

For a portable, durable, economical shelter or additional bedroom, set up a tepee! Practical yet beautiful, your tepee can easily be constructed of canvas, poles, and rope using instructions in *The Indian Tipi: It's History, Construction, and Use,* Reginald and Gladys Laubin, New York, Ballantine Books, 1970. Or, purchase a readymade tepee or tepee kit from Nomadics, Star Route, Box 41, Cloverdale, Oregon 97112. Prices start at $115, including waterproof liner, for a tepee with a side slope (or radius when lying flat on the ground) of 16 feet. Ready-to-sew kits are $20 cheaper.

A somewhat more expensive supplier: Goodwin-Cole Company, 1315 Alhambra Boulevard, Sacramento, California 95816.

ON THE SHACK TRACK

Deep down in our hearts, many of us adults would really rather live high in a tree house, nearer the stars. For details on how to build a tree house, fagot shack, Indian building, or other wilderness home—using nothing but ingenuity and free scrap or natural materials—get *Shelters, Shacks and Shanties,* D. C. Beard, Totowa, New Jersey, Scribner's, 1972.

CONDOMINIUM CONVENIENCE

That comfortable compromise between the spaciousness of a private home and the carefree maintenance of the apartment—the condominium—is an excellent buy for the would-be homeowner with limited funds. The cost is as much as one fourth less than that of a private home, and condominiums appreciate in value almost as fast as the latter. Many condominiums also accept down payments of as little as $500, compared to the $2,000 or more that is customary for the private home.

For further information:

How to Buy a Condominium, Patricia Brooks and Lester Brooks. New York, Stein & Day, 1975.

SLOOP FROM SCRAP

Build your own live-on 20-foot plywood sailboat for $300—$1,700 less than retail! Bill Hyslop did just this, using scrap lumber—with a bit of good ol' Yankee ingenuity thrown in. The result, the "Hina," proved thoroughly seaworthy in two and a half months of live-on Lake Michigan cruising.

For further information:

"Hina: We Built a Live-on Boat for $300!" Bill Hyslop, *The Mother Earth News,* No. 37, June 1976, pages 68–72.

TRAILER TALK

These days, mobile home parks come in a wide assortment of shapes and sizes. You can live in a family-operated, 10-space park with simple bathroom, shower, and laundry facilities. Or you can live in a swanky 100-space park by the sea or nestled in the mountains with every recreational facility from table tennis to riding stables.

What the mobile home park lacks in privacy, it makes up for in rock-bottom rental costs (which usually include utilities), and recreational and socializing opportunities. Spaces are available from San Francisco to Savannah, and prices of only $50 a month for the more Spartan facilities are not uncommon.

For further information:

Woodall's Mobile Home and Park Directory, Curtis Fuller. Highland Park, Illinois, Woodall (annual publication).

SEASONAL SALES

Mobile home dealers, like automobile dealers, have end-of-summer clearance sales to make way for next year's models. If you get the urge for a spiffy mobile home in July, wait a few months! Seasonal sales strategy can save you $1,000 to $3,000 on the brand-new mobile home of your choice.

For further information:

Good Shelter: A Guide to Mobiles, Modular, and Prefabricated Homes, Bernard Rabb and

Food, next to shelter, comprises the second greatest financial expenditure in the everyday life of the average citizen. If your family's income is $10,000, you'll spend over $2,000 for grocery products in the next year—unless you make a conscious and aggressive effort to conserve those food dollars.

At first glance, any success in saving substantial amounts of money at the supermarket checkout stand appears to be hopeless. After all, what can we do when we reach toward the supermarket shelf for a can of peaches or a pound of sugar and—before our hand touches the product—the stockboy appears out of nowhere to stamp a new, higher price on the item?

Well, our financially beleaguered friend, there's a lot that can be done. In fact, there are an infinite number of ways to skin the supermarket cat. Take your hand away from that can of peaches! Don't you know that you can get a whole *lug* of cull peaches in the country for the price of one supermarket can? And you can easily buy *ten* pounds of rolled oats in a feed store for less than you'd pay for a pound of supermarket oat cereal.

But these are just a few of the many ways to slash your food costs drastically. Follow the tips given in the succeeding pages and learn how easy it is to do. The only thing you have to lose is your supermarket manager's love.

Outsmarting the Supermarket

SERVE REDI-RESERVE

At about $1.45 a day, you can enjoy two daily servings each of fruit, protein, and milk supplements, three vegetable portions, and enough wheat to make a half loaf of bread. You get 70 grams of protein and 1,535 calories daily, plus vitamins and minerals, in the form of canned, dehydrated, but tasty edibles. Request Item #1698, 12-Month Redi-Reserve

Pak ($525.50), from Mother's General Store, Box 506, Flat Rock, North Carolina 28731.

CONVENIENT COST CUTS

While it is often true that fresh or home-prepared foods cost less than frozen, canned, dehydrated, and ready-to-serve products, a U.S. Department of Agriculture survey has shown that more than half of the popular convenience foods cost the same as *or less than* fresh home-prepared or equivalents.

Into this category fall such canned or frozen produce as orange juice, cherries, cut corn, spinach, lima beans, and green peas and beans; frozen fish sticks; lasagna, macaroni-chili-beef, and beef stroganoff TV dinners; pound cake, yellow cake, waffle, pancake, brownie, corn muffin, chocolate frosting, and chocolate pudding mixes.

For a list of prices for various forms of products, see "Some Convenience Foods Do Save Money," *Changing Times*, January 1975, pages 13–15.

COOPERATE

If you have a little more time than money, join a food-buying cooperative. In exchange for a minimal amount of time donated to help run the co-op—helping to take orders and buy, sort, and distribute groceries to other members—you can latch onto substantial food savings—what amounts to a wholesale discount.

A similar idea on a smaller scale is to organize a food alliance among several families in the neighborhood, or members of your apartment house. Duties can be shared or rotated.

Buy your produce directly from the farm, and your dairy goods from the dairy. Other grocery items can be obtained at discounts of up to 30 percent by purchasing in bulk from one of the new bulk supermarkets. One such outfit, the Hippopotamus chain, currently has one store in Santa Ana, California, and two stores in Memphis, Tennessee. Other bulk supermarkets are springing up all over the country.

For further information:

The Food Coop Handbook: How to Bypass Supermarkets to Control the Quality and Price of Your Food, Co-Op Handbook Collective. New York, Houghton Mifflin, 1975.

COUPON COUP

Strategic coupon shopping can stretch your food dollar 20 percent farther, but the pitfalls of coupon shopping are numerous. Don't let coupon shopping "hook" you on higher-priced luxury foods, or beguile you into buying unneeded types or quantities.

With these cautions in mind, and instructions from the book below, you'll be ready to scoop up free cash, coupons, and merchandise offered by thousands of eager manufacturers.

For further information:

The Coupon Way to Lower Food Prices, Carol Kratz and Albert Lee. Documentary Books, 1775 Broadway, New York, New York 10019 ($2.45).

SANDRICHES

Last year, in organizing a weekend block party, Cricket ingeniously came up with an idea that provided ample food for the event—for next to nothing! On Friday at 5 P.M., she simply made the rounds of local mobile catering firms, which supply offices and factories with sandwiches and other edibles. Since these firms cannot legally hold their perishable goods until Monday, they willingly sold here, at a 50 to 75 percent discount, all their leftover sandwiches, macaroni salads, cakes, and pies.

You can get the same deal from similar firms in your area. To find them, check your Yellow Pages under "Caterers."

STABLE STAPLES

A hundred pounds of basic people food for under ten dollars? This is *not* the impossible dream. Pick up a sack of rolled oats, barley, corn, rye, brown rice, whole wheat, or dried beans at your local feed, seed, or grain dealer. Store it in a clean garbage can with a lid to keep out insects and rodents. Grind it yourself for flour or breakfast cereal. *The Whole Earth Catalog* recommends the Quaker City Hand Grain Grinder, available for $12 plus postage from Nelson and Sons, Inc., P.O. Box 1296, Salt Lake City, Utah 84110.

For stable staple recipes, see Edyth Cottrell's *The Oats, Peas, Beans, and Barley Cookbook: Much More for Your Money with Nature's Basic Foods*, Santa Barbara, California, Woodbridge, 1974.

MOLASSES IN JANUARY (OR ANYTIME)

You can't buy a cheaper sweetener than blackstrap molasses. If you buy your molasses by the gallon from a stock-feed mill, you will pay less than *one fifth* of the cost of white sugar. Heat this partially processed molasses product just to the boiling point and it's ready to use.

In baking, substitute one cup of molasses for each cup of sugar. Use no baking powder, but add ½ teaspoon soda and subtract ¼ cup liquid from the recipe, for each cup of molasses. Best results come from using half the sugar your recipe calls for, then substituting molasses for the other half.

For further information:

Out of the Molasses Jug, Cindy Davis. Berkeley, California, Cloudburst Press (orders to Book People), 1974.

HEALTH FOOD STORE LORE

There are two distinct types of health food stores: Those that are in business solely for profit and those run by kind souls whose main concern is simply to contribute to a better way of life. The former are to be avoided. The latter, usually nonprofit co-ops with volunteer staff, are a boon to the budget-minded. You will find that many co-op staples, such as flour, grains, rice, and nuts, sold in bulk—in old-fashioned bins and bags—are shockingly cheaper than at the supermarket.

Many times these "people's" co-ops have no telephone listing. Our experience has been that the best way to track them down is to call your friendly vegetarian restaurant or check with your local underground newspaper for their whereabouts.

For further information:

"Food," *People's Yellow Pages of America*, Scott French. New Rochelle, New York, Richard Heller & Son, 1974.

A DENT IN YOUR BUDGET

Back in our San Francisco days, we saved a third to a half on all our canned goods by shopping at an out-of-the-way supermarket which specialized in slightly dented cans. If no such store exists in your area, make a deal with your grocer to relieve him of dented cans at a discount. The best buys along this line are canned fruits and vegetables, which can be stored and used when the fresh produce is out of season. Avoid any cans that are punctured, bulging, or black around the rim or dent.

For further information:

How to Cut Your Food Bill by Half or More, Kurt Saxon. Mother's Bookshelf, P.O. Box 70, Hendersonville, North Carolina 28739.

RAINCHECKS

If a supermarket advertises an item for sale without indicating a limited quantity, and then runs out of the item, the law entitles you to a raincheck on the item at the sale price. This raincheck can get you even greater savings on *seasonal* items such as fruits and vegies if you hold onto it until the end of the season, when prices are considerably higher.

Raincheck tactics can be used not just on food but on other types of products as well —for example, sportswear and lawn-care equipment.

For further information:

The Supermarket Survival Manual, Judy Lynn Kemp. New York, Bantam, 1974.

BABY YOUR BUDGET

Slash store prices of baby food in half by making your own. Simply strain, mash, or grind a small portion of tonight's vegetables, fruit, or meat and add a little water. Make the mixture very bland—salt is not good for the high-chair set.

You can get the portable, efficient Happy Baby Food Grinder ($5.45) through Bowland Jacobs Manufacturing Company, 9 Oakdale Avenue, Spring Valley, Illinois 61362.

For further information:

Making Your Own Baby Food, James Turner, Des Plaines, Illinois, Bantam, 1973.

BURGER BARGAINS

Ever tried using oatmeal as a meat stretcher in your meatroll? It's tastier than bread and far easier on your pocketbook than such convenience mixes as Hamburger Helpmate and Butchered Beef Broadener.

In fact, you needn't limit your meat stretchers to oatmeal. We have a frugal and ingenious friend who uses such items as sesame seed, cornmeal, wheat germ, ground matzo crackers—even bird seed—in her burger recipes.

For further information:

Meat Stretcher Cook Book, Better Homes and Gardens, editor. Des Moines, Iowa, Meredith, 1974.

Protein Power

BE AN INSECTIVORE!

According to leading nutritional authorities, the ideal solution to the pressing problem of feeding an already overpopulated world is right under your nose (or at your feet). The solution—insects! Locusts, termites, and houseflies contain 75 percent protein—much more than meat—and they can be delicious if properly prepared. The taste, contrary to popular opinion, is rather like crispy lettuce.

Next meal, why not serve fried baby bees, locusts, crickets, caterpillars, or midges—all free for the gathering—instead of that tiresome beef, pork, or fish?

For further information:

Butterflies in My Stomach: Insects in Human Nutrition, Ronald Taylor. Santa Barbara, California, Woodbridge Press, 1975.

AMAZING ALGAE

A far-out source of protein, vitamins, and minerals, a small pond of algae can be grown right in your backyard. Algae, in powdered form, supply 14,000 pounds of protein per acre per year, compared to 269 a year for wheat and a measly 54 a year for meat. In fact, an algae-growing project in the southern part of India has actually provided the growers with twice as much nourishment at half the price of the community's standard milk-vegetarian diet.

All algae require to live and multiply are water, a little sea salt, and a source of nitrogen such as cow or human urine, malt waste from breweries, or vegetable oil extraction waste from mills. In fact, one person's urine, fed to algae, can provide that person with 60 percent of his daily protein requirement!

For further information:

"Algae Research in Auroville," Robert Lawlor, *Alternative Sources of Energy*, Number 16, December 1974, pages 2–9.

MULTIPURPOSE FOOD

It looks like flour, tastes like whole-wheat cereal, and a five-ounce serving provides *all* of the U.S. recommended daily allowance for protein and 75 percent of the RDA for 13 essential vitamins and minerals. At $4.50 for a four-pound can of multipurpose food (MPF), you will be paying 42¢ for a full day's worth of protein—a mighty far cry from the cost of that steak or roast beef you might otherwise buy.

Before using MPF, mix it with an equal amount of water and let it stand ten minutes.

Then add to tomato juice, cereal, scrambled eggs, waffles, salad, soup, or baby food, or use it to fortify casseroles, vegetables, baked beans, spaghetti, sauces, or puddings.

Order from General Mills, Inc., 400 Second Avenue, South, Department 175, Minneapolis, Minnesota 55440.

GLUTEN GLUTTONY

A good source of protein at one-third beef prices, wheat gluten is the basic ingredient of commercial vegeburgers, vegetarian dinner cuts, and other meat dinner substitutes.

Make your own with little effort by mixing 2½ to 3 cups of water with 8 cups of gluten flour or white flour. Roll into a ball, and soak in water overnight. The following day, knead off and on, pouring off starchy water and replacing with cold water. When the water remains clear on kneading the gluten, season with soy sauce, salt, wine, onion, or garlic. Then cut it into pieces, and fry or steam, or grind and use like hamburger.

For further information:

"Meat," Ann Liston, *The Updated Last Whole Earth Catalog*, Pam Cokeley, ed. *The Whole Earth Catalog*, Box 428, Sausalito, California 94965, May 1974, page 195.

BEEF RELIEF

For thirteen times as much protein per dollar as a rib roast of beef, learn to cook with soybeans, which you can pick at up any health food store.

After you've concocted such dishes as Welsh rabbit, mock lasagna, Southern bisque, and applesauce cake—all made with this miraculous little bean—you'll wish you'd have gotten into the soybean habit years ago.

For further information:

Soybean Cookery, Virg and Joanne Lemley. Wilderness House, 2656 Circle Drive, Escondido, California 92025, 1975.

SOY PLOY

Soybean meat stretchers! Not only do they save you 25 percent on hamburger costs, but they also boost the nutritional value of your meat proteins, as well as lowering your cholesterol and fat intake, thus helping prevent diseases associated with a diet high in these foods.

These miracle soy products are marketed under such brand names as TVP (textured vegetable protein); Burger Plus (Cargil); Burger Builder (General Mills); and Burger Bonus (A. E. Staley).

For further information:

"Now There's 'Meatless Meat,' " *Changing Times*, February 1974, pages 53–54.

MEAT MIRACLES

Slash a third off your meat bill by purchasing the less expensive, tougher cuts of meat and marinating in red wine overnight. The result will be a much more tender cut of meat than you'd get by paying top prices at the meat counter.

Or, marinate the meat for a few hours in salad dressing or plain old vinegar and oil. The fastest method: Pound the meat with a tenderizing hammer or a regular hammer wrapped in cloth.

For further information:

Money Saving Meat Cookery, Ted Kaufman and Jean Kaufman. New York, Warner, 1974.

BE A CUT-UP

Never buy lamb chops, veal chops, pork chops, individually cut beef steaks, or chicken pieces. Instead, buy lamb or veal shoulders, end-cut pork, pork steaks, chuck roast, and whole chickens. Cut them yourself, or have your butcher cut them into chops and steaks.

The savings involved in "bulk" meat buying and doing your own cutting are substantial. You can get $4 worth of roast, steak, and stew meat or ground beef, plus a soup bone and scraps from one $2.70 chuck roast. A family of four can save over $250 a year using this plan.

For further information:

How to Shop for Food: Practical Tips for the Family Food Buyer, Jean Rainey. New York, Barnes & Noble, 1972.

SPREADING SAVINGS

Canned sandwich spreads cost upwards of $2 a pound, yet they often contain as little as 50 percent meat. Thus, you pay $4 a pound for the meat content in these spreads. Buy a secondhand meat grinder and make your own sandwich spreads with leftover chicken, ham, and beef roast, plus mayonnaise and seasoning. This maneuver will easily save you $2.00 to $3.50 per pound.

For further information:

Joy of Cooking, Irma S. Rombauer and Marion Rombauer Becker. Indianapolis, Bobbs-Merrill, 1964.

EAT DOG FOOD?

We're not suggesting that you fry up a batch of canned Doggie Delight—a dog should deserve such a fate! But for a savings of about 90¢ a pound or $110 a year for even a meager meat-eater, try out some of the "variety" meats smart pet-owners have been feeding their animals for years.

Liver, heart, tongue, sweetbreads, kidneys, brains, tripe—these are nutritious protein foods enjoyed worldwide by gourmets. Their bargain prices are due to the fact that the general public has not yet developed a taste for them.

For further information:

Innards and Other Variety Meats, Jana Allen and Margaret Gin. San Francisco, 101 Productions (orders to Scribner's), 1974.

TURKEY TALK

Thinking of buying a turkey? It will pay you to buy a large one, even if your family is small. A 10-pound turkey yields about 10 servings, while an 18-pounder yields about 36 servings, or twice as much for your money. Cut your large bird in half and freeze one side for a feast another day!

After all, why fowl up your budget unnecessarily?

For further information:

How to Buy Food, Valerie Moolman. New York, Cornerstone Library, 1970.

FISH TRICKS

Here's how to preserve all the fish you need—for pennies—without the high operational expense of freezing your food: Smoke it!

For your "smokehouse," you'll need either a wooden box lined on the inside with aluminum foil or a foil-covered frame in the shape of a box. Suspend the fish on wires from the inside of the box or place them on a grate inside. To produce smoke, simply keep a few wood chips smoldering inside the box at all times. The whole process takes only a day, and the delicious results keep indefinitely.

For further information:

The Art of Curing, Pickling and Smoking Meat and Fish, James Robinson. New York, Gordon Press, 1973.

HORSING AROUND

Want to know how to slash meat prices by 70 percent? Eat horsemeat! Contrary to popular belief, the meat of the horse is cleaner, tastier, and more tender than that of the cow (or steer). In fact, in many foreign cultures, only horsemeat is eaten, as other types of meat are considered unclean. In our country, horsemeat is government inspected with the same strict standards as for beef.

For suppliers, check your Yellow Pages under "Horsemeat," or contact any animal food dealer or large pet store.

SEASONAL PROTEINS

Take advantage of meat and egg price fluctuations to slash your protein bill drastically. You'll find large cuts of meat on sale in the summertime, when most people are buying smaller cuts. Stock your freezer with steak in June to avoid high July and August steak prices. Buy lamb in the spring, when the supply is plentiful. And eggs are cheaper in the winter, when chickens are more prolific layers.

For further information:

How to Shop for Food, Jean Rainey. New York, Barnes & Noble, 1972.

THE EGG AND YOU

Since eggs provide excellent quality protein at far lower prices than meat, stock up on them at your next supermarket sale. The quantity you buy need not depend on the keeping interval of this perishable food. You can preserve and keep eggs indefinitely.

Separate the whites from the yolks and freeze both separately. Or, pour melted wax over the intact eggs. Or stick them in a bottle of water under a layer of water glass (sodium silicate) from your hardware store.

For further information:

How to Get the Most from Your Food Dollar, Rudolph Wurlitzer. New York, Universal Publishing and Distributing, 1970.

LEFTOVER LUXURIES

Why pay a premium for a pittance of work? Make your own cheese spread from leftovers and save $2.40 a pound. Just let your hardened odds and ends of cheese soften in a covered jar with a little wine, then mash and serve!

For an out-of-sight dip for cauliflower, celery, or carrots, mix a little cream cheese with milk and add bacon bits, onions, bleu cheese, chopped artichoke hearts, anchovies, smoked oysters, or caviar. It's half as expensive as the tinfoil packets of dip, and infinitely tastier!

For further information:

The Cheese Guide and Cookbook, Ann Chandonnet. Concord, California, Nitty Gritty Productions, 1973.

BUTTERMILK BLESSING

Cut your buttermilk costs in half by making your own buttermilk! Steam a pint-sized jar with lid for ten minutes to sterilize. Next, place a starter cup of buttermilk in the jar, then fill with powdered (reconstituted) skim milk and add a pinch of salt. Place at room temperature overnight.

The next morning you will awaken to a pint of the best danged buttermilk you ever tasted! In addition, one cup of this mixture plus more powdered milk will yield another pint of buttermilk, and so on indefinitely.

For further information:

Homesteader's Handbook, Rich Israel and Reny Slay. Israel and Slay, P.O. Box 416, Keddie, California 95952, 1973.

MILK FOR BABY

Aside from the aesthetic and psychological aspects of the breast versus bottle dilemma, we offer this unique aspect to the debate: Bottle feeding your child will save you $160 a year! Why? Essentially, because cow-milk is much less expensive than the extra nutrients a woman needs to breast feed.

For further information:

How to Bring Up a Child Without Spending a Fortune, Lee Benning. New York, David McKay, 1975.

SOUR POWER

Vivo's mother's money-saving motto: Never throw out good nutrition! You can even use milk that has turned sour in almost every kind of cooking. It's especially good as a substitute in recipes that call for buttermilk, such as pancakes and waffles, corn bread, biscuits, and spice cupcakes.

If you have no sour milk, don't waste precious pennies on whole milk for cooking. Use a cheaper form of milk, such as skim, evaporated, or dry.

For further information:

Evaporated Milk: A Good Choice for the Thrifty Family (FNS number 15) and *Instant Nonfat Dry Milk: A Good Choice for the Thrifty Family* (FNS number 16), U.S. Food and Nutrition Service. Superintendent of Documents, U.S. Government Printing Office, Washington, D.C. 20402, 1971.

HOMEMADE YOGURT

Make your own delicious yogurt at home for pennies, using milk and a few teaspoons of leftover yogurt for a starter! First, insulate the inside of a largish pot with one-inch-thick foam rubber—top, bottom, and sides. Next, in another pot, heat a pint of milk to 180° F. Pour into a sterilized pint jar and let cool in a separate container to 109° F. Quickly mix ½ teaspoon yogurt with 1 tablespoon of the heated milk, then stir it into the rest of the milk before it cools to 106° F. Cover the top of the jar with foil, place in the insulated pot, and cover. In eight hours you will have a pint of scrumptious homemade yogurt at one third of store prices.

For further information:

Making Your Own Cheese and Yogurt, Max Alth. Totowa, New Jersey, Funk & Wagnalls, 1973.

Produce and Other Edibles

IT'S IN THE CAN

You can find great bargains in such canned produce as pineapples and tomatoes in the height of the pineapple (March to May) and tomato (June to August) seasons. Stock up the cans while they're cheap. Enjoy fresh produce in season, and save the cans for winter, when they'll be higher priced.

For a produce buying calendar, see Jean Rainey's *How to Shop for Food*, New York, Barnes & Noble, 1972, pages 54–55.

For further information:

How to Buy Food, Valerie Woolman. New York, Cornerstone Library, 1970.

RICE RULES

Slice two-thirds off the cost of packaged pre-seasoned rice by purchasing the unseasoned variety and cooking up your own delicious seasonings. For Spanish rice, add ¼ cup of tomato sauce per cup of rice. Add chopped mushrooms and olives; season with salt, pepper, and thyme or rosemary.

Or, try curried rice: Add a liberal tablespoon of curry per cup of rice, a pinch of chervil, salt and pepper to taste, and bacon bits.

Here's our favorite: Chop, sauté, and add to each cup of rice one good-sized onion. Add ¼ cup pine nuts (health food store) and serve with oyster sauce (supermarket gourmet department) or soy sauce. Out of this world!

SPROUT SAVINGS

The dry bean is an extraordinary vegetable. Costing only 30¢ a pound, this magical legume can be converted to six times its weight in edible produce.

It's done simply by soaking the beans in water overnight, then placing them on a moist cloth in a dark place and flushing with water three to five times a day. In three days you will have three-inch sprouts chock full of vitamins B and C.

For further information:

The Complete Sprouting Cookbook, Karen Whyte. San Francisco, Troubador, 1973.

DRESSING DETOUR

Save half the cost of bottled salad dressings or salad-dressing mixes by making your own gourmet concoctions. Mix two parts safflower oil with one part vinegar and add salt, cracked peppercorns, dried parsley, dill and celery seeds, a pinch of ground cumin.

For creamy dressing, add two tablespoons of mayonnaise and a tablespoon of ketchup. And for out-of-sight blue cheese dressing, simply add a three-ounce package of crumbled bleu cheese to a small jar of mayonnaise and let sit in the refrigerator for a day or two.

For further information:

Salads and Salad Dresssings, Eulalia Blair. Boston, Cahners, 1974.

IN A PICKLE?

Fresh cucumbers, onions, carrots, tomatoes—bought by the crate in the height of their respective seasons at half the off-season price—can be preserved indefinitely *at no cost*, and without the high electrical bills involved in freezing food! How? By pickling them in the leftover liquid from store-bought pickle and chili jars.

For a homemade substitute for this liquid, costing only pennies, mix one part vinegar to two parts water. You may wish to add a little garlic, a few peppercorns, tarragon, or other herbs for seasoning.

For further information:

The Pleasures of Preserving or Pickling, Jeanne Lesem, Westminster, Maryland, Knopf, 1975.

A FRUITFUL IDEA

At farmers' markets and food stores, you can pick up slightly overripe fruit by the lug at fantastic savings. Canning or freezing it will provide you with nutritious, economical food the year round.

The low-cost, low-labor alternative is to slice the fruit, place it on screens in a sunny, breezy place protected from insects, and dry it. You can use the same technique on beef to create that outrageously overpriced delicacy, beef jerky. Great for camping trips, power failures, and just plain hard times.

For further information:

The ABC's of Home Food Dehydration, Barbara Densley. Garden City, New York, Doubleday, 1975.

USE YOUR NOODLE!

For truly spectacular noodle savings (80 cents on the dollar), roll your own noodles from a mixture of flour, eggs, water, salt, and oil. Mix and knead 1⅓ cups flour, 2 eggs, 2 tablespoons water, 2 teaspoons oil, and 1 teaspoon salt. For a really far-out noodle, add ¼ cup dried parsley (or cooked, chopped and dried dandelion leaves from your backyard), ground sesame seeds, curry, chili powder, poppy seeds, or chopped caraway seeds. Let stand for an hour, then roll out paper-thin. Next, dry until almost brittle (about a half hour), then cut into strips.

For further information:

"Cook's Adventure: Making Your Own Noodles," *Sunset*, Vol. 142, January 1969, pages 90–91.

BARLEY COFFEE?

During World War II, coffee shortages forced many nations to use rye, wheat, or barley as a coffee substitute. The cost, compared to that of coffee, is infinitesimal. The product contains no caffeine, thus helping to keep both your heart and your pocketbook healthy.

Just grind the grain coarsely, roast it in the oven, and either boil or percolate it.

For further information:

Eat Well on $1 a Day, Bill and Ruth Kaysing. San Francisco, Chronicle, 1975.

WINE WINDFALLS

You don't have to spend a fortune to enjoy excellent wines. For those in the know, fantastic bargains are everywhere. Yugoslavian wines, for example, produced by the government of that country under the names Adriatica, Slovin, and Navip, are equivalent to French, Italian, and German wines with similar names, at a fraction of the price. For just $1.60 to $1.80 a bottle, purchase Yugoslavian Refosk instead of Italian Refosco; Yugoslavian Rizling instead of Rhine Riesling.

You can often purchase a wine nearly identical to that of an expensive famous vineyard by looking for a label from a nearby vineyard. For example, try Château Brane-Cantenac, at one third the cost of its $25 to $40 neighbor, Château Margaux. For a good list of fine wines, bargain-priced at under $5 a bottle (many at $2 or under), read "Good Wines at Moderate Prices," *Changing Times*, October 1973, pages 33–35.

SOUR DOUGH

Sour over prices for that deliciously different sourdough bread? Make your own using Sourdough Starter, Item #0672 ($1.60), from Mother's General Store, Box 506, Flat Rock, North Carolina 28731. This package, used in place of yeast, will allow the dough to rise with its own fermented souring. One package lasts a lifetime—in fact, it improves with age!

A FORTUNE IN TEA LEAVES

After conducting some research of our own in area supermarkets, we've discovered the shocking fact that a major brand of tea costs *nine* times more per serving individually bagged than when it is in the form of loose tea leaves. Furthermore, you'll pay 20 to 35 times more for tea in instant form than you would for loose tea leaves.

TEA TAB

Don't get teed off about having to pay $2 or more an ounce for imported specialty teas in your local supermarket. Instead, order direct from the grower. You can get 2 kilos (4.4 pounds) of Flowery Orange Pekoe for only $7 by ordering this tea from R. N. Agarwala and Son, Nehru Road, Darjeeling, India.

LIQUID LOGIC

Odd as it seems, the cheapest beverages are the most nutritious! Here's a list of popular drinks, from least to most expensive: frozen orange juice, milk (by the gallon), Diet-Rite Cola (16-ounce returnable 6-pack), Hawaiian Punch (46-ounce can), off-brand soft drink (12-ounce 6-pack), and Coke (16-ounce returnable 6-pack). To give you an idea of the price range, an 8-ounce glass of frozen orange juice costs about 7¢, and Coke, at about 11¢ an 8-ounce glass, costs 60 percent more.

ROOT BEER RUBLES

Root beer, that old-fashioned drink concocted of yeast, sugar, and flavoring, can be made and bottled at home for less than half of store prices. Order root-beer extract, Item #0581 (90¢—enough for five gallons); bottle capper, Item #0235 ($14.60 plus $1.10 shipping); and a package of 144 caps, Item #0236 ($2.45) from Mother's General Store, Box 506, Flat Rock, North Carolina 28731. The bottle capper will work with any recycled bottles such as beer or wine bottles.

A FEW SALTY REMARKS

Instead of wasting $10 or more a year on the seasoned salt products sold in your supermarket, mix your own unique blends at a savings of 50 percent or more. For an absolutely delicious seasoning concoction, mix together in a salt shaker or an old seasoned salt container three parts garlic powder or dried onion flakes, one part celery seed, and one part salt; mix equal parts fresh-ground pepper, paprika, parsley flakes, and salt; seven parts coarsely ground sesame seeds and one part salt; or even five parts powdered seaweed, one part cumin, and one part salt.

For further information:

Herbs, Spices and Flavorings, Tom Stobart. New York, International Publications Service, 1972.

NICE SPICE PRICES

For extremely economical mail-order herbs, spices, and scents, request a price list from Mother's General Store, Box 506, Flat Rock, North Carolina 28731. These folks sell four ounces of the ever-popular rosemary for 70¢—one fourth of the store-bought price. They also feature four ounces of such scented herbs as patchouli, pennyroyal, frankincense, and myrrh at $1.10 to $2.40.

WOOD WISDOM

You can buy smoked meat flavoring in a bottle for $1 or you can easily manufacture it yourself by sprinkling a handful of sawdust (any kind of wood) that has been soaked in water over a charcoal fire just before putting the meat on to cook. It's cheap and it makes meat taste good!

For further information:

Heloise's Kitchen Hints, Heloise Cruse. New York, Pocket Books, 1971.

Free Food

MINE MUSHROOMS!

With mushrooms rapidly approaching the price of sterling, it will pay you handsomely to seek out and pick your own. This delectable vegetable can be had for the taking in just about any damp, shady spot.

How to tell edible from poisonous? Take an illustrated mushroom field book with you on your forays to identify your quarry on the spot. Most edibles have a smooth, tapering base. Never eat a mushroom with a bulging, fringed base.

For further information:

Introduction to Mushroom Hunting, Vera Charles. New York, Dover, 1974.

FREE FOOD FROM THE FARM

The next time you take a Sunday ride in the country, keep in mind the fact that you're in Free Food Heaven. If you see a crew of workers harvesting strawberries, oranges, spinach, or nuts, stop and ask the foreman how much he'll charge for a basket or a bag of culls.

A couple we know scavenged enough tomatoes on one trip to provide them with five years' worth of stewed tomatoes, tomato paste, and delicious homemade tomato juice. The foreman gave them the raw material free for the asking.

For further information:

Eat Well on $1 a Day, Bill and Ruth Kaysing. San Francisco, Chronicle, 1975.

TEAS FOR THE TAKING

You don't have to pay a mint to stock your larder with an exotic assortment of herb teas. Simply hie yourself out to the country—or the nearest vacant lot—and pick a few of these favorites of Early America: catnip (thought to alleviate nervous headaches), fennel for indigestion, wild mint for colds. Other herb teas: balm, chickweed, dandelion, elder leaf, elder blossom with peppermint, eyebright, feverfew, ground ivy, horehound, hyssop, mugwort, nettle, plantain, rosemary, scurvy, speedwell, strawberry leaf, tansy, violet, and yarrow.

For further information:

A Garden of Herbs, Eleanour Rohde. New York, Dover, 1969 (cookbook).

Weeds of Lawn and Garden: A Handbook of Eastern Temperate North America, John Fogg. Philadelphia, University of Pennsylvania Press, 1956.

How to Know the Weeds, R. E. Wilkinson and Harry Jaques. Dubuque, Iowa, William C. Brown, 1972.

MEALS FOR MOTHERS

Free food is available for needy pregnant or nursing mothers and also for children under four years of age. Ask your State Health Department, or if you are an Indian, your Indian Health Service Area office or your tribal office, about the Special Supplemental Food Program for Women, Infants, and Children (WIC).

SALAD FIXIN'S

With the price of lettuce rising faster than a New York cabbie's temper in a July traffic jam, you'll want to avoid this costly vegetable as much as possible. A wealth of greenery is yours for the taking in just about any vacant field.

For a gourmet's delight, try the tender spring leaves of pigweed (green amaranth), the young peeled stems of burdock, or one of the members of the cress family (including watercress). Add a dash of vitamins A and C to the salad with wild violet leaves.

For further information:

Eat the Weeds, Ben Harris. Barre, Massachusetts, Barre Publishers, 1969.

Why Wild Edibles?, Russ Mohney. Seattle, Pacific Search, 1975.

SEED STORY

Don't pay $3 a pound for seed snacks at the supermarket! Make your own by washing pumpkin, cantaloupe, or squash seeds thoroughly, coating with oil or butter, and roasting in a moderate oven until light brown. Season with garlic salt or onion salt.

For further information:

Nuts and Seeds, the Natural Snacks, Organic Gardening and Farming Staff Editors. Emmaus, Pennsylvania, Rodale Press, 1973.

WINES FROM THE WILD

You can have the most unique wine cellar in town for practically nothing. How? Wild flowers can supply you with wines that can't be bought anywhere. Clover, daisy, dandelion, goldenrod, rose—all make excellent grist for your own special blend. You might try such herb wines as chickweed or balm; walnut or hickory nut leaf, oak or grape leaf wine; the ever-popular blackberry and raspberry, and the less renowned but equally delicious wild strawberry.

For further information:

Folk Wines, Cordials and Brandies, M. A. Jagendorf. New York, Vanguard, 1963.

TAKING STOCK OF THE SITUATION

Instead of paying 40¢ a pound for beef stock, a "stock" ingredient in such recipes as stew, casseroles, and soups, make your own with ease by using what would ordinarily be termed garbage!

Keep a pot of salted water simmering on your stove while you fix supper. Into it throw bone scraps, meat skin, fat trimmings; juices, vegetable tops, potato peels; and wilted or leftover salad fixings. In the evening, cover the pot and let it cook, then refrigerate.

Continue the process each night until the mixture thickens; then boil ten minutes, strain, place in sterile, lidded jars, and pop into the fridge. The next time your recipe calls for stock, you'll have a stock response!

For further information:

The Simmering Pot Cookbook, Alice Loebel. Riverside, New Jersey, Macmillan, 1974.

LILY LURE

The common day lily, as often found growing wild along streams or in lowlands as in a garden, is a versatile, free nutritional substitute for asparagus, green beans, even potatoes. Dig up the crisp new tuber roots in spring or summer and eat raw in salads, or creamed or boiled.

Chop up the new spring shoots and add to salad, or steam the piths like asparagus. In the summer, boil the unopened flower buds or the full-fledged flower and fry in batter, or add at the last minute to soups and stews. Blossoms can also be dried for winter use. Talk about exotic!

For further information:

The Wild Gourmet: A Forager's Guide to the Finding and Cooking of Wild Foods, Babette Brackett and Mary Ann Lash. Boston, David R. Godine, 1975.

GETTING FAT—FREE

Why flatten your wallet for fat fees? Pork fat trimmings, available free from your butcher, can be cooked slowly until the fat is rendered out and used in any recipe that requires shortening.

Save your bacon drippings for cooking eggs or potatoes, add them to cooked greens or baked beans for a meaty flavor, or use them instead of that expensive canned dog food to flavor puppy's kibble.

For further information:

Joy of Cooking, Irma S. Rombauer and Marion Rombauer Becker. Indianapolis, Bobbs-Merrill, 1964.

CATTAIL TALE

In the diet of many budget-conscious families, over $50 a year goes to the lowly potato alone. Anyone who lives near a pond, lowlands, or swamp can eliminate this cost completely by digging up and preparing that scrumptious starchy food always found in such places—the root of the cattail. This root can be stewed or roasted whole as you would cook potatoes; boiled with wild greens; or ground and dried for meal. In addition, cattail pollen is a tasty nutritional supplement to soups, cereals, and stews.

Tasting like tender celery hearts, new shoots of cattail are a gourmet's delicacy once enjoyed by the Chumash Indians of California. The pith of the cattail stem, otherwise known as "Cossack asparagus," can be added to stew or casseroles or eaten raw in salads. Free corn? Boil up the green spikes atop summer and fall cattails for a delicious helping of "roasting ears."

For further information:

"Wild Foods: The Common Cattail," *The Mother Earth News Almanac, The Mother Earth News* Staff. New York, Bantam, 1973, pages 10–11.

FOOD STAMP SAVINGS

Bet you didn't know that a person who supports a family of eight can make well over $1,000 a month and still be eligible for food stamps! If you're having trouble making ends meet, why not find out if you're eligible?

A medium-sized family that qualifies can save several hundred dollars on food bills each month. Even a single person can receive enough stamps to buy $50 worth of food every month. For details, contact your local welfare office.

For further information:

The Food Stamp Program (079D), Public Documents Distribution Center, Pueblo, Colorado 81009, 1975.

WHAT'S UP, DOC?

They don't call Queen Anne's lace the "wild carrot" for nothing. Cook up a batch of the young roots—it tastes just like the real thing. In the summer, use the leaves of this omnipresent weed for tea, and in the fall, save the seeds for soup, stew, and bread-crust flavoring.

For further information:

"Wild in the City," *The Mother Earth News Almanac*, *The Mother Earth News* Staff. New York, Bantam, 1973, pages 60–63.

BERRY BONUS

The elderberry bush contains more vitamin C than oranges, more vitamin A and calcium than any comparable wild plant, and a goodly amount of iron and potassium. Almost every part of this plant is edible—flowers, young shoots, juice, piths, and of course, the berries.

The flowers can be dried and made into a delicate pale yellow wine; fried; eaten as a salad; used as a garnish for duck or flavoring for sherbet or fritters; or distilled with orange flower and used as seasoning. Young shoots, preserved in vinegar, can be eaten like bamboo shoots. The juice, combined with vinegar, anchovies, spices, and shallots, makes "Pontac ketchup." The piths can be cooked like asparagus, chilled, and eaten with a sauce of one part vinegar to two parts safflower oil (or one part lemon to two parts butter), with onion and parsley for seasoning. The berries make the famous elderberry wine, or can be combined with crabapples for zap.

For further information:

"The Underappreciated Elderberry," *Los Angeles Times*, 22 April 1976, Part VI, pages 24–25.

THE CROUTON CRUNCH

What a gyp for a few ounces of fried bread! Save your bread heels and ends for the week, toast them lightly, cut into cubes, and sauté them with garlic, salt, and your favorite herb. Your croutons will taste better than the store-bought version, and they're made with what you usually throw out. By the way,

preseasoned bread cube "dressings," sautéed lightly in butter, make excellent croutons at a third the price.

For further information:

The Impoverished Student's Book of Cookery, Drinkery, and Housekeepery, Jay Rosenberg. Long Island, New York, Doubleday, 1965.

POTHERB POTENTIAL

Never buy those expensive chemical-laden store-bought seasonings again! Instead, pick a few wild potherbs—strongly flavored plants which add nutritional value as well as seasoning to your foods—for a unique down-to-earth touch that literally can't be bought. You're probably already familiar with most of these savory seasoners: sorrel, wild mustard, cowslip, cress, fireweed, evening primrose leaves, dayflower, pigweed, mallow, milkweed buds and flowers, sassafras leaves. There are many more!

For further information:

A Sampler of Wayside Herbs: Rediscovering Old Uses for Familiar Wild Plants, Barbara Pond. Riverside, Connecticut, Chatham Press (orders to E. P. Dutton), 1974.

Eating Out

KRISHNA KONDIMENTS

For a truly unique free meal, and a glimpse into a fascinatingly different life-style, enjoy Sunday dinner at one of the Hare Krishna Society chapters located in any large city. When we dropped by the San Diego chapter, we were treated to chanting and dancing, an extravagantly costumed play from the life of Krishna, and a discussion of the sexual positions favored by same. Moreover, the food was abundant, a gourmet's delight and, needless to say, favored by Krishna.

See your White Pages under "International Society for Krishna Consciousness."

PEANUTS FOR LUNCH

Looking for an inexpensive, clean place to get food? Check out the cafeterias of hospitals, colleges, and government office buildings in your area. They're practically always open to the public, and mealtime savings are substantial. In San Francisco, for example, the cafeteria of St. Mary's Hospital offers a salad, meat dish, vegetable, milk, and dessert for as little as $1.

Not to be overlooked: These tipless self-service restaurants automatically save 10 to 15 percent on your food bill.

EATS FOR THE ELDERLY

If you are sixty or older, you and your spouse qualify for daily free meals under the Nutrition Program for the Elderly sponsored by the Administration on Aging. This program also offers home-delivered meals for those who cannot leave home.

To find out if such meal programs operate in your area, contact the local senior citizens' organizations, which can be found in the Yellow Pages.

SUPPER SAVINGS

During their lunch hour, many restaurants offer, at a sizeable discount, suppers that might normally be out of your financial limits. And although they don't advertise it, a large number of dinner houses offer an "early bird" dinner menu. Patrons who arrive prior to the hectic supper hour (usually before seven) can find meals for one-third to one-half the normal price.

To find such bargains, walk your fingers through the Yellow Pages, making inquiries of local eateries before planning your evening meal out on the town.

TWOFER ONE

If you dine out a lot with a friend, you can save a bundle by buying and using dinner club booklets. The $10 membership fee for San Diego's Let's Dine Out, for example, entitles you to one free meal for every meal you buy in any of forty-five San Diego restaurants. In addition, many times these booklets entitle you to discounts on entertainment, sporting events, and lodgings.

See your Yellow Pages under "Dinner club booklets" or "Clubs."

3

MEDICAL MARKDOWNS

There's a story about a man who went to the doctor for a lengthy series of tests. Although the man was found to be perfectly healthy, his doctor, nevertheless, ordered him into the hospital as a heart-attack patient. The man protested. "But doctor," he said, "I don't understand. All my tests show that I'm in perfect health, yet you're sending me to the hospital for a heart attack. I've *never* had a heart attack." The doctor replied, "I know it, but you *will* have when you get my bill!"

Almost every city and county across the land offers *some* type of free health care. Services may include prenatal and child care; gynecological and birth-control services; immunization shots; tuberculosis and venereal disease treatment; smoking, alcoholism, and weight-reduction clinics—even psychiatric counseling—all at no cost! For a list of free facilities throughout the country, see "Appendix II, Free Clinic Directory," *The People's Handbook of Medical Care*, Arthur Frank and Stuart Frank, New York, Random House, 1972, pages 399–409.

Your union, employer (if you work for a large corporation), or professional association may also offer free or low-cost X rays, laboratory work, or vaccinations.

Some hospitals offer free or extremely low-cost access to their outpatient and inpatient services if one can prove need.

Many fine research hospitals offer the most advanced medical care—at no cost—to individuals suffering from physical and psychological maladies in which the hospital is interested.

The main thing to remember when you consider free medical service: Habit is a great builder of prejudice. Don't assume, just because you are accustomed to paying high medical costs, that you are getting better health care. We have found free service more than adequate. And, according to the example cited above, simply eliminating the stress of high medical bills can help you recover sooner—or prevent you from getting sick in the first place!

Hospital Bill Killers

OPERATING EXPENSES

Minor operations such as removal of tonsils, which formerly required hospital admission, can now be done on an outpatient basis. If your health insurance covers such treatment, you can dispense with those high-priced room fees. And if your doctor won't perform the operation on an outpatient basis, find yourself one who will! Saves 25 to 75 percent on your hospital bill!

For further information:

"One-Day Surgery Cuts the Expense," Leonard Sloane, *Moneysworth*, 1 September 1975, page 12.

"Outpatient Surgery," Helen Silver, *McCall's*, Vol. 102, September 1975, page 39.

A PAT ANSWER

If you must enter the hospital, you can still cut down drastically on those outrageous in-patient bills by having as many tests as possible run on an outpatient basis—before you check into that financially unhealthy hospital.

This sensible system is known as Pre-Admission Testing (PAT). For every day you avoid being in the hospital, you will save $100 on semiprivate room and board at even the low-priced community hospitals.

For further information:

How you Can Get Better Medical Care for Less Money, Morris Placere and Charles Warwick, New York, Walker and Company, 1973.

CHEAP CONVALESCENCE

Is your impending hospital stay likely to involve a long period of convalescence? Then find yourself a hospital with "progressive" patient care. Such hospitals offer intensive-care, intermediate-care, extended-care, and self-care units, in decreasing order of medical attention, ranging in cost from scandalously exorbitant to the price of a middle-range motel room. Use of self-care units during the final stretch of recovery from an illness can save you 25 percent or more per day over the cost of a hospital that lacks such units.

Ask your physician for the name of the nearest progressive patient-care hospital.

For further information:

Save Your Health and Your Money: A Doctor's Answer to Today's High Health Costs, Patrick Doyl. Washington, D.C., Acropolis, 1971.

HOSPITAL HORSE SENSE

Hospitals, like doctors, can be high-priced or economical. Generally speaking, hospitals affiliated with universities and large medical centers charge more for their services. If your medical problem is unusual or your condition critical, such prestigious hospitals will offer you special care along these lines.

If your medical problem is commonplace, however—having a baby, tubal ligation, removal of an appendix or tonsils—you will get perfectly adequate treatment from a local, less-renowned hospital at less than half the price. For example, at University Hospital in San Diego, a sophisticated hospital affiliated with the University of California San Diego School of Medicine, a routine childbirth costs $850–$1,000 for a three-day stay, excluding doctors' fees. But at Bay General Hospital, in the San Diego suburb of Chula Vista, the cost for a three-day childbirth stay is $395. Obviously, the money saved here will go a long way toward feeding and clothing that welcome—but expensive—new addition.

For further information:

How to Reduce Your Medical Bills, Ruth Winter. New York, Crown, 1970.

A TESTY TESTIMONIAL

Are you one of those people who turn regularly and unquestioningly to the hospital as the only source of efficient medical testing? It may surprise you to learn that such medical tests as X rays, complete blood counts

(CBC's), thyroid tests, and electrocardiograms (EKG's) can be had for less than half the inflated hospital price at medical and X-ray laboratories (see your Yellow Pages under these headings).

Why are independent labs so much less expensive? Because hospitals invariably mark these services up in order to compensate for budget losses in other departments, whereas private labs incur no such losses.

For further information see *How to Reduce your Medical Bills,* above.

KUT-RATE KIDDIE KARE

If your child must enter the hospital, by all means find out if any hospitals within a reasonable distance have care-by-parent units. Under this program, the parent is allowed to stay with the child—in his room—and care for him. The University of Kentucky Hospital is presently offering this plan with great success.

Not only does this arrangement help to calm the child's fears in these strange surroundings, but since this care by the parent frees hospital staff for other work, the average hospital bill, including the *parent's* room and board, is a merciful 40 percent less.

For further information see *How to Reduce Your Medical Bills,* above.

HOSPITAL HAZARD

Sometimes a doctor will unthinkingly have you check into a small hospital on a Thursday or Friday, then lie around until Monday waiting for tests, while the hospital's X-ray or laboratory technicians take the weekend off. While they play golf, you pay hospital-room rates. If this is the case in your hospital, and if you are able to wait, it will be far more economical for you to check in on Monday.

For further information:

Save Your Health and Your Money: A Doctor's Answer to Today's High Health Costs, Patrick Doyle. Washington, D.C., Acropolis, 1971.

HERNIA HELP

If a hernia operation is inevitable, check into the low rates of Shouldice Hospital, Thorn Hill, Box 370, Toronto, Canada. Even considering transportation costs to Toronto, most people living in the northeastern United States find it far cheaper to fly to this hospital, which specializes in treating hernias, than to get the job done at their local hospital.

Shouldice's specialization and streamlined patient care allow the average patient to leave the hospital after four days, as compared to a week or more at other hospitals. At about $60-a-day hospital costs (including everything but doctor's fees), the shorter stay lops $180 to $240 off your bill.

A HOSPITAL WITH A HEART

The Deborah Hospital, Browns Mills, New Jersey 08015, will treat people with lung diseases and heart defects without regard for their ability to pay for the services. To gain admission, you must be sponsored by one of several hundred chapters of this organization.

For further information:

Deborah Hospital, National Office, 901 Walnut Street, Philadelphia, Pennsylvania 19107.

FREE TREATMENT

If you have a chronic disease—asthma, heart trouble, schizophrenia, or just about any of the more common serious diseases—you may be able to get the most advanced treatment for free at the National Institutes of Health Clinical Center, Bethesda, Maryland 20014. Your physician must recommend you to this research center and supply the necessary medical information.

While the center will not pay for your transportation to them, they will pay all the hospital costs for your stay, provided your symptoms correspond to one of their research programs.

RESPIRATORY RELIEF

Free treatment for chronic respiratory diseases is available through the National Jewish Hospital and Research Center, 3800 East Colfax, Denver, Colorado 80206. The center uses the most advanced research techniques to treat emphysema, TB, and such allergic disorders as asthma. This organization will accept individuals of all faiths.

BLOOD PRESSURE TESTS

These tests are available free several times a year through many affiliates of the American Heart Association, 44 East 23rd Street, New York, New York 10010.

Some of these affiliates offer penicillin *at cost* to prevent complications from rheumatic fever. If you have a heart problem for which you cannot afford treatment, they will help you find the funds. Recovering from a stroke? Their trained volunteers will help you carry out your rehabilitation program.

Doctors, Dentists, Shrinks

LAYMAN, HEAL THYSELF!

You may be surprised to learn that, because of spiraling health-care costs, an increasingly large segment of our population is practicing effective, do-it-yourself medical care. How do these dilettante doctors learn their skills?

There are many avenues of approach. Red Cross chapters across the land offer valuable low-cost first-aid training. Many county health departments loan films and provide free literature on health care. The U.S. Public Health Service offers special medical training programs for lay people. The ubiquitous adult schools and university extensions often include in their programs classes in medicine for the layman. And, finally, there is a wealth of books on the market dealing with all aspects of home medicine.

For further information:

The Well Body Book, Mike Samuels and Hal Bennett. New York, Random House/Bookworks, 1973.

Home Medical Handbook, E. Russel Kodet and Bradford Angier. New York, Association Press, 1970.

NURSING YOUR NEST EGG

Home visits by your doctor are to be avoided, not only because they are expensive, but also because they limit the doctor to a small fraction of his or her medical equipment and diagnostic techniques.

If you are just too ill or too feeble to make it to the doctor, consider calling a visiting nurse. Under such limiting circumstances, the nurse is able to perform many services, and the cost will be about half as much as the doctor. You may also find that a visiting nurse's fee is covered by your health insurance, while a visiting doctor's fee is not.

See your Yellow Pages under "Nurses and nurses registries."

FREE MEDICAL INFORMATION

No need to spend $25 for an office visit just to get simple medical information. A program called Tel-Med is available in 37 major U.S. cities. You can call the Tel-Med number for taped information on over 100 medical topics ranging from acne to varicose veins.

To find out if a Tel-Med program is available in your area, call your local medical association or lung society.

GETTING AHEAD

Project Headstart, a program begun in 1965 under the auspices of the Department of Health, Education and Welfare, offers a multitude of free health services as well as free educational opportunities for children of financially deprived families.

Medical care, including speech, hearing, and vision testing; laboratory work, and follow-up treatment; dental X rays, examination, and treatment; a daily hot lunch, and a dynamic learning situation through classroom activities are among the benefits of this outstanding program.

For further information:

Headstart, Main Office, 1021 Fourteenth Street, N.W., Washington, D.C. 20005, or contact your local Headstart office.

A FAR-SIGHTED PLAN

Need an eye exam? You don't have to pay a specialist $20 or more for the service. Such organizations as hospital vision clinics, community health agencies, vision associations, and labor unions often provide no- or low-cost eye care—including examination, treatment, and glasses.

For more information, contact your city or county health department. One source of free eyeglasses for those who cannot otherwise afford them is New Eyes for the Needy, Inc., 549 Millburn Avenue, Short Hills, New Jersey 07078.

DO-IT-YOURSELF ALLERGY TEST

Before you shuck out the $200 or so a specialist requires to pinpoint your allergies, pick up a copy of Dr. Arthur Coca's *The Pulse Test*, New York, Arc (distributed by Arco), 1958. The book shows you how to discover your allergies simply by taking your pulse rate, a technique even more accurate than the traditional expensive, painful, long drawn-out skin tests.

DESENSITIZING DOLLARS

You can desensitize yourself to hayfever, poison ivy, even germs in a wound, without paying for shots from an allergist or doctor. For hayfever, beg "cappings," or honeycomb wax trimmings from a local beekeeper before pollen season gets into full swing. Chewing on these, which contain traces of pollen, will accustom your system to the stuff and moderate or alleviate the later allergic reaction.

For poison ivy immunity, Euell Gibbons has recommended *eating* one of the triple-leaves of the plant a day for two weeks, commencing with the first day the tiny leaves appear. Over the weeks, the leaves will increase in size, until you are accustomed to them. *We don't recommend this for those who suffer extreme allergic reactions to the weed.*

Under field conditions, if no antiseptic is available for a wound, we suggest licking the wound, as other animals do. The theory goes that germs from the wound are introduced to the system through the mouth, allowing your body to build up its defenses and heal you faster. If you have any *raw* honey, smear it on the wound (yuck!). It is antiseptic and contains enzymes that promote healing.

For further information:

"Natural Health Saving Tips," *The Mother Earth News Almanac, The Mother Earth News* Staff. New York, Bantam, 1973, pages 304–305.

BIRTH CONTROL

Excellent birth-control education and advice are available at over 500 Planned Parenthood–World Population offices. You pay little or nothing for pills, diaphragms, IUD insertion and follow-ups, and in some cases vasectomies. If an abortion is necessary and legal, they will help you find funding for it. For more information, call a local office or write their headquarters at 300 Park Avenue South, New York, New York 10010.

If you're considering voluntary sterilization, but haven't the funds for the operation, contact the Association for Voluntary Sterilization, Inc., 708 Third Avenue, New York, New York 10017. They will help you get the service free.

TOOTHSOME FEES

If you want ultramodern dental care at about half the rate of the most reasonable dentists,

try out one of the forty dental schools in the United States.

Students at these schools are bucking for grades and are often more familiar with the newest technical developments than old-time practitioners. Some of the best dental work we've had is the product of dental schools.

Optometry schools likewise offer high-quality services at cut-rate fees.

For a list of dental schools in the United States, write to the American Dental Association, Commission on Accreditation of Dental and Dental Auxiliary Educational Programs, 211 East Chicago Avenue, Chicago, Illinois 60611. For a list of optometry schools, write to the Council on Optometric Education, American Optometric Association, 7000 Chippewa Street, St. Louis, Missouri 63119.

DENTURE DEAL

A dental clinic in South Carolina attracts people from all over the world by offering a full set of dentures for $40. (The usual fee elsewhere is about $480). After you pay for transportation to this unique clinic, you will probably still come out way ahead of the game. For further information, write to Dr. C. L. Sexton Dental Clinic, 377 West Palmetto, Florence, South Carolina 29501.

PSYCHIATRIC COUNSELING

Before you shuck out $50 or so for an hour's conversation with that Beverly Hills psychiatrist, check with the psychology department of your local university. These often offer counseling and testing by graduate students for next to nothing.

For example, the San Diego State University Psychological Clinic offers free or low-cost counseling, psychotherapy, and other mental health services for families, groups, and individuals—including nonstudents as well as students.

To find out about other free and low-cost psychological services, check with your state or county mental health department.

For further information:

People's Yellow Pages of America, Scott French. New Rochelle, New York, Richard Heller & Son, 1974.

GETTING IT TOGETHER

Excellent low-cost or free supportive aid in recovering from mental illness can be had through local chapters of national self-help groups such as Recovery, Inc., 116 South Michigan Avenue, Chicago, Illinois 60603. Recovery sponsors small group meetings at which former mental patients act as group leaders. Families of patients can attend, but are not allowed to participate. The low annual membership fee will be waived for those who cannot afford it, and the collection taken at each session is purely voluntary.

Professional and volunteer counseling, special education programs, and transporting families to visit a patient in a hospital, as well as transporting patients from the hospital into town, can be arranged through the National Association for Mental Health. If no local chapter exists in your area, write to their headquarters at 1800 North Kent, Roslyn Station, Arlington, Virginia 22209.

See your Yellow Pages under "Social service and welfare organizations" for other sources of possible help in this area.

Drugs and Sickroom Equipment

WHOLESALE DRUGS

Most savvy buyers of medications and vitamins today buy these goods through reputable mail-order firms rather than over the counter. Why? Because it's possible to save a third to a half of the retail price this way.

For both prescription and nonprescription drugs, contact Celo Direct Drug Services, Burnsville, North Carolina 28714.

For mail-order vitamins at a third to a half of retail prices, write to the following: Nutri-

tion Headquarters, 301 West Main, Carbondale, Illinois 62901; Great Earth Vitamin Discount Center, 10739 West Pico, Los Angeles, California 90064; Vitamin Quota Incorporated, West Coast Mail Order Center, 800 Stillwell Avenue, Reno, Nevada 89502, or East Coast Mail Order Center, Vitamin Quota Incorporated, Fairfield, New Jersey 07006. All will send a free catalog upon request.

GENERIC GENEROSITY

Thanks to the U.S. Food and Drug Administration, you can be fairly sure of the quality of all drugs on the market these days. So when your doctor prescribes your drugs by brand name, ask him to write down the *generic* name of the drug. Then ask the druggist for the cheapest drug with the generic name.

You can often get drugs for as little as a tenth of the brand-name price this way. For example, an antihistamine that costs $20 under the brand name Chlor-Trimeton, costs just $2 as chlorpheniramine maleate. The tranquilizer Miltown costs $57; its generic equivalent (meprobamate) costs $8. And the arthritis medicine Meticorten ($90) costs $9 as prednisone.

For further information:

The New Handbook of Prescription Drugs, Richard Burack. New York, Ballantine, 1975.

Consumer's Guide to Prescription Prices, William Gulick. Syracuse, New York, Consumer Age Press, 1973.

NATURE'S SLEEPING PILL

Aside from bedtime sex, nature's most effective sleeping pill is L-tryptophane, an amino acid that is abundantly present in meat, milk, and cheese. If sleeping pills are putting a big dent in your budget, find yourself a lover, or eat more meat.

For further information:

"Nature's Sleeping Pill?" *Newsweek,* Volume 86, No. 15, 13 October 1975, page 69.

LAXATIVE LOGIC

With proper diet and exercise, it should never be necessary to use laxatives, especially not habitually. However, if you must use one from time to time, for heaven's sake, don't contribute to the hundreds of thousands of dollars Americans spend *daily* on the drugstore variety!

Instead, create your own *natural* laxative by preparing any of a number of herbs which will do the job just as effectively. Cook up a batch of young, peeled burdock shoots, or try white mustard leaves, raw or cooked; seed tea of white or black mustard; root tea or cooked leaves of yellow dock; and spring leaves of wild lettuce, raw or cooked.

For further information:

Just Weeds, Edwin Spencer. New York, Scribner's, 1957.

Wild Edible Plants of the Western United States, Donald Kirk. Healdsburg, California, Naturegraph, 1970.

A PEACHY IDEA

Plain peach tree leaves, free for the taking in many backyards and gardens, reportedly cure a wide range of ailments that might otherwise require treatment with expensive drugs. Many herbalists agree that tea from these leaves will cure bladder and uterine infections, upset stomach, jaundice, and abdominal inflammation.

The powdered leaves or bark will help heal skin injuries or sores. Buds from the peach tree may be bruised, boiled in vinegar until thick, and used as a quinine substitute. This concoction is even reputed to cure blindness!

For further information:

Back to Eden, Beneficial Books, Box 404, New York, New York 10016.

MEDICAL MEDLEY

You can spend a lot of money on the contents of your medicine chest, or you can spend a little on simple, old-time, proven remedies that work just as well. For example, use 3

percent hydrogen peroxide as mouthwash and as an almost painless antiseptic for external cuts; an old-fashioned shaving soap bar and brush instead of aerosol-can shaving cream; dishwashing detergent instead of bubble bath; petroleum jelly to soothe chapped lips or as cold cream. Douche with two tablespoons of vinegar in a quart of warm water. Rinse your hair with lemon juice or cider vinegar.

For further information:

Van Nostrand's Practical Formulary, William Minrath, ed. Princeton, New Jersey, Van Nostrand, 1952.

PLANT PANACEA

An excellent home remedy for a wide variety of skin and internal ailments is a plant called Aloe Vera, which can be purchased at any nursery. The soothing juice of its leaves serves as an ointment for burns, or for treating diaper rash, sunburn, and skin blemishes. Use it as a facial lotion to prevent wrinkles, or as a scalp and hair conditioner before shampooing. Or chew up a piece of the leaf to relieve indigestion, ulcers, and arthritis and rheumatism.

For further information:

"Aloe Vera: The Drugstore You Grow on a Windowsill," Nancy Chute. *The Mother Earth News*, No. 37, January 1976, page 95.

BAY BANISHER

Banish headaches, depression, or a stuffy nose with that well-known herb, the bay leaf! For headache or depression, boil up a tea of two to four leaves in a pot of water. Let the concoction cool, then bathe forehead and neck with it. This actually works!

To cure a stuffy nose, take in a few breathsful of the steam from the boiling tea. (Take care not to scald yourself in the process.)

GARLIC PENICILLIN

Garlic may not keep away werewolves, but eating it will relieve fungus and skin infections, typhoid, wound infection, paratyphoid, and cholera. The curative effect is caused by the combination of a garlic substance called alliin with enzymes in garlic (as well as in onions and leeks) to form allicin, an antibacterial agent. One milligram of allicin is as effective as 25 units of penicillin. Moreover, allicin, unlike penicillin, kills only the "bad" bugs, allowing the good bacteria necessary to your body's health to thrive.

Onions, also containing a substance that helps dissipate blood clots, just may save the life of folks with a history of thrombosis or apoplexy, both of which are caused by blood clots.

For further information:

"Amazing New Facts about Onions, Radishes, and Garlic," *The Mother Earth News Almanac*, *The Mother Earth News* Staff. New York, Bantam, 1973, pages 34–35.

ASTHMA ATTACKER

An asthma remedy with a tiny appetite that can be had free from your animal shelter? That's right—a Chihuahua. One of those facts that are stranger than fiction, reported by Tom McCahill, *Mechanix Illustrated*'s automotive editor, and verified by hundreds of readers: These little pets prevent asthma!

Does the dog filter the asthma-producing particles out of the air through its own lungs, or secrete a substance that represses the sufferer's symptoms? The cause remains a mystery, but the fact is that this "medicine" *does* work. Keep the pooch on or near the sufferer.

For further information:

The Mother Earth News Almanac, *The Mother Earth News* Staff. New York, Bantam, 1973, page 249.

AMAZING ACUPRESSURE

Acupressure is an age-old Chinese method of relieving pain and discomfort without harmful drugs. This method, now becoming fairly popular in America, is quite similar to the better-known acupuncture technique, but instead of needles, simple finger pressure is applied to certain strategic points of the body.

Headaches and backaches, as well as discomfort from colds, hay fever, bronchitis, menstrual cramps, constipation, and many other ailments can be effectively and easily eliminated through proper acupressure techniques.

For further information:

Finger Pressure, Pedro Chan. Westminster, Maryland, Ballantine Books, 1975.

INTESTINAL FORTITUDE

We can't say much for the taste of this cure for indigestion, but a lot can be said for the price—about a penny a dose compared to who-knows-what for commercial remedies. It's a home recipe for mineral water, an alkaline concoction that neutralizes excess stomach acid just like they say in the ads.

Place one teaspoon of calcium hydroxide (powdered slaked lime—buy it at a drugstore) in a quart of cold water and shake well. Refrigerate and allow the lime to settle to the bottom. Pour off and save the liquid, and throw out the residue. Drink one-third cup to soothe your dissatisfied duodenum.

For further information:

"Down Home Medicine for Nervous Stomach," *The Mother Earth News Almanac*, *The Mother Earth News* Staff. New York, Bantam, 1973, page 171.

MEDICINE MAGIC

Considering the cost and efficacy of conventional drugs for the following maladies, you have everything to gain by trying these natural remedies, which may well be growing right in your backyard.

For poison ivy, forget the calamine lotion. Instead, smear on juice of jimson weed (don't eat it; it's poisonous!). To banish warts, use milkweed juice. Staunch the flow of blood from a deep wound with cobwebs (nice clean ones, please). Soothe blisters with a strong tea of boiled oak bark.

For further information:

Nature's Cures, Carlson Wade. Hauppauge, New York, Universal Publishing and Distributing (orders to Award), 1972.

TOOTHY TALLY

Take a big bite out of toothpaste tolls by making your own at 15 percent off retail prices. Just mix one part glycerine (drugstore) with two parts powdered pumice (hardware store), using a drop or so of peppermint oil (drugstore or chemical supply house) for flavoring.

For further information:

The Chemical Formulary (Vols. 1–15), H. Bennett. New York, Chemical, 1972.

DON'T GET SORE

If the price of suntan lotion burns you up, you can create your own natural sunscreen by eating plenty of yellow fruits and yellow and green leafy vegetables. These foods contain a pigment—beta carotene—which vastly improves the skin's ability to withstand the sun even for extra-sensitive persons.

Doctor Michelin Matthews-Roth injected this pigment into a group of sun-sensitive patients, and as a result 87 percent developed natural sunscreens.

SUNTAN SAVINGS

Make your own simple, inexpensive suntan lotion that will help you tan and protect you from burning at the same time! You'll need two tablespoons of phenyl salicylate crystals, which you can buy at a drugstore or from retail chemical suppliers. Mix this with a cup of vegetable oil. Add a little brown food coloring and perfume, if you like. That's all you need to make a whole cup of suntan lotion!

For further information:

The Standard American Encyclopedia of Formulas, Albert Hopkins, ed. New York, Grosset & Dunlap, 1953.

SKIN SOLUTION

For people with sensitive skin, or those who have been overexposed to wind, cold, or sun, a fine skin cleanser costing pennies instead of dollars is *mayonnaise*. The light vegetable oil cleanses more thoroughly than the heavy oils in most commercial cleansers; the vinegar in the mayonnaise helps maintain proper skin pH; and the egg yolk ingredient provides vitamin A to nourish your skin.

For tired skin, a little cornmeal added to milk soap suds will gently remove that thin layer of dead cells and revitalize the skin —again, for just a few cents!

For further information:

Cosmetics from the Kitchen, Marcia Donnan. New York, Holt, Rinehart & Winston, 1972.

LIP TIP

No drugstore item is more outrageously overpriced than that little stick of chapped-lip soother. It should hardly come as a surprise that you can save $3.70 per *ounce* by cooking up your own brand of lip-soothing ointment.

You'll need 4 parts beeswax (hobby shop); 4 parts castor oil (drugstore); 3 parts sesame oil (grocery store); and 2 parts anhydrous lanolin (drugstore or chemical supply house). Melt the beeswax in a double-boiler. Remove from heat and add other ingredients. For a pleasing taste, add oil-soluble food flavoring of your choice. Stir well and store in small ointment or jelly jars. Apply sparingly to lips with finger.

For further information:

Nature's Way to Beauty, Benassi Enterprises, 1350 Ferndale, Highland Park, Illinois 60035.

SHEEP STROKES

This remedy for chapped hands is easy to come by down on the farm, or at the children's section of your zoo. Find yourself a sheep, and stroke its back. The lanolin in the sheep's wool will soften your hands, and the additional aroma will make you irresistibly attractive to other sheep. Much more fun than buying lanolin at the drugstore.

Too sheepish to try the above? Hie yourself to a farm supply store and purchase a little Bag Balm for your poor hands at 10 percent off drugstore hand-lotion prices.

For further information:

"Folk Medicine," *The Mother Earth News Almanac, The Mother Earth News* Staff. New York, Bantam, 1973, page 163.

OIL YOUR PALM

Save $7.75 per quart of baby oil by substituting U.S.P. grade white mineral oil. Add a few drops of oil-base perfume to fancy it up. This is a fine way to pamper baby's bottom and oil your palm at the same time.

For further information:

Nature's Way to Beauty, Benassi Enterprises, 1350 Ferndale, Highland Park, Illinois 60035.

CLEANSING CONCOCTION

Why put out a small fortune for cleansing lotion when you can make your own for half as much using drugstore ingredients? Here's how: You'll need distilled water, borax, witch hazel, and denatured ethyl alcohol. Measure out ½ cup distilled water, plus 4 teaspoons. Dissolve ¼ teaspoon borax in it—you may have to heat it to dissolve. Then cool the mixture, and add 1²/₃ tablespoons of witch hazel and 10 teaspoons of denatured ethyl alcohol.

Voilà! A cup of cleansing lotion as good as or better than you'll find in the swankiest boutique!

For further information:

New Cosmetics Formulary, H. Bennett. New York, Chemical, 1970.

DEODORANT DODGE

Up in arms over deodorant prices? Make your own at ¹/₁₄ the cost by using denatured or isopropyl alcohol, powdered alum, and

zinc oxide, all available at your friendly drugstore. Mix ⅝ cup water with ⅛ cup alcohol and ¾ teaspoon each of alum and zinc oxide. Shake well before each use.

For further information:

Nature's Way to Beauty, Benassi Enterprises, 1350 Ferndale, Highland Park, Illinois 60035.

ARMPIT PLOY

An inexpensive and very effective natural underarm deodorant containing chlorophyll can be made by steeping fresh pine needles, strawberry leaves, and/or peppermint leaves and stems in alcohol for a few days. Add an equal part of water to this mixture to protect tender underarms.

FOOT POWDER POWER

Here's a deodorant foot powder that really fills the bill and fits the feet—at a third off retail prices. Get yourself some powdered alum, boric acid, and talc from the drugstore. Mix 3 parts alum with 12 parts boric acid and 16 parts talc. Place in an old powder container or salt shaker.

By the way, this mixture will keep your pet smelling sweet as a rose as well. And your roses, well, they may end up smelling like your pet!

For further information:

The Up-With-Wholesome, Down-With-Store-Bought Book of Recipes and Household Formulas, Yvonne Tarr. Westminster, Maryland, Random House, 1975.

TOAST PROPOSAL

Why spend a mint on store-bought breath-freshening tablets? Chewing a little burnt toast or fresh parsley will banish even the most pungent garlic, onion, and liquor odors at a fraction of a cent!

For further information:

"Twenty-five Crafty Ways to Save Money," *Mechanix Illustrated*, August 1974, pages 11–12, 98–99.

CONTACT CLEANER

For a penny or less, compared to the retail price of 60¢ per ounce, you can make your own contact lens cleaning fluid. You probably already have the ingredients: salt, baking soda, and distilled water.

To four tablespoons of distilled water, add a few grains of salt and a few grains of baking soda. Stir well, and drain through a coffee filter into your old contact lens fluid bottle or into an eyedropper.

For further information:

The Chemical Formulary (Volumes 1–15), H. Bennett. New York, Chemical, 1972.

SPLIT TRICK

No need to buy a new thermometer if the mercury in your old one has divided. Instead, use a magnet, touching the glass to pull the separated mercury back down into the bulb.

For further information:

"Twenty-five Crafty Ways to Save Money," *Mechanix Illustrated*, August 1974, pages 11–12, 98–99.

LUNG POWER

Breathing assistance (intermittent positive pressure breathing) devices for lung-disease patients who cannot otherwise afford them can be borrowed without charge from affiliates of the American Lung Association, 1740 Broadway, New York, New York 10019.

Examples of other services offered: Reconditioning programs for children with asthma, payable on a sliding scale; free recreational activities for hospitalized TB patients; and a wealth of free information in the form of films, literature, and lectures.

CANCER CARE

Two nonprofit organizations will be helpful to cancer patients and families both financially and from the standpoint of emotional support. The American Cancer Society, 777 Third Avenue, New York, New York 10017, with chapters in every state, will loan or give outright sickroom equipment and supplies. They will also transport patients and family to and from the hospital and visit at home. Some chapters also offer outright financial aid.

Advanced cancer patients who live within fifty miles of New York City should contact Cancer Care, Inc., National Cancer Foundation, 1 Park Avenue, New York, New York 10016. This group gives professional counseling. For those with low and middle incomes, they offer financial help, including the cost of home care, nursing and nursing homes, and medicine.

Nursing, Physical Therapy

NURSING YOUR POCKETBOOK

If you have been advised that nursing care is necessary, ask your doctor if a highly trained registered nurse (RN) is a must, or whether the licensed practical nurse (LPN), whose salary is close to $20 less for an eight-hour shift, will do. This applies whether the nurse's services are needed in a hospital or at home.

One word of warning: If your health insurance covers, or partly covers, nursing service, you may be outfoxing yourself to try this approach, as some insurance plans will not pay for the services of an LPN.

For further information:

Family Handbook of Home Nursing and Medical Care, I. J. Rossman and Doris Schwartz. New York, M. Evans (orders to J. B. Lippincott), 1968.

HOME HOSPITAL

From a financial standpoint, as well as an emotional one, the sooner you can get out of the hospital and back in familiar surroundings, the better. Even if you need the use of hospital equipment and trained personnel, it's quite likely that you can receive this help at home through the services of a home health care agency.

The more progressive agencies bring a mobile hospital laboratory—a specially equipped truck—and trained hospital personnel right to the patient's home.

Your county health department may offer such a service at cut-rate prices. If not, ask your family doctor for the name of such an agency, or see your Yellow Pages under "Home health services."

For further information:

"Two Ways to Beat High Hospital Costs: Home Care," J. D. Ratcliff, *Reader's Digest*, Vol. 104, February 1974, pages 33–34.

NO COST NURSING CARE

Under Medicare, a senior citizen can get free nursing care for twenty days and half-price care for another 80 days—but only under certain conditions which you and your doctor can help bring about: You must enter the nursing facility, on doctor's orders, within 14 days of a hospital stay of three days or more.

For further information:

A Brief Explanation of Medicare, DHEW Publication Number (SSA) 75–10043, January 1975, Social Security Administration. Superintendent of Documents, U.S. Government Printing Office, Washington, D.C. 20402, or available from your local Social Security Administration office.

ARTHRITIC ASSISTANCE

If you suffer from a rheumatic disease, check with your local chapter of the Arthritis Foundation, 221 Park Avenue South, New York, New York 10003. Not only can they keep you up to date on the latest developments in the treatment of arthritis, but many chapters have facilities for occupational therapy with costs based on ability to pay.

For further information:

Arthritis: Complete Up-to-Date Facts for Patients and Their Families, Sheldon Blau and

Dodi Schultz. Garden City, New York, Doubleday, 1974.

AID FOR THE CRIPPLED

A wide range of free or low-cost services is available for crippled children and adults. Crippled Children Services (see your White Pages under this heading) offer free diagnostic help for children crippled by cerebral palsy, heart and kidney disease, bone diseases, and illnesses leading to blindness. Depending on the family income, they may also meet the cost of medical and occupational therapy for these children.

The Easter Seal Society is a major source of help for crippled adults and children. They sponsor rehabilitation and treatment centers, and mobile and home therapy units offering physical and speech therapy; speech, hearing, and general physical evaluation; psychological testing; personal and family counseling; and referral and follow-up programs. They treat people with cerebral palsy, blindness, amputation, learning disabilities, arthritis, birth defects, and other crippling conditions.

To learn more about their services, write to the National Easter Seal Society for Crippled Children and Adults, Washington Building, 1435 G Street, N.W., Suite 1031–32, Washington, D.C. 20005.

For further information:

How to Get Money for: Youth, the Elderly, the Handicapped, Women, and Civil Liberties, Human Resources Network. Radnor, Pennsylvania, Chilton, 1975.

HEAR, HEAR!

For free speech and hearing evaluation and therapy, including professional advice on the type of hearing aid best suited to you and therapy for speech problems, contact your local affiliate of the National Association of Neighborhood Health Centers, Inc., 1625 I Street, N.W., Suite 403, Washington, D.C. 20006.

In our area, the San Diego affiliate, Neighborhood Health and Support Services, offers free examinations that normally cost $25 or more commercially.

NEUROMUSCULAR DISEASES

If you have any one of several dozen neuromuscular diseases, including the various muscular dystrophies and myasthenia gravis, you can get a wide range of invaluable free medical assistance from the Muscular Dystrophy Association, Inc., 810 Seventh Avenue, New York, New York 10019.

On a doctor's recommendation, they will pay for a stay of up to three days in the hospital for a diagnostic workup. If they find that you do indeed have one of the diseases they cover, you'll be eligible for their patient care program, including free weekly physical therapy sessions; individually tailored braces; the loan of wheelchairs, hospital beds, commodes, walkers, crutches, and hydraulic lifts; and participation in their recreational programs.

For further information:

How to Get Money for: Youth, the Elderly, the Handicapped, Women, and Civil Liberties, Human Resources Network. Radnor, Pennsylvania, Chilton, 1975.

DON'T GET BURNED

Before you put out several hundred dollars for enrollment in a commercial stop-smoking clinic, check with your local lung association. These often offer complete smoking cessation programs for only $5 or $10. If not, they can tell you what commercial clinics charge least with best results.

If no affiliate of the American Lung Association exists in your community, write their headquarters at 1740 Broadway, New York, New York 10019.

For further information:

How to Stop Smoking, Herbert Brean. New York, Simon & Schuster, 1975.

UTILITY AGILITY

The most efficiently heated house that one can imagine would be so perfectly insulated, weather-stripped, and draft-proof that it would require no more to heat it than the body warmth of its inhabitants. The only fault with this heating system is that right around the time the people got warm, they'd all suffocate!

Reality seldom approaches such extremes. Be that as it may, the authors can nevertheless easily show you how to slash your heating bills—indeed, all your utility bills—by at least 50 percent. We did it. Our friends have done it. You can do it, too.

For instance, an inexpensive aluminum-silicate liner in your old oil furnace will lower your fuel bill 20 percent. Place an inexpensive transparent silver film over your windows to cut ¼ off heating and air-conditioning bills. Install a turbine ventilator in your attic to save 20 percent on air-conditioning costs. Plug a certain inexpensive gadget into your light-bulb socket for 12½ percent electricity savings. Other simple gadgets will cut in half the water your toilet and shower consumes. We have a legal way for you to make hundreds of long-distance calls—at no charge.

The list is endless, the methods simple. Let's get started. . . .

Heat and Juice

TREE TRUTHS

About to select a house? You can cut heating bills 28 percent in a cold climate by selecting a home with a windbreak (preferably a staggered double row) of evergreens on its north and northwest sides. In addition, deciduous trees on the south side of the house will shed their leaves in winter to allow solar heating, and will cool your home in summer with their shade. Just one moderate-sized tree can cool your house daily as much as 5 room air conditioners operating for 20 hours!

For further information:

"Save Fuel With Insulation Plus . . .," William Morrell, *Mechanix Illustrated*, December 1975, pages 72–73, 104.

THREE IN ONE

Your electric dryer can help lower your heat bill in the winter if you relocate the outlet to your dryer vent *inside* the house. Then, simply secure an old nylon stocking over the vent with a rubber band to prevent lint from escaping. Presto! A combination dryer-heater-humidifier!

Warning: This trick should only be used with an electric dryer—never with a gas dryer, which releases products harmful to humans.

CIRCULATION COSTS

The Thermocycler, a verticle pipe attached at the base to a small fan, recirculates the air inside your home by pulling hot ceiling air down to the floor, where it warms you. This little device can slash 25 percent off your heating bill. Write Brown Manufacturing, Hartford, Wisconsin 53027, for details.

ANTIFREEZE, PLEEZ!

If your home is heated with a hot-water system, you can save 5 percent on your heating bill by using one part ethylene glycol (that's glycol antifreeze; get the kind with corrosion inhibitors but without anti-leak) to four parts water in the hot-water system. The antifreeze, a surface-wetting agent, provides smoother boiler operation and faster extraction of heat from water for improved efficiency, increased radiator heat, and a corresponding decrease in fuel costs.

For further information:

"Coping with the Energy Crisis," *Family Handyman*, April 1974, pages 36–37.

A CAULKULATING CAPER

Did you know that an insignificant gap of ¼ inch under your front door causes a heat transfer equal to a 9-square-inch hole in your

wall? Caulking windows and weatherstripping doors takes little time and money. Yet it can save 10 percent on heating bills in the winter, and the same amount in summer air-conditioning bills.

While you're at it, make sure your fireplace flue is closed. An open flue, like an open window, can really put a damper on winter heating bills!

For further information:

In the Bank . . . or Up the Chimney? Superintendent of Documents, U.S. Government Printing Office, Washington, D.C. 20402 ($1.70).

How to Save Money by Insulating Your Home, National Mineral Wool Insulation Association, Inc., 382 Springfield Avenue, Summit, New Jersey 07901 (30¢).

GLAZED GAME

If you live in the northern United States, and if your old single-glazed house windows are slowly rotting away, replace them with modern double-glazed windows. The initial cost of such windows will be recouped in five to seven years, leaving you with a better-looking home and yearly heat and cooling savings of up to $36.

For further information:

"Replace Your Old Energy Losers With Modern Insulating Windows," Erik Arctander. *Popular Science*, September 1975, pages 106–108, 110, 112–113.

PLASTIC STORM WINDOWS?

It's a fact that storm windows cut down your fuel costs in the winter, and air-conditioning costs in the summer. Why? Windows, because they lack insulation, are major culprits in the case of heat and cold transfer. But if you don't want to put out the money for storm windows, the gas and electric company suggests a low-cost substitute that is just as effective. Just buy some clear plastic sheets and attach them to window frames with masking tape. This is a cheap, workable way to help keep your home at the desired temperature.

For further information:

"New Light on Conserving Energy," Mel Mandell, *Money*, October 1973, pages 66–68.

OILS WELL THAT ENDS WELL

Use oil to heat your home? Here's how to slice 10 to 15 percent off those astronomical winter oil bills. Gather a group of disgruntled fellow consumers and form an oil cartel. Greater buying power—or the threat of an oil embargo—will get you that discount.

A recent newspaper article documented the formation of such a group in Maryland. After bartering with the local oil company, the group effected a 12 percent discount on bulk oil purchases.

You can also wangle a discount, as an individual, by purchasing over 300 gallons of oil (if your tank will hold that much) at one time. For those with smaller tanks, buying oil in the off-season—summer or early fall—will score a 10 percent discount.

INSULATE YOUR ATTIC

If heat (or air-conditioning) bills have your temper boiling, lower your utility bills—and your blood pressure—by insulating your attic. First, protect yourself with gloves, a mask, and thick clothing. Then pad your attic floor with six inches of mineral wool, cellulose, or fiber glass insulation. This will automatically knock 25 percent off your heating bill. If you have an air conditioner, it will lower the cost of air conditioning as well.

For further information:

You Fix It: Insulation, Carmine Castellano and Clifford Seitz. New York, Arco, 1975.

Insulate Your Home Yourself, National Mineral Wool Insulation Association, Inc., 382 Springfield Avenue, Summit, New Jersey 07901 (free).

BRIGHT HEAT

This trick saved our next-door neighbors $45 in heating bills last winter. Instead of at-

tempting to warm their bathroom with heat from their bedroom, they simply installed a heat lamp, available at any hardware store, in their bathroom light socket. These lamps radiate both heat and light, and therefore satisfy two needs for the price of one.

In addition, this trick will allow you to comfortably keep the rest of the house at 66° F. instead of the usual 72° F. The six-degree temperature drop will chop 15 percent off your winter heating bill.

For further information:

Tips on Saving Energy, Council of Better Business Bureaus, Inc., 1150 Seventeenth Street, N.W., Washington, D.C. 20036, 1974.

FANNING THE FLAME

If you don't already have continuous air circulation in your forced-air system, consider converting to it. Conversion, which involves installing a fan that runs on high speed while the furnace is operating, and on low at other times, is inexpensive.

This constant circulation prevents cold air from settling near the floor, and provides more even heating, with a subsequent fuel bill reduction of 15 to 30 percent.

For further information:

"Convert to Continuous Air Circulation," J. M. Matthewman, *Popular Science*, Vol. 203, October 1973, page 128.

THE RADIATOR ROUTE

Although radiators are rapidly going the way of high-button shoes and five-cent cigars, there are still enough of these clanking old relics around to warrant mention.

If you should find yourself sharing a home with some of these low output heating devices, here are three simple ways you can increase their efficiency and lower your heat bill: Apply a fresh coat of oil-base paint, place aluminum foil or a metal reflector and one inch of insulation between radiator and wall, then keep the radiator well-dusted or vacuumed. These measures will prevent 35 percent of your radiator's heat from disappearing into the wall.

INSTALL A NIGHTWALL

To cut nighttime heat loss through metal-frame windows by 75 percent or more, insulate them with "Nightwall," a low-cost insulation panel consisting of easily removable, magnetic clip-on beadboard. Zomeworks Corp., P.O. Box 712, Albuquerque, New Mexico 87103, will custom-make these panels to your specifications.

FIREBOX FOXINESS

The fire chambers of oil furnaces manufactured prior to 1963 can easily be lined with aluminum-silicate ceramic-fiber. This liner, which can be purchased from your heating supply company for around $35, was specifically created to protect astronauts from extreme cold and heat in space. It will increase your furnace's combustion efficiency 25 percent, thus slashing 20 percent off your fuel oil bills.

For further information:

The Homeowner's Survival Kit: How to Beat the High Cost of Owning and Operating Your Home, A. M. Watkins. New York, Hawthorn, 1971.

FURNACE FRUGALITIES

A few hints for getting the most furnace heat for your money: Clean or replace your furnace filters every three months. Use adhesive or duct sealing tape to patch leaks in your heating ducts. If your gas furnace doesn't serve as your water heater, cut off the pilot light in the summer. Having your furnace serviced every fall can net you $100 in savings a year!

For further information:

"Tune Your Heating System to Peak Efficiency," Evan Powell, *Popular Science*, Vol. 203, October 1973, pages 124–128.

BEATING THE HEAT

If you use an old-fashioned, free-standing coal, gas, wood or oil space heater for your home, you can increase heater efficiency 30 percent for the amount of energy a 40-watt light bulb would use, by installing a waste heat circulator.

This device passes stovepipe air through a tube system, and uses a thermostatically controlled fan to blow hot air back into the room, rather than letting it escape up the chimney. The cost? Only $84, which should make up for itself in fuel costs within two to three months. Order 2188 Waste Heat Circulator, six-inch flue, or 2189 Waste Heat Circulator, eight-inch flue, from Mother's General Store, Department 112, P.O. Box 506, Flat Rock, North Carolina 28731.

A less effective, but far less expensive system to increase stovepipe heat radiation involves a $9.95 set of sixteen slip-on aluminum fins, sold by Patented Manufacturing Company, Bedford Road, Lincoln, Massachusetts 01773.

For further information:

"Stovepipe Power," A. Michael Wassil, *The Mother Earth News Handbook of Homemade Power*, *The Mother Earth News* Staff. New York, Bantam, 1974, pages 50–55.

WINDOW WONDER

Magic Stick is a unique reusable transparent silver film which, when applied to windows, cuts heat transfer through them by 80 percent. Thus, placed on north windows in winter, or south windows in summer, it will cut your heating/air-conditioning bills by a good 25 percent. Although the material allows light to enter the house, it effectively blocks almost all of the sun's ultraviolet rays, thus protecting drapes and furniture from fading.

Order from Ain Plastics, Inc., 160 South Macquesten Parkway, Mount Vernon, New York 10550 at $14.95 (18 inches by 10 feet); $9.95 (26 inches by 5 feet); or $18.95 (36 inches by 6½ feet).

A HOT TIP

Has it become catastrophically clear that your old heating system has wheezed its last? While you're calling around for estimates on a new system, check with your local gas, electric, and fuel oil companies. Such concerns often will install a new system at a cut-rate price in return for receiving a long-term customer for their energy source.

For further information:

Three-Hundred-Fifty Ways to Save Energy (and Money) in Your Home and Car, Henry Spies. New York, Crown, 1974.

CHIMNEY CHOICE

Whether you're building a new house or installing a new heating system in an older one, you can shave $100 off these costs by using the fireplace chimney as an outlet for the furnace or boiler as well. Quite a savings for a few minutes' forethought!

For further information:

The Home Owner Handbook of Plumbing and Heating, Richard Day. New York, Crown, 1974.

WATER HEATER WAMPUM

Next to house heating and cooling, your hot-water heater is your greediest energy consumer. Here's how to reduce its appetite: Insulate the hot water tank and pipes with asbestos-fiber cellular coating and seal all joints with asbestos-fiber tape. These materials can be purchased at large hardware stores. Keep the hot-water heater set at 140° F. (medium), its most effective setting.

For further information:

"Practical Ways to Run a House for Less," *Changing Times*, August 1974, pages 24–28.

ATTIC ANTIC

If you live in an area like New York City or Houston, Texas, where summers are fierce, save 20 percent or more on air-conditioner energy costs by installing a turbine ventilator (air-conditioning equipment outlet) in your attic. This wind-driven device removes hot attic air, thus exerting a cooling effect on the entire house.

For further information:

"Save Energy and Keep Cool This Summer," *Family Handyman*, June 1974, pages 36–37.

THE REPULSIVE ROOF

In the southern United States, where summer heat is more of a problem than winter chill, a low-cost alternative to air conditioning is reflective roof paint. Tiny flakes of aluminum in this paint repulse the heat of the sun, and lower the temperature inside your house an average of 10°F., without increasing your electricity bills.

Purchase the paint at your neighborhood paint dealer.

For further information:

Painting and Paper Hanging for the Home Owner, Charles Moore. Garden City, New York, Garden City Publishing Company, 1949.

KOOL KIT

Save up to 70 percent on air-conditioning bills with an "economizer kit" from your local Honeywell distributor. This device, which automatically feeds outside air into the house to cool it at night or at other times when the weather is cool and dry, works with maximum efficiency in low-humidity areas.

For further information:

"Add an Economizer to your Central Air Conditioner," *Popular Science*, May 1975, page 114.

ENERGY-SAVING AIR CONDITIONERS

Contrary to what many appliance salesmen would have you believe, the biggest, most expensive air conditioner is not necessarily the best. To know what size air conditioner would be most efficient for the area you plan to cool, you must know the heat gain of that area (the amount of heat the unit must be able to remove). If you would like a form for calculating this heat gain, send a self-addressed, stamped envelope to the Association of Home Appliance Manufacturers, 20 North Wacker Drive, Chicago, Illinois 60606.

Once you have the size narrowed down, compare energy efficiency ratings (EER) for the various makes. The EER number, which may be calculated by dividing the model's BTU (British Thermal Units—a measure of temperature) by the watts (power) it takes, ranges from one to twelve. A model with an EER of five uses *twice* as much energy as a ten. Paying a little more for an energy-saving air conditioner will save you some cool cash for years to come. According to the U.S. General Services Administration, the air conditioners that cost least in purchase price and energy consumed are Fedders' ACL 16E, 17E, 18E, and 19E ACL 7H.

For further information:

"Cutting This Summer's Air-Conditioning Bill," and "Get Your Money's Worth in Air-Conditioning," *Changing Times*, April 1975, page 4, and August 1974, page 26.

Ways to Reduce Energy Consumption and Increase Comfort in Household Cooling, Superintendent of Documents, U.S. Government Printing Office, Washington, D.C. 20402 (40¢).

UP IN THE AIR?

Undecided about whether to install a central air conditioner or several small units in individual rooms? Not only will a central air conditioner save you 20 percent on your electric bill, but it will cool 50 percent more efficiently, and also provide more even cooling.

For further information:

"Central Air Conditioning: Buy Now and Save," *Better Homes & Gardens*, Volume 50, April 1972, page 72.

"What You Ought to Know About Central Air Conditioning Now," *House & Garden*, Vol. 141, June 1972, page 12.

MORE LIGHT FOR LESS

This little device cuts down voltage to an incandescent light by 12½ percent, thereby decreasing light-bulb energy costs by the same amount. In addition, it increases your light bulb's life. Called the Ener-G-Saver, it can be ordered from Aladdin Products, 2128 Alvarado Street, San Leandro, California 94577 ($3).

LUMINOUS LOWDOWN

Instead of using electric lights on porches, walkways, halls, and basement stairs, buy yourself a pint of fluorescent paint from your paint store ($1), and mark keyholes, walk edges, house numbers, and ends of steps. The marks will glow steadily in the dark, preventing accidents and lowering your light bill accordingly. If you'd rather not mar these surfaces permanently, simply paint strips of masking tape, then apply the tape to these areas. One zip and your "paint job" disappears.

For further information:

"Coping with the Energy Crisis," *Family Handyman*, April 1974, pages 36–37.

SWITCH RICHES

Leaving a few lights on around the house when you're going out for an evening or weekend is an excellent deterrent to a potential housebreaker, but sakes' alive, can this practice eat up precious kilowatts!

If you're wise, you'll buy an electric timer at your local hardware store (under $10) and use it to turn your lights on and off automatically for you when you're out.

For further information:

Hot to Get More for Your Money in Running Your Home, Merle Dowd. West Nyack, New York, Parker, 1968.

"How to Cut Your Gas, Electric and Water Bills," Hubbard Cobb, *Woman's Day*, October 1975, pages 48, 181–182.

"The Nearly Burglarproof House," *Changing Times*, May 1975, pages 45–47.

INCANDESCENT VS. FLUORESCENT

In the energy efficiency fight, fluorescent bulbs win over their incandescent counterparts hands down. A 40-watt fluorescent bulb gives more light than a 100-watt incandescent one, uses less than half as much energy, and lasts ten times as long. So if you're remodeling your home or adding on, by all means have fluorescent fixtures installed in bathrooms, kitchen, studies, and work areas.

What's the best incandescent-lighting buy for workrooms and studies, where extra brightness is required to prevent eyestrain? One 100-watt light bulb, which costs less than two 60-watt bulbs, uses less energy and gives more light than both the smaller watt bulbs combined.

For further information:

"For Ecology, Fluorescent Light Shines," Bernard Gladstone, *Moneysworth*, 26 May 1975, page 16.

PRESSURE COOKER CUTS

Since a pressure cooker takes one-third as long to cook a meal and does so at a lower heat than ordinary pots, your initial investment in this handy utensil will more than make up for itself in long-term energy savings.

For further information:

"Pressure Cooking," *Joy of Cooking*, Irma S. Rombauer and Marion Rombauer Becker. Indianapolis, Bobbs-Merrill, 1964, pages 128–129.

PANHANDLING

When you cook on top of the stove, use pans that cover the burner and keep a tight lid on your concoctions to minimize heat loss. Pots with flat bottoms and straight sides cook more evenly and preserve more heat energy. Medium-weight aluminum pots are more economical for cooking quick meals on the range, but heavy pots, since they retain and distribute heat more effectively, are best for slow-cooking dishes like soup and stews.

The best saucepans are Farberware, Flint

Radiant Heat Core Saucepan #3701, and Sears Harvest Saucepan, Catalog #605–1071. Recommended frypans are Country Inn Breakfast Skillet, #3338 by West Bend; Enterprise, #5082-BH; and Griswold Ware Early American Cast Ironware Skillet.

For further information:

"Saucepans and Fryingpans," *Consumer Bulletin*, Vol. 55, April 1972, pages 21–26 (plus correction in *Consumer Bulletin*, Vol. 55, June 1972, page 27).

FRIDGE FACTS

A frequent cause of high electric bills is worn refrigerator door seals. Test your fridge by placing a piece of writing paper between door and gasket near the door handle. If the paper pulls out easily when the door is closed, the gasket should be replaced.

To avoid paying a repairman $15 or more, do the job yourself using a length of rubber weatherstripping to replace the worn area. Glue it on with adhesive cement. Bring the remaining original gasket up to the thickness of the new section by wedging a paper towel coated with adhesive cement under the old gasket.

For further information:

"Tips You Should Know About," *Family Handyman*, October 1974, pages 42–43.

REFRIGERATOR FIGURES

In the market for a new refrigerator? Here are a few energy facts to contemplate along with the purchase price. The cheapest refrigerator you can buy, energy-wise, is the regular 12-cubic-foot variety. If you get a frostless 12-cubic-foot model, or a 14-cubic-foot refrigerator/freezer, your operating costs will be one and a half times as high. And the electric bill for a 14-cubic-foot frostless refrigerator/freezer will run you two and a half times that for the small, plain model. Since the refrigerator is one of the six biggest energy consumers in the home, you'll want to carefully weigh the facts *before* you buy.

For further information:.

Directory of Certified Refrigerators and Freezers, Association of Home Appliance Manufacturers, 20 North Wacker Drive, Chicago, Illinois, 60606.

TV TABLES

The initial purchase price of a TV set is small in comparison to the amounts you'll spend just supplying it with electricity during its lifetime. You can lower your kilowatt costs substantially, however, by choosing a set with a smaller energy appetite.

Transistorized black-and-white sets, for instance, use half as much electricity as old-fashioned black-and-white tube models. But beware of the color TV set. It gobbles up four times as much energy as the transistorized black-and-white set.

For further information:

The 1976 Buying Guide Issue of Consumer Reports, Consumers Union of United States. Mount Vernon, New York, Consumers Union of United States, 1975.

A SHOCKING FACT!

You've heard of a water leak and a gas leak, but how about an electricity leak? According to our local electrician, as many as half such appliances as radios, TVs, and microwave ovens "leak" electricity because of a short circuit inside the appliance. This can cost you needless dollars every month.

Here's how to check: Unplug all the electrical appliances in your house. Then plug in one at a time, leaving the switch on each turned off. Check your electric meter after plugging each one in. If the dial on your meter starts turning around, the last appliance you plugged in is the culprit.

If you suspect some scoundrel of tapping your electric line for free juice, turn off the switch that controls all the power for your house. If the dials on your electric meter are still turning, better have the police trace the tap and throw that rapscallion in the pokey!

For further information:

Twenty Ways to Save Electricity, Federal

Energy Administration, Publications Distribution Office, Office of Communications and Public Affairs, Washington, D.C. 20461 (free).

Telephone

NEW PHONE FRILLS

Moving day? There *are* ways to cut down on the phone installation fee at your new home. If, for instance, you want one of those handy plug-in phones with a spare jack, place an order for one phone and one extension phone, both with jacks. A few weeks after installation, tell the phone company you don't want that extension phone after all. They will remove it, leaving you with an extra jack at one-fourth the regular installation fee.

Want a Trimline, Princess, or Touchtone phone? If the old inhabitants of your new abode left such equipment behind, or if you've had such equipment in the past, ask the phone company for an equipment fee credit. That's about $5 in your pocket.

PORT-A-PHONE SAVINGS

In Columbia, South Carolina, the phone company has instituted a plan whereby people who are about to move can simply cut the phone cord and take the phone along with them when they move. Naturally, this lowers the installation fee at their new residence. The plan is rapidly spreading to new areas of the country.

Call your phone company and find out if they will allow you to join the great phone rip-off plan.

LOW-USE LOWDOWN

If you're getting a phone, and plan to make 60 local calls or less a month, save a third of your basic-service phone bill by switching to 60-call measured service. And if you make 30 local calls or less each month, you'll lop more than 50 percent off your basic-service phone bill by switching to 30-call measured service.

A TOLL TALE

The newest thing in individually tailored telephoning is the optional residence telephone service. If a high percentage of your phone bill goes for local-area toll calls, you'll cut costs drastically by arranging to get unlimited or semi-limited calling to certain nearby communities. Check with your local phone company to see if they offer this plan, called optional residence telephone service, and to find out how much you can save with it.

NUMBERS RACKET

You don't have to pay $12 a year for an unlisted phone number. Instead, tell the phone company to bill you but list the phone in the name of your friend Blue Sky, Psyche Delic, or—if you want to be inconspicuous—Tom Smith. Also, they will leave out your address on request.

For further information:

The "Steal Yourself Rich" Book, Abbie Hoffman. Insider's Mailbox, Inc, 595 Madison Avenue, 29th Floor, New York, New York 10022, 1971.

PHONE PHRIPPERY

Designer phones, which are available from the telephone company for $50 to $100, can be purchased at a 30 percent discount from electronics supply houses. However, if you tell the phone company you are buying an "outside" phone, they will charge you $10 to $25 in modifications to "protect" their equipment. To avoid this charge, get a regular plug-in phone from the phone company and substitute your fancy phone yourself.

For free extension phones, first have extra jacks installed around the house by the telephone company. Since unathorized extensions are detected by running a line check on the number of phones ringing, you can avoid detection by having the ringers disconnected from phones you have purchased on your own.

For further information:

"How Smart Operators Fool the Phone Company," *Moneysworth*, 11 November 1974, page 2.

WHAT'S WATS?

If your long-distance phone bill runs into a sizeable sum each month, you can save a passel by switching to Wide Area Telephone Service (WATS). This service allows unlimited calls either to or from (or both to and from) a certain area for a specified number of hours every month, with fees varying accordingly.

Normally, WATS service is available only to the business community, rather than to noncommercial subscribers. But if you use a business name, and take in laundry, sell insurance, or fix bicycles in or from your home, you will qualify.

A LARGE CHARGE

For years, whenever we made a long-distance call from someone else's home, we'd automatically have the operator give us time and charges, so we'd know how much to reimburse our hosts for the call.

Recently, however, we discovered that this service is not free. Now, in order to save money, we simply time ourselves on these calls, then call the operator afterwards for the *rate*. You'll save yourself up to 70 percent on each long-distance call by doing the same.

GIVE YOUR PHONE A VACATION

If you're going on vacation for one to eight months, save 50 percent on your phone bill by having your service temporarily disconnected. People who call while you are away will be informed that the disconnection is only *temporary*.

LONG DISTANCE FOR FREE

To find out if a distant business that you wish to contact has a toll-free (prefix 800, Zenith, or Enterprise) number, dial (800) 555-1212. You may also find such numbers displayed occasionally in company advertising or in your local phone book.

Use them and let the company you do business with foot the bill.

PHONY PHONE BILLS?

A recent survey of timed telephone calls on 16 phone lines by the New York State Public Service Commission showed errors in *50 percent* of the telephone company's bills. If, as the commission suggested, phone companies in other areas are guilty of such sloppiness, you can avoid being thusly cheated by double-checking your telephone bill on all long-distance calls.

If your phone bills are running more than $150 a month, and you suspect the phone company of errors, Interconnect Telephone Services, Inc., 32 Union Square East, New York, New York 10003, will audit your bills for a nominal fee, plus half of any refund due you. Some clients have gotten refunds of up to $12,000 as a result of this company's audits!

To verify gas, electric, and water bills, write for *Checking Your Utility Bills* (183D), Consumer Information, Public Documents Distribution Center, Pueblo, Colorado 81009, 1974 (free). Double-check the meter man's figures each month, and figure up the bill yourself.

JACK DOUBLER

If you decide—after your phone has been installed—that you want more jacks, but don't want to pay Ma Bell that $23 installation fee for same, you can purchase your own jack doubling device for just $2 in many electronic supply stores. Jack-in-a-Plug connects to your present phone outlet and also allows you to plug another extension into it.

Check with your local electronic equipment distributor, or write to Saxton Products, 215 North Route 303, Congers, New York 10920, for the name of a distributor near you.

Water

RAIN WATER WONDERS

Save an average of 300 barrels of water yearly by placing a barrel under your roof drainspout to catch rainwater. During dry spells, this water will then keep your lawn and garden wet and happy.

An easy watering technique: Coil up a garden hose in the barrel until the hose is full of water. Taking care to keep one end of the hose in the water, put your thumb over the other end and place this end on the ground. Gravity will then make the water flow.

For further information:

In Celebration of Small Things, Sharon Cadwallader. Boston, Houghton Mifflin, 1974.

USE YOUR HEAD

Decrease shower-water waste by using the fine spray setting for your shower head. If you have a nonadjustable nozzle, place a sink-faucet-type neoprene washer (available at your hardware store) between pipe and shower head. Not only will this save you $10 to $15 over the cost of a new adjustable shower head—but you'll cut down on water bills as well.

For further information:

"Save Energy," Chris Logan, *Alternative Sources of Energy*, No. 18, July 1975, page 49.

SOFT SELL

If you own a home in a hard water area, you'll save about $57 a year in water, detergent costs, longer-lasting water pipes, and improved clothing life by installing a water softener. The Chicago YMCA has found that linens washed in soft water last up to 40 percent longer than those washed in hard water.

When you connect the equipment, make sure that it bypasses lawn and toilet water. For maximum savings, connect it only to the hot water supply.

Companies carrying conditioners awarded the Water Conditioning Foundation's Gold Seal include Bruner-Calgon Corp., 4767 North 32nd Street, Milwaukee, Wisconsin 53209; Reynolds Water Conditioning Co., 12100 Cloverdale Avenue, Detroit, Michigan 48204; and Water Refining Co., Inc., Middletown, Ohio 45042.

For further information:

"Who Needs Soft Water," *Money*, January 1976, page 20.

FOIL THAT TOILET

A leaky toilet can waste hundreds of gallons of water every day. Yet these leaks can be difficult or impossible to detect just by looking. Here's a simple way to spot this sneak thief: Dump a little laundry bluing into the toilet tank after it has filled up and stopped running. If a slow leak is present, the dye will soon show up in the toilet bowl.

Sometimes a simple adjustment of the float level will solve your problem. Or you may have to replace worn valve parts or a waterlogged float to patch up that hole in your water bill.

For further information:

Be Your Own Plumber, Jean Krenzer. Los Angeles, Nash Publishing (orders to E. P. Dutton), 1972.

A BRICK TRICK

You can save 3 to 4 gallons of water each time you flush your toilet (a family of four will save 200 to 400 gallons of water a week) by putting a brick or two, or a plastic bottle full of water, in the toilet tank. Make sure these objects don't interfere with your toilet's operation.

Or, simply bend down the float in your toilet tank so that it turns off the water at a lower level. If you have a flushometer toilet, reset it at 3½ gallons per flush. Ask your plumbing supply store for details. Another water saver: Send $4.98 to Savway Company, 52 Copley Street, Staten Island, New York 10314, for their ingenious device which allows you to flush just a half tank for liquid wastes and a full tank for solid.

For further information:

"How to Cut Your Gas, Electric and Water Bills," Hubbard Cobb, *Woman's Day*, October 1975, pages 48, 181–182.

5

ALTERNATE ENERGY:
FREE UTILITIES

You've just learned how to cut utility prices in half. This chapter will allow you to kiss your utility company good-bye.

To date, there is no limit to the staggering amounts of energy provided us by the sun and wind. Also in plentiful supply are human and animal wastes and streams of running water. These free, alternate sources of energy can be cheaply harnessed to heat or cool your home, cook your food, wash your clothes, provide electric power, or perform any number of other functions for which you now must pay your utility company a pretty penny. In fact, the day is not far off when our fatigued environment will force whole communities into utilizing such accessible energy sources.

Meantime, you can get a head start on the rest of the world—and save a bundle in the bargain—by tapping nature's plenteous supply of free energy sources.

Sun

UNIQUE HEAT

If you're just now building your home, you can arrange to spend as little as *$7 a year* on heat for the rest of your life, even if you live as far north as southern Minnesota or northern New York State. How? By harnessing the heat of the sun to take over 75 percent or more of the work of heating your home.

One design for utilizing the sun's energy involves pumping water over or through a black, heat-absorbing surface exposed to the sun. A layer of glass prevents the heat from escaping. The heated water is pumped down to holding tanks, such as insulated, stone-filled vats. One family in Washington, D.C., paid $18.75 in heating bills over three years' time—a savings of around $750 over their neighbors' heating bills.

Plans for this solar heating system can be had for $10 from Edmund Scientific, 623 Edscorp Building, Barrington, New Jersey 08007. *Drum Wall Plans* for another solar heating sys-tem that uses water-filled drums placed in the south wall of a house, as well as *Beadwall System* plans and license, which use Styrofoam beads blown into double, glazed translucent walls to prevent heat loss at night can be had from Zomeworks Corp., P.O. Box 712, Albuquerque, New Mexico 87103, for $5 and $15 respectively. Plans for constructing a $150 solar hot-air heat collector or hot-water collector are $5 from Hadley Solar Energy Co., P.O. Box 1456, Wilmington, Delaware 19899.

Incidentally, tax write-offs for installation of solar heating are now given by the states of Montana, Maryland, New Hampshire, North Dakota, South Dakota, Colorado, and Oregon.

For further information:

Direct Use of the Sun's Energy, Farrington Daniels. Westminster, Maryland, Ballantine, 1964.

SUN BATHING

Even if your home is already built and the heating system already installed, you can save hundreds of dollars a year by employing the sun's energy to provide hot water for your bath, dishes, and so on. Simple solar water-heating units are selling like rice in price-conscious Japan. Using one only three months out of the year, at a rate of 40 gallons a day, will save you $150!

For further information:

Bulletin 5513.2 (50¢, do-it-yourself plans), Volunteers in Technical Assistance, 3706 Rhode Island Avenue, Mount Rainier, Maryland 20822.

Energex Corp., 3030 South Valley View Boulevard, Las Vegas, Nevada 89102 ($395 for a unit).

SOLAR SWIM

A commercially installed solar heating system for your pool will pay for itself in three years. After that, pool heating costs will be almost nonexistent. Such systems, which generally involve a rooftop set of black panels through which pool water is pumped, warmed by the sun, then returned to the pool, can keep you in the swim year-round in such mild climates as California without the help of gas heat. The ready-made cost is $2.50 to $3.25 per square foot of pool area. See your Yellow Pages under "Swimming pool equipment and supplies" for dealers near you.

For further information:

How to Heat Your Swimming Pool Using Solar Energy, A. Whillier. Brace Research Institute, MacDonald College of McGill University, Ste. Anne de Bellevue 800, Quebec, Canada, January 1965 (50¢).

COOL POOL?

For even cheaper pool heating, build your own solar pool heater using your house or patio roof, covered with black vinyl to warm the water. Parts, including a pump to lift water to the roof and clear plastic cover to prevent water evaporation, cost just $60, a savings of $450 or more over the cost of commercially installed units. It takes two weekends to install the equipment.

For further information:

How to Design and Build a Solar Swimming Pool Heater, Francis De Winter, Copper Development Association, Inc., 405 Lexington Avenue, New York, New York 10017 (free). Also ask for appendix of sample calculations.

WARM WORK

You can save up to $15 a month in winter heating bills for houses with large window areas by using your windows as solar heat traps during the day and insulating with drapes at night. To learn how to calculate net heat gain for your windows, as well as steps to take to improve solar window heating, see "How to Trap Solar Heat with Your Windows," Edward Allen, *Popular Science*, February 1975, pages 108–110, 114, 116.

AUTOMATIC SKYLIGHT

This ingenious contraption will save you many dollars in heating costs. Once installed, the Skylid automatically allows the sun to enter through a skylight when necessary, and closes to insulate the skylight and trap warm air inside the house when the sun goes down. It consists of large, insulated louvres which perform silently, without the aid of electricity.

Prices start as low as $180 FOB Albuquerque, New Mexico, from Zomeworks Corp., P.O. Box 712, Albuquerque, New Mexico. 87103.

HOSE HEAT

If you live in a sunny climate and have access to water under pressure, you can easily eliminate the cost of heating shower water by using a solar shower. Ever noticed how hot the water gets in a hose lying out in the sun? This phenomenon has been put to use by Mike Oehler, a homesteader in the rural United States, to produce piping hot showers every day.

Coil up a long length of garden hose and place it under clear plastic in a sunny spot. Run the end of the hose into your shower, or build a shower stall of scrap lumber outdoors. The sun will heat the water in the hose and provide you with a steaming shower every afternoon.

For further information:

"The Homestead Solar Shower," Mike Oehler. *The Mother Earth News Handbook of Homemade Power*, The Mother Earth News Staff, New York, Bantam, 1974, pages 246–248.

INSTANT WATER PRESSURE

For campers, boaters, and back-to-the-landers without access to water pressure, a pressurized hot shower—shampooer—dishwasher can be yours for just $20. How? At the hardware store, pick up a pump-type garden sprayer (3½ gallons); a sink hose; and sink, shampoo, and dishwashing sprayer heads. (Be sure *not* to use a sprayer in which pesticide has been placed.) Replace the hose and nozzle that come with the sprayer with your sink hose, adding whichever sprayer head you need at the moment.

The water can be solar heated by painting the sprayer black and placing it outdoors on tinfoil, with another piece of tinfoil nearby reflecting the sun onto it. Or, simply dump a few quarts of stove-warmed water in the sprayer.

For further information:

"Portable Shower," John McGeorge, *Alternative Sources of Energy*, No. 18, July 1975, page 28.

SUN SHOWER

Another inexpensive solar shower for people without access to pressurized water is the sun shower. This 2½-gallon plastic bag, painted black on one side and with a hose and shower head attached, warms up from 70° F. to 110° F. after being in the sun for three hours. A temperature-sensitive dot changes color when the water gets hot.

At $8.95 from Basic Designs, Inc., Box 287, Muir Beach, California 94965, it sure beats the price of a hot-water heater!

A STRANGE RANGE

Every year the average kitchen range consumes a minimum of 1,200 kilowatt-hours of electricity—costing at least $50 annually. This expense can be cut 25 percent or more by harnessing the sun as a source of energy instead.

The following book will tell you how to make your own sun-powered reflector cooker using materials that cost less than $10: *Fun With the Sun*, D. S. Halacy, Jr. New York, Macmillan, 1959.

SOLAR OVEN

Now that you have a solar range, why not build a solar oven and free yourself al-

together from that kilowatt-consuming stove?

You can make a solar oven by using materials that cost about $20—galvanized iron sheets, fiber glass insulation, and other inexpensive odds and ends garnered from your local hardware store.

For further information:

Fun With the Sun, D. S. Halacy, Jr. New York, Macmillan, 1959.

CELESTIAL DISTILLATIONS

You can distill your own water with absolutely no operating costs by using a solar still. For $20, a still can be built using a 2½ by 4 foot shallow, insulated box covered with black polyvinyl and a top cover of glass. The box is placed at right angles to the sun, and water is allowed to trickle down over the plastic. The pure water which condenses on the inside of the glass is then drained off. The still makes two gallons of distilled water a day in warm, sunny climates, and one gallon a day during the wintertime.

For further information:

Direct Use of the Sun's Energy, Farrington Daniels. Westminster, Maryland, Ballantine, 1964.

Wind

GENERATING SAVINGS

Don't sit by helplessly as utility rates rise to outlandish proportions! Unless you're living on an island in the "horse latitudes"—where the wind is practically nonexistent—you can generate your own electricity by using wind power.

Build your own 500-watt wind charger—which will supply enough electricity for a small house—for less than $200. For plans, see "Wind Generators: Here's an Advanced Design You Can Build," Hans Meyer, *Popular Science*, November 1972, pages

103–105, 142. Plans for a deluxe $350 model are available from Jim Sencenbaugh, 678 Chimalus Drive, Palo Alto, California 94306.

Or, you can buy your own ready-made generator plant, including a mill, AC-DC converter, batteries, and a backup generator for those windless days, for as little as $665. Maintenance requires only one half gallon of lubricating oil a year and the mill lasts up to 40 years.

For further information:

Heller-Aller Co., corner of Perry and Oakwood, Napoleon, Ohio 43545.

Dyna Technology, Inc., P.O. Box 3263, Sioux City, Iowa 51102.

Solar Wind Co., Bar Harbor Road, P.O. Box 7, East Holden, Maine 04429 (catalog of generators they sell, $2).

WINDFALL

Across the Great Plains, wind generators perch unused on spindly towers, slowly rusting to death. Careful bargaining can often get you one of these potential gems from their owners for as little as $20 or $30. The trick is to buy one that can be restored without too much trouble, to get it down from its perch, and to get the generator back into working condition.

For full instructions, read James DeKorne's "The Answer Is Blowing in the Wind," *The Mother Earth News Handbook of Homemade Power*, *The Mother Earth News* Staff, New York, Bantam, 1974, pages 162–185.

BATTERY BONANZA

An amazingly cheap battery for your personal wind power plant is the used forklift truck battery. With only one weak or dead cell, these 300–2,400 AH capacity units become unserviceable for forklifts, but they can power your plant for 3 to 5 years thereafter. The cost? About 6¢ per pound from the scrap battery dealer, who will buy them back at 4¢ per pound when you're through!

For further information:

"Batteries," Ron Neely, *Alternative Sources of Energy*, No. 18, July 1975, page 51.

WIND-POWERED WASH

If you live in an area where a fair breeze often blows, circumvent the high purchase price and maintenance of a commercial washing machine by building your own wind-powered model. The investment? Ten dollars' worth of scrap lumber, some pipe odds and ends, and a 55-gallon drum.

For further information:

"A Simple Wind-Powered Washing Machine That You Can Build," Ed Seelhorst. *The Mother Earth News*, No. 37, January 1976, page 94.

Wood

SELF-HEATING, SELF-COOLING HOUSE

This home, designed by Wendell Thomas of North Carolina, contains only a wood stove and maintains a constant year-round indoor temperature of 60–75°F. The cost? About $40 for the year.

The house has a basement, which is completely underground, and a surface-level story. In the floor of the upper story are a series of vents around the perimeter, and another series around the stove, which is in the center of the room. These vents allow a figure-8-shaped flow of air from the cooler basement to the warmer area upstairs which very efficiently warms the house in winter, and reverses flow to cool the house in summer.

For further information:

"The Self-heating, Self-cooling House," *The Mother Earth News Almanac*, *The Mother Earth News* Staff. New York, Bantam, 1973, pp. 224–226.

PASS ON GAS!

For a $1,200-a-year fuel savings, convert your liquified petroleum gas forced-air furnace to a wood-burning one. A Minnesota couple did just this, by adding a firebox to the cold-air-returning duct of their existing furnace. Their firebox features a large, off-center door for fast, twice-a-day stoking with large pieces of wood.

For conversion instructions, see "Our $100 Wood-burning Furnace Saves Us $1,200 a Year!" David Bleed, *The Mother Earth News*, No. 36, Vol. 75, pages 116–118.

STOVE SENSE

Using such discarded containers as a steel drum or 5-gallon paint can (or anything in between), plus a few steel and brick scraps and lengths of stovepipe, you can make your own combination cook-stove and space heater. Necessary tools: tin shears and a hacksaw or power saber saw.

An amateur can follow with ease the directions in *Making Do: Basic Things for Simple Living*, Arthur Hill, New York, Ballantine, 1972. The author also shows how to make a portable stove out of an old smoke pipe or piece of air-conditioning duct.

AUTOMATIC WOODBURNERS

While the initial cost of woodburning heaters with automatic thermostatic control is a little higher than for those without this feature, you more than make up for this expense in operating savings. These heaters, which feature air-tight fireboxes and temperature-sensitive devices to regulate air intake and room temperature, burn wood more efficiently, with a savings of up to 50 percent in fuel costs.

For prices on the basic Ashley Thermostatic Woodburning Circulator and King Automatic Wood Circulators (these vary depending on your location), write King Stove & Range Co., P.O. Box 730, Sheffield, Alabama 35660. Somewhat more expensive and more efficient are the Riteway Wood and Coal Heaters, Marco Industries, Inc., P.O. Box 6, Harrisonburg, Virginia 22801 ($261 FOB Harrisonburg, Virginia). For a deluxe, enameled version ($185–$450), get information on the Norwegian-made Jøtul from dealers David Lyle, South Acworth, New Hampshire 03607; and L. L. Bean, Inc., Freeport, Maine 04032.

HEAT INCREASER

If you use your fireplace to heat your house, you can increase the room-heating capacity of the fireplace 500 percent by using a U-shaped pipe with a fan inside. This device, which is attached to the top of the fireplace, draws cold air from the room into the fireplace, where it is warmed to 400°F. and fanned back out into the room at 120 cubic feet a minute. Costs $59.95.

What does this mean to you? That $100 cord of wood will go five times as far, thus saving you $80 per cord.

Order from Thermalite Corp., P.O. Box 69, Hanover, Massachusetts 02239. Ask for information on Hearth-Aid. A similar device, the Thermogate D–0670 ($79.50) can be ordered freight-collect from Mother's General Store, Department 112, Box 506, Flat Rock, North Carolina 28731.

For further information:

"Fireplace Heat Savers Warm the Room, Not the Chimney," Wayne Leckey, *Popular Mechanics*, December 1974, pages 174, 176.

A HOT NEWS ITEM

Instead of giving your old newspapers to the neighborhood recycler, consider rolling them into tight cylinders to use as logs for your winter fireplace. When rolling, leave an air passage in the center for ventilation, then tie a metal wire around the logs to prevent them from flopping open when they catch fire.

FIREPLACE FORTUNES

You can draw three times as much usable heat from fireplace logs by remodeling your fireplace to take advantage of the heat-intensifying principle used in blacksmith forges. A controllable amount of cold air is drawn into the fireplace from a duct under the house. Sliding glass doors are installed in front of the fireplace to prevent drafts through the house and to control air intake. Warm air—an output of as much as 150,000 BTU's (a measure of heat quantity)—is then systematically fed into the room through a duct in the side of the chimney.

For further information:

"Bill Wells: Fireplace under Glass," Edward Moran, *Popular Science*, March 1976, pages 111, 153.

LOWCOST COVERUP

The biggest problem, energy-wise, with using your fireplace to complement your regular heating system is what to do after the fire dies down and you're ready to retire.

The best bet, aside from flooding your fireplace with water, is to purchase a fireplace cover of tempered glass at your fireplace equipment dealers. Placed in front of the fireplace opening, this cover will prevent heat dollars from escaping, will allow the fire to die down naturally, and will eliminate the fire hazard of flying sparks while you sleep.

For further information:

Save Energy, Save Money (303C—free), Consumer Information, Public Documents Distribution Center, Pueblo, Colorado 81009.

STOVEPIPE OVEN

Ever heard of a stovepipe oven? As you may have already guessed, it's a heat-retaining box designed to fit between the first and second joints of the stovepipe of your wood-burning heater. The oven uses heat escaping up the stovepipe to cook bread, cakes, a chicken, or what-have-you.

It costs just $40, a far cry from the $400 price tag on a new wood-burning range.

For further information:

Mother's General Store, Department 112, Box 506, Flat Rock, North Carolina 28731 (1640—stovepipe oven).

Louisville Tin and Stove Company, 737 South 13th Street, Louisville, Kentucky 40210.

INSTANT WATER HEATER

Convert the stovepipe of your wood-burning heater or stove to a hot-water heater using nothing more than a steel drum and a spigot!

It's done by cutting holes in the top and bottom of the drum, then slipping the stovepipe through. Then weld to create a waterproof bond. Next, add a removable lid to the top of the barrel or a pipe with a float valve to fill the container with water automatically. A spigot near the bottom of the drum will complete your contraption and provide you with hot water through the winter months, when the wood stove will be burning constantly.

For further information:

"Stovepipe Power," A. Michael Wassil, *The Mother Earth News Handbook of Homemade Power*, The Mother Earth News Staff, New York, Bantam, 1974, pages 50–55.

PIPE DREAM

If you now heat your home with a wood-burning stove, you can make one stove heat your whole house, rather than just one or two rooms. How? By utilizing a trick invented by early settlers in this country.

Redesign your stovepipe so that it runs horizontally the length of the house, then up through the ceiling. Or, if you have a multistory home, place the stove on the ground floor and have the stovepipe extend upward through several stories. The majority of heat that normally goes up through the pipe will then radiate from the pipe and warm the rooms through which it passes. See "Stovepipe Power," above.

CANNY KNACK

What's in an old tin can? A heat-reflecting candleholder and a jim-dandy one-burner camp stove, to name just two things. To make the candleholder, first cut off the top of the can with a can opener. Then, with tin snips, cut diagonally down each side of the can to the far side, leaving the bottom intact. Nail the back of the container to the wall, drip a little melted wax into the bottom, and stick in the candle.

To make the camp stove, clip a hole in the side of the can near the bottom large enough to place twigs, a candle, or a Sterno can inside and to allow air to enter. Using a beer-can opener, sprong several triangular holes in the opposite side near the top of the can. This will allow a cross-draft to help the fire burn. Now just place the fuel in the can, put an open can of beans, or whatever, on top, and get cooking!

For further information:

"Tin Can Candle Holder," "Tin Can Cook Stove," *The Mother Earth News Almanac*, *The Mother Earth News* Staff. New York, Bantam, 1973, page 157.

THE GREAT FIREWOOD GIVEAWAY

National Parks offer firewood for the paltry sum of $5 a cord, or free for the taking at certain times of year. At this rate, you can rent a chain saw and an open trailer for a day to cut and transport the wood, and still end up paying only a third of the $120 or so charged by retail firewood outlets. Talk about cheap heat!

For further information:

National Park Service, U.S. Department of the Interior, C Street between 18th and 19th Streets, N.W., Washington, D.C. 20240. Or, contact your regional National Park Service.

"How to Cut Free Firewood in the National Forests," Barry Lopez, *Popular Science*, December 1974, pages 93–95.

WOOD WONDERS

How much heat you get from a cord of wood depends on the type of wood you buy. You will get twice as much heat per cord from

such hardwoods as black birch, hickory, ironwood, black and honey locust, swamp white oak, shad bush, and dogwood as you would from softwoods like grey birch, chestnut, cucumber, white elm, sassafras, hemlock, and Norway pine.

For further information:

"Relative Heat Value of Some of the Important Woodlot Species. . . ," *The Naturalist's Almanac and Environmentalist's Companion*, Northern Pacific Region Edition, John Gardner, ed. New York, Ballantine, 1973, page 146.

KNOTTY PROBLEM

If you've run out of firewood scavenging sources, try the nearest glass company. These receive glass that has been crated in such poor-quality wood that it can serve no useful purpose except as firewood. We found one such company with tons of the stuff, which they were only too happy to give away.

For further information:

"All the Good Wood You Want—Free (or Very Cheap)," C. Wayne Close, *Family Handyman*, April 1975, pages 50–51.

Water and Other

FREEWHEELING

For property on which even a small stream flows year-round, a homemade dam and waterwheel can generate enough electricity to supply a homestead. Moreover, the pond that backs up behind the dam will serve as a water reservoir for livestock, fire fighting, and fish raising; a wild bird attractor (roast duck!); and a swimming-recreation area.

To find out if your stream will produce adequate electricity, as well as for detailed instructions on building a dam and waterwheel, see "Build Your Own Water Power Plant," C. D. Basset, *The Mother Earth News*

Handbook of Homemade Power, The Mother Earth News Staff, New York, Bantam, 1974, pages 68–109.

Some manufacturers of waterwheels and turbines: Asea Electric, Inc., 2 Kaysal Court, Armonk, New York 10504; Davis Foundry and Machine Works, Rome, Georgia 30161; J. W. Jolly, Inc., Holyoke, Massachusetts 01040; and Sulzer Brothers, Inc., 19 Rector, New York, New York 10006.

For further information:

Low-Cost Development of Small Water Power Sites, Hans Hamm, Volunteers for International Technical Assistance, College Campus, Schenectady, New York 12308, 1967.

WELL WATER WELCHING

If you own a well, you can get the jump on home cooling bills by using the well water to cool your house. This unique setup involves pumping cold well water through a system of three auto radiators, which cool the surrounding air. The cooled air is then blown into the house using a squirrel cage type air blower. The well water is then fed to lawn sprinklers or recirculated to the well.

Morgan Powell, who built such a system for $100 in 1957, was paying $3 a month to cool his Oklahoma house effectively during 100°F. weather, an amazingly low figure even in that year.

For further information:

"Well Water Air-Conditions Our Home," Morgan Powell, *Popular Science,* Volume 170, June 1957, page 202.

NIGHT SKY LARK

For $15, you can create your own outdoor refrigerator, using the night sky rather than expensive electricity, to keep your perishables cool.

First, construct a wooden box containing a hinged door on the side. Insulate top, bottom, sides, and door with three inches of fiber glass batt, Styrofoam scraps, or shredded newspaper. Build into the top a three-

inch-deep tray, suitable for holding water. The water top should be covered before sunrise with an insulated, tinfoil-covered outer lid to prevent solar heating. At nightfall, the outer cover is removed and the heated water allowed to cool off under the night sky.

For further information:

"Night Sky Refrigeration," George Helmholz and Larry Wheat. *Alternative Sources of Energy,* No. 18, July 1975, page 15.

FREE FRIDGE

The following is an old-fashioned, no-cost refrigeration method that cools by water evaporation—rather than by expensive electricity.

Get a shallow granite-ware pan, fill it halfway with water, and place it in an open window in the shade. Wrap containerized items to be refrigerated—milk, cream, beer—in cloth, and stand them in the water. To keep butter cool, place in an earthen dish (to keep out water) and cover with an earthen flowerpot. Put a cloth over the pot and place the container in the water so that the cloth touches the water.

This device won't work unless there's water in the pan and the cloths touch the water, so check water level twice a day. The constant evaporation of the water from the cloth keeps the items cool—just as people cool off when they perspire or take a shower.

For further information:

"A to Z Worry Free Make Your Own Book," *The New Earth Catalog: Living Here and Now,* Scott French, ed. New York, Putnam/Berkley and Heller & Son, 1973.

MANURE MANEUVER

With a 275-gallon tank and 100 gallons of manure (horse, cow, human, or otherwise), you can heat an average two-bedroom house. When the manure is mixed with water, it generates methane gas, which serves as an energy source just as does oil or kerosene.

Impossible, you say? Not at all. Inventor Harold Bate of England has used "manure power" to heat his home for the last 18 years. While you may think that the stench involved in using such a system would drive you from your house, recent refinements have made this method a practical choice for home use—and at what a savings!

For further information:

Composting, Harold Gotaas. Q Corporation, 49 Sheridan Avenue, Albany, New York 12210, 1959.

SELF-POWERED WATER PUMP

If you wish to transport flowing water on your property up a hill for crop irrigation, stock watering, or storage for use on the homestead, you can do so without the constant operating costs of an electric pump by installing a hydraulic ram pump. This amazing device, costing $200 or less, utilizes the power of running water itself to lift the water to a higher level. As a result, operating costs are zero!

Hydraulic ram manufacturers include Edward Barberie, Box 104, Green Spring, West Virginia 26722; Ce Co Co Chuo Boeki Goshi Kaisha, P.O. Box 8, Ibaraki City, Osaka, Japan; and Rife Hydraulic Engine Manufacturing Co., Box 367, Millburn, New Jersey 07041.

For further information:

"Perpetual Motion for the Homestead . . . the Hydraulic Ram," William Hebert, and "How it Works," Don Marier, *The Mother Earth News Handbook of Homemade Power*, *The Mother Earth News* Staff, New York, Bantam, 1974, pages 110–113, 113–115.

FREE HEAT

With oil prices soaring higher than an amorous bartender's hopes at closing time, you can nevertheless heat your home with oil absolutely free—by hauling away old crankcase oil from gas stations. In fact, they may even pay you for taking it off their hands.

Once you have located a source of supply, build a stove for it out of a discarded bottled-gas cylinder or steel drum. For complete instructions, see "Cheap Heat," Bill Cheney, *The Mother Earth News Handbook of Homemade Power*, *The Mother Earth News* Staff, New York, Bantam, 1974, pages 57–61.

To learn of a special atomizing technique used to heat one home with crankcase oil, read "Max Ordway Burns Discarded Crankcase Oil," E. F. Lindsley, *Popular Science*, June 1975, pages 112–113.

CLOTHES AND COSMETICS

Assuming you didn't take seriously our suggestion in Chapter 1, that you cut shelter costs by moving into the nearest cave, suitable clothes and flattering cosmetics are indeed necessary items. And how we pay for them! A newspaper article recently reported that it was not uncommon for some clothes manufacturers to mark up their goods by 1,000 percent, and for makers of top of the line beauty aids to mark up their products by as much as 5,000 percent!

One way you can avoid these outrages is by getting your material directly from the wholesaler, then designing your own clothes. Or, by inexpensively purchasing your clothes in kit form, and then assembling them yourself.

Perfumes, makeup, and fine skin creams can easily be concocted in your own kitchen using ingredients whose cost is but a fraction of store-bought cosmetics. Not only will these be suitable for personal use, but they will make fine presents, saving you valuable dollars at gift-giving time.

You'll find that by taking a creative approach to clothes and cosmetics, not only you but your bankbook as well will look tip-top in no time.

Buying Clothes

GETTING THEATRICAL

Costume shops, as well as legitimate theaters, are an excellent little-known source of cheap but spectacular clothing. In many instances, elaborate but no longer needed costumes will go for as little as $10.

See your Yellow Pages under "Costumes—masquerade and theatrical."

FUR FINAGLING

Oddly enough, you can often get a *custom-made* fur from a furrier for less than what *ready-made* furs cost in high-class department stores. Languishing for lack of business in these inflationary times, furriers are anxious to lower prices in order to attract business.

Discounts of 25 to 50 percent—cuts of up to $1,500—are not unusual. In addition, January and August markdowns of 10 to 50 percent are customary for furs, the most seasonal of haute couture *habillements*.

A STITCH IN TIME

One big difference between inexpensive, poorly made goods and the higher-quality, higher-priced variety is the stitching. Save a bundle by buying cheaper merchandise, then reinforcing seams, removing tacky ornaments and button thread, and adding binding where necessary. Be sure that the cloth in the apparel you buy is of good quality, preshrunk, and permanent-press.

For further information:

Make Your Own Alterations: Simple Sewing the Professional Way, Miriam Morgan. New York, Arco, 1970.

BRAND NAMES AT BARGAIN PRICES

Better brands of clothing can be obtained cheaply through factory outlets or bargain houses. The goods you find at these stores are often unpopular, damaged, or out-of-season, but the customary markdown of 50 percent or more can bless the wary shopper with any number of rare bargains.

Call businesses listed in your Yellow Pages under "Men's (and Women's) wearing apparel—wholesale and manufacturers" and ask if they will sell to the public.

For further information:

S.O.S. Directory: Directory of Factory Outlet Stores in the Entire United States and Canada, Iris Ellis. Jacksonville, Florida, S.O.S. Directory, 1975.

Factory Outlet Shopping Guides (for various East Coast areas), Jean Bird. Oradell, New Jersey, Factory Outlet Shopping Guide, 1975.

SEASONAL SAGACITY

Taking advantage of seasonal clothing sales will allow you to buy all new apparel at a third to a half of the retail price. Here's a seasonal sales summary: Buy dress fabrics in January and February, winter sports clothes in March, men's summer suits and coats in June, women's summer sportswear in July and August, hosiery in October, women's wool dresses in November, men's winter clothing in November and December, women's coats in December, cocktail dresses after Christmas, and lingerie Christmas through January.

CLOTHES CO-OP

Get together with friends, relatives, neighbors—even strangers—and arrange a monthly clothes-swapping session. Here, everyone will bring their old get-ups and—at no cost—will acquire a completely new wardrobe.

STRONG SOLES

Shoe soles treated with butyl, an oil derivative, last twice as long as ordinary soles, and are more water- and puncture-resistant and more flexible. So, cut down on shoe repairs by purchasing the butyl-treated shoes manufactured by such companies as Hanover.

For further information:

"Consumer's Guide to Men's Shoes," *Mechanix Illustrated*, November 1975, page 24.

Make Your Own!

BIKINI BUCKS

Even if you have never sewed before and never will again, sew yourself a bikini this summer. Simplicity itself to make, using, at the most, $2 worth of material, your one-

of-a-kind swimwear project will save you $23 or more over the store-bought variety!

For further information:

Cheap Chic, Caterine Milinaire and Carol Troy. New York, Harmony, 1975.

SKIN SUIT

But why even go to the expense and bother of making and donning swimwear at all? After all, your swimsuit can't produce vitamin D under the sunshine! There are many, many beaches, both here and abroad, that allow you simply to shuck and go bare!

For locations and descriptions, get a copy of *Nude Resorts and Beaches*, Rod Swenson, Jr., New York, Popular Library, 1975.

WRAP IT UP

If sewing just isn't your bag, pick up some really inexpensive fabrics at Goodwill and "wrap" your clothes instead. For instructions on imaginative, exotic wraparounds—blouses, sarongs and mini-sarongs, pantarounds, evening wear, scarves, and halters—see *Cheap Chic*, Caterine Milinaire and Carol Troy, New York, Harmony, 1975.

SPINNING A YARN

You can get wool yarn in any of six natural colors—white, light or medium grey, tan, and rusty or dark brown—for one-half domestic prices from Rammagerdin, Hafnar Straeti 5 and 17, Reyk Javik, Iceland. The quality is outstanding.

For good, cheap embroidery yarn, write to Olympus Thread Mfg. Co. Ltd., 8–9, Nishiki 3, Naka-ku, Nagoya, Japan.

SANDAL SOUS

To whip up completely free sandals that will last a lifetime, scavenge an old tire and inner tube from a tire dealer or dump. Chalk in the outline of your feet on the smooth inner surface of the tire and cut out your sandals, leaving ⅜ of an inch extra all round. Cut slits around the edge and insert strips of inner tube for straps, gluing with contact cement.

DRESS FORM FUN

No need to pay $30 or so to enjoy the convenience of a dress form for your sewing. You can make your own for pennies using some cotton tubing, rolls of gummed paper, a little shellac, and a willing helper.

Fit the cotton tubing over your body from your neck to below the hips. Then have your helper paste overlapping strips of the gummed paper over the tubing until this part of your body is completely covered. After the strips dry, have your helper cut all the way up the back of the form so you can slip out. Seal the back cut, reinforce the openings of the form, and coat with shellac inside and out. Voilà! A personalized, handmade dress form!

LOOM LESSON

The retail price of $200 and up for a loom is enough to discourage even the most avid amateur weaver. For less than $50 in materials—consisting of scrap lumber, fishing-line heddles, pulleys, and the teeth from six used grass rakes—you can make your own floor-pedal loom.

See instructions in *Making Do: Basic Things for Simple Living*, Arthur Hill. New York, Ballantine, 1972. Also included are instructions for making a simple hand loom using $10 worth of lumber and some old coat hangers.

TAN YOUR HIDE

If you don't want to pay the $25 or so charged by leather companies for tanned cowhides, purchase a hide at $3 or so from a local slaughterhouse and tan it yourself. See your Yellow Pages under "Meat Packers."

For further information:

Home Tanning and Leather Making Guide, A. B. Farvham. Harding's Books, 2878

East Main St., Columbus, Ohio 43209, 1950.

SEWING FOR THE SCHOOL SET?

Teach your child sewing-machine embroidery while creating useful objects at the same time by requesting the free children's embroidery instruction guide offered by White Sewing Machine Co., Cleveland, Ohio 44111 (enclose 35¢ for postage). Projects include school and kitchen aprons, blotter pad, stuffed dog, smock, bib, oven mitt, and napkin/napkin ring set. It's a steal!

CROCHET COURSE

For high fashion at a tenth of store prices, crochet your own clothes, afghans, and rugs. Two free instruction guides, *The ABC's of Crochet* and *Crocheting Projects for the Beginner*, can be had for the asking from Coats & Clark, P.O. Box 495, Fair Lawn, New Jersey 07410.

JUMP INTO THIS!

Want a free pattern for a shift and shirt outfit featuring removable buttons and trim for a variety of styles? Send a self-addressed, stamped, long envelope to William Prym, Inc., Dayville, Connecticut 06241, and request their free swing shift pattern and instructions.

THE ZIGZAG BAG

If you're thinking of trading in your old sewing machine for a new one with a zigzag feature, think again. You can buy yourself a new zigzag attachment for your old machine for under $20, or a used one for half that, at a local sewing machine repair and parts center.

These attachments are hard to come by because sewing machine manufacturers would much rather sell you a new machine with the zigzag feature at $150 than the attachment for $15, so keep on plugging. A little perseverance will pay off handsomely.

FABRIC FUN

If you happen to stumble upon a bargain, you might just find block-printed fabrics, draperies, and wall hangings at $20 a yard. Instead, buy yourself some cotton cloth at $2 a yard and print your own, using a design carved out of linoleum.

Write to Hunt Manufacturing Co., 1405 Locust Street, Philadelphia, Pennsylvania 19102, for the nearest outlet selling their *Creative Print Making Book* (75¢).

MACRAME MAGIC

We all know how expensive that lovely handmade macrame work is: $25 for a small handbag, $10 for a belt, up to $100 for a wall hanging. Make your own with a bit of string, a little ingenuity, and free instructions from The Beadcraft Club, P.O. Box 5754, Augusta, Georgia 30906 (include 25¢ to cover postage; request #C23, *Basic Macrame*).

THIMBLE THOUGHT

A thimble can cost you a quarter at the dime store, or it can cost you nothing. Just tape a coin to your finger. Voilà! A free thimble that won't slip off or allow the needle to puncture your pinkie.

OVERALL HAUL

What to do with a pair of overalls with worn-out knees? First, cut off the legs above the knees for summer "overshorts." Now, make the discarded pant legs into a tote bag!

Cut five 1-inch-wide strips of material from one of the discarded pant legs and sew together the ends to form the tote-bag strap. Then sew the other pant leg into a bag and attach the strap to opposite sides of the bag's open end.

For further information:

"Mother's Newspaper Column," *The Mother Earth News*, No. 37, January 1976, pages 57–60.

NEEDLE KNOWLEDGE

Knit your own shawls, sweaters, caps, blankets, and skirts at a third of store prices. Instructions, along with diagrams of stitches, advice, and explanations of terminology are available in a free booklet, *The ABC's of Knitting*, from Coats & Clark, P.O. Box 495, Fair Lawn, New Jersey 07410.

Care and Cleaning

SOLE SAVER

To make your shoe soles last ten times longer, coat them with Sole Saver, a black paste that hardens into a durable, skid-, water-, and fire-resistant surface. Order one pint—enough to coat four pairs of shoes—at $4.50 plus 90¢ shipping from Mother's General Store, Box 506, Flat Rock, North Carolina 28731 (order number 0661).

DYE NATURALLY!

Why buy your dye when you can pick it for free? Onion skins, lichens, dahlia flowers, camomile, coreopsis, and barberry root bark will dye your clothes orange or buff. Apple bark, marigold, zinnia flowers, goldenrod, or aster will give you yellows. And a mixture of barks, flowers, and leaves will give you still other colors.

For further information:

Home Dyeing with Natural Dyes, Margaret Furry and Bess Veirmont. Santa Rosa, California, Thresh, 1973.

THE WELL-HEELED BOOT

Here's an item for the ladies who wear rubber boots over shoes with heels during the rainy season. If you put a little money into the boots you wear, they will last two to three times as long as usual. And you can recover your financial outlay when you chuck the boots out.

How? Just place a quarter in the heel of each boot to prevent your shoes grinding a hole in the rubber.

STORE CASH, NOT FURS

Don't fork over $20 to your friendly fur storage company to keep your fur on ice. Hang it all in a cloth garment bag in the coolest part of the house—the cellar, for example. Place mothballs and dehumidifying crystals at the bottom of the bag.

The cheapest dehumidifying crystal is calcium chloride, available at your retail chemical supply house for around $3 a pound. Check periodically, and when this chemical gets gooey with moisture, just chuck it out and put fresh crystals in. At the same supply house you can purchase the more expensive silica gel or drierite. These dehumidifying compounds are blue when dry, red when wet. You can place red ones in your oven for a spell to dry out, then reuse them.

TSP ESP

Instead of buying Spic and Span, Oakite, and other cleansers whose main ingredient is TSP (trisodium phosphate), purchase this chemical, which also acts as a water softener, from your paint store at a 15 percent savings. For a similar discount, combine a little TSP with whiting (a nonscratch powder) from the paint store. You concoction will be basically identical to retail scouring powders.

For further information:

Home Cleaning Guide, Barbara Molle and Irv Charles. Tucson, Arizona, Sincere Press, 1972.

DIAPER DUCATS

Since diaper services charge in multiples of 5, 7, and 10, you will save by rounding out each week's load to one of their multiples. For example, if your service charges for multiples of 10, and you used 73 diapers, return 70 diapers, holding back three until next week. Cunning counting will save you at least two weeks' worth of service costs a year.

For further information:

How to Bring Up a Child Without Spending a Fortune, Lee Benning. New York, David McKay, 1975.

SUEDE SAVER

Before you send that suede coat, jacket, vest, or pair of trousers to the cleaners', try cleaning it yourself with a washcloth dipped in vinegar. Then use a suede brush to renew the nap. Saves $15 in cleaning fees for a simple suede jacket.

For further information:

Heloise's Housekeeping Hints, Heloise Cruse. Englewood Cliffs, New Jersey, Prentice-Hall, 1964.

SHOE SHINE DIMES

Next time you run out of shoe polish, try this substitute at a fraction of the price: plain old lemon juice! Just rub it on and buff. It works!

For further information see *Heloise's Housekeeping Hints*, above.

FUR FOXINESS

Before you pay a furrier $30 or so to revamp your flagging fur coat, try this simple, economical, do-it-yourself cleaning method. Wet some cornmeal or sawdust with dry-cleaning solvent, which you can find under "Cleaners and dyers' supplies" in your Yellow Pages, and rub it gently into the fur. Shake the fur and allow to dry in a cool room, then brush it.

The solvent dislodges dirt and grease, and the cornmeal or sawdust acts as an abrasive. Your fur will look like new for a mere pittance!

To find out how the experts do it, read *Fur Storage, Fumigation, and Cleaning*, Boston, National Fire Protection Association, 1969.

WASHDAY WOES

Most of us have experienced the frustration of buying a real "bargain" laundry detergent, only to find the extra soap required for a wash more than cancels out the sales-price savings. Judged on the basis of cost per washload, the five cheapest detergents, ranging in price from 4 cents to 6.5 cents per washload, are Bio-D (nonphosphate), King Kullen, Arm & Hammer (nonphosphate), Bold, and Rinso. The six most expensive detergents, ranging in price from 7.5 cents to 12 cents per washload, are Gain, Fluffy All, Bestline, Fab, Drive, and Duz.

For further information:
How to Live with Inflation: A Guide to Saving Money When Buying, Joseph Newman, ed. Washington, D.C., Books by *U.S. News and World Report,* 1974.

DETERGENT DISCOVERY

Believe it or not, using a paltry *tenth* of the washload detergent amount indicated on the package will get your wash *cleaner* and place less wear on your washing machine as well, thus helping to eliminate costly appliance repairs.

To find out exactly how much detergent your washer requires, check the wash two minutes after adding soap. If there's more than a half inch of suds around the edge of the wash water, reduce the soap allowance further next wash, and so on, until you get the suds level down to the half-inch standard.

Good Looks: Cosmetics and Jewelry

DISCOUNT DIAMONDS

To save 25 to 50 percent on fine diamonds, order them from Empire Diamond Corp., Empire State Building, New York, New York 10001. This wholesaler, which also caters to retail customers, offers a moneyback guarantee that an appraisal of their merchandise will confirm their cut-rate prices.

PERFUME PLEASURES

Perfumes are simplicity personified to make, but the ingredients are expensive for one person to get, due to the relatively large quantities in which they must be purchased. If you can get a group of women on your block, campus, or in your office to chip in to buy the ingredients, you will end up with perfume at just a few dollars an ounce—that's a savings of about *95 percent* on well-known, exorbitantly priced perfumes.

Here's the formula for making a smell-alike of Jean Patou's famous Joy: 3 ounces of medium perfume oil base, blended with neroli oil and musk (4 drops each); angelica and vetivert (8 drops each); synthetic bergamot oil (1 dram, or $1/16$ ounce); oil of rose ($2\frac{1}{2}$ drams); ambergris and artificial jasmine ($1/5$ dram each); and heliotropin ($\frac{1}{2}$ dram). Makes a little over 3 ounces.

Ingredients can be ordered from Florasynth Laboratories, Inc., 1150 Bronx River Avenue, Bronx, New York 10472; Norda Essential Oil and Chemical Co., 475 Tenth Avenue, New York, New York 10018; or Synfleur Scientific Laboratories, Inc., 33 Oakley Avenue, Monticello, New York 12701.

FAKE FRAGRANCES

If you don't want to go to the trouble of making your own perfume, it is still possible to enjoy the rich fragrance of Joy, Bal à Versailles, and other famous perfumes for as little as one-eighth of their going price. The Tuli-Latus (a firm specializing in low-cost duplication of expensive perfumes) products are so good that it is impossible to distinguish them from the originals.

The Tuli-Latus version of Joy ($85 an ounce) sells for only $10 an ounce. Their copy of Bal à Versailles ($90 an ounce) goes for $12, and of L'Air du Temps ($40) for $8.

For further information:

Tuli-Latus, 146-36 Thirteenth Avenue, Whitestone, New York 11357.

MASK MAGIC

For a first-rate skin mask at one twentieth of retail prices, warm a little honey with egg white, dry skim milk, or cream. This mask will tone and tighten facial skin. Lie down and place raw potato, cucumber slices, or moist, used tea bags over the eyelids as the mask hardens. Remove the mask and rub your face with cream, avocado oil, or almond oil to moisten.

AVOCADO ALL OVER

Avocados, which contain 25 percent oil, 11 vitamins, and 17 minerals, make fine skin and hair conditioners. They soften dry skin on elbows, hands, and feet, and add lustrous body to hair after a shampoo. Just mash an avocado into a cream, add a little water, and apply to hair and skin. After a half-hour, wash off and admire yourself. This mask saves half the cost of beauty counter equivalents.

For further information:

Guide to Natural Cosmetics, Connie Krochmal. New York, Quadrangle, 1973.

BUBBLE BATH BARGAIN

When you buy bubble bath in the store, you're paying a slew for the fancy wrapper. The ingredients are cheap and easily prepared. All you need is 1 teaspoonful of borax and ⅜ cup each of distilled water and tri-ethanolamine lauryl sulfate. The last-named item, which is a detergent, can be purchased from a retail chemical supplier or from Continental Chemical Co., 270 Clifton Boulevard, Clifton, New Jersey 07015.

Simply swirl the ingredients together until the borax dissolves. Fancy it up with a drop of perfume and food coloring. Because of the low cost, ease of preparation, usefulness, and the impressiveness of the finished product, this makes an excellent gift idea. To add flair, paint or otherwise decorate the outside of the gift bottle.

For further information:

Formulas, Methods, Tips and Data for Home and Workshop, Kenneth Swezey. New York, Times Mirror Magazine, 1969.

HAND LOTION

Save a third or more of the cost of hand-care lotion by making your own. You'll need a few teaspoons of soluble rose water and a little over a fourth of a cup of glycerin, both available at your drugstore. Simply mix these with a cup of distilled water. Soak your hands in this solution for a few minutes daily to keep them smooth and soft.

For further information:

Van Nostrand's Practical Formulary, William Minrath, ed. Princeton, New Jersey, Van Nostrand, 1957.

EGG SHAMPOO

Forget about store-bought egg shampoo at $2 a bottle. Make your own for a nickle by mixing one egg yolk and a pinch of borax in a pint of warm water. Rinse hair well first in hot water, then in cold, after shampooing.

For further information:

"More Cosmetics from the Kitchen," *The Mother Earth News Almanac, The Mother Earth News* Staff. New York, Bantam, 1973, page 119.

GREEN SHEEN

For an excellent old-fashioned shampoo at half the prevailing price, try Tincture of Green Soap from your drugstore. This shampoo should be used only for normal or oily hair. People with very dry hair should use a shampoo with lanolin to correct the condition.

For further information:

How to Live with Inflation: A Guide to Saving Money When Buying, Joseph Newman, ed. Washington, D.C., Books by *U.S. News and World Report*, 1974.

DRY SHAMPOO NEWS

An instant dry shampoo at one tenth of commercial prices is cornmeal from your kitchen. Work into your hair and leave it on for five minutes to give your hair new life before that last-minute appointment.

For further information:

"Readers' Tips," *Consumer Life*, Vol. 1, No. 4, June 1976, page 33.

BEET BLUSH-ON

Here's a tip from a struggling actress friend who, out of necessity, has learned to cut many corners in the area of makeup purchases. Instead of paying $4 a jar for blush-on creams, she simply brushes on beet juice left over from cooking or liquid from canned beets. In front of the cameras *and* on the street, it looks as natural as a real blush!

COLD CREAM CAPER

At $4 for an 8-ounce jar, costs for cold cream can really add up. Why not make your own cold cream using ingredients available at your drugstore? Get yourself ½ cup mineral oil, 1 ounce beeswax, some borax, and distilled water. Heat the first two ingredients in a double-boiler until the wax melts. Combine ⅙ teaspoon of borax and slightly over ¼ cup distilled water. Bring to a boil in a separate container, then pour slowly into the oil mixture, stirring vigorously.

The result: a cup of fine-quality cold cream for pennies!

For further information:

New Practical Formulary, Mitchell Freeman. New York, Chemical, 1955.

TAKE A POWDER

As is the case with many consumer items, those $6 to $7 prices for fancy bath powder are charged on the basis of the beautiful packaging. Outsmart the manufacturers by concocting your own fancy bath powder at just one fifth of retail prices.

You'll need talc and boric acid from the drugstore and cornstarch from your supermarket. Simply combine 1 part boric acid with 4 parts cornstarch and 16 parts talc. Next, add a few drops of food coloring and non-oil-base perfume, mix thoroughly, and presto, your own personal bath-powder creation!

For further information:

Guide to Natural Cosmetics, Connie Krochmal. New York, Quadrangle, 1973.

HALF-PRICE HAIRDOS

For a third of the price of a swanky hair "analyst," and half the price of the run-of-the-mill beauty salon, you can get your hair cut, shampooed, and set by an aspiring apprentice at a beauty school. Cricket's experience with these schools is that the students, who are graded on their work, do a fine job for the money. Check your Yellow Pages under "Beauty schools."

LEG LOTION

Cook up a soothing hand and leg lotion at a 90 percent savings by simmering a big handful of pine needles, lettuce leaves, or cucumber slices in water for a half hour. For cooking, use a stainless steel or glass container in order to avoid a chemical reaction with the metal of the pot. Strain into a jar and add benzoin ($1 at your drugstore) drop by drop until the concoction turns milky.

For further information:

Complete Herbal Guide to Natural Health and Beauty, Dian Buchman. Garden City, New York, Doubleday, 1973.

HAIR CARE

Making your own hot oil conditioner for brittle, dry hair costs only a few pennies. Just mix two parts castor oil with one part olive oil, warm in a double-boiler, and apply to hair for twenty minutes or so before washing.

For further information:

Cosmetics from the Kitchen, Marcia Donnan. New York, Holt, Rinehart & Winston, 1972.

NAIL POLISH PENNIES

Purchase a gallon of acetone at your hardware store for the price of a tiny bottle of nail remover. It's the same stuff! It is useful as a solvent for removing contact cement and wood glue, or for cleaning fiber glass off equipment as well.

For further information:

"Twenty-five Crafty Ways to Save Money," *Mechanix Illustrated,* August 1974, pages 11–12, 98–99.

BATH SALT BONUS

Scented bath salts, which soften the water for a more enjoyable bath, cost about $5 a pound retail. You can make them at a fraction of the price. Just purchase some sodium carbonate, sodium sesquicarbonate, or borax at a drugstore or retail chemical supplier. Add a drop of food coloring and perfume per pint of salts, then mix thoroughly. Use about two tablespoons per bath. A personalized, inexpensive gift idea as well!

For further information:

Formulary of Perfumes and Cosmetics, Rene Gattefosse. New York, Chemical, 1959.

SHARPENING SORCERY

With this technique, you'll never have to buy new razor blades again. The mysterious device described below, which apparently concentrates ambient magnetic fields, will magically sharpen dull razors.

Out of heavy cardboard, cut four triangles with a base 15.7 inches long and sides 14.94 inches high. Tape these together to form a small pyramid, the tip of which should stand 10 inches high. (Proper proportions are important!) Make a stand $3^{1}/_{3}$ inches high to hold the razor blade. Using a compass, place this under the center of the pyramid so that the razor edge faces east-west. Set the pyramid over the stand with base edges facing exactly east-west and north-south. In a few days, your razor will be sharp.

For further information:

"Create a Pyramid, Mummify a Slug," *The Great Escape—A Source Book of Delights and Pleasures for the Mind and Body,* Min Ye, ed. New York, Bantam, 1974, page 211.

ORGANIC FACE LOTIONS

If you have normal or dry skin, apply cucumber, bell pepper, cabbage, strawberry, or grape juice as a soothing lotion after washing the face. A fine astringent lotion for oily skin, at half store prices, is plain grapefruit juice.

WATCH WORRIES

Repair costs for inexpensive watches and clocks often exceed the cost of a replacement. Escape from this dilemma by repairing your own timepiece! With the step-by-step instructions in H. G. Harris' *Handbook of Watch and Clock Repairs,* Buchanan, New York, Emerson, 1972, even an amateur can succeed in this tricky business with ease.

HAIR RINSE HINTS

Make your own hair rinse/skin conditioner at one third of retail prices. Pick a cup of lavender, violet, honeysuckle, lemon verbena, mint, geranium, or carnation leaves or petals. In a stainless steel or glass container, bring a pint of water to a boil. Add the greenery, and simmer two minutes. Add one cup cider vinegar, place in a jar, seal, and leave two weeks.

Now strain your cosmetic vinegar through a cloth.

Use as a hair rinse to remove soap residue and restore the scalp's acid balance, or to relieve sunburn or dry, itching skin.

For further information:

"Cosmetics from the Kitchen," *The Mother Earth News Almanac*, The Mother Earth News Staff. New York, Bantam, 1973, pages 55–57.

7

EDUCATION ECONOMICS

Today, the average cost of a four-year college education in our country, including tuition and living expenses, is $17,600—and steadily rising! If the high cost of a higher education has taken you by surprise, don't despair! Scholarships, fellowships, grants, and low-cost loans from federal, state, city, and private sources literally go begging in the United States.

Why? Mainly because many people simply don't know that they are available or are hesitant to apply for them. But there is no doubt about it. If you truly need the money, you can get it! One sure way to impress the people that hold the pursestrings is to study the various college entrance examination preparation books diligently—then score highly on the tests. And, of course, you'll want to apply for funds to many different sources. After all, if you splatter enough peanut butter on the wall, some of it's bound to stick!

In the books below and the chapter that follows, you'll discover a plethora of free money possibilities—in fields from accounting to zoology. Just ask!

Student Aid Annual 1974–75. Moravia, New York, Chronical Guidance Publications, 1974.

Student Financial Help: A Guide to Money for College, Louis and Joyce Scaringi. Garden City, New York, Doubleday, 1974.

Scholarships, Fellowships, and Loans, S. Norman Feingold. Arlington, Maryland, Bellman, 1972.

Meeting College Costs, College Board Publications Order Office, Box 592, Princeton, New Jersey 08540 (free).

Financial Assistance for College Students. Superintendent of Documents, U.S. Government Printing Office, Washington, D.C. 20402 (50¢).

"Need a Lift?" The American Legion, Department S, P.O. Box 1055, Indianapolis, Indiana 46206 (50¢).

Federal and State Student Aid Programs. Washington, D.C., Superintendent of Documents, U.S. Government Printing Office, 1972.

Grants of Aid to Individuals in the Arts. Washington International Arts Letter, 1321 Fourth Street, S.W., Washington, D.C. 20024.

Study Abroad. United Nations Educational, Scientific and Cultural Organization, UNIPUB, Box 433, New York, New York 10016.

Barron's Handbook of American College Financial Aid, Nicholas Proia and Vincent Di Gaspari. Woodbury, New York, Barron's Educational Series, 1971.

Guidance to Financial Aids for Students in Arts and Sciences for Graduate and Professional Study, Aysel Searles, Jr. and Anne Scott. New York, Arco, 1974.

A Selected List of Major Fellowship Opportunities and Aids to Advanced Education for United States Citizens. Fellowship Office, National Academy of Sciences, 2101 Constitution Avenue, N.W., Washington, D.C. 20418.

Financial Aids for Graduate Students, 1972–73, Lewis Hall, ed. Cincinnati, Educational Horizons Publishers (annual publication).

Annual Register of Grant Support 1973/1974, Deanna Sclar, ed., and The Staff of Academic Media. Orange, New Jersey, Academic Media, 1973 (United States).

The Grants Register 1975–1977, Roland Turner, ed. New York, St. Martin's Press, 1975 (worldwide).

Scholarships and Loans

CANADIAN CUTBACK

You can save $2,000 a year by attending a private Canadian college rather than a private American one. While tuition and living expenses at private colleges in America average out to $4,400 a year, these costs run $2,300 in such top-notch Canadian institutions as the University of Toronto, McGill

University, and the University of New Brunswick.

For further information:

Universities and Colleges of Canada. Ottawa, Canada, Information Canada (annual publication).

"Splitting to Canada Halves College Fees," Loretta Larrabee, *Moneysworth*, 4 August 1975, page 1.

CLIP COSTS WITH CLEP

If you have managed to acquire academic knowledge without a formal college education—either through experience or through diligent self-study—there *is* a way you can receive credit for it without attending college.

Through the College-Level Examination Program (CLEP), you can take a series of tests that will enable you to obtain credits for as much as two years of college, thus cutting college expenses in half. With the average cost of a college education approaching $20,000, this is no mean feat!

For further information:

CLEP May Be for You. College Board Publication Orders, Box 2815, Princeton, New Jersey 08540, 1975.

Barron's How to Prepare for the College-Level Examination Program (CLEP), William Doster et al. New York, Barron's Educational Series, 1975.

THE CO-OP OPTION

Forming a student cooperative is an excellent way to shave up to $500 a year off the cost of college room and board. With the approval of school authorities, your co-op will take over such chores as preparing cafeteria meals and maintaining dormitories, thus eliminating costly hired help.

To find out if your college has such an arrangement, simply check with your student affairs office. If it doesn't, form your own co-op!

For further information:

A Guide to Student Co-Ops, Student Division of the Cooperative League, 59 East Van Buren Street, Chicago, Illinois 60605.

CALCULATED CRAMMING

If you don't need to work summers to support yourself through college, attending a trimester—rather than a two-semester—college will save you thousands of dollars. Here's how: On the two-semester plan, you can work each summer, earning altogether around $4,000 at the minimum wage. On the trimester plan, you will study in the summer but you'll graduate a year early. During the fourth year, as a college graduate, your earning power will increase to $10,000 or more a year, thus saving you $6,000.

For further information:

"Reducing College Costs," B. Robert Anderson, *Reader's Digest*, Vol. 105, September 1974, pages 123–125.

"How to Beat the High Cost of a College Education," *Senior Scholastic*, Vol. 105, 23 January 1975, page 14.

TUITION TRICKS

Shave $2,500 off the first two years of college by taking advantage of the low-cost or free education provided by community colleges and state university extension centers. Here, you can take all the general subjects needed for your degree, saving that valuable tuition money for a major university during the last two years, where you can get specialized training in your field of interest.

Besides saving on board by living at home during the first half of your college years, you will pay only a few hundred dollars—and in some states, nothing—for tuition.

For further information:

Barron's Guide to the Two-Year Colleges, two volumes, Woodbury, New York, Barron's Educational Series, 1975.

1975 Community, Junior, and Technical College Directory, Sandra Drake, ed. American Association of Community and Junior Colleges, One Dupont Circle, N.W., Suite 410, Washington, D.C. 20036, 1975.

CLASSROOM CANNINESS

Not only do "free," or alternative, schools offer a wide variety of unconventional subjects, including mystic arts, experimental-living philosophies, and avant-garde arts and crafts, but the tuition is either low or, in many cases, nonexistent. For a complete list of such schools, write for *Directory of Free Schools*, Alternatives!, 1526 Gravenstein Highway North, Sebastopol, California 97452 ($1).

SCHOLARSHIPS OF MERIT

Merit Scholarships, offered by the National Merit Scholarship Corporation for college students, involve full scholarships plus a stipend of from $100 to $1,500 a year. Based on need, they must be renewed each scholastic year. The *National* Merit Scholarships offered by the same corporation differ from the above in that they confer a one-time award of $1,000 during your college years.

If you wish to be considered for a Merit Scholarship or a National Merit Scholarship, you must take the Preliminary Scholastic Aptitude Test/National Merit Scholarship Qualifying Test in your junior year of high school. (See your school counselor.) You will then automatically be considered for the scholarships.

For further information:

Scoring High on National Merit Scholarship Tests—Preliminary Scholastic Aptitude Tests, Harry Tarr. New York, Arco, 1974.

Guide to the National Merit Scholarship Program. National Merit Scholarship Corporation, 990 Grove Street, Evanston, Illinois 60201, 1975.

A STATE REBATE

Many states offer a scholarship program, either on the basis of a competitive exam, or on the basis of your high-school grades alone. An example is the famous Regents College Scholarships program of New York State, offering scholarships of $250 to $1,000 a year for up to five years. Information on programs in your state can be had from your high-school counselor.

If you are unable to get a state scholarship, ask a local bank if a state-sponsored loan program is available. Such loans are often easier to get than federally funded loans, and the states often foot part of the interest for you. Such programs as the Michigan Guaranteed Loan Plan offer loans of up to $1,500 per year, provided you have the approval of your state college and lending institution.

For further information:

How to Locate All Federal and State Student Aid Programs. Superintendent of Documents, U.S. Government Printing Office, Washington, D.C. 20402 (45¢).

FUNDS FOR FREE

If you don't have top-notch grades and cannot afford college, don't give up hope. The Supplemental Educational Opportunity Grants Program, funded by the Federal government and distributed through school financial-aid offices, may be able to provide you with up to $1,500 a year for your college education! Although it is called a grant, the money is actually a gift, no strings attached. The funds are available, on the basis of exceptional financial need, to undergraduates who are studying at least half-time.

For further information:

HEW Fact Sheet (DHEW Publication No. [OE] 76—17907), U.S. Department of Health, Education and Welfare, Office of Education, 330 Independence Avenue, S.W., Washington, D.C. 20202.

BASIC BOOTY

If you aren't penniless enough to qualify for a Supplemental Educational Opportunity Grant, try for the Basic Educational Opportunity Grant Program. On the basis of financial need, basic grants of up to $1,000 a year are offered to undergraduate students enrolled on at least a half-time basis. The money need not be repaid.

For further information:

Basic Grants Application, Basic Educational Opportunity Grant Program, U.S. Department of Health, Education and Welfare, Office of Education, 330 Independence Avenue, S.W., Washington D.C. 20202 (annual publication).

SOCIAL SECURITY SCHOLARSHIPS?

You may be automatically entitled to over $100 a month in social security benefits to cover your educational expenses. Are you an unmarried, full-time college student between the ages of eighteen and twenty-two? If the parent that supports you receives Social Security retirement or disability payments, or if your deceased parent worked long enough under Social Security, you may qualify under the Social Security Act student Benefits Section.

For further information:

Social Security Checks for Students 18 to 22, Social Security Administration, P.O. Box 57, Baltimore, Maryland 21203, or contact your local Social Security office.

CASH FROM CORPORATIONS

These are a significant source of scholarships for college students. Firms offer them mainly in an effort to promote their name to the businessman of tomorrow. One of the more famous is the General Motors Scholarship Plan, with awards of up to $2,000 a year, depending on need.

In another program, the National Coal Association offers Coal Company Scholarships of up to $1,500 a year to students in general, or specifically for students of certain majors, schools, or states. Other scholarships are for children of company employees.

Find out if your school participates in the General Motors Scholarship Plan by contacting your college director of admissions.

For Coal Company Scholarship information, write the National Coal Association, 1130 Seventeenth Street, N.W., Washington, D.C. 20036.

For further information:

Scholarships, Fellowships, Grants, and Loans, compiled by Lorraine Mathies. New York, Macmillan, 1974.

PRESBYTERIAN PRIZES

Of the various church-sponsored educational aid programs, the United Presbyterian Church offers perhaps the most far-reaching. Students at Presbyterian colleges can apply for National Presbyterian College Scholarships awards of from $100 to $1,400, depending on need. College students from ethnic minority groups may apply for a Student Opportunity Scholarship of up to $1,200. Students at a Presbyterian college who can recite the Westminster Shorter Catechism may receive a Samuel Robinson Scholarship for $300 on the basis of a religious essay.

Loans are also available through the church. Children of Presbyterian religious leaders may receive from $400 to $1,400, depending on need and availability, through the Educational Assistance Program. And finally, students preparing for a church occupation may borrow as much as $1,500 a year, at 3 percent interest, with repayment beginning six months after graduation, under the Student Loan Fund.

Request information on the program in which you're interested from Financial Aid for Studies, United Presbyterian Church in the United States of America, 475 Riverside Drive, New York, New York 10027.

RICHES FOR THE RELIGIOUS

Many other religious groups offer financial-aid programs for their members. The United

Methodist Church, for example, offers scholarships and low-cost loans to college students who are members. The Knights of Columbus offer scholarships for KC members or children of members who are studying at a Catholic college. College students who are Lutheran may qualify for a scholarship under the Aid Association for Lutherans All-College Scholarship Program. Scholarships are available for students at any Lutheran college through the AAL Lutheran Campus Scholarship Program. Interest-free loans for those of the Jewish faith can be had through the Lemberg Scholarship Loan Fund.

For further information:

Section of Loans and Scholarships, Board of Higher Education and Ministry, The United Methodist Church, P.O. Box 871, Nashville, Tennessee 37202.

Director of Scholarship Aid, Knights of Columbus, Supreme Council, Columbus Plaza, P.O. Drawer 1670, New Haven, Connecticut 06507.

AAL All-College Scholarship Program, Educational Testing Service, P.O. Box 176, Princeton, New Jersey 08540. For information on the AAL Lutheran Campus Scholarship Program, see the financial aid office of the Lutheran college involved.

Lemberg Scholarship Loan Fund, 838 Fifth Avenue, New York, New York 10021.

DEPENDENT DOLLARS

Most everyone knows that many veterans and servicemen can get several hundred dollars a month for four years of education under the GI bill. But did you know that a number of programs are available for the children and wives of disabled or deceased veterans, prisoners of war, and servicemen missing in action?

Under the Dependents' Educational Assistance Program, such dependents who are full-time students can receive up to $220 a month for up to four years of college! Under the AMVETS Memorial Scholarship Program, children of disabled or deceased vet-

erans can obtain scholarships of up to $1,000 for four years of college.

For further information:

Veterans Administration, 810 Vermont Avenue, N.W., Washington, D.C. 20420, or contact a local Veterans Administration office.

AMVETS National Scholarship Program, 1710 Rhode Island Avenue, N.W., Washington, D.C. 20036.

LOOT FOR LIBRARIANS

A veritable plethora of financial assistance in the form of scholarships, grants, and loans has been set aside for students in library education. You can get the lowdown from librarians, guidance counselors, or financial-aid officers at your college.

Or, send a self-addressed label to Library Education Division, American Library Association, 50 East Huron Street, Chicago, Illinois 60611, for a copy of the booklet *Financial Assistance for Library Education.*

LABOR UNION LUCRE

If you are the child of a union member, a young union member yourself, or even a nonmember high-school student, you may be able to qualify for one of the many scholarships—up to $10,000 for four years of college—offered by international, national, state, district, and local labor unions across the nation.

For a list of scholarships and application information, send $2 for the *Student Aid Bulletin*, Chronicle Guidance Publications, Inc., Moravia, New York 13118.

BLACK BONANZA

Quite a few scholarships, many sponsored by individual colleges, are available for black students. On the national level, there are the well-known National Achievement Scholarships and the Achievement Scholarships. To apply for these, you must take the Preliminary Scholastic Aptitude Test/National Merit

Scholarship Qualifying Test in your junior year of high school and indicate on it that you are black. The National Achievement Scholarship is a $1,000 one-time award. The Achievement Scholarship is a full scholarship, plus a stipend of $250 to $1,500 a year, depending on need. This scholarship must be renewed every scholastic year.

See your high-school counselor or principal for details. For information on other scholarships and aids available to black students, contact the National Scholarship Service and Fund for Negro Students, 1776 Broadway, New York, New York 10019.

For further information:

Preparation for College Board Examinations: Scholastic Aptitude Test and College Board Achievement Tests. Chicago, Henry Regnery, 1972.

Scholarships Available to Black Students, American Indian Students, Spanish-Speaking Students. The Reader Development Program, The Free Library of Philadelphia, 236 North 23rd Street, Philadelphia, Pennsylvania 19103, 1971.

FOR EVANS SAKE

If you're planning to attend one of the twelve universities which have Evans Scholars Chapter Houses (University of Colorado, University of Illinois, Indiana University, Marquette University, University of Michigan, Michigan State, University of Minnesota, University of Missouri, Northwestern University, Ohio State, Purdue University, and the University of Wisconsin) or in states where there is no chapter, any state university—by all means look into the Evans Scholars Foundation Scholarship Program.

Set up and administered by the Evans Scholarship Foundation for the benefit of students who excel academically, these scholarships cover the cost of both tuition and housing. You must meet stringent academic and personal requirements, need the money, and be recommended by a club member.

For further information:

Western Golf Association, Golf, Illinois 60029.

HEALTH STUDENT WEALTH

For those of you planning to study medicine, pharmacy, osteopathy, optometry, podiatry, or veterinary medicine, excellent financial help is available through the Health Professions Scholarship and Student Loan Program sponsored by the National Institutes of Health. If you're a U.S. citizen or permanent resident, or plan to become one, and really need the money, you may qualify for a scholarship of up to $3,500 a year. If you can't get the scholarship, look into their low-cost loans available for students of the health professions. If you can show need, you can receive up to $3,500 a year, at 3 percent interest. Interest doesn't begin to accumulate until you start repaying the loan—a year after graduation.

Not only that, but you may defer repayment and interest accrual three years by joining the Public Health Service or the Peace Corps. The loan can be deferred indefinitely by going on to advanced training in the field of health. You can work off up to 60 percent of the loan by practicing in an area where there is a shortage in your field.

For further information:

National Institutes of Health, Division of Physician and Health Professions Education, Bureau of Health Resources Development, Bethesda, Maryland 20014.

FUNDS FOR FUTURE NURSES

Excellent programs of financial aid are available to those who wish to study nursing. Outright scholarships of up to $2,000 a year are granted on the basis of availability and need. Also, loans of up to $10,000 are available at only 3 percent interest.

You don't have to start repaying the loan until nine months after graduation. If you go on to advanced nursing study, the payments can be deferred another five years. If you join the military or the Peace Corps, the payments may be deferred up to three years. Not only that, but you can work off up to 85 percent of the loan by working as a nurse in a public or nonprofit institution, or in an area where there is a nursing shortage.

For further information:

Division of Nursing, Bureau of Health Manpower Education, National Institutes of Health, Bethesda, Maryland 20014.

Scholarships, Fellowships, Educational Grants and Loans for Registered Nurses, National League of Nursing, 10 Columbus Circle, New York, New York 10019.

JOURNALISTS' JEWELS

For the student of journalism, over 3,000 scholarships in all shapes and sizes, and millions of dollars' worth of loans, are offered through The Newspaper Fund, P.O. Box 300, Princeton, New Jersey 08540.

Journalism majors with a good track record can also apply for one of the scholarships offered by the William Randolph Hearst Foundation, Suite 218, Hearst Building, Third and Market Streets, San Francisco, California 94103. Writing them may be the first bit of journalism for which you get paid. And what a payment!

For further information:

Journalism Scholarship Guide, The Newspaper Fund, P.O. Box 300, Princeton, New Jersey 08540.

DENTAL DOLLARS

Planning to go into dentistry or a related field? In many states, scholarships and loans are available for dental students either through the state dental association or society or through a specific college or university financial-aid office. Financial aid is also available through the American Fund for Dental Education (dental laboratory technology), the American Dental Assistants' Association, and the American Dental Hygienists' Associ-

ation, all located at 211 East Chicago Avenue, Chicago, Illinois 60611.

For minority dental education students, generous scholarships are offered through the American Fund for Dental Education, Suite 1630, 211 East Chicago Avenue, Chicago, Illinois 60611.

Best of luck in locating your real-life tooth fairy!

INCOME FOR INDIANS

For Indians, Eskimos, and Aleuts, especially those living on reservations, scholarships and loans awarded on the basis of need and ability can be had for college or university education. The average scholarship grant amounts to $1,300; loans amount to $500 or more a year.

The agency office that has a record of your tribal membership must apply for you to your area office of the Bureau of Indian Affairs.

For further information:

U.S. Department of the Interior, Bureau of Indian Affairs, Division of Student Services, 123 Fourth Street, S.W., P.O. Box 1788, Albuquerque, New Mexico 87103.

Scholarships Available to Black Students, American Indian Students, Spanish-Speaking Students. The Reader Development Program, The Free Library of Philadelphia, 236 North 23rd Street, Philadelphia, Pennsylvania 19103, 1971.

FREE LOANS

Under the National Direct Student Loan program, you can get up to $5,000 for undergraduate work, plus an additional $5,000 for graduate work. No interest is charged on this loan while you're in school. Nine months after you graduate, you begin to repay the loan, over a five- to ten-year period—at the fantastically low interest rate of 3 percent!

If you continue your studies at another institution, or join Vista or the Peace Corps, you may wait three years before beginning your loan repayments. Moreover, if you teach in a school with pupils from low-income families or with handicapped children, or if you become a member of Head Start, your loan obligation will be eliminated at the rate of 15 to 30 percent a year.

To apply for this loan, contact the financial-aid office of the institution you plan to attend.

For further information:

How to Beat the High Cost of College, Claire Cox. New York, Dial, 1971.

LOW-COST LOANS

If you are unable to qualify for a scholarship or for a National Direct Student Loan, you can still qualify for a low-cost deferred loan regardless of your family's income. The Guaranteed Student Loan Program available in some states allows you to get a higher educational loan from a bank, savings and loan association, credit union, or other source for up to $7,500 for an undergraduate and $10,000 for a graduate student. The interest is lower than can generally be obtained elsewhere, and you don't have to start repaying until nine to twelve months after you graduate. If you continue your education at another institution, or join the Peace Corps or Vista, the repayments will be deferred up to three years.

To apply for a United Student Aid Fund Loan, a similar loan available in some states, write to United Student Aid Funds, Inc., 5259 North Tacoma Avenue, Indianapolis, Indiana 46220.

Grad Bag

GADABOUT GRADS

Does the thought of a $4,600 Roman scholarship, an all-expense paid German fellowship, or a $4,500 ten-month Belgian fellowship whet your traveling appetite? These and many more stupendous stipends await the eager European academic adventurer.

For details, write the *Fellowship Guide for Western Europe*, Council for European Studies, 156 Mervis Hall, University of Pittsburgh, Pittsburgh, Pennsylvania 15260 ($2.00).

ARCTIC ADVENTURE

How about an all-expense paid vacation to the mysterious Arctic, land of the midnight sun? As a qualified investigator of oceanography, cold weather physiology, permafrost, geophysics, or many other Arctic conditions, you will stay at the Naval Arctic Research Laboratory, Barrow, Alaska, or one of its field stations. Apply for your grant-in-aid through The Arctic Institute of North America, 1619 New Hampshire Avenue, N.W., Washington, D.C. 20009.

COMMON WEALTH

One of the nicest things about fellowships to British Commonwealth countries is that the native language can be learned in a few weeks' time! All kinds of freebies await the scholar-visitor to the United Kingdom. A small sample: The Marshall Scholarships, British Embassy, 3100 Massachusetts Avenue, N.W., Washington, D.C. 20008, allows $3,800 a year stipend to United Kingdom university students.

For men studying at the University of Oxford, thirty-two Rhodes Scholarships are available each year, covering full tuition and a maintenance allowance. Contact The Rhodes Scholarship Office, Wesleyan University, Middletown, Connecticut 06457.

For details on other Commonwealth opportunities: *Scholarships Guide for Commonwealth Postgraduate Students*, The Association of Commonwealth Universities, 36 Gordon Square, London WCIH OPF, England ($6).

LATIN LEARNING

Did you major in Latin American studies? Here's your ticket to a year or two of advanced study in the land of your dreams. Doherty Fellowships for Latin American

Studies, Doherty Fellowship Committee, Program in Latin American Studies, 240 East Pyne, Princeton, New Jersey 08540, offers one-year social studies grants covering travel, living, and research costs.

Up to two years' worth of travel, tuition, and living expenses in OAS (Organization of American States) countries are paid to advanced students in many fields by the Office of Fellowships and Training, Secretariat for Technical Cooperation, Organization of American States, Washington, D.C. 20006.

FULBRIGHT-HAYS FORTUNES

A fortune in grants and fellowships for study abroad is offered through the various Fulbright-Hays programs. For predoctoral work there are the Fulbright-Hays Full Grants and Fulbright-Hays Travel Grants administered by the Institute of International Education, 809 United Nations Plaza, New York, New York 10017. Write for their booklet *Grants for Graduate Study Abroad*.

For doctoral dissertation research in modern foreign languages, world affairs, and area studies for countries all over the world, apply to the Division of Foreign Studies, Institute of International Studies, Office of Education, U.S. Department of Health, Education and Welfare, 330 Independence Avenue, S.W., Washington, D.C. 20202.

RUSKIE RESEARCH

If you have a deep-seated desire to test the scenic authenticity of *Doctor Zhivago*, free research trips of up to ten months to the stolid Soviet Union, romantic Romania, beautiful Bulgaria, and other Communist countries can be had through the International Research and Exchanges Board, 110 East 59th Street, New York, New York 10022. Most candidates for this program must be advanced doctoral candidates or teachers. Teachers of Russian may apply for this board's summer language program in Russia.

PACIFIC PLEASURE

For an idyllic graduate study program at the University of Hawaii, with field study on a lovely Pacific isle or Oriental area of your choice, apply for a graduate study grant through the Office of Participant Services, The East-West Center, Honolulu, Hawaii 96822. The office will foot all bills related to your study of language and culture, population, the effects of technology, and other human problems affecting the United States, the Pacific, and Asia.

FEMALE FELLOWSHIPS

Aren't you glad you're a woman! The American Association of University Women, Educational Foundation, 2401 Virginia Avenue, N.W., Washington, D.C. 20037, offers fifty awards a year of up to $5,000 each to enable women to complete their dissertations.

Another boon to womankind, Career Advancement Scholarships offered by the Business and Professional Women's Foundation, 2012 Massachusetts Avenue, N.W., Washington, D.C. 20036, assists mature women to enter a career area or to advance their professional status. Financial assistance is available for part-time or full-time study.

Female college graduates who are planning to teach high school or college and whose career has been interrupted for three years or more should apply for one of thirty-five fellowships offered yearly for master's or doctoral study from The Danforth Foundation, 222 South Central Avenue, St. Louis, Missouri 63105.

LAW LOOT

For law-school graduates, and for social science students who have completed doctorate requirements (except for the dissertation), up to $9,000 a year in Russell Sage Residencies in Law and Social Science is ripe for the picking. These residencies are offered to those wishing to apply social science methods to research on legal processes and institutions by the Director, Law and Social Science Residency Program, Russell Sage Foundation, 230 Park Avenue, New York, New York 10017.

If legal history is the love of your life, fellowships of up to a year for its study can be obtained through Project in Legal History, American Bar Foundation, 1155 East 60th Street, Chicago, Illinois 60637. You must either be working on your dissertation or already have a law or doctoral degree.

WILDLIFE WELTER

The study of wildlife conservation and management is popular not only with many students these days, but also with the men who hand out the free study money. For example, The Theodore Roosevelt Memorial Fund, American Museum of Natural History, Central Park West at 79th Street, New York, New York 10024, will pay graduate students' travel and living expenses for field studies anywhere north of the Mexican border. They will pay for trips to New York City to study the museum's collections, and trips to the museum's field stations as well.

Doctoral-degree candidates can obtain fellowships of up to $4,000 for nine months of wildlife conservation study from the Executive Director, National Wildlife Federation, 1412 Sixteenth Street, N.W., Washington, D.C. 20036.

Grants of up to $1,500 are offered graduate students of wildlife management by the Wildlife Management Institute, Wire Building, Washington, D.C. 20005. Just pick up a pen: The wild life will be yours!

SCIENTIFIC? TERRIFIC!

If you just obtained your Bachelor of Science degree, and wish to continue your education in a scientific field, write to the Fellowship Office, National Research Council, 2101 Constitution Avenue, N.W., Washington, D.C. 20418. If you can convince them that your goals are worthy, one of their $3,600 a year, three-year fellowships will be yours!

FEDERAL ARTS AND HUMANITIES

The U.S. Office of Education is a prime sponsor of a multitude of financial-aid programs for students of the arts and humanities. Get yourself a copy of *U.S. Office of Education Support for the Arts and Humanities, Catalog Number HE5.2:AR 7|5|72,* Superintendent of Documents, U.S. Government Printing Office, Washington, D.C. 20402 (35¢), and drink in the details.

For students of the humanities who have finished a year of graduate school and wish to learn an East European language such as Greek, Yugoslavian, or Polish in the native land, the East European Language Program sponsored by the American Council of Learned Societies, 345 East 46th Street, New York, New York 10017, is well worth investigating. These folks offer an all-expense paid summer of language study in the country of your choice.

PSYCH OUT

Graduate students of psychology can choose from a host of governmental and private stipends and financial-aid programs. An example: The Veterans Administration Psychology Training Program, Veterans Administration, Department of Medicine and Surgery, Psychology Division 116C, Washington, D.C. 20420, offers standard stipends of up to $6,790. These folks will give you up to $9,000 a year provided you work a year for them beforehand.

For details on other psych stipends, get *Graduate Study in Psychology,* Educational Affairs Office, American Psychological Association, 1200 Seventeenth Street, N.W., Washington, D.C. 20036 (annual publication).

MIXED BLESSINGS

What do Byzantine, Polish, and American studies have in common? In each of these fields, generous fellowships are available for graduate students. You can get up to $4,000 (single person) or $4,500 (married) for the study of Byzantine civilization from the Dumbarton Oaks Center for Byzantine Studies, 1703 Thirty-Second Street, N.W., Washington, D.C. 20007. You must know Latin, and if you have studied Greek your chances will be significantly increased.

The cost of transportation to Poland, tuition for Polish studies, and room and board are covered by the Polish Studies and Exchange Scholarships offered by The Kosciuszko Foundation, 15 East 65th Street, New York, New York 10021.

All kinds of information on financial aid for graduate students of American civilization can be had from the annual summer supplement of *American Quarterly*, American Studies Association, Box 30, Bennett Hall, University of Pennsylvania, Philadelphia, Pennsylvania 19104.

FOOTING THE BILL

As much as $4,000 a year can be yours in the wonderful world of podiatry through American Podiatry Association Fellowships. A requirement: 4 hours of work every week at a college of podiatric medicine; or 120 hours during the summer.

Get your foot in the door by writing to the association at 20 Chevy Chase Circle, N.W., Washington, D.C. 20015.

OSTEOPATH MATH

Each year, twenty-seven $750-a-year scholarships are awarded to students at any of seven osteopathic medical colleges. Pave your pathway to this lucrative field of treatment with a National Osteopathic College Scholarship from the American Osteopathic Association (address below).

For further information:

Education Annual (The Journal of the American Osteopathic Association, March issue), Office of Education, American Osteopathic Association, 212 East Ohio Street, Chicago, Illinois 60611.

TRAVEL TICKET

The Social Science Research Council, 230 Park Avenue, New York, New York 10017, is your ticket to graduate studies anywhere in the world. For foreign studies in the humanities and social sciences, they pay all transportation, maintenance, research, health insurance, and some tuition costs as well. Through their Fellowships and Grants for Training and Research on Foreign Areas, you can go to Africa, the Caribbean, the Orient, Latin America, Europe—practically anywhere. Bon voyage!

SMITHSONIAN SIMOLEONS

Does an all-expense-paid study trip of up to one year at the famed Smithsonian Institution in historic Washington, D.C., strike your fancy? If you are a graduate student, doctoral candidate, or postdoctoral scholar in one of the multifarious fields into which the museum delves, grab this chance to work closely with a professional museum staff in the area of your choice . . . for free!

For further information:

Smithsonian Opportunities for Research and Study in History, Art, Science, Office of Academic Studies, Smithsonian Institution, Washington, D.C. 20560.

MONEY MAGIC

Are you working on a doctorate in a social, environmental, or field science? You can obtain all the money you need for travel, field research, and supplies through that magnanimous magician, The National Science Foundation (NSF), Washington, D.C. 20550. Let them turn your laboratory rats into chinchillas!

EARTHLY ECSTASIES

For both graduate and undergraduate students in the exciting field of geophysical exploration, the Society of Exploration Geophysicists Foundation, P.O. Box 3098,

Tulsa, Oklahoma 74101, offers a grant of up to $1,000 a year. Loans can also be obtained through this organization.

The Ph.D. candidate in geology can obtain funds for field or laboratory work, including travel, living expenses, and research supplies through The Geological Society of America, 3300 Penrose Place, Boulder, Colorado 80301. Pay dirt—dig it!!

ART START

You can get $6,000 a year from the Metropolitan Museum of Art, New York, New York 10028, to study one of their collections! You must have obtained your master's degree and approach them with a specific topic of research.

Art history fellowships are also offered by the National Gallery of Art, Washington, D.C. 20565. You must be well on your way to a doctoral degree before applying.

ACCOUNTING AFFLUENCE

Graduate students of accounting who plan to teach this discipline can obtain up to $500 a month (single) or $550 a month (married) while they pursue their education.

For details, write to:

Committee on Relations with Universities, American Institute of CPA's, 666 Fifth Avenue, New York, New York 10019.

HUGHES NEWS

If you majored in engineering, physics, or math, you can get a $2,300-a-year-lift toward your master's degree through Hughes Aircraft Company, Scientific Education Office, Building 100, Mail Station U-614, P.O. Box 90515, Los Angeles, California 90009.

For doctoral candidates in these subjects, this organization offers up to $3,100 a year, and up to $13,000 a year for a work-study program. Awards are made on the basis of academic excellence.

SMOG SOLUTIONS

An annual $6,500 can be yours for graduate study of one of the most pressing problems of our day—air pollution. Write to the Manpower Development Staff, Controlled Programs Development Division, Office of Air Quality Planning and Standards, Research Triangle Park, North Carolina 27711, for Air Pollution Control Office Fellowship information.

SOCIAL SERVICES SUGGESTIONS

Graduate students in social services can obtain free grants to continue their education from a number of sources. You can get up to $6,000 a year from the Chief, Staff Development and Education Division, Social Services Work (122), Department of Medicine and Surgery, Veterans' Administration, Washington, D.C. 20420, for study in a VA hospital.

For students willing to work for the B'nai B'rith Youth Organization after their schooling, up to $2,500 a year can be had through this organization's Klutznick Scholarships. Write them at 1640 Rhode Island Avenue, N.W., Washington, D.C. 20036.

For further freebies, check: *Family Service Grants to Students in Graduate Schools of Social Work*, Family Service Association of America, 44 East 23rd Street, New York, New York 10010; *Scholarships, Fellowships, Work-Study Plans for Graduate Social Work Education*, Personnel Services, National Jewish Welfare Board, 15 East 26th Street, New York, New York 10010; and *Career and Traineeship Information for Graduate Study in Rehabilitation Counseling*, National Rehabilitation Counseling Association, 1522 K Street, N.W., Washington, D.C. 20005.

TEACHER TREASURES

If you're planning to become a teacher, one of the following fellowships may well allow you to attend graduate school for free: The famous Danforth Fellowships and Kent Fellowships are offered to graduate students who wish to become college teachers by The Danforth Foundation, 222 South Central Avenue, St. Louis, Missouri 63105.

Future college teachers can obtain a $3,000-a-year stipend, plus tuition, from the Higher Education Personnel Training Programs, Division of University Programs, Bureau of Higher Education, U.S. Office of Education, Washington, D.C. 20202.

The Richard M. Weaver Fellowship Awards Program, Intercollegiate Studies Institute, Inc., 14 South Bryn Mawr Avenue, Bryn Mawr, Pennsylvania 19010, offers twenty fellowships a year, including a $2,000 stipend, plus full tuition at the school of your choice.

Among more specialized awards are the dissertation fellowships offered by The Richard D. Irwin Foundation, 1818 Ridge Road, Homewood, Illinois 60430, to potential business, social science, and economics teachers.

Future political science teachers can obtain Congressional Fellowship Program awards of $6,500 and up from The American Political Science Association, 1527 New Hampshire Avenue, N.W., Washington, D.C. 20036. For potential foreign language teachers, NDEA Graduate Foreign Language Fellowships are funded by the U.S. Department of Health, Education and Welfare, Division of Foreign Studies, Institute of International Studies, Office of Education, Washington, D.C. 20202. Write HEW for details.

Work-Study Savvy

COLLECTING CREDITS

With the average private college education costing $20,000, college credits are indeed money. Under the Cooperative Education Work-Study Program, not only do you get paid for working full time at the occupation for which you are studying, but you'll get academic credit for the work as well.

Some public high schools offer a Career Development Program with college credit for past work done. Another public high-school and adult-education program, the Regional Occupation Program, offers on-the-job training for academic credit.

Inquire about these programs at your high-school or college-counseling office, or send for a copy of *Undergraduate Programs of Cooperative Education in the United States and Canada,* The Cooperative Education Research Center, National Commission for Cooperative Education, 360 Huntington Avenue, Boston, Massachusetts 02115.

For further information:

Handbook of Cooperative Education, Asa Knowles and Associates. San Francisco, Jossey-Bass, 1971.

HOME-STUDY HINTS

Private home-study schools are a good, low-cost solution to needed educational courses, eliminating payment for transportation, room, and board for those living in out-of-the-way places. However, there are quite a few correspondence schools around that promise you the moon for astronomical prices, then fail to get you off the ground. To avoid getting hoodwinked by these bamboozlers, find out if the school you're considering is a reputable one. A free *Directory of Accredited Private Home Study Schools* can be obtained from the National Home Study Council, 1601 Eighteenth Street, N.W., Washington, D.C. 20009. For a ten-cent catalogue of inexpensive *used* correspondence courses, write Smith Instruction Exchange, 124 Marlborough Road, Salem, Massachusetts 01970.

CHEAP CORRESPONDENCE COURSES

For only a few dollars each, you can take any of a number of correspondence courses offered on such subjects as business administration, engineering, education, athletics, agriculture, home economics, and various arts and sciences. These and other useful subjects are offered through land-grant college-extension services across the nation.

Get full information on these courses and other special study programs at your state college.

For further information:

Guide to Correspondence Study in Colleges and Universities. University of California Extension Service, Berkeley, California, 1970.

WAMPUM FOR WOMEN

If you're a mature woman who's trying to get back into the job market, or already have a job and are trying to get a better job, a scholarship from Soroptimists international may help you acquire the necessary skills. This organization, whose aim is to help women live more productively, offers $30,000 in scholarships a year.

For further information:

Soroptimists International of the Americas, 1616 Walnut Street, Philadelphia, Pennsylvania 19103.

TECHNICAL TRAINING

Before you put out hard-earned money for a technical, business, or other vocational course at a commercial school, check into the wealth of courses offered free of charge through joint state-federal vocational programs. Subjects include medical assistant, merchandising, and agricultural training; nursing, homemaking and child-care courses; and technical training in plenteous profusion.

Courses are available through public schools, community organizations, and vocation-technical schools. Contact your high-school counselor, state employment service, or state vocational-education department for further information.

For a list of U.S. vocational schools, including fees, see *Lovejoy's Career and Vocational School Guide: A Source Book, Clue Book and Directory of Institutions Training for Job Opportunities*, Clarence Lovejoy, New York, Simon & Schuster, 1973.

BUSINESS BRIEF

Valuable business courses are available for a nominal fee through the U.S. Small Business Administration's management assistance program. This agency co-sponsors with local colleges and universities, trade and professional associations, and professional experts, courses on a wide range of business related subjects.

For more information, contact your local Small Business Administration office or write the U.S. Small Business Administration, 1441 L Street, N.W., Washington, D.C. 20416.

TRANSPORTATION
TALENTS

The average bloke works 300 long hours a year just to pay for carting himself back and forth to work every day. The major factor in this astounding expense for basic transportation is the high cost of *status*—the prestige of owning a new car every year, and the resultant heavy penalty of depreciation incurred.

It *is* possible to cut down on transportation costs and still own a new car every few years. But your major transportation savings—thus reducing those long transportation-earning hours from 300 to 30 or even less—will come from such alternative forms of transportation as the electric car, the motorcycle, and the bicycle. For that matter, you can even own a helicopter for less than the cost of a new car!

Getting Your Wheels

There are two main ways you can buy a reliable used car. You can go to a dealer and spend a *lot* of money for what you get. Or, you can buy from a private party—whose existence doesn't depend on selling cars —and get a bargain.

Look for used-car bargains in newspaper classifieds and through supermarket, laundromat, and college bulletin boards. Another good bet lies in the public auto auction. If there's one in your area, you might look over their stock and bid for what you want.

If you happen to find the car of your dreams on a dealer's lot, and you simply *must* have it, here are some tips. If you have a trade-in, keep it under your hat while you bargain for the car you want. When you've got what you think is a rock-bottom figure, *then* ask what you can get for your old car. By using this method, you'll readily determine how much the dealer is *really* giving you for your trade-in. And for land's sake, don't be afraid to haggle. Bargaining may not be the custom at Macy's or Sears, but at a car dealership—it's no holds barred.

Take your time and shop around at several dealers. Drop a hint to the salesman that you've been looking elsewhere and don't allow yourself to get pushed into a sale by falling for the "today-only" ploy or the "I've almost got another buyer" gambit that so many car salesmen use.

CHEAP CARS

Want to know how to buy just about any new domestic car at $125 over dealer cost, with manufacturer's warranty and full service? Order it from United Auto Brokers, 1603 Bushwick Avenue, Brooklyn, New York 11207.

This is an association composed of auto dealers throughout the country who have agreed to participate in the plan. Naturally, you'll have to pay transportation costs to your locality, but you'll still be saving hundreds of dollars on a $3,000 car.

If there is no participating dealer in your area, and you're forced to walk into a dealership "cold," here's an excellent tool to use in your bargaining negotiations. Before approaching the dealer, find out what price *he* paid for the car. You can get this information by sending $10 along with the make of the car and options desired, to Car/Puter International Corporation, 1603 Bushwick Avenue, Brooklyn, New York 11207.

For further information:

"Knocking Down the Sticker Price on a New Car: This Simple, Step-by-Step Approach Will Get the Car You Want at Hundreds of Dollars Less," *Changing Times*, October 1975, pages 11–13.

55 MPG??

That's what you get with Urbacar, a 2-passenger, 700-pound auto with top speeds of 50 miles per hour. You can make it yourself for $1,500. For Plans Package C–4–75, send $15 to *Mechanix Illustrated* Plans, Greenwich, Connecticut 06830.

BOX BUCKS

A California firm is marketing The Box, a build-it-yourself auto kit including chassis, streamlined body, extra-wide tires, and interior, at $945. Combined with an economy engine (not included), this do-it-yourself car will get 75 miles per gallon. For details, send $1 to Monocoque Engineering Inc., Box 906, Costa Mesa, California 92627.

VERSATILE VW

Bug owners who need a pickup or camper can actually convert their VW into one, at a savings of thousands of dollars over the cost of a new model, with the help of kits from Danurs, 312 East 17th, Kansas City, Missouri 64108. Kits cost $399 (pickup) and $549 (camper).

ERSATZ MG

If you long for a classic MG roadster on a Beetle budget, this may be the answer to your prayers. Buy the VW Bug, then purchase an MG fiber glass body ($3,195) to fit over it from Fiberfab, Inc., 548 Baldwin Street, Bridgeville, Pennsylvania 15017. Or, the un-assembled body in kit form at $1,395 sure beats that up-to-$10,000 price tag on the real thing.

LESS FOR MORE

When choosing between a six- and eight-cylinder automobile, don't let the feeling of mastery and power that the eight-cylinder implies overwhelm your rational and highly commendable inclination to economize.

Consider, first of all, that the purchase price of a new six-cylinder is $100 to $250 less than that of an eight. And secondly, the six will cost far less to service and will save you well over $50 a year on gas.

For further information:

How to Save Money When You Buy and Drive Your Car, Merle Dowd. West Nyack, New York, Parker, 1967.

AUTO ANTICS

Which new car is cheaper to own and operate—compact or subcompact? U.S. Department of Transportation figures surpris-ingly show the total cost of owning a 1974 subcompact to be 11.2 cents per mile —compared to 10.8 cents per mile for the compact car.

For further information:

Cost of Operating an Automobile, Office of Public Affairs, Federal Highway Administration, HPA–1, Washington, D.C. 20590.

AXLE FAX

Your best buy for economy is a car with a low axle ration, 2.5:1 being about the lowest you can get and 4.5:1 the highest. With the lower ratios, the car's engine turns slower than with the faster accelerating high-ratio models. Thus, the lower ratios don't waste energy on fast getaways and needless speed spurts.

You can obtain this technical information directly from the manufacturer or from dealers' spec sheets. If the axle ratio information is not available, ask the car salesman for the standard as opposed to the optional ratio, or for the economy as opposed to the performance or trailering ratio.

For further information:

How to Get Your Money's Worth in New and Used Cars (No. 4). World-wide Books, P.O. Box 404, Radio City Station, New York, New York 10019 ($1 plus postage, *print* return name and address).

AUTOMATIC SOLUTIONS

If you are presently faced with the decision of whether to buy an automatic transmission or stick shift, bear in mind that the latter offers a hefty 14 percent increase in power-transmitting efficiency, saving you, as an average driver, about $50 worth of gas per year.

For further information:

Save Money, Save Gas, Robert Irvin. Chicago, Enterprise (orders to Newspaper Enterprise Association), 1974.

COOLING OFF

As a no-cost alternative to the auto air conditioner which gobbles up two or three miles per gallon of gasoline in city driving, consider the flow-through ventilation system found on some of the new model cars.

Vents, front and rear, allow a cooling air flow throughout the entire length of the car. So why not just keep the windows open you say? Open windows cause "wind-drag" which serves to decrease engine efficiency, thus, like the air conditioner, increasing gasoline consumption.

IGNITION CONDITION

Here's a point worth considering in choosing between a standard ignition and a solid-state electronic ignition, which lacks breaker points. The improved design of the newer system will keep those sparks plugging away for longer than the standard ignition, lengthening service intervals, with a corresponding decrease in maintenance costs.

ACCESSORY AGILITY

Just agreed with a dealer to purchase a new car from him? Don't think he'll suddenly soften up and give you a good deal on selling and installing such additional equipment as optional ignition system, radio, or stereo. Heavens to Aunt Betsy's busted bustle! A firm that specializes in such installation can put in that stereo for a whole $100 less! Or, for rock-bottom prices, pick up a how-to book and the parts at your auto parts store, and install your own extras.

For further information:

Auto Radio Servicing Made Easy, Wayne Lemons. Indianapolis, Bobbs-Merrill, 1969.

Auto Stereo Service and Installation, Paul Dorweiler and Harry Hanson. Blue Ridge Summit, Pennsylvania, TAB Books, 1974.

How to Install Your Own Auto Transistor Ignition System, Brice Ward. New Augusta, Indiana, Editors and Engineers, 1965.

Saving on Gas

HOW TO DROWN IN A CAR POOL

Back in her nine-to-five days, Cricket once had the bright idea of starting a car pool with five querulous working ladies and an equally querulous 1962 lilac Cadillac. At the end of this bold experiment, the Cadillac had cost $200 in repairs, gas, and parking fees, and the ladies had paid $80 for her services. This left Cricket with what would have been the cost for bus fare to work three times over, a broken-down car, four disgruntled and one irate former passenger, and several years off an already harried life.

Obviously, other people tackle this venture with more success than she. Your best bet is to attempt it with a reliable economy car. Better yet, join someone else's car pool and leave the expense to them!

For further information:

Carpools for Fun and Profit (O11D), Consumer Information, Public Documents Distribution Center, Pueblo, Colorado 81009, 1974 (free).

CLEAN AIR

It need cost you nothing to revamp your air cleaner, but a dirty one can cost you fully half your usual gas mileage. If you don't know where the air cleaner is, ask your friendly service-station attendant. Take it off and tap it to loosen up dirt. Blow dirt out from the inside out with a gas station air hose, being careful not to apply too much pressure to the fragile filter paper.

Or, you can buy a new air cleaner at your auto parts store for $3 or $4 and easily install it yourself.

For further information:

How to Keep Your Car Running, Your Money in Your Pocket, and Your Mind Intact, Ross Olney. Chicago, Henry Regnery, 1973.

OIL SPOILS

The lighter weight oil you are able to use, the more you will save on gas mileage. Why? Lightweight oil allows faster engine warm-up and reduces friction inside your engine. Unless you live in Alaska, 10W–30 oil will do you all year long. In the northern United States, where winter temperatures don't usually exceed 68°F. (or go lower than −48°F.), 20W oil will do nicely for the cold months.

For further information:

How to Save Money When You Buy and Drive Your Car, Merle Dowd. West Nyack, New York, Parker, 1967.

FAN-DANGO

Your auto heater-defroster fan consumes up to twenty-four amperes of electricity. This load on the alternator results in a gas mileage loss of a half mile per gallon—no joke at today's gas prices! If your car is traveling at forty or more miles per hour, turn off the fan and let normal air resistance force air through the intake of your ventilation-heating system.

ARCANE OCTANE CHICANE

Check your owner's manual to see what kind of gas is recommended. If a 91 research octane number is quoted, as is the case for many newer cars, hop down to your local gas station and check the octane numbers posted on the gas pumps.

If the low lead and unleaded pumps say 89, as is often the case, you don't necessarily have to switch to high-test, which may have an octane rating of over 100. Instead, fill your tank with the correct mixture of high-test and regular which will, when averaged out, give you the octane rating your car requires.

For further information:

Gasoline: More Miles Per Gallon (012D), Consumer Information, Public Documents Distribution Center, Pueblo, Colorado 81009, 1974 (35¢).

HIGH PRESSURE PROBLEMS

Could be that a fuel pump forcing gas into your carburetor at too high a pressure is partly to blame for that monstrous gas bill. This can easily be checked out with a pressure gauge, which you can get at an auto parts store for under $5. If the pressure is too high, get yourself a new fuel pump, and you'll be back in the high-mileage ballgame!

Some checks and minor adjustments on your engine can result in unexpectedly high fuel savings. These include the following: Adjust the idle speed and idle mixture screws on your carburetor until the engine hums happily. Then reduce the engine idle speed until the engine is just on the verge of stalling (but doesn't). Check your automatic choke for proper operation. Lubricate the linkage and butterfly valve if necessary.

Finally, and simplest of all, check your carburetor and fuel lines for wetness and gassy smell—symptoms of gas leaks. If these are not repaired, the road may literally be eating up your gas!

For further information:

Auto Repairs You Can Make, Paul Weissler, ed. New York, Arco, 1971.

A CASE FOR THE SUITCASE

The worst place to put the luggage for a car trip is on a luggage rack. Why? The increased drag, by making your engine work harder, wreaks havoc with your gas consumption.

The best and most economical place to stow that gear is inside the car itself, preferably in the space between front and rear seats.

EXHAUSTING THE POSSIBILITIES

One way to stretch each gallon of gas by several miles is to replace standard exhaust manifolds and baffled muffler with smooth headers and straight-through muffler. These increase fuel efficiency by facilitating exhaust removal.

They are costly, however, and increase engine noise. But if you're a heavy driver and can stand the extra racket, you'll save yourself a bundle on gas consumption.

For further information:

Hot Rods: How to Build and Race Them, John Christy. New York, Bobbs-Merrill, 1960.

PCV PROBLEMS

While, admittedly, the PCV (positive crankcase ventilation) valve is a boon to the environment, it is anything but a boon to the pocketbook. Once these little gadgets get clogged with dirt, they will lower your mileage by 10 to 15 percent, as well as contribute to engine problems.

Since we cannot legally remove these devices, it makes sense to make the best of a bad situation by keeping them at peak operating efficiency. Replace them when you get your car tuned, every 10,000 miles or so.

For further information:

Modern Guide to Auto Tuneup and Emission Control Servicing, Paul Dempsey. Blue Ridge Summit, Pennsylvania, TAB Books, 1974.

A TIMELY TIP

Does your car take regular gasoline? You can improve mileage by switching to premium! How? The richer gas will allow you to advance your ignition timing, which will increase mileage.

To advance ignition timing, turn the distributor one or two degrees, then road test the car. If your car does not knock or ping, advance the timing another degree or two. Continue this procedure until the car begins to knock or ping, then back off on the timing.

For further information:

Chilton's More Miles-per-Gallon Guide, Ronald Weiers. Radnor, Pennsylvania, Chilton, 1974.

MOLECULE MISERY

During the heat of the day, the molecules of which gasoline is composed grow restless and jounce against each other with increas-

ing ferocity as the thermometer rises. The result is that the liquid gas expands, decreasing the actual amount of gas per gallon that is pumped into your tank. In Hawaii, for example, where the average temperature is 80°F., gas buyers lose 1½ pints of gas per fill-up compared to residents of more moderate climates.

It would thus appear that those of us who live in Florida, Arizona, and other warm states are perpetually short-changed on our gas bills. The best way to remedy this problem, short of moving to Alaska, is to buy your gas in the early morning or late evening when the gas molecules are more compliant. (Natch, don't fill up all the way, or you'll lose that savings in the afternoon as the gas expands and leaks out onto the ground.)

BARING THE BEARING

You wouldn't think that wheel bearings have *any* bearing on your gas tank, but they do. Poorly greased bearings cause friction which diverts more energy than necessary into the process of turning the wheel, thus wasting gas. Rear wheels are usually self-lubricating, but front wheels should be repacked every 15,000 miles or so. A service station or garage will do it for less than $10.

For further information:

What You Should Know Before You Have Your Car Repaired, Anthony Till. Los Angeles, Sherbourne Press, 1970.

MORE FUELISHNESS

We've often wondered if it's worth it to sit forever before a malignantly uncooperative stoplight with the idling auto engine consuming gas as usual. Or would it be cheaper just to turn the ignition off when a long wait is anticipated? Here's the answer: Professional tests have shown that shutting off the engine and restarting is more economical if the wait will last *more than a minute*.

Since starting the engine is one of your car's fastest gas-spending moments, a weak battery, which prolongs the starting process, likewise contributes to gas guzzling. You can get your battery recharged for less than $5 at any gas station. Before you do that, however, check battery cables for wear, and clean and tighten battery terminals, in case these problems should be causing a "weak battery" effect.

For further information:

"A Driver's Guide to Gasoline Economy," *Money*, March 1975, page 36.

WHAT A DRAG!

Those of us who experienced the trauma of bicycle brake failure at unpredictable moments in our youth have invariably tried the oldest known emergency brake: the outstretched foot. Unbeknownst to you, the mechanical equivalent of the outstretched foot may well be wreaking havoc with your gas consumption. This is the dragging drum brake shoe.

This culprit can be discovered by placing the car on a rack and checking to see if the wheels turn freely. If they don't, get a service-station man to adjust the brakes. The job will cost you only $2 or $3, and it may save your life!

TANK TACTICS

You may be surprised to know that if you only use your car for occasional driving, it actually costs you money to keep your gas tank less than three-quarters full at all times. How? A low tank allows far more gas to evaporate than a full one, and every bit of evaporated gas is wasted.

Naturally, if you do a lot of freeway driving, you won't want to stop frequently to fill your tank. No need to either, as you'll be using up the gas so fast that it won't have a chance to evaporate!

KNOCKING DOWN GAS PRICES

Even if your car knocks with regular gasoline, you can avoid those superlative super prices by feeding it a tablespoon of this antiknock concoction with every fillup.

You'll need benzene from a chemical sup-

ply or solvent dealer, and denatured alcohol and hydrogen peroxide from your drugstore. Mix one part hydrogen peroxide with eight parts benzene and sixteen parts alcohol.

For further information:

Henley's Twentieth Century Book of Formulas, Processes, and Trade Secrets, T. O'Conor Sloane. New York, Books, 1965.

CD SPREE

You can get up to 20 percent more gas mileage, go 70,000 miles on one distributor, and ensure that your car will always start instantly! How? By installing a CD (capacitive discharge) ignition system. Such systems as Tiger SST CD, Tri-Star Corporation, Grand Junction, Colorado 81501 ($42.95) and Del Mark Ten B, Delta Products, Inc., Grand Junction, Colorado 81501 ($59.95), are easily installed in ten minutes and include a switch that allows you to change back to standard ignition whenever you like. CD's without this optional switch are available for as little as $30 at your auto parts store.

For further information:

"New Auto Ignition Is a Key to Savings," *Moneysworth*, 26 May 1975, page 11.

SCRAMBLED EGGS

Other gas-savers worth considering: Replace your old cooling system thermostat with a 180–195°F. thermostat for maximum operating efficiency. Replace that clunky old radiator fan with a lightweight fiber glass or aluminum model to allow your engine to work less.

Have a tachometer and/or manifold vacuum gauge installed to help you determine just when you are driving uneconomically and correct the situation on the spot. Replace bad shock absorbers to improve mileage and tire life.

Consider buying a "cruise control" kit at your auto supply store. This gadget, which maintains your car at an economical preset speed unless you manually override it, can put a big dent in your gas bill.

And last but certainly not least: Observe that 55-mile-per-hour speed limit. Better yet, try to cut your top speed to 50. U.S. Department of Transportation tests have shown that steady 50 mph driving gives you three and a half more miles per gallon of gas than 60 mph driving. Tooling along at the lower speed, then, will net you a solid $2 savings every time you fill your gas tank.

For further information:

The Gas Saver's Guide, Johnny Callender and Douglas Woods. New York, Pinnacle Books, 1974.

POOR MAN'S TACHOMETER

While a tachometer, which indicates the speed of your car's engine, is a very useful device in improving gas economy, you may hesitate to invest $15 in a store-bought model. You can make your own tach using no more than a tape measure, a little white shoe polish, and the instructions in Ronald Weiers' *Chilton's More Miles-Per-Gallon Guide*, Radnor, Pennsylvania, Chilton, 1974.

GASOLINE MACHINE

Believe it or not, you can simply and inexpensively manufacture your own gasoline! How? By extracting methane gas from the manure of cows, horses, people—or whatever. The methane gas can then be used as fuel for any internal combustion engine.

Complete instructions are available from Earth Move, P.O. Box 252, Winchester, Massachusetts 01890.

For further information:

Bio-Gas Plant: Generating Methane from Organic Wastes, Ram Bux Singh. Mother's Bookshelf, P.O. Box 70, Hendersonville, North Carolina 28739 (biogas plant plans).

PROPANE PROPOSAL

Increasingly more economy-minded motorists are converting their cars to propane. Reason? When bought in bulk, this fuel costs only 42¢ a gallon. Furthermore, it sub-stantially reduces engine wear, runs cooler, and causes less pollution.

You can convert your car for $100, and easily transfer the arrangement to your next car as well. The technique described in the reference below also allows auxiliary use of gasoline in a pinch.

For further information:

How to Convert Your Auto to Propane: A Manual of Step by Step Procedures for the Complete Idiot, Jerry Friedberg, Arrakis Volkswagen, P.O. Box 531, Point Arena, California 95468 ($2).

Maintenance and Repairs

Contrary to popular belief, it doesn't take a mechanical genius to repair most auto ailments. And naturally, the do-it-yourselfer comes out far ahead of the game in dollars saved. All you need is a repair manual for your particular make of car—which you can find at any large public library—and some used or reconditioned parts from a wrecking yard or parts supplier.

If you need special tools for a major repair job, enroll in one of the auto repair courses offered by many high-school adult programs these days. These courses will get you free access to tools as well as unlimited advice on all aspects of auto repair and maintenance. Also, read Michael Lamm's article "You'll Get Real Bargains Buying 'Recycled' Car Parts," *Popular Mechanics*, January 1976, pages 70–72, 156–158.

CAR COINS

Want to know how to slash $120 off the cost of a valve job on your car? Take it to school! Automotive schools across the nation provide first-class repair work at cut-rate prices.

For example, the automotive school of American Business College in San Diego,

California, will remedy any kind of automotive problem for the price of parts plus 20 percent of the standard labor cost.

For more information, see your Yellow Pages under "Schools—industrial, technical, and trade."

A LOYAL OIL

Beginning to make its appearance on the market is one of the most revolutionary auto maintenance products of all time: synthetic oil. This substance, which is put together in the lab from animal or vegetable oil, or from components similar to those found in mineral oil, is presently being marketed under the trade names of Eon-11, Frigid-Go, Amzoil, and L.T.D.

Although the initial cost of the product is two or three times as much per oil and filter change as natural oil, you can go five to ten times as long between oil changes with reduced engine wear, cleaner running, and longer spark plug life. That means an overall savings to you of up to $60 over 50,000 miles of driving.

If you can't find synthetic oil at your auto supply store, it can be ordered from Certified Labs, 1300 Northgate Drive, Irving, Texas 75062, under the brand name Tetrol (10W–40).

RING STING

Before you waste $100 on a ring and valve job for your clunker, try this unusual remedy. It's an alloy compounded of antifriction metals which is dropped in the gas tank. As the alloy slowly dissolves, it removes carbon from the auto's combustion chamber and coats worn parts in the combustion chamber with metal. Old cars are said to drive "five years younger" within 500 to 1,000 miles. Order Motaloy, Item #0573 (autos—$6.00, plus 50¢ postage) or Item #0574 (trucks and tractors—$7.50, plus 50¢ postage), from Mother's General Store, Box 506, Flat Rock, North Carolina 28731.

BUDGET BALANCER

Pacer Products, 680 East Taylor Street, Sunnyvale, California 94086, markets a device that automatically balances your wheels during operation. Each Road Hugger is a hollow ring in which suspended lead weights compensate for imbalance as you drive. At $40 for a set of four, these beauts will more than pay for themselves in savings on service-station balancing, which often runs $20 a shot.

THE REASONABLE RADIAL

While radial tires cost twice as much as ordinary tires, their hard, firm tread area makes them last four times as long. This leaves you with twice as many miles for your money. As if this weren't enough, their superior construction decreases friction against the road and stretches every gallon of gas you use a couple of extra miles.

Incidentally, no matter *what* kind of tires you have on your car, if they're soft, they can cost you a mile a gallon in gas—and they'll wear out faster. So be sure to keep those tires inflated to the manufacturer's recommended poundage.

For further information:

The 1974 Buying Guide Issue Consumer Reports, Consumers Union of United States. Mount Vernon, New York, Consumers Union of United States, 1973.

BALL JOINT BLUES?

If your car is out of alignment because of loose ball joints, there *is* a way you can correct the problem without paying a mechanic $100 or more to replace the parts. Using the Shimmy Stop kit, at $17 to $18 in discount parts houses, and an adjustable wrench, you simply inject resin into the joints to take up play. The job will last for up to 50,000 miles.

For further information:

"Repair Your Car's Ball Joints and Save Up to $100," Paul Weissler, *Family Handyman*, April 1974, pages 44–45.

DEFRAY DEFROST COST

Spray cans of windshield defroster will set you back $2 to $3 each. Save money and time by purchasing at the drugstore a bottle of glycerin (eighty cents) with which to coat your car windshield inside and out. This will prevent moisture, and consequently frost, from forming on the glass.

For further information:

Formulas, Methods, Tips and Data for Home and Workshop, Kenneth Swezey. New York, Harper & Row, 1969.

BATTERY BRILLIANCE

Repeated car battery failure is often due to the buildup of pastelike flakes from the plates at the bottom of a cell chamber. When this gook reaches the plates, the battery shorts out. To remedy the problem, dump out the electrolyte, being careful not to contaminate eyes or skin with this caustic solution. Next, flush the bad cell with a hose. Then have a garage refill with electrolyte, or mix your own, using sulfuric acid from a storage battery company.

Almost like getting a new battery for free! For further information:

"Batteries," Dave Metz, *Alternative Sources of Energy*, No. 18, July 1975, page 51.

A TESTY TALE

Why pay $40 for a dwell-tach and voltmeter at your auto supply store? Instead, purchase the 707 Portable Multitester, which combines these functions for $34.50. Order from R. J. Shuler, Box 8537, Kensington Station, Detroit, Michigan 48224.

WINDOW WONDER

Does your car window annoyingly drop open an inch or so after you close it? Stop this bothersome habit without doling out $25 to your neighborhood mechanic by rolling the window up all the way, then reversing the position of the window handle, so that gravity cannot pull it down as you bounce along.

LIGHTER RIGHTER

Before you pay $5 to replace that deceased cigarette lighter in your auto, check to see if the fault lies in a poor ground connection between the lighter base and the dash. Do this by wrapping a tapered piece of broom handle with emery cloth and twisting it around inside the lighter to clean off the grounding surface. In many cases, this is all that's needed!

For further information:

175 Money Saving Tips for Every Car Owner, Carl Sifarkis. New York, Tower, 1970.

PARTS SMARTS

At tuneup and repair time, the car owner theoretically pays for two distinct things: parts and labor. Believe it or not, most mechanics make a tidy profit just from the sale of parts.

Buy your own spark plugs, points, and condensers at discount parts houses, and present them to your mechanic at tuneup time. Also, if you've got a major repair job coming up, find out from your mechanic what's needed and tell him you'll secure these parts yourself. Saves 20 to 50 percent on parts costs, depending on the greediness of your mechanic.

For further information:

How to Get Your Car Repaired Without Getting Gypped: The Car Owner's Survival Manual, Margaret Carlson. New York, Harper & Row, 1973.

Alternative Transportation

200 MILES PER GALLON?

Yep, that's what you get with a motorized bicycle. The lightweight two-cycle engine can putt along at 18 miles an hour on level ground. On steep hills, you must walk your bike, but the motor will allow it to pull its own weight up.

If you need transportation mainly for tooling around town, by all means consider this simple, energy-conserving alternative to the auto. You can't beat the price: about $120 for the motor, new, which can be attached to just about any kind of bicycle. The motor is available through bicycle dealers, who will sometimes install it for free.

For further information:

"Motorized Bikes—They Get Up to 200 mpg!" *Changing Times*, Vol. 30, No. 1, January 1976, pages 21–23.

PLANE POWER

For about half the cost of an economy car, you can get yourself a kit for a single-seat airplane that gets up to 50 miles per gallon and cruises at 18 to 60 miles an hour. The plane weighs only 100 pounds, including a 15-horsepower, 2-cycle engine. The manufacturer claims that you can take off and land right in your own backyard. Costs $1,395. For information ($5), write Birdman Aircraft, Inc., 1280 Wildcat Street, Daytona Beach, Florida 32015.

Other home-built models can be had from Stewart Aircraft Corp., Marten Road, Clinton, New York 13323 (Headwind—kit, $990); Stolp Starduster Corp., 4301 Twining, Riverside, California 92509 (Acroduster I—kit, $5,500); M.B. Taylor, Box 1171, Longview, Washington 98632 (mini-IMP—plans, $200, kits available); P. H. Spencer, 8725 Oland Avenue, Sun Valley, California 91352 (Spencer Air Car, amphibian—plans, $185, kits available); Rutan Aircraft Factory, Box 656, Mojave, California 93501 (VariEze —plans and kits available); Yvan Bougie, 11 Terrasse-Robert, Nitro-Valleyfield, Quebec, Canada (Hauscat—plans, $125); Chris Heintz, 236 Richmond Street, Richmond Hill, Ontario, Canada (Mono Z—plans, $130); Peter Bowers, 13826 Des Moines Way S., Seattle, Washington 98168 (Namu II —plans available); and George Pereira, 3741 El Ricon Way, Sacramento, California 95825 (Osprey 2—plans, $150).

COPTER CRAFTINESS

The cheapest-to-run aircraft around ($3-an-hour operating costs) is the gyro copter. Plans ($35) and kits ($2,000) can be purchased from Benson Aircraft Corporation, Raleigh-Durham Airport, P.O. Box 2746, Raleigh, North Carolina 27602.

Once you've got your copter assembled, why not try for the $5,000 prize these people are offering to the first person to fly around the world in one?

For further information:

"New Build Your Own Copters: More Power, Looks, Convenience," Sheldon Gallager and Howard Levy. *Popular Mechanics*, Vol. 140, December 1973, pages 143–145.

LEASE LESSON

If you use your car for weekend driving or for only a few months out of the year, leasing will actually cost you less than buying a car. Such expenses as depreciation, insurance, maintenance, tires and oil, licenses and registration, even for an older model car, cost about $1,000 a year. These expenses, which cannot be recouped when you sell your car, will of course be much higher if your car is new or almost new.

Car rental rates include the cost of all these headaches. You can plan to take up to thirty 100-mile weekend jaunts or two vacation months of driving 100 miles a day (at a discounted monthly rental rate) and still get off with less down-the-drain expenses than you would have owning a car that is not in constant use.

For further information:

"When It Makes Sense to Lease a Car," William Flanagan, ed., *Business Week*, 20 January 1975, pages 73–74.

CHARGE IT!

The average suburban family can save $140 a year on fuel bills for a second car by purchasing one of the many electrical models available. Operating costs on these are only 1.5 cents a mile rather than the 3.2 cents typical of gas-powered autos. Range is 30 to 45 miles on an 8- to 12-hour overnight charge of the car's large batteries, making them ideal for shopping and errand running.

Manufacturers of the less expensive models include Sebring-Vanguard, Inc., Sebring, Florida 33870, at $2,500 (two-seater, 28 mph tops) and $2,700 (38 mph); and Elcar Corporation, Elkhart, Indiana 46514, at $3,000 (25 mph) and $3,400 (35 mph). Or check your Yellow Pages under "Electric cars."

For further information:

"Charged Up Cars," *Money*, February 1975, pages 14–15.

VOLTS WAGON

Believe it or not, for only $500 you can convert your Beetle, Ghia, Squareback, or VW Bus to electric power! And once the conversion is made, you'll own a vehicle that'll tool along at a neat 30 mph with a 25-mile range before recharging.

For further information:

"Volts Wagon," Jary Squibb, *Alternative Sources of Energy*, No. 18, July 1975, pages 16–19.

FURNISHINGS AND
APPLIANCES

Here, we're not only concerned with saving money on the purchase of household goods, but also with cutting costs on their construction and repair. As is the case with other valuable items, you have the choice of buying and having them repaired at the normal commercial establishments or of exercising your creativity, your imagination, and by cutting corners, drastically decreasing your expenditures. After all, why buy your new furniture and appliances from that high-priced department store when you can get the same thing from a wholesale showroom at half the price? For that matter, why buy brand-new merchandise at all? Big-ticket items, like automobiles, depreciate greatly in their early life. Picking up slightly used goods at an auction, then, or slightly damaged merchandise at a freight outlet will save you untold dollars.

In the case of furniture, even more money can be saved by building your own from scratch or from a kit, or by buying unfinished goods, and then painting or varnishing them according to your own tastes.

In the area of appliance repair, even if you're not handy with a screwdriver or pliers, cut corners by seeking out that old, semiretired handyman down the street, rather than dealing with that high-priced, union-run repair shop.

The following books will give you much valuable help in the area of stretching your furniture and appliance dollars:

Secondhand Is Better, Suzanne Wymelenberg and Douglas Matthews. New York, Arbor House, 1975.

The Plain Man's Guide to Second-Hand Furniture, Frank Davis. Levittown, New York, Transatlantic Arts, 1972.

How to Buy Major Appliances, Charles Klamkin. Chicago, Henry Regnery, 1973.

Underground Shopper, SusAnn Publications, P.O. Box 10124, Dallas, Texas 75207 (one book for each of these areas: Dallas–Fort Worth, St. Louis, Minneapolis, Houston, Miami, Boston, Atlanta, Seattle, Kansas City, San Francisco, Portland, Los Angeles, Toronto, Philadelphia, and Mexico City).

How to Fix Almost Everything: The Standard A to Z Guide to 1001 Household Fix-It Problems, Stanley Schuler. New York, M. Evans (orders to J. B. Lippincott), 1975.

Buying Them

TURN OFF TURN ON

At washing machine buying time, save a bundle of greenbacks on future soap and water consumption by purchasing a machine that allows you to regulate the water level in the wash. After all, why use a whole tankful of water and a cupful of soap for a quarter-load?

Shopping for a frostless refrigerator? Purchase one with a switch to turn off the defrost heater during low-humidity days and save 16 percent on energy costs.

When purchasing a new dishwasher, weigh the fact that models featuring a switch to omit the final hot air drying phase can save you 40 percent on electricity. KitchenAid, General Electric, Sears, and Hotpoint, among others, have such models.

For further information:

The 1976 Buying Guide Issue of Consumer Reports, Consumers Union of United States. Mount Vernon, New York, Consumers Union of United States, 1975.

$40 SAUNA

You won't find a cheaper sauna than this lightweight, portable steam bath of vinyl over an aluminum tubing framework, with vaporizer inside. Order the Sauna Mist from Stevens and Company, 1005 Thomas Street, Abbeville, Louisiana 70510.

PRINTS TO PAINTINGS

Why pay hundreds of dollars for quality oil paintings? Using the technique described in Instruction Sheet #C25, *Make "Oil Paintings" from Prints,* free from The Beadcraft Club, P.O. Box 5754, Augusta, Georgia 30906 (enclose 25¢ for postage), you can lend brushstroke realism to your favorite art prints and posters for less than $1 a picture.

FREE FURNITURE?

That's right! Every morning across the land thousands of tons of good or repairable chairs, desks, sofas, mattresses, TV sets, and kitchen appliances sit outdoors on sidewalks awaiting collection by local trashmen.

Get the jump on them by hopping in your car or pickup truck at sunrise and proceeding on your own shopping spree!

For further information:

How to Fix Almost Everything, Stanley Schuler. New York, M. Evans (orders to J. B. Lippincott), 1963.

How to Fix It, Ann Singerie. Garden City, New York, Doubleday, 1975.

WITHIN RANGE

In the market for a gas range? Caloric's new automatic pilotless-ignition systems will save you an average of 30 percent on fuel!

For further information:

"Now! Energy-Saving Appliances," Frank Coffee, *Mechanix Illustrated,* January 1975, pages 64–65.

GRAND SAVINGS

You don't have to plunk down the retail price of $500 to $1,000 to own that elegant relic of bygone days, the grandfather clock. With no special watchmaking skills, even the amateur assembler can make his own grandfather clock for just $150.

For further information:

Westchester Clock Co., 260 Keeler Building, Division Avenue North, Grand Rapids, Michigan 49502.

Mason & Sullivan, Osterville, Cape Cod, Massachusetts 02655.

KALENDAR KONSCIOUSNESS

Almost everyone knows about January and August linen sales. But how about Washington's Birthday (February) and Columbus Day (October) for appliances and housewares? March and September are also good times to buy housewares, as well as glassware and china. May—spring cleaning time—sees sales of rugs, wax, and mops. Furniture is often on sale in June. Look for July and August sales of lawn furniture, garden supplies, and barbecue sets. Rugs and bedding are often on sale in August and September.

Keeping these traditional sale times in mind will help prevent that sinking sensation when you buy at list price, then find your item advertised at half price the following week.

MINCING WITH MUSLIN

About to buy new upholstered furniture? Ask the furniture store to have muslin-covered furniture in the style you want shipped from the factory. Then make or purchase your own slipcovers for the furniture. You can easily save $50 on a chair and $100 on a medium-priced sofa this way.

For further information:

How to Buy Furniture, Donna Difloe. Riverside, New Jersey, Macmillan, 1972.

POOL PRUDENCE

Swimming-pool construction is such a seasonal affair that people in this business practically starve to death in the winter. Take advantage of this unbalanced situation by calling your local pool builder in midwinter—when he's wondering how he'll be able to afford Christmas presents for his kids—and making him an offer he can't refuse.

These crafty tactics can save you several hundred dollars on an above-ground pool. And for the sunken type, you can cut costs to the tune of the better part of a grand.

For further information:

Shopper's Guide: How to Get the Most for Your Money, U.S. Department of Agriculture. Woodbury, New York, Barron's Educational Series, 1975.

DISTINGUISHING EXTINGUISHERS

In the market for a new fire extinguisher? Before you buy, check the date on the item. Extinguishers must be tested every five years, at a fee of around $5. So, if you buy a model that is already two years old—and this happens more often than we care to think —you will be shelling out close to twice as much in maintenance fees the first three years you have it, due to the fact that you must have it serviced two years sooner than a new model.

For further information:

Fire Extinguishers: The ABC's and the One, Two, Three of Selection, Consumer Information Series, Number 3, U.S. General Services Administration. Superintendent of Documents, U.S. Government Printing Office, Washington, D.C. 20402, 1972.

RUGS FROM REMNANTS AND RAGS

The ability to create an eye-catching patchwork carpet and save half or more over the cost of an ordinary carpet is right at your fingertips. Call around to carpet dealers in your area for rug remnants and mill ends at a hefty discount—occasionally even *free*.

Arrange your patches in a pleasing pattern over an old carpet pad, which can be purchased cheaply at a secondhand store and cut to size. Glue the rug patches to the pad with a white glue (not paste) such as Elmer's.

Another possibility: Make your own rag rugs, using the contents of your scrap basket. Or, rags can be picked up at secondhand stores. Cut your heavy rags into thin strips and your light rags into wider strips so that all the strips are of about the same bulk. Then separate according to color, and begin braid-

ing. Arrange the braids in a tight spiral, and sew together adjoining edges.

For further information:

How to Live Cheap but Good, Martin Poriss. New York, American Heritage Press, 1971.

Rug Hooking and Braiding for Pleasure and Profit, Dorothy Lawless. New York, Thomas Y. Crowell, 1962.

CHIME IN

Wind chimes and mobiles to liven up your home run $5 and up in gift stores. Make your own unique creations by using throw-away plastic containers from the supermarket, scraps of ribbon, and instructions from Hazel Williams' *Making Things from Discards*, New York, Bounty Books, 1974, and Edna and John Clapper's *Pack-o-Fun Make It from Odds 'n' Ends*, New York, Hawthorn, 1973.

FRAME FOXINESS

As anyone knows who has priced these items, a custom-made picture frame costs almost as much as an original work of art. It is sometimes possible to find low-cost frames in the size you need at secondhand stores. For a lush antiqued look, you can gild these with gold paint and rub with oil. If you want a more modern frame, tack together some fruit crate wood and cover with leather or wind twine around it.

Some frame shops now offer do-it-yourself framing at a 40 percent discount off ready-made prices. You buy the frame wood and use their equipment to make the frame. Occasionally, you can also purchase tag ends of frame wood from these shops at a considerable saving.

For further information:

Professional Picture Framing for the Amateur, Barbara Wolf and Jack Wolf. Blue Ridge Summit, Pennsylvania, TAB Books, 1974.

PROTECTION MONEY

Don't let a fast-talking salesman get you to buy a fully installed fire-, smoke-, or burglar-alarm system for $500 to $1,000—or more. This is highway robbery in your own home! Instead, purchase your own equipment and install it yourself—or even hire a handyman to install it for you—at a fraction of the price. Effective, easy-to-install smoke alarms, for example, can be purchased at discount department stores for about $40. Burglar alarms to cover five windows and a door can be bought at electronic equipment dealers for $70.

For further information:

How to Install Protective Alarm Devices, Donald Brann. Briarcliff Manor, New York, Directions Simplified, 1973.

SCREEN SHENANIGANS

Last summer the flies waged an all-out war to take over our three-bedroom screenless abode. As they gradually gained ground, we made a last-ditch plea to our landlords for screens. They grudgingly consented to pay a limit of $12 for twelve needed screens. Naturally, at this price, pre-framed screens were out of the question.

How did we solve our dilemma? By galloping off to our local hardware store and purchasing a length of wire screen which we then cut to size and stapled over the outsides of the windows.

PLAQUE POWER

Make beautiful wall plaques out of old greeting cards, magazine pictures, or calendars! Just mount on wood and glaze, following free instructions from A. Taylor, Pactra Industries, 6725 Sunset Boulevard, Los Angeles, California 90028. Ask for *Crafty Hint #5.*

WINDOW WIT

By using ready-made windows as replacements for old ones—rather than paying to have new ones custom-made—you'll save $15 per window. For older homes, replacement windows are difficult, but not impossible to find. If a search through conventional channels doesn't work, check used home furnishing stores and salvage shops.

For further information:

Family Handyman Home Improvement Book, Family Handyman Magazine. Totowa, New Jersey, Scribner's, 1973.

FURNITURE FACTS

In any large city, huge showrooms exist for the wholesale furniture trade. There, you can find anything from armchairs to zebra-skin cabinets. Some showrooms are open only to the wholesale trade. However, many of them will not only allow entry to the general public, but will sell their floor samples at unbelievable discounts.

Cricket once bought a houseful of fine furniture at Western Contract Furnishers, an inconspicuous showroom off Market Street in San Francisco, for *half* the retail price.

Check the Yellow Pages under "Furniture—wholesale" for the location of showrooms in your area.

CHEST QUEST

With a little discarded wood and plans from Stanley Tools, Advertising Services Department, P.O. Box 1800, New Britain, Connecticut 16050, you can easily make a $50 treasure chest for a few dollars. Send 25¢ for *Anything Chest* plans.

SUNCLOCK SAVVY

Want a clock-calendar accurate to within a few minutes, made to last with durable stainless steel, aluminum, and translucent plastic, which will never increase your electric bill —all for $9.95? The Universal Sunclock/Calendar can be mounted outside a south-facing window and read from indoors.

Time is told by noting the point at which the shadows of two wires intersect on the plastic.

It's offered by Lighthearted Company, 30801 Northgate Drive, Southfield, Michigan 48076.

CLOCK STOPPER

Even more economical than the foregoing, you can create your own combination clock-calendar for the price of a hand mirror! The mirror, placed horizontally in the window of a south-facing wall, reflects sunlight on the ceiling. Hour lines are drawn on the ceiling to tell time as the reflected sunlight moves across the ceiling.

For details, read *Sundials: Their Theory and Construction*, Albert Waugh, New York, Dover, 1973.

TILE TIP

Here's an inexpensive shortcut to buying decorative tiles for accent tile work. Tile appliqués ($1.98 for twelve) in nine styles and colors can be had from Comark Plastics Division, United Merchants and Manufacturers, Inc., 1407 Broadway, New York, New York 10018. Simply place the appliqué over existing tiles for no-fuss fancywork at a third of the cost of ready-made patterned tiles.

TABLE TRICKS

Old cable reels are often available free from utility companies or found abandoned along roadsides. After sanding and finishing, these can be fashioned into uniquely stylish and serviceable kitchen- and dining-room tables. And as conversation pieces, they're tops!

If you have need of a large kitchen table or worktable, pick up a new door, with a defect on one side, for half price, at your home improvement center. Place it over an old smaller table or use a couple of sawhorses as legs.

Rather than plunking down $50 or more for a new coffee table, spruce up that trunk in the attic with a covering of tree bark or fur.

Glue pebbles, ceramic tile, or bits of broken mirror glass to the top and cover with clear plastic sheeting or glass. Or, glue on family photographs and protect with clear acrylic spray from your photo supply store.

For further information:

How to Make Furniture Without Tools or Skill, Clement Meadmore. New York, Pantheon Books (orders to Random House), 1975.

POOL PESOS

Not only do above-ground swimming pools save you up to $7,000 over the cost of their below-ground counterparts, but their portability makes them nontaxable in many areas and allows you to take them with you when you move. Moreover, the sides of an above-ground pool present a natural safety barrier to small children and pets.

Prices for 18-foot economy do-it-yourself models run as low as $200; 18 by 36 foot deluxe models run $1,300.

For further information:

"There You Are, Basking in Your Own Pool," *Changing Times*, April 1973, pages 45–47.

MAKE AMERICANA

If you fancy colonial decor and "doing it yourself," all kinds of useful accessories can be yours for as little as 10 percent of store prices! Plans for *60 Early American Designs* ($2.50)—everything from small footstools to big plate racks and cabinets—can be had from Stanley Tools, Advertising Services Department, P.O. Box 1800, New Britain, Connecticut 06050.

WE MEAN BUSINESS

Pick up rare bargains in furniture for every room in your house at secondhand office furniture stores. An old-fashioned wooden desk makes a fine bedroom bureau. Wooden swivel chairs make comfie, stylish dining-room seats. A file cabinet, with a bright new coat of paint, will neatly store anything from pots and pans to sweaters. Best time to buy is right after political campaigns, when nearly new campaign headquarters furniture sells for a third of retail prices.

For further information:

Starting Out, The Guide I Wish I'd Had When I Left Home, Lili Krakowski. New York, Stein & Day, 1973.

TRASH SMASHER

How to get around paying the retail prices for that handy gadget, the trash compactor? Get yourself a do-it-yourself Trash Compactor Kit from Heath Inc., Benton Harbor, Michigan 49022. At $199.99, it saves you $80 over ready-made prices.

For truly compact prices ($12.95) plus a little elbow grease on your part, you can get a hand trash masher that utilizes your garbage can and people power to reduce trash volume by 50 percent. Write Akens-Adornetto, 6725 Pike West, Zanesville, Ohio 43701.

WOODEN WONDERS

Nothing can be sillier than paying store prices for wooden shelves, dividers, and storage units. You can shave $50 or more off the cost of these handy furnishings by making your own, and they are among the easiest to make of all home projects! For free copies of plan sets T541 (shelving) and T540 (storage areas), write to Stanley Tools, Advertising Services Department, P.O. Box 1800, New Britain, Connecticut 06050 (include 10¢ each for postage).

SPEAKING UP!

A 20-watt build-it-yourself hi-fi speaker, with 8-inch woofer and 2 tweeters can be yours for less than $25—just half of retail prices. Carefully follow the instructions in "Build a True Hi-Fi Speaker for Under $25,"

David Weems, *Mechanix Illustrated*, August 1974, pages 28, 30–31.

THREAD BREAD

Pin and thread artwork, those seemingly elaborate geometrical picture patterns created with thread or wire strung on pins or nails, can cost you a bundle in a gift shop. While do-it-yourself hobby kits cost half as much, you can make these fashionable fantasies for less than $1 each using the inexpensive ingredients and the easy instructions in Warren Farnworth's *Pin and Thread Art*, New York, Taplinger, 1975.

RACK UP

Make yourself a free, stylish wine rack using large juice tins, sturdy cardboard mailing tubes, or cylindrical drain tiles. These may be placed in an apple crate set on its side, or bound in a circular or square shape using coat-hanger or bailing wire. Glue on cardboard backing (mailing tubes) or string wire across the back (drain tiles) to prevent the wine bottles from slipping out the end.

For further information:

In Celebration of Small Things, Sharon Cadwallader. Boston, Houghton Mifflin, 1974.

DELIVERY DOLLARS

When you buy home furnishings, large appliances, or other big-ticket items at a store that provides "free" delivery, offer to pick up the merchandise at the store yourself, in exchange for a price reduction. Our next-door neighbor knocked $25 off the price of an easy chair with this trick.

TURN THE TABLES

Cut the cost of high-quality tables, desks, and chairs by 80 percent by making your own. Send 25¢ to Stanley Tools, Advertising Services Department, P.O. Box 1800, New Britain, Connecticut 06050, for their Butcher

Block Table plan. Or, request plan set SS–12 ($1.25), including complete plans for corner tilt-top, coffee, and game tables. Or, send $1.25 for plan set SS–16 or SS–17, each of which includes plans for three desks and a variety of tables.

WOOD WONDERS

According to the U.S. Department of Commerce, about four billion feet of lumber is used annually to build wooden containers. This staggering amount of perfectly good wood, after serving its purpose, is simply thrown into trash bins behind retail and wholesale outlets.

Literally hundreds of unique pieces of furniture can be made from nail kegs (stools and stands), orange crates (bookcases), and the sturdy wooden boxes, imprinted with enigmatic Chinese characters, found behind Oriental markets (storage shelves, medicine cabinets). Cardboard shipping cartons, which are even more plentiful than the wooden variety, can be covered and used as nightstands or accent tables. The long cardboard rolls often found behind stationery stores make great clothes racks or coffee-table legs (use six or eight of these for support). Even a few egg cartons can be stood up end to end in a circle, topped with a paper plate, and used as centerpiece stands or decorative shelving.

For further information:

Scrap Craft, Michael Dank. New York, Dover, 1969.

How to Have a Prettier Room. Johnson Wax, Consumer Education Department, Racine, Wisconsin 53403 (free).

SHEET SENSE

Make your own decorator curtains at $1 a pair using white sheets from a secondhand store, split in half lengthwise, and dyed to contrast with wall color. Ruffles are easily concocted of two-inch-wide strips of the same material, pleated and sewed on as a border.

For further information:

In Celebration of Small Things, Sharon Cadwallader. Boston, Houghton Mifflin, 1974.

FOXY FURNITURE FROLIC

You can buy perfectly good furniture at rock-bottom prices through city and county governments. The government obtains furniture either as unclaimed stolen items that the police recover, or from the estate of people who have left no local heirs. Also available at such auctions: bicycles, stereos, sets of fine dishes, and beautifully made draperies for under $10.

For more information, contact your public administrator.

CANDLEHOLDER CUNNING

A highly original, stylishy effective, *free* candleholder can be fashioned from an old furniture leg, either refinished or torch-burned. Stick the candle to the upper part of the leg with a little melted wax. For a grand effect, convert an old floor lampstand into a candelabra!

For further information:

In Celebration of Small Things, Sharon Cadwallader. Boston, Houghton Mifflin, 1974.

How to Make Something from Nothing, Ruth Egge. New York, Coward-McCann, 1968.

AUCTION CAUTION

According to authors Jean and Cle Kinney, who have seen a lot of auctions in their time, the type of auction you go to can make a big difference in the purchase price of various items. If you go to a court, estate, or farm auction where many practical, middle-class people are buying, even a commonplace bed may get top dollar. But at a gallery specializing in rare books, a handcrafted bed may go for under $10. Why? Because the bidders are interested in rare books—not in furniture.

The moral: Frequent auctions where the item you're seeking is the exception, rather than the rule. Watch your newspaper for all types of auctions.

For further information:

How to Get 20 to 90 % Off on Everything You Buy, Jean and Cle Kinney. New York, Award, 1967.

How to Buy at Auction, Michael De Forrest. New York, Cornerstone Library (orders to Simon & Schuster), 1974.

SOME KNOCKERS!

You can make a distinctive door knocker for less than $1 out of an old door hinge and a wide-headed thumb screw. Screw one side of the hinge longways on the door, with the other side of the hinge flapping loose over it. Place the screw in the center hole of the loose hinge flap for a knocker handle. Sure beats the $5 or more you'd pay for the hardware-store variety!

For further information:

"Second Uses for Discards," *Family Handyman,* February 1974, pages 48–49.

CARPETING CAPER

Recarpeting a large area? In carpeting her home, Cricket once saved $37 on the price of the carpet she selected by offering to take a whole (90 to 140 foot) roll of carpet off the salesman's hands. It was well worth a 20 percent discount to him to avoid cutting the carpet up and dealing with remnants. You can do the same!

For further information:

"Carpets," *Changing Times,* December 1975, pages 41–43.

Maintenance, Repairs, and Moving

HOT TOP TIP

Driveway need resurfacing? For $2 a ton (that's $22 a ton cheaper than conventional asphalt), you can buy "hot top reject" from tar and gravel dealers.

This substance, which packs down well for a dust-free driveway, is composed of unscreened gravel plus leftover tar from road surfacing jobs. For details, see your Yellow Pages under "Contractors—paving."

WORKSHOP WOODWORK

Slash store prices in half for a home workshop by banging together your own. Request Dream Workshop Plans DW1, DW2, and DW3 ($2.50) from Stanley Tools, Advertising Services Department, P.O. Box 1800, New Britain, Connecticut 06050.

NEVER CALL THE PLUMBER!

If you're not able to perform home repairs and maintenance yourself and must depend on outside help in these matters, *never* call a plumber, electrician, or carpenter. Instead, call a handyman.

Why? Nine times out of ten, the handyman knows as much or more about home repairs than the so-called "specialists." In addition, he'll tackle small jobs that nobody else will touch. Furthermore, a nonunion handyman will charge one half to two thirds less than his specialized counterpart.

See your Yellow Pages under "Fix-it service."

For further information:

Super Handyman's Encyclopedia of Home Repair Hints: Better, Faster, Cheaper, Easier Ideas for House and Workshop, Al Carrell. Englewood Cliffs, New Jersey, Prentice-Hall, 1971.

APPLIANCE APTNESS

You don't need an electrician to repair such simple problems as a broken or frayed electrical cord, faulty plug, wall outlet, or light switch. Repair them yourself using the simple instructions in Sharon Cadwallader's *In Celebration of Small Things,* Boston, Houghton Mifflin, 1974.

Warning: Before attempting wall outlet or switch repairs, cut off all house current at your fuse box or circuit breaker!

COVERING EXPENSES

To reduce your pool-heating costs up to 35 percent and simplify pool maintenance as well, purchase one of several types of pool cover. Plastic bubble sheets such as the Solar Quilt or another system involving one-quarter inch polyurethane strips which are heat-sealed into single sheets allow the sun to pass through them and warm the water. These cost about 75¢ per square foot.

A chemical pool cover only one molecule thick which cuts heat loss and stops evaporation is acetyl alcohol. You may buy it as a liquid or as a brick. All of the above are available through any swimming-pool supply house found in the Yellow Pages.

For further information:

"Pools: The Facts of Solar Heating," *Los Angeles Times Home Magazine*, 14 March 1976, pages 20–22.

A BORING BUSINESS

Build your own pedal-operated horizontal boring machine at half of retail prices! Plans are just $6.95 from *Popular Mechanics* Plans Library, Department D5, Box 1014, Radio City, New York 10019. Ask for PL 1400.

LOCK LUCRE

Need a new lock on your door? Save several ten-spots by getting your own lock from a hardware store and installing it yourself. In our town, for instance, two locksmith-installed single-cylinder locks cost a whopping $54. In a hardware store, you can buy your own locks, plus the simple tools necessary for the installation, and save nigh onto $30.

If you lack lock-luster, the book below will give you a free education on the subject.

For further information:

Practical Course in Modern Locksmithing, Whitcomb Crichton. Chicago, Nelson-Hall, 1943.

CANE CARE

Instead of buying new cane furniture at a whopping $100 or more per set, find old, sagging cane furniture cheaply at swap meets, garage sales, and secondhand stores. Then refurbish it with this simple trick: Just sponge a hot mixture of one part vinegar to one part water on the sagging areas, and place the furniture in the hot sun to dry. Voilà! Like new!

For further information:

How to Repair and Reupholster Furniture-Caning Simplified, Donald Brann. Briarcliff-Manor, New York, Directions Simplified, 1974.

PAINT PLOY

Before painting such porous surfaces as acoustical tile, coat them with a penetrating sealer. This will prevent the paint from soaking into the surface, saving you up to 50 percent on painting costs.

ECONOMIC RECOVERY

If you're planning on having your furniture recovered, you can stretch your refurbishing dollars substantially by purchasing upholstery fabric at a mill end shop or discount fabric house.

At such outlets in our area, for example, heavy-weight cotton velvet mill ends run $6 a yard—a savings of *up to $25 a yard* over fabric prices charged by commercial upholsterers. See your Yellow Pages under "Upholstery fabrics."

Take your cut-rate cutups to the upholsterer, and let him take it from there—or do your own slipcovers for even greater savings.

For further information:

Upholstering for Everyone, William Parker and Alice Fornia. Englewood Cliffs, New Jersey, Reston (orders to Prentice-Hall).

CUNNING CANING

Caning is simplicity itself, yet a professional will charge you nigh onto $100 to recane a set of four square railed chairs. Keep most of this loot in your pocket by purchasing your own caning at a fourth of the price through a chair caning supplier, found in your Yellow Pages. Wet the caning and thread it through the holes in the chair rails, up and down, across, and diagonally.

For further information:

How to Restore Antiques, Raymond Yates, New York, Harper, 1948 (at your library).

RUSHING FOR NOTHING

Although the professional rushing of chair seats costs twice as much as caning, the technique is so simple that a first-timer can do a fine job, and the materials are available free for the picking.

Find yourself a pond where narrow-leaf cattails grow. As fall approaches, when the tips of the leaves start to brown, pick yourself a bundle of uniform, unbroken leaves about seven feet long. Let dry in a cool place for three weeks. Then sprinkle with water and cover with wet burlap overnight. Wring excess water out of the rushes with an old-fashioned clothes wringer, and you're ready to weave.

For further information:

Seat Weaving, L. Day Perry. Peoria, Illinois, Charles A. Bennett, 1917 (at your library).

WASTE MONEY

If it has become odiously obvious that your cesspool urgently needs draining, take a tip from us to eliminate the problem. Calculate your cesspool's capacity, and call around for a disposal truck with the same capacity as your tank. A larger truck will charge you more for unused space because the sewage disposal plant charges *them* more, even if they're only half full.

Putting it crudely, the smaller truck's price to you will get a rough edge of $10 to $15 over that of the larger truck.

SEPTIC SUGGESTION

Next time your septic tank gets sluggish, save $40 or more by resisting that urge to call in a septic tank serviceman. Instead, use this old-time home remedy that'll cost you only a fraction of a dollar.

Mix a pound of brown sugar and a tablespoon of dry yeast in a quart of water. Flush this solution down the toilet. When it reaches your septic tank, it'll serve as a veritable feast—and an activator for those millions of bacteria, helping to decompose the waste material therein.

For further information:

Henley's Twentieth Century Book of Formulas, Processes, and Trade Secrets, T. O'Conor Sloane. New York, Books, 1965.

BLANKET BRILLIANCE

Two old, worn-out blankets can be recycled thus: Cut them into squares and quilt them together. Line them underneath with a preshrunk cotton sheet. Use your revamped coverlet as a combination bedspread-blanket.

Or, piece the two blankets together and use as a warm inner lining for a homemade quilt. You can also use ripped-up old wool clothing (all of the same thickness) for this.

Or, piece the blankets together and cover with a patterned material on one side and a solid material on the other. Voilà! A reversible, versatile coverlet!

SHABBY SHADES?

If your window shades are worn and dirty, don't put out good money for a new set. Yours can be the classiest shades in the neighborhood for just a few dollars simply by applying a coat of rubber-base paint to them to match your decor. For flashy shades, add stripes or flowers. Or cover with leftover fabric, as many home decorators do.

For further information:

Do-It-Yourself Ideas for Window Shades, Window Shade Manufacturers Association, 230 Park Avenue, New York, New York 10017 (25¢).

PLYWOOD POWER

Need a small piece of plywood for a project? Before you buy that over-large standard-size sheet of plywood, check your lumberyard's secret cut-up bin. In our local lumberyard, this bin, located in the darkest, innermost recesses of the shed, contains plywood odds and ends at one third the cost of standard plywood sheets.

For free lists of pamphlets on plywood uses, write the American Plywood Association, 1119 A Street, Tacoma, Washington 98401. Ask for their literature indexes on consumer and do-it-yourself topics, residential construction, general construction, or agriculture.

You will also find these odds and ends can be transformed into imaginative handmade toys for children. See Grete Petersen's *Making Toys with Plywood*, Newton, New Jersey, Carstens Publications, 1967.

DRILL THRILL

Turn your electric drill into a $30 router with a $5 attachment marketed by Stanley Tools. This device, the Electrichisel, can do a professional job of joining two pieces of wood, and make vee-cuts and slots. Get it at your hardware store.

WINDOW WIZARDRY

Repairing old window sashes on an average-sized house, as opposed to buying new ones, will fatten your pocketbook to the tune of over $100! Repairing window sashes is easy. Just pry loose the little strips of wood that hold in the upper and lower sashes, and then remove the window sashes from the opening.

Paint remover will remove old paint and soften crumbling putty. New panes of glass are fixed in place with triangular bits of metal called points, which can be obtained in any hardware store. Next, apply new putty and paint.

If the window won't stay up when you open it, chances are the rope is broken in the pulley-rope-weight system at the side of the window (the frame). Nine times out of ten, all you have to do is pry loose a piece of wood in the frame to expose the pulley, replace the rope, and tack the wood back in place.

For further information:

Basic Home Repairs Illustrated, Editors of Sunset Books and *Sunset Magazine*. Menlo Park, California, Lane, 1973.

LINOLEUM SIMOLEONS

Does your kitchen or bathroom floor's sheet linoleum look like a herd of elephants have been using it for a battleground? Here's how to give your floor a brand-new look for next to nothing. Just turn the linoleum over to expose the unscuffed underside and scrape off any dried-up gunk adering to this. Try painting an unusual design on it for a farout floor. Or, use up your odds and ends of paint by creating a multicolor spatter-paint pattern.

For further information:

Home Remedies: Fixing up Houses and Apartments, Mostly Old but Also Otherwise, Christopher Fahy. Totowa, New Jersey, Scribner's, 1975.

DRAIN DOCTORING

Household drain problems, like dental cavities and pregnancies, are best dealt with by practicing prevention, rather than attempting to effect a cure. But accidents *do* happen, and if you are suddenly confronted with a recalcitrant drain, don't pay a plumber $30 for help.

First remove the drain plate, then try unblocking the drain mechanically with a long screwdriver or a piece of stiff wire. If this doesn't work, try a chemical such as Drano, a "plumber's friend" (rubber plunger), or a snake (long wire), all available at your hardware store.

Get details on these and other drain-repair techniques by sending 35¢ and a 13¢ stamp to Plumbing-Heating-Cooling Information Bureau, 35 East Wacker Drive, Chicago, Illinois 60601. Ask for the booklet entitled *Plumbing Care and Repair*.

DRILL THRILL

A drill press with ball-bearing spindle, good torque for drilling up to one-fourth inch, with an adjustable worktable—for only $76.95? Definitely, if you make your own, using parts from hobby shops and hardware stores ($70) and plans (PL 1401—$6.95) from *Popular Mechanics* Plans Library, Department D5, Box 1014, Radio City, New York 10019. Saves $200 over the store-bought variety.

GAS COMPANY GOODNESS

Your local gas company is an excellent source of free advice and no-cost minor repair work on your gas-operated appliances. The last time our gas floor heater broke down, we called the gas company and explained the problem. Their repairman crawled under the house, shut off the supply of gas to the heater, and found out what part was broken—all free of charge. We then bought the part for a few dollars and installed it ourselves. To make sure we'd done a good job, we called the repairman back for another free inspection. The serviceman told us that a similar repair job had cost a little old lady he knew several hundred dollars through an unscrupulous commercial repairman. A word to the wise . . .

For further information:

Appliance Service Handbook, George Meyerink. Englewood Cliffs, New Jersey, Prentice-Hall, 1973.

JEEP WHIZ!

If you own a jeep with power takeoff, you'll be happy to know that you can convert it to a cement mixer (temporarily, of course) by using an old tire, a standard mixing drum, and a five-inch-diameter drive pulley.

First the drive pulley is attached to the power takeoff. Then the drum is bolted to the tire, which is attached to the rear of the jeep above the pulley. Contact of the rotating pulley with the tire turns the mixing drum. Sure beats that $65-a-day rental fee for a portable mixing drum!

TRUCKING TRUTHS

Here's a trick we tried in moving our personal belongings from Los Angeles to Columbia, South Carolina. Pack the items carefully in sturdy cardboard cartons and have them trucked to your destination by freight forwarder rather than by a professional moving company. You'll have to deliver the goods and pick them up at the truck terminal, but this method will easily save you two-thirds on a cross-country move.

See your Yellow Pages under "Freight forwarding."

For further information:

Do-It-Yourself Moving, George Sullivan. Riverside, New Jersey, Macmillan, 1973.

SEASONAL SILVER

Save up to $60 on commercial moving rates for a typical three rooms (3,000 pounds) of furniture by making your interstate move in the "off-season"—October to May. The discount of a dollar or two per hundred pounds of goods during these months is the only rate cut allowed by the Interstate Commerce Commission.

For further information:

A Common-Sense Guide to Relocating Your Family, Edith Ruina. New York, Funk & Wagnalls (orders to Thomas Y. Crowell), 1970.

TARE SNARE

Moving companies weigh their trucks before and after they pick up your stuff to determine the weight of the load. To guard against possible deception—even blatant larceny—arrange to be with them when they weigh. Check the scales yourself, and make sure nothing is in the truck on second weighing except your stuff. If they fill up their gas tank before the second weighing, and two burly movers remain in the truck while it's weighed, you'll end up with an extra 500 pounds on your bill. At $35 per hundred pounds for the typical cross-country move, that's a hefty $175 rip-off!

For further information:

The Ins and Outs of Moving, Robert Rosefsky. Chicago, Tollett, 1972.

FROM POTHOLDERS
TO PAINT REMOVERS

Within the pages of this chapter, you'll be presented with a cornucopia of knickknacks, formulas, recipes, gadgets, and hints to help you stem the tide of those rapidly diminishing household dollars. Many are original ideas. Others have been chosen selectively as the best of thousands of household suggestions which have been passed down through many generations.

In either case, the following have saved countless coins for ourselves, our relatives, and our friends. We know they will for you too.

Around the House

TOOL TAKE

You can make your own tools—everything from screwdrivers and tinsnips to one-of-a-kind seedling transplanters and vegetable harvesters—using junk steel found along roadsides.

With a forge and anvil, a drill press, and a little imagination, you'll save hundreds of dollars over the store-bought variety.

For further information:

The Making of Tools, Alexander Weygers. Cincinnati, Van Nostrand Reinhold, 1973.

ANT AUDACITY

If you, like us, had spent one long, dry California summer trying to evict ants from your kitchen, using every deadly weapon from flyswatters to cleanliness to those expensive spray insecticides, you might swear that those little critters are invincible. Imagine our surprise when we recently discovered the ultimate ant weapon—common salt! Just sprinkle it across their path, preferably in corners so it won't get in your way. Works like a charm.

Another solution, which country people used in days gone by, is to plant an herb called tansy around your house or pot it in your kitchen. Ants find the acrid odor of this herb repulsive, and therefore take special pains to avoid it.

Tansy seeds can be ordered from Greene Herb Gardens, Greene, Rhode Island 02827, for 50¢.

BRUSH UP

The newest thing in paintbrushes is the Astrobrush, made entirely of one-piece polypropylene. Use it to paint, varnish, or enamel; it will even baste turkeys. It won't shed, and costs just 25¢—half the price of ordinary brushes. Order from Edy Brush Company, 81 Brookside Avenue, Amsterdam, New York 12010.

COCKROACH CONTROL

Despite the fact that a plague of cockroaches is unmentionably depressing—and probably most depressing because it's unmentionable—don't let the depths of despair drag you into hiring one of those expensive pesticide people to get things in hand. Riddance might be good for the soul, but it's not worth a $30 exterminator's fee. No need to buy expensive bug sprays either.

The answer? Just get yourself some powdered boric acid at the drugstore and sprinkle it on floors and shelves. While it may be harmless to humans, bugs hate the stuff. Costs only about $1 for an eight-ounce bottle.

FOUR-IN-ONE

Want a level, tape measure, square, and scriber, all rolled into one, at a $7 savings over the individually bought items? Order Versatape ($8.95) from Better Ideas, P.O. Box 225, Dayton, Ohio 45401.

DEBUNKING THE SKUNK

You can believe us, having a pair of skunks make their abode in the air vents of your heating system to escape from the winter cold is *no* laughing matter! When the heat comes on in the middle of the night and the stench of surprised and slightly scorched escaping skunk fills the house, it's enough to drive you to the nearest pest exterminator foolhardy enough to undertake this risky enterprise.

Before you fork over $50 for professional help, call your animal shelter or pound and ask if they have skunk traps to loan out. You can catch the critters live in these (they're odor-proof) and return them to the pound for disposal. Or, if you feel sorry for them, you can turn them loose in the country far from your house. Then block up all means of access to the space under your house. Sprinkle mothballs (whose odor skunks dislike as much as we dislike theirs) liberally around the skunks' former entrance place.

RATS!

As an alternative to investing in expensive rat poisons, we offer the following effective alternative—guaranteed to kill those offensive little (and sometimes not so little) beasts *dead*.

Simply mix, in equal portions, cement powder and kitchen flour. Gives the greedy things a fatal case of indigestion and costs about a third as much as commercial poison. Moreover, household pets and children seldom find this meal tempting. To be on the safe side though, place the meal in a hard to reach place.

For further information:

The Standard American Encyclopedia of Formulas, Albert Hopkins, ed. New York, Grosset & Dunlap, 1953.

GET THE HANG OF IT?

Hangers for lightweight pictures need cost nothing. Just attach a soft-drink or beer-can tab to the back of each picture with a dab of epoxy glue. Beats those $1-a-package variety-store prices by a country mile!

For further information:

"Second Uses for Discards," *Family Handyman*, February 1974, pages 48–49.

FLYPAPER FOXINESS

To make an effective heavy-duty flypaper at practically no cost, melt equal parts castor oil (drugstore) and resin (hardware store). Then apply to a magazine cover or other heavy, slick paper, and hang it up. Saves 75 percent over ready-made prices!

For further information:

The Mother Earth News, No. 37, January 1976, page 10.

PINING AWAY

Want to know of a preposterously inexpensive stain to use on pinewood? Tea! Just make some strong tea, apply it to the wood, and let dry. Then brush on two coats of white shellac, polish with wax, and you have a fine "antique" piece of pinewood.

For further information:

Heloise's Work and Money Savers, Heloise Cruse. New York, Pocket Books, 1971.

THE ULTIMATE MOUSETRAP

If your abode is overrun with rodents and you simply haven't the wherewithal to buy a mousetrap or keep a cat, try this ingenious little contrivance. Fill a bucket or a high pot two-thirds full of water. Next, place a short plank leading from the floor to the top of the bucket. Now balance a piece of paper on top of the bucket with a morsel of cheese right in the middle of the paper. In the dead of night, your pesky little rodent will leap greedily onto the paper to get the cheese, fall into the water, and drown.

Better yet, for ease of disposal, use your toilet as a bucket. We've tried this and it works!

MOUSE REPELLENT

Since mice hate the smell of peppermint, you can repel the willful rodents and keep your kitchen smelling fresh at the same time, at a cost of just a penny or two, simply by placing fresh peppermint sprigs from your garden in drawers and cupboards. Change the cuttings weekly.

For further information:

Common Sense Pest Control, Helga Olkowski. Berkeley, California, Consumer Cooperative (orders to Book People).

THINNER WINNER

Use mineral spirits, rather than turpentine, as paint thinner. This goes for painting everything from walls to portraits. Mineral spirits cost about 40 percent less than turpentine.

You can save half again on the shelf price of mineral spirits by toting your own bottle or can to the hardware or paint store and having it filled there.

TERMITE TERMINATION

Avoid the high cost of hiring a professional exterminator to termite-proof your house, or even of buying ready-made chemical solutions. You can easily—and cheaply—whip up your own termite repellent.

You'll need mothballs (paradichlorobenzene) from your hardware or variety store, and denatured alcohol from your drugstore. Simply dissolve one part mothballs in eight parts alcohol. Apply two liberal coats to foundations.

Warning: The strong smell of this solution limits its use to the outdoors.

For further information:

Van Nostrand's Practical Formulary, William Minrath, ed. Princeton, New Jersey, Van Nostrand, 1957.

REMOVING PAINT PROBLEMS

For a paint remover at less than half the price charged in a hardware store pick up some water glass (sodium silicate) at your drugstore. Brush on, leave for 15 minutes, then wash off.

Here is an old-fashioned solution to the stiff paintbrush problem that will cost you next to nothing. Simply place the brush in

boiling vinegar, simmer a few minutes, and wash with soap.

For further information:

Dick's Encyclopedia of Practical Receipts and Process, William Dick. New York, Funk & Wagnalls, 1975.

FLEA AND TICK SHTICK

There are a passel of low- and no-cost solutions to the age-old problem of controlling fleas and ticks on your pet. Low-cost: Sprinkle brewer's yeast on your pet's food. Fleas hate vitamin B_1, of which this food supplement is full. No-cost: Boil up some pennyroyal, mint, or sassafras and wash your pet in the solution. Or, hang a bunch of the herbs in the doghouse, or stuff a pillow with camomile flowers and place therein. The easiest solution: Soak a piece of clothesline in oil of pennyroyal and use as an effective flea collar. Replace every few weeks.

For further information:

"Natural Flea and Tick Control for your Dog," *The Mother Earth News Almanac, The Mother Earth News* Staff. New York, Bantam, 1973, page 206.

FILE FRANCS

The 4-in-Hand File is four files in one—flat and round, each fine or coarse grained. At $3.25 from Nicholson, Box 728, Apex, North Carolina 27502, it will save you $3 over the cost of separately bought files with the same functions.

ALL JUICED UP

Has it become odiously obvious that your dog has just encountered a skunk? Instead of wasting a $2 bottle of dog shampoo in a vain attempt to placate your nose, smoosh a 50¢ bottle of tomato juice all over your pet and let sit for an hour. Rinse off the guck with a concoction of one part vinegar to one part water. Not only will your dog stop smelling like a skunk—he won't even smell like a *dog* for a week or two! Pet-shop owners in our areas, who frequently deal with this problem, swear by the above remedy.

For further information:

"P.S. Readers Talk Back," *Popular Science*, April 1975, page 4.

Cleaning and Cooking

FIRELESS COOKER

While stores will charge you up to $35 for a crock pot, the modern-day version of the old-time fireless cooker, you can make the real thing for free. Simply construct a well-insulated box with a tight-fitting lid. Your cooking pot should slip snugly into a cylindrical hole in the center of the box, with room for a one-inch thick heating stone (cast concrete will do nicely) beneath. Bring your food to a boil in the pot, heating the stone at the same time. Then place the stone and pot in the cooker immediately and leave it there up to twelve hours.

For further information:

Cache Lake Country, John Rowlands. New York, Norton, 1959.

IT'S NO LYE!

Lye, the caustic chemical which runs 70¢ a pound at the hardware store, can be made at home for nothing by filtering water through hardwood ashes, straw, and gravel in a barrel. The resultant lye is drained off through holes in the bottom of the barrel into a container (*not* aluminum, through which it eats).

For further information:

"The Many Uses of Lye," *The Mother Earth News Almanac*, The Mother Earth News Staff. New York, Bantam, 1973, pages 200–203.

POACH COACHING

An easy, no-cost egg poacher: With a can opener, remove the top and bottom from a used tuna or anchovy can. Place the resulting ring of metal in your skillet, add water to the skillet outside the ring, and place the egg to be poached in the dry spot inside the ring.

Works just like a $10 egg poacher!

For further information:

Heloise's Housekeeping Hints, Heloise Cruse. Englewood Cliffs, New Jersey, Prentice-Hall, 1964.

BRILLO AU NATUREL

We all know how much those little pot-scouring pads cost and how soon they need replacing. Make your own natural scouring pads free by using a tightly tied bundle of common horsetail ("scouring rush," a primitive plant) stems, which grow abundantly in vacant lots and fields.

The cell structure of these plants is stiffened by silica (glass), which accounts for its fine scouring ability. When the edges of your horsetail scouring brush wear down, simply cut them off for a stiff new brush.

For further information:

"Common Horsetails," *The Mother Earth News Almanac*, The Mother Earth News Staff. New York, Bantam, 1973, page 120.

SCOURING SALT

At 10¢ a pound, plain household salt is a great bargain not only for all-round seasoning, but also for an amazing variety of household chores. It makes an excellent scouring powder for cutting boards, baking dishes, and coffee pots. To clean an enamel pot, fill it with cool water and a few tablespoons of salt. Let it stand overnight, then bring to a boil for a few minutes.

To keep your sink drain odorless and greaseless, heat ½ cup water with ½ cup salt, and pour it down the drain. For tired feet ½ cup of salt in a basin of water also makes a soothing soak; a cup in your bath water will refresh your whole body.

A pinch of salt in coffee will remove a bitter taste; in tea and hot cocoa, it will add a mellow full taste; and in milk, it preserves freshness and sweetness.

For further information:

"Plain Salt: The Cheapest Cure for 15 Household Chores," Lucille Goodyear, *The Consumer Gazette*, December/January (1975–76), page 66.

FUNNEL MONEY

To make a funnel with a handle, simply cut in half an empty plastic bleach jug. Line the cut edge with masking or adhesive tape to prevent injuries. The top half, minus the cap, makes a funnel. The bottom half can be used to make ice or freeze food. Saves several dollars on the funnel alone.

For further information:

Heloise's Housekeeping Hints, Heloise Cruse. Englewood Cliffs, New Jersey, Prentice-Hall, 1964.

SHOW YOUR METAL

Polish zinc counters, as well as copper and brass kitchen utensils, with inexpensive kerosene applied with newspapers. Works just like store-bought specialty metal cleaners, at one fourth the cost!

For further information:

Home Cleaning Guide, Barbara Molle and Charles Irv. Tucson, Arizona, Sincere, 1972.

KITCHEN FLOOR KARE

Make your own linoleum wax at a 17 percent savings over store prices! Get yourself some carnuba wax and yellow beeswax from a hobby shop, paraffin from the grocery store, and turpentine from the hardware store.

In a double-boiler, melt ¼ cup carnuba wax, 1 tablespoon paraffin, and 2 tablespoons of beeswax. Remove from heat and add 2 cups turpentine. After this solution has cooled, bottle your liquid booty for future use as a superb linoleum polish.

For further information:

The Up-With-Wholesome, Down-With-Store-Bought Book of Recipes and Household Formulas, Yvonne Tarr. Westminster, Maryland, Random House, 1975.

TOWEL TIP

At half the price of conventional dish towels, pick yourself up a dozen diapers at your local department or variety store. You will find these inexpensive substitutes better and more absorbent than many a legitimate dish towel.

For further information:

Heloise All Around the House, Heloise Cruse. Englewood Cliffs, New Jersey, Prentice-Hall, 1965.

WOOD WAX WISDOM

You can make yourself a year's supply of wood floor wax for the same price as three months' supply of the store-bought variety.

Melt two tablespoons of paraffin (grocery store) in a double-boiler, remove from heat, then stir into a quart of mineral oil (drugstore). The mixture is ready to use as soon as it cools.

For further information:

Dick's Encyclopedia of Practical Receipts and Processes, William Dick. New York, Funk & Wagnalls, 1975.

GET FRESH

Those aerosol room deodorants with which blissful TV housewives burden the air inside their homes are not only expensive, but usually smell as bad or worse than the odor they were meant to eliminate! So, make your own zingy room deodorant by cutting up leftover orange or lemon peels and placing them strategically about the room. Or, place a few drops of vanilla extract in a bowl of water and let the aroma waft through the room. And for those truly terrible smells, place an open bottle of ammonia in the offending area for a few hours.

By the way, if you perspire at the mere thought of underarm deodorant prices, try this simple substitute: Mix well ¼ cup of denatured or isopropyl alcohol, 1¼ cups water, and ½ tablespoon each of alum and zinc oxide. (All the ingredients can be bought at the drugstore.) Shake before using.

For further information:

The Formula Book, Norman Stark. Kansas City, Sheed and Ward, 1975.

JAR JIVE

One of the most useful but least-seen kitchen gadgets of all is that handy jar-opening device. But why pay $4 or $5 for the hardware store variety? Make your own out of an old leather belt and a ruler.

Place the middle of the belt around a stubborn jar lid. Next, place one end of the ruler, with the ruler jutting out at a 90° angle from the jar, against the lid where the sides of the belt meet. Pull the loose belt ends the length of the ruler, then fold them over the ruler's free end. Grip the jar with one hand and grip the ruler-belt handle with the other hand to twist off even the most stubborn lid.

For further information:

"Mother's Newspaper Column," *The Mother Earth News*, No. 37, January 1976, pages 57–60.

POLISH PRUDENCE

Duplicating at home that store-bought $1.20 bottle of lemon oil furniture polish is easier than jumping off a log—and you'll save a pretty penny in the bargain.

Get a bottle of lemon oil (drugstore) and a quart of mineral oil (hardware store). Mix one tablespoon of lemon oil with the mineral oil and place the mixture in a discarded spray bottle.

If you like a heavier furniture polish, here's an excellent formula for a low-cost wax variety: Melt 1½ teaspoons of carnuba wax (hobby shop) and 1 cup mineral oil together in a double-boiler. After the polish cools, store it in jars.

CLEANSING AGENTS

Surprisingly enough, you probably already have on hand many excellent, low-cost substitutes for cleansing agents which are every bit as effective as those sold at a premium in stores. Use a paste of vinegar, flour, and salt to clean copper. Just smear it on, let it set an hour, and wash off. Vinegar, kerosene, ammonia, or old tea and water do a fine job of washing windows. Vinegar can also be used to soften your laundry water, remove water spots from glassware, and brighten up aluminum. Put soap scraps in your toilet tank to keep it clean. A teaspoon or so of ammonia in a glass of warm water will clean brushes and combs. And an overnight bath of sour milk will clean your fine silver.

Check the back of your cookbook for simple household stain removers. Did you know that salt can help remove fresh wine stains; alcohol can erase grass stains; cornstarch can soak up oil or grease stains; and ice cubes can dissolve scorches?

For further information:

Removing Stains from Fabrics (054D), Consumer Information, Public Documents Distribution Center, Pueblo, Colorado 81009, 1968.

POTHOLDER POTENTIAL

Those blue jeans that just breathed their last have excellent potholder potential. Just fold them over three or four times, stitch the edges together with string or macrame cord, and save yourself nigh onto a dollar. For a fancy touch, cut out an apple or orange from a scrap of red or orange material and appliqué it on. A good gift idea as well.

For other potholder ideas, see Better Homes & Gardens' *100's of Ideas, Crafts and Sewing 1972*, Des Moines, Iowa, Meredith, 1972.

BISCUIT BUCKS

No need to pay $1 for store-bought biscuit cutters. Instead, remove the top and bottom from an empty tuna can and pound down any remaining ragged edges of metal. Or, for a fancier shaped biscuit cutter, remove the ends from an empty anchovy can.

OIL STRETCHER

Mineral oil is generally recommended to clean and renew tile floors. We have a tip that can stretch your mineral oil supply almost twice as far, saving you around 45 percent on tile-cleaning costs.

Over a double-boiler, mix one quart of mineral oil with three cups of water and three-eighths cup (or six tablespoons) of ammonia soap (ammonium oleate) from your drugstore or chemical supply house. Blend the mixture with an egg beater and store in jars.

CHALK TALK

No need to buy metal polish ever again! Use leftover chalk ends to shine everything from stainless steel cutlery to brass doorknobs. Also, put them in with your costume jewelry to prevent tarnishing.

Is there a hole in your plaster wall? Instead of putting out hard-earned dollars for a plaster patch, drive an old piece of chalk into the hole and snap it off even with the wall.

This and That

AN INVITING SUGGESTION

For high-quality invitations to weddings and other formal occasions, order thermographed rather than engraved work from your printer. Thermographed letters are raised, as are the engraved kind, for a luxurious look. But lower costs result because a costly engraving plate need not be made. Only a professional engraver and your pocketbook will know the difference. Saves you $36 per hundred invitations!

For further information:

Barbara Quint, *Glamour*, April 1975, page 130.

BAKING SODA BONANZA

People who take a year or two to use up one box of baking soda must not be aware of the plenteous panorama of uses for this vastly versatile product. Naturally, you can use it in cooking, but what else? Make a paste of it with a little water to soothe insect bites, bee stings, prickly heat, and poison ivy. Add a few tablespoons to your bath water and soak in it to relieve sore muscles. Half a teaspoon in a glass of water will relieve indigestion and colds. Dissolve a little in water for mouthwash or mix dry baking soda with salt for toothpaste. For a douche, use one tablespoon of baking soda in a quart of warm water. For underarm deodorant, pat on soda directly. A teaspoon of soda in your shampoo will remove hairspray. Shaving cream for tender skin is easily concocted of three tablespoons soda in one-half basin of warm water.

Keep an open box in the fridge to absorb odors. After a few months, replace with a new box, pour part of the contents of the old one down the drain to eliminate that nasty smell, use the rest to clean glass, ceramic tile, pots and pans, bathtubs, sinks, stoves, and garbage can interiors. Mix a little with warm water to clean your coffeepot or china.

For auto battery and terminal corrosion, apply one tablespoon in one quart water, rinse, let dry, and smear on petroleum jelly. To clean rusty, clogged auto radiators, dump in a pound of baking soda, operate the car for an hour or so, then flush with water and refill with water/antifreeze. To "bleach" nylons before washing, soak five minutes in a basin of warm water to which three tablespoons soda have been added. And finally, baking soda, in a pinch, makes an excellent fire extinguisher!

COPY CLUES

A single Xerox copy can cost up to 15¢. Your best bet for really economical copying is at the library of your local college or university. Five cents is the current going rate at San Diego State University.

For volume offset printing, shops in the vicinity of a college are often cheapest.

REPRO INFO

If you do a lot of copying, you can beat copy-shop prices by purchasing your own electricity-less, crankless, portable copier that turns out twenty copies a minute for only the cost of mimeograph paper (¼ cent a sheet).

This economical (34.95) unit will save you a whopping $585 over the cost of a regular mimeograph machine, and hundreds more over the cost of a photo copier.

For further information:

Press N Print, Art Nilsen Company, 1225 South Biscayne Point Road, Miami Beach, Florida 33141.

SPRING STING

Don't pay $15 for a scale when you can make your own out of a stiffish spring (such as an old auto throttle spring) and a container (such as an old bucket). Tack one end of the spring onto a shed roof beam or porch rail. Attach the container to the bottom end of the spring. Next, tie a hairpin or wire to the spring between the bottom coil and the container as a pointer and tack a sheet of cardboard onto the beam next to the spring.

The scale can be calibrated up to nine pounds by placing known quantities of water in the container and marking the card accordingly (one gallon of cold water weighs eight and one-third pounds). Zero on your scale is the point indicated on the card when the container is empty.

For further information:

"Quick and Easy Homestead Scales," Gordon Solberg, *The Mother Earth News*, No. 38, March 1976, pages 24–25.

GAIN WEIGHT

If you need a hanging scale with which to weigh objects up to, say, 50 pounds, you can save $15 by purchasing a model with a 25-pound limit and converting it to double capacity. Here's how: Hang up the scale; attach one end of a heavy string to the wall a foot or so to one side of the top of the scale; attach the other end of the string to the bottom of the scale, leaving a foot of string extra for leeway.

Now find an object that you know weighs, say, 30 pounds and hang it on the string, sliding it along till the scale registers 15 pounds. Mark this place on the string where the wall (to which the string is nailed) supports exactly half the weight of an object. From now on, if you want to weigh an object between 25 and 50 pounds, hang it on the string at the mark, find the reading on the scale, and multiply by two for the weight of the object. Got it?

For further information:

The Mother Earth News Almanac, The Mother Earth News Staff. New York, Bantam, 1973.

GLUE CUE

Make your own glue at just half of retail prices! You'll need only gelatin, which you can buy in your local supermarket, and glacial acetic acid from a chemical supply company.

Soak the gelatin overnight in an amount of water equal to twice its weight. Then dissolve the gelatin in the water by heating it very gently. To this mixture, add glacial acetic acid equal in weight to the amount of gelatin you used. Instant glue!

For further information:

"The Fully Illustrated, Worry-Free A to Z, How to Make Your Own Book," *The New Earth Catalog: Living Here and Now*, Scott French, ed. New York, Putnam/Berkley and Heller & Son, 1973, pages 131–143.

TINT HINT

If you want the effect of tinted light bulbs without paying more than double the cost of ordinary bulbs, buy the plain kind, and then tint you own. Use either food coloring (preferred) or poster paints (somewhat murkier in color).

Light the bulb *just* before painting. If you let the bulb get too hot, it will explode as the cold paint touches it, so be careful. This do-it-yourself technique saves 65¢ per 60-watt bulb!

For further information:

"Painting and Craft Tips," Chuck Kennedy, *The New Earth Catalog: Living Here and Now*, Scott French, ed. New York, Putnam/Berkley and Heller & Son, 1973, page 72.

COOL SPOOL SPIEL

Instead of buying those fancy, expensive cabinet or bureau knobs, save yourself some bucks by using empty thread spools instead. Or, use them as butcher-knife holders by nailing them into your kitchen wall in pairs.

STAMP SAVVY

We've used a lot of stamps in our time, and we're delighted to hear of this postage ploy. Use phone shopping to locate stamp dealers who will sell you older mint commemoratives for as low as 80 percent of their face value. Other discount offers can be found in the classified ads of stamp collectors' magazines.

For further information:

Stamps: A Weelky Magazine of Philately, H. L. Lindquist Publications, Inc., 153 Waverly Place, New York, New York 10014.

Linn's Weekly Stamp News, Sidney Publishing Company, P.O. Box 29, Sidney, Ohio 45365.

LINT PICKER LOGIC

You can shave the cost of lint removers down from a dollar to just a penny or two! Just wind some cellophane tape or masking tape, sticky side out, around an old piece of shirt cardboard or cardboard tube. Pressing against fabric picks up lint and hairs just like the expensive kind!

For further information:

"Tips You Should Know About," *Family Handyman*, October 1974, pages 42–43.

TYPEWRITER WIPER

Know that two- or three-ounce bottle of typewriter cleaner that costs you the better part of a dollar? You can make your own for a few pennies by mixing two parts water with three parts denatured alcohol (from your drugstore). Store in a tightly sealed bottle.

This solution can be used to clean all your typewriter parts, including the type and platen.

For further information:

New Practical Formulary, Mitchell Freeman. New York, Chemical, 1955.

DISPENSER DEFTNESS

Those poultry water dispensers which store water in an upside-down plastic bottle and dispense it gradually into a tray cost $3 at the farm supply store. Make your own for nothing using an old bottle or can and dish or aluminum throwaway pie plate. Fill the can or bottle with water, place the dish or pie plate over the top, and turn the whole thing over quickly, keeping the lid firmly in place. Ain't that the ritz?!

For further information:

The Mother Earth News Almanac, The Mother Earth News Staff. New York, Bantam, 1973.

POST OFFICE PICKIN'S

Your friendly local post office stocks a burgeoning inventory of stationery supplies—some at prices that would shock a stationery supplier right out of his ream.

Last year alone we saved over $50 on such items as prestamped postcards (sold for the price of the stamp only), manila envelopes, postage scales, and those handy little stamp dispensers (a nickle compared to $1.50 at your stationery store). Also available *free* at the post office: mail sacks, tags, wrappers for mail bundles, and special delivery stickers.

CLASSY GLASSES

Convert your old soda and beer bottles into elegant glasses for next to nothing! All you need are a glass cutter, a little gasoline, some string, and a carborundum sharpening stone.

Score a circle around a likely bottle with a glass cutter where you want the break to be. Next, tie a string soaked in gasoline (or kerosene or turpentine) around the scored circle. Set the string on fire and turn the bottle slowly for even heating. When the neck is very hot, dip it in ice cold water, tap lightly, and the neck will break where the string was tied. Smooth the cut glass with your sharpening stone for a one-of-a-kind recycled no-cost drinking glass!

For further information:

Making Do: Basic Things for Simple Living, Arthur Hill. New York, Ballantine, 1972.

SCRAP PAPER SOURCES

To avoid spending $3.50 a ream for scrap paper at your stationery store, you can find huge quantities of computer paper at the data processing centers at your city or county government, school district, college computer science department—even at a local accounting firm. One Modesto, California, writer picked up enough paper to keep him busy for six months with one trip to his county office.

Another good source of scrap paper: the wastebaskets next to Xerox machines.

For further information:

"The Writing Life," *Writer's Digest*, January 1976, page 5.

POULTRY POINTERS

Don't spend $2 for poultry delousing powder. Instead, attract the lice *away* from the birds by hanging banana stems in the poultry house. As lice accumulate on the stems, dispose of them.

Or, if you live in tobacco country, you can repel these nasty little critters by placing leaves of dried tobacco in poultry nests.

Your poultry will love you for it!

For further information:

The Bug Book: Harmless Insect Controls, John Philbrick and Helen Philbrick. Charlotte, Vermont, Garden Way, 1974.

ASSAULTING BATTERY COSTS

What kind of battery is best for small appliances such as transistor radios, toys, and flashlights that receive normal use? The heavy-duty carbon-zinc battery costs only a dime more than the ordinary carbon zinc variety and lasts two or three times longer.

If you need batteries for a photo flash unit, large tape recorder, or other heavy-duty equipment, your best buy is a rechargeable nickel cadmium battery. While each battery costs $3 or $4, and the recharging device costs around $15, the battery can be recharged a thousand times.

For further information:

"Mind Your Money: Best Batteries for the Job," Peter Weaver, *Los Angeles Times*, Part IV, 18 December 1975.

TRY AEROGRAM, SAM!

If your letters to foreign shores tote up to a considerable amount, purchase aerograms at your post office instead of sending ordinary letters. These are pre-stamped, lightweight sheets of stationery which, when folded over, become their own envelopes.

The advantage? Not only will you save on the cost of stationery, but an aerogram costs about one-fourth less in postage than an ordinary letter.

FREE BABYSITTING

You need never pay for a babysitter again. Get together with other parents in your community and form a babysitting pool. If you can get only six parents interested, each will entertain the lot one day a week. In exchange for one day a week of intensive babysitting, you will have six blessed days or evenings of freedom—without blowing your budget.

For further information:

Caring for Children: A Symposium on Co-Operation in Child Care, M. L. Pringle. Atlantic Highlands, New Jersey, Humanities Press, 1969.

KNICKKNACK KNOWLEDGE

What's in a box? Anything your imagination dictates. The most beautiful jewelry box can be made from an old cigar box covered with cloth, leather, or fur, partitioned with pieces of cardboard, and lined with rich velvet. Before you chuck out that dozen or so boxes and cans in odd shapes and sizes every week, consider: An old cake or pancake flour box can be cut down and covered with contact paper for use as a kitchen napkin holder. Old match boxes covered and decorated with sequins make excellent knickknacks and gifts. Oilcloth-covered coffee cans with plastic lids can be transformed into cannister sets for your kitchen staples or matching flowerpots for your window, all for pennies.

Once you get the knack of this idea, you won't have to nick your budget on these items!

For further information:

Pack-O-Fun Treasury of Crafts, Gifts and Toys, Edna and John Clapper. New York, Hawthorn, 1971.

BLIND BARGAINS

If you can't read normal-size print, or if you are legally certified as blind, the U.S. Post Office will foot the postage for any large-type Braille literature you order. "Free Matter for the Blind or Handicapped" should be written in the stamp space. Leave the envelope unsealed so the post office can check up on you.

Note: This freebie doesn't apply to correspondence that includes advertising.

GETTING THE SCOOP

If you buy grain in quantity for yourself or your animals, you'll need a feed scoop with which to handle the grain. Instead of plunking down $5 at a feed store, convert an empty gallon plastic container—bleach, antifreeze, or otherwise—to a scoop for free.

Pick a spot below the handle to cut half way through the container. Then cut lengthwise from your first cut to the bottom. Now cut off the bottom of the container for a durable plastic scoop.

For further information:

"Ask Poppy George," "Poppy George" Pitt, *The Mother Earth News,* No. 27, May 1974, page 74.

GREEN SAVINGS
FOR GREEN THUMBS

Nothing beats that lazy summer afternoon relaxing on your own chaise lounge, mint julep in hand, on a carefully manicured, well-nourished lawn, watching tomatoes in your soon-to-be-self-sufficient garden ripen in the sun. The question is, how to enjoy burgeoning outdoor greenery without depleting the green in your pocket? Forethought is the answer.

It doesn't take much physical effort to purchase $100 worth of exotic shrubs for your home at a plant nursery. But that careless decision will cost you plenty in soil additives, special fertilizers, and the tons of water needed to keep those shrubs alive in soil and climatic conditions to which they are not accustomed. On the other hand, you can obtain shrubs ideally suited to your area, which will require far less costly pampering, by carefully transplanting native varieties growing wild in outlying areas.

Another technique is to obtain cuttings free from a neighbor. We recently latched onto ground cover for an entire hillside by finding a neighbor whose yard was overrun with iceplant. A truckload of starter plants, which would have cost a small fortune at the plant nursery, cost only the effort of trimming the plants and hauling them away.

If you're just now planning a lawn, make it dichondra and eliminate the considerable expense of a lawn mower and other accoutrements. If you're planting a vegetable garden, read up on companion planting, a method of eliminating garden pests without the expense and effort involved in using pesticides. Or, if your garden is already in the ground, the ideas contained in this chapter will offer a variety of organic, inexpensive weed- and pest-control alternatives.

Lawn and Garden

POST HASTE

While a store will charge you $13 or so for a fence-post driver, you can make one with a four-foot length of scrap pipe and a heavy nut and bolt. Just drill two holes on opposite sides of the pipe an inch from the top, insert the bolt, and secure it with the nut. Or, use an old axle housing with a steel plate welded across one end.

Now, slip the unobstructed end of the pipe over the post and let go. When the bolt or welded plate hits the post top, the force of gravity will drive the post into the ground.

POND POWER

If you'd like to have a small fish pond or lily pool in your garden or lawn, but can't see putting out $200 for a professional job, try one of these low-cost do-it-yourself alternatives.

For this one, all you need is an old barrel, some soil, water lilies, a little sand, and some flat stones for a border. Dig a hole and place the barrel in it, flush with the ground, fill halfway with soil, plant your lilies, add an inch or two of sand, fill with water, and place the stones around the brim.

An attractive, inexpensive pool can be constructed of heavy vinyl sheeting from your hardware store. Place the vinyl in a depression, place stones around edges to hold in place, add dirt near the bottom, plant lilies, fill with water, and add fish as desired.

For further information:

"The Barrel Lily Pool," *The Naturalist's Almanac and Environmentalist's Companion*, Northern Pacific Region Edition, John Gardner, ed. New York, Ballantine, 1973, page 154.

"Instant Pool for your Garden," Arthur Glowka, *Popular Science*, August 1975, pages 108–109.

MOW IN STYLE

Save $400 over the price of a store-bought sit-down lawn mower by building your own from a kit. Ten-horsepower model TR–10–ALE is available from Heald, Inc., P.O. Box 1148, Benton Harbor, Michigan 49022, costs $700, compared to $1,100 retail, and takes only a few weekends to assemble.

For further information:

"A Mower You Build from a Kit," Robert Beason, *Mechanix Illustrated*, November 1975, pages 94, 96.

BARROW BARGAIN

A new wheelbarrow needn't cost you $30. Arthur Hill, in *Making Do: Basic Things for Simple Living*, New York, Ballantine, 1972, tells you how to make your own out of $15 worth of lumber and some steel strips. The man even tells you how to make the wheel out of a few pieces of scrap lumber.

MULCTING MULCH

Why pay $50 or more at a plant nursery to obtain compost for your yard? A little finagling will get you this stuff for free. Call the stables in your area. At least one will be happy to get its excess manure out from underfoot. Now call your local sawmill, and casually offer to remove some of that sawdust that litters their property. When you get your booty home, mix it all together with kitchen garbage, grass clippings, and weeds. After six months, you'll have plenty of compost for yard and garden.

You can also use some of the sawdust straight as a ground cover to help retain moisture for your growing things.

For further information:

Let It Rot! The Gardener's Guide to Composting, Stu Campbell. Charlotte, Vermont, Garden Way, 1975.

ORGANIC ODYSSEY

Into organic gardening? For a free packet of seaweed fertilizer or vegetable seeds, as well as a "Grow Organic" banner and an organic gardening newsletter, send 30¢ (for postage) to Mr. Reindeer, Reindeer's Organic Company Ltd., 5307 Patricia Bay Highway, R.R. 5, Victoria, B.C., Canada.

WEATHER VANITY

Make your own one-of-a-kind weathervane at one fourth of ready-made prices! Send 50¢ to Stanley Tools, Advertising Services Department, Box 1800, New Britain, Connecticut 06050, and request T314, four weathervane ornaments. These lovely ornaments can also be adapted as wall plaques and porch or patio fashion accents.

GOING TO POT

No need to pay $20 or more for a bit of greenery inside your home. Instead, grow your own potted plants from seeds you would otherwise throw in the trash. Lovely avacado, orange, mango, grapefruit, tangerine, and tamarind trees; edible garlic and onion sprouts; lush pineapple tops; prodigiously fast-growing potato vines; and fern-like carrot tops are only a few of the many grow-your-own greeneries that can be salvaged from your garbage can.

For further information:

"Indoor Greenery from Kitchen Leftovers," *Money*, February 1975, pages 66–67.

SLED SAVVY

Even a small wagon or sled with which to cart stones or produce through fields and over dirt roads costs several hundred dollars. A no-cost substitute is a sled made of a junk auto hood, flipped over, with an old chain attached to the front. Pull with people, horses, or auto.

For extra-heavy loads, place logs or pipes crosswise underneath to prevent friction as you pull.

For further information:

"A New-Fangled Version of an Old Idea," *The Mother Earth News Almanac*, *The Mother Earth News* Staff. New York, Bantam, 1973, page 177.

PATIO PLAN

Thousands of dollars' worth of repairable patio furniture is thrown out every year simply because the owners didn't know how to fix it or feared that the cost of repairs would be more than the price of a new set. Learn to repair your own easily with a minimum of tools by reading "Fixing Metal Patio Furniture," *Family Handyman*, June 1975, pages 46–47.

MOWER POWER

Lawn mower wheels won't turn? A repairman will charge you $10 to fix the trouble, but you can do it yourself for a quarter! Follow instructions in the reference below to disassemble the wheels and remove the pinion gear rachet. A replacement part from a mower repair shop will solve the problem.

For further information:

"Repair Your Power Mower for a Quarter," Parry Yob, *Family Handyman*, June 1975, pages 30–31.

LEAF BAG BLUES

At $1.10, the frugal homeowner will think twice before buying those heavy-duty lawn and garden trash bags. A no-cost substitute: plastic bags from the cleaners, placed one inside the other for triple or quadruple strength.

WAGON WAGES

For $75, compared to $500 retail, you can construct your own carry-all flatbed wagon to tow behind your car. You'll need an old auto chassis and scrap metal from your junk dealer, rough lumber for the wagon bed from a sawmill, and the instructions in "Make Hay . . . With a $75.00 Build-It Yourself Wagon," Larry Brumfield, *The Mother Earth News*, No. 38, March 1976, pages 40–42.

ROOT LOOT

Store your root crops underground all winter at *no* cost in a discarded refrigerator, buried up to the door, with a layer of hay or other insulation on top. Be sure to remove the door

lock so that children cannot trap themselves inside.

PLANTER PAINTER

Lovely five-gallon planters need not cost you $10 at a garden shop. Make your own using scrap lumber and the simple instructions in *Gifts You Can Make*, Editors of Sunset Books and *Sunset Magazine*, Menlo Park, California, Lane, 1971.

LAND SCAPES!

Why pay out hundreds of dollars for a professional landscaping job for your lawn? Instead, become a plant design pro yourself by studying the free booklet *Home Planting by Design*, available through the Publications Information and Agricultural Marketing Service, U.S. Department of Agriculture, Washington, D.C. 20250.

TRACTOR TALK

Make your own 10-horsepower Yard Bronc garden tractor for $599.95 and save $400 over the normal retail price. Coming in kit form, this unit can be assembled in just ten hours. Order from Heald, Inc., Box 1148, Benton Harbor, Michigan 49022.

SPRINKLER TINKERING

To install an underground lawn sprinkler system covering 800 square feet, all you need is $32 worth of supplies, a pipe wrench, a shovel, and the determination to save the several hundred dollars' worth of labor charged by professional installers.

Do-it-yourself starter kits, complete with detailed instructions, are available at hardware stores everywhere.

For further information:

"The Do-it-yourself Kit Route to Underground Sprinklers," William Hawkins, *Popular Science*, June 1975, pages 96–99.

SAWBUCKS

Renting a chain saw for garden work, cutting up firewood, or making home improvements can cost you a pretty penny—up to $25 a day. Even if you only use this tool three or four times a year, it will pay you to buy your own.

What type is the best buy for your money, the electric or the gas model? The electric saw will cost you $15 to $30 less than the gas variety. Also, it is much quieter. You can use it indoors in the winter without asphyxiating yourself on gas fumes, and you don't have to keep cans of gas stashed dangerously near your house. It starts on cue every time, and it doesn't require periodic tuneups, as does the gas type.

Believe us, this argument has got *teeth* in it!

For further information:

"Buying a Chain Saw That Won't Cost You an Arm and a Leg,"*Moneysworth*, 29 September 1975, page 20.

ROTOTILLER THRILLER

Add $100 to your till by purchasing a Groundhog Semi-Kit tiller from Heald, Inc., P.O. Box 1148, Benton Harbor, Michigan 49022. Kits start at $200 for a five-horsepower model. They can be assembled with simple tools in six hours.

POT PERSPICACITY

No need to pay a garden shop $5 for a set of seed-starting flats or pots. Instead, use cardboard egg cartons, which you can pick up free in any restaurant. Because these cartons disintegrate in the soil, there's no need to remove the seedling before planting. Or, place half an egg shell in each pocket of a Styrofoam egg carton and plant a seed in the shell. Seedlings can be transplanted in the shell, which will protect the fragile root system, as well as adding minerals to the soil.

Start tomato or cabbage seeds in discarded Styrofoam cups (check the trash basket of any fast-food outlet). On transplanting, cut the bottom half of the cup away from the soil inside, then use the top half as a collar to protect the plant from cutworms. Tin cans with bottom or top removed also make good collars.

For further information:

"The Art of Early Planting," *The Mother Earth News Almanac, The Mother Earth News* Staff. New York, Bantam, 1973, pages 6–7.

Organic Pesticides

SLUGGEROO

A low-cost, highly effective insecticide for garden slugs is plain old everyday beer. An experiment by an entomologist (insect specialist) has shown that beer killed 300 slugs compared to 28 for the traditional metaldehyde/arsenic poison. The slugs just fall in the beer and drown—presumably in a state of euphoria.

For further information:

"Dead Drunk Slugs," Floyd Smith, *Time*, 9 February 1970, page 46.

SKIRTING THE ISSUE

To protect your trees from gypsy moths without paying for a professional spray job, just wrap a six-inch-wide burlap skirt around each tree trunk three feet above the ground. In the late afternoon, shake the caterpillars, which will hide under this skirt during the day, into a bucket with an inch or more of light oil such as kerosene, in which they'll drown.

To get rid of elm spanworm, which spin their way down from branches and then crawl back up the trunk, just mix some molasses with axle grease, petroleum jelly, or other sticky or greasy substance, and generously smear it around the tree trunk. Even with yea many legs, the critters can't get a purchase on the gooey stuff.

INSECT INSIGHT

You can keep such harmful insects as aphids and cutworms out of your garden without the expense or risk of using chlorinated hydrocarbons. Just plant garlic, chili pepper, and onion around the border of the garden and at intervals in the middle. These strong-tasting plants will then act as a "fence." Bugs take one bite and turn away, overlooking your tomatoes, lettuce, and so on.

If your garden is already in the ground, don't despair! Crush a chili pepper and a clove of garlic into a quart of water, mix thoroughly, strain, place in an old window-cleaner bottle or plant sprayer and squirt on your plants. Gives those pesky garden critters heartburn!

For further information:

"Bug Heartburn," R. D. and J. L. Hamilton, *The Updated Last Whole Earth Catalog: Access to Tools*, Pam Cokeley, ed. *The Whole Earth Catalog*, Box 428, Sausalito, California 94965, May 1974.

EDIBLE INSECTICIDE

An effective garden insect-killer, so harmless to humans that they can eat it and costing just half as much as the conventional dangerous type, is readily available to the insect-beleaguered consumer.

Diatomaceous earth is a white powder composed of the fossil skeletons of trillions of microscopic sea creatures. How does it kill insects? They cut themselves on its sharp edges and (ugh!) bleed to death. Buy the stuff from swimming-pool suppliers, plant nurseries, or rock and sand suppliers.

ROSE RUSE

No need to spend $3 on an insecticide to rid your roses of aphid infestation. Instead, simply steep tobacco in water, add a little soap, and spray on the plants. The tobacco-water is harmless to your roses, but acts as a strong repellent to these destructive garden pests.

For further information:

"For the Household," *The Naturalist's Almanac and Environmentalist's Companion*, Northern Pacific Regional Edition, John Gardner, ed. New York, Ballantine, 1973, page 123.

GARDENIA GARDENER

To make the soil properly acidic for healthy gardenia growth without spending $3 on special additions, use this down-home, cheap substitute. Simply water the plants with a solution of a half teaspoon of white vinegar in a quart of warm water. Works like magic!

For further information:

"Your Spring Garden," *Family Handyman*, March 1975, pages 60–61.

HOMEMADE PLANT SPRAY

Tomato mosaic virus is a costly disease for which there is no conventional cure. Rather than spending $5 or so for replacement plants, spray your tomatoes with milk—dry, whole, or diluted—which poisons the virus.

Spider mites in your apple trees? Spray them with a gooey homemade mess—1 cup flour, 2 ounces buttermilk, and 1¼ gallons water. Try it, they'll hate it!

WEED WOES

Walk and driveway weeds can be eliminated at one fourth the cost of conventional weed eradicators by sprinkling a strong, non-poisonous rock salt/water solution on them.

Caution: Don't use this method in gardens, as it will kill regular plants too.

For further information:

"Tips You Should Know About," *Family Handyman*, June 1974, pages 44–45.

MOLE MASTERY

Rid your lawn of moles without investing in $2 mole or gopher killing contraptions. All you need is a few cents worth of sulfur (drugstore), a rag, a match, and a board.

First plug up all the mole holes on your property except one. Next dig down into the one open hole, place the sulfur-soaked rag inside and light it. Then cover the hole with the board so that no smoke escapes. The mole's own tunnel will conduct the vile smell of the burning sulfur throughout and asphyxiate him.

CORN SAVER

To keep raccoons and groundhogs from raiding your corn, at half the cost of conventional poisons, place mothballs at three-foot intervals around the border of your corn patch once a week as the corn is reaching maturity. This humane pest-control device works by repelling the animals, which hate the smell, rather than by poisoning.

For further information:

The Natural Way to Pest-Free Gardening, Jack Kramer. Totowa, New Jersey, Scribners', 1972.

PEST PRUNERS

Forget about expensive garden pesticides! Instead, herbalize your garden. For every vegetable you plant, there is an herb, flower, or common weed, called a companion plant, that deters pests and enhances growth. For example, horseradish deters the potato bug; sage discourages the carrot fly and cabbage moth; marigold keeps away Mexican bean beatles, nematodes, and insects throughout the garden. Moreover, the horseradish and sage will provide you with seasoning, and the marigolds grace your table at 1/100 of store prices.

If you've already planted a garden, the companion concept can still be carried out by mashing up the companion in water and spraying it on the infested plant.

For further information:

"A Companionate Herbal for the Organic Garden," *The Mother Earth News Almanac, The Mother Earth News* Staff. New York, Bantam, 1973, pages 80–83.

SLIPPERY SPRAY

A harmless-to-humans insecticide for white flies and other tree pests is Zip Wax Car Wash (Turtle Wax Company), purchased at your auto parts store. Mix with water and spray on fruit, citrus, and magnolia trees. The wax ruins the pests' appetite and costs half as much as harmful pesticides.

For further information:

"Farm and Garden," *Family Handyman*, April 1975, page 48.

12

A TORRENT OF TRAVEL TIPS

Ah, the adventure of the open road! The exhilarating pace, the change of scenery, the opportunity to make new friends, a breath of fresh air in our often stagnant lives! But travel—and especially its cost—is what you make it. Believe it or not, there are multitudes of frugal vagabonds roaming the earth who have learned to live for less on the road than they would in their hometown.

After you've decided where in the world you want to go, contact the tourist offices of the countries of your choice for a wealth of free travel information. A complete list of these follows.

Australia: Australian Tourist Commission, 3550 Wilshire Boulevard, Los Angeles, California 90010.

Austria: Austrian National Tourist Office, 3440 Wilshire Boulevard, Los Angeles, California 90010.

Bahamas: Bahamas Island Tourist Office, 510 West 6th Street, Los Angeles, California 90014.

Belgium: Official Belgian Tourist Bureau, 720 5th Avenue, New York, New York 10019.

Brazil: Brazilian Trade Center, 333 South Flower Street, Los Angeles, California 90017.

Canada: Canadian Government Office of Tourism, 510 West 6th Street, Suite 712, Los Angeles, California 90014.

Caribbean: Caribbean Travel Association, 20 East 46th Street, New York, New York 10017.

Central America: Central America Tourist Bureau, 616 West Commonwealth, Fullerton, California 92632.

Ceylon (Sri Lanka): Ceylon Tourist Board, 2007 Wilshire Boulevard, Room 820, Los Angeles, California 90057.

Chile: Chilean National Tourist Board, 510 West 6th Street, Los Angeles, California 90014.

Colombia: Colombian Government Tourist Office, 140 East 57th Street, New York, New York 10022.

Czechoslovakia: Cedok, 10 East 40th Street, New York, New York 10016.

Dominican Republic: Dominican Tourist Information Center, 485 Madison Avenue, New York, New York 10022.

Egypt: Egyptian Government Tourist Office, 3001 Pacific Avenue, San Francisco, California 94115.

Fiji: Dailey & Associates, 574 Pacific Avenue, San Francisco, California 94133.

France: French Government Tourist Office, 9401 Wilshire Boulevard, Beverly Hills, California 90212.

Germany: German National Tourist Office, 323 Geary Street, San Francisco, California 94102.

Great Britain: British Tourist Authority, 612 South Flower Street, Los Angeles, California 90017.

Greece: Greek National Tourist Organization, 627 West 6th Street, Los Angeles, California 90017.

Guatemala: Guatemala Tourism Commission, 412 West 6th Street, Room 1008, Los Angeles, California 90014.

Lebanon: Lebanon Tourist and Information Office, 405 Park Avenue, New York, New York 10022.

Malaysia: Malaysian Tourist Information Center, 600 Montgomery Street, San Francisco, California 94111.

Mexico: Mexican Government Tourism Department, 3106 Wilshire Boulevard, Los Angeles, California 90005.

Morocco: Moroccan National Tourist Office, 597 5th Avenue, New York, New York, 10017.

Netherlands: Netherlands National Tourist Office, 681 Market Street, San Francisco, California 94105.

New Zealand: New Zealand Government Tourist Office, 10960 Wilshire Boulevard, Suite 1530, Los Angeles, California 90024.

Pacific: Pacific Area Travel Association, 228 Grant Avenue, San Francisco, California 94108.

Panama: Panama Government Tourist Office, 3900 West 3rd Street, Los Angeles, California 90020.

Philippines: Far East Express, 617 South Olive Street, Suite 811, Los Angeles, California 90014.

Poland: Polish National Tourist Office, 500 5th Avenue, New York, New York 10036.

Portugal: Portuguese National Tourist Office, 1 Park Plaza, Suite 1004, 3250 Wilshire Boulevard, Los Angeles, California 90010.

Puerto Rico: Puerto Rico Tourism Development Company, 10100 Santa Monica Boulevard, Suite 1520, Century City, Los Angeles, California 90067.

Russia: U.S.S.R. Intourist, 45 East 49th Street, New York, New York 10017.

Scandinavia (Finland, Sweden, Norway, Iceland, Denmark): Scandinavian National Tourist Offices, 3600 Wilshire Boulevard, Los Angeles, California 90010.

Singapore: Singapore Tourist Promotion Board, 251 Post Street, San Francisco, California 94108.

South Africa: South African Tourist Corporation, 9465 Wilshire Boulevard, Beverly Hills, California 90212.

Spain: Spanish National Tourist Office, 209 Post Street, Suite 710, San Francisco, California 94108.

Switzerland: Swiss National Tourist Office, 661 Market Street, San Francisco, California 94105.

Tahiti: Tahiti Tourist Development Board, P.O. Box 3720, Hollywood, California 90028.

Taiwan: Republic of China Tourist Bureau, 3660 Wilshire Boulevard, Los Angeles, California 90010.

Thailand: Tourist Organization of Thailand, 510 West 6th Street, Suite 1212, Los Angeles, California 90014.

Trinidad and Tobago: Trinidad and Tobago Tourist Board, 400 Madison Avenue, Suite 712, New York, New York 10017.

Turkey: Turkish Tourism and Information Center, 500 5th Avenue, New York, New York 10036.

Virgin Islands: Virgin Islands Government Information Center, 16 West 49th Street, New York, New York 10020.

Yugoslavia: Yugoslavia State Tourist Office, 509 Madison Avenue, New York, New York 10023.

For students who plan to travel, the Student Identity Card ($2.50), available from Student Travel Services, 777 United Nations Plaza, New York, New York 10017, is a *must* for a spectacular range of travel discounts.

The books listed below will give you valuable information on stretching your travel dollar to its utmost.

Whole World Handbook: A Student Guide to Work, Study and Travel Abroad, 1976–1977, Council on International Educational Exchange, 777 United Nations Plaza, New York, New York 10017.

Latin America for the Hitchhiker, Bramsen and Hjort ($2.95) and *Student Guide to Asia,* Australian Union of Students ($3.95). Student Travel Services, 777 United Nations Plaza, New York, New York 10017.

Africa for the Hitchhiker, Bramsen and Hjort ($4.95). Student Travel Services, 777 United Nations Plaza, New York, New York 10017.

Vagabonding in Europe and North Africa, and *Vagabonding in America,* Ed Buryn. Berkeley, California, Bookworks (orders to Random House), 1973.

Europe on $10 a Day, Arthur Frommer. New York, Arthur Frommer, Inc., 1975. See also Arthur Frommer travel guides on specific countries and cities.

For dirt-cheap accommodations, both here and abroad, many of which include meals, refer to the next chapter: *Cheap Sleep: Motels and Monasteries.*

Bargains by Air

TOUR DE FORCE

Here's a relatively easy way to get free transportation to practically anywhere in the world. Get together a group of fifteen people who will agree to go on a trip with you and approach your airlines in the capacity of "tour conductor." The airlines will let you travel free in exchange for bringing them so much business, and they may be able to arrange free ground accommodations for you as well. If you can get a group of thirty together, you can also bring a friend along free.

For further information:

Consolidated Air Tour Manual (I), 3850 N.W. 30th Avenue, Miami, Florida 31142 (semiannual publication).

IT'S SMARTER TO CHARTER

If you're not the tour conductor type, a no-cost way to fly to Europe is to persuade 75 couples from a club to which you belong to charter an airplane. While the rental of a plane and crew is astronomically expensive, a flight to Europe averages out to less than $300 per person, round trip, split 150 ways. Naturally, as organizer, you'll include yourself and a friend in at no charge.

Warning: Travel clubs cannot charter, and one member of a family flying charter must have been a member of the club for at least six months. (The airlines don't want to make it too easy for you to take advantage of this spectacular moneysaver.)

For further information:

"Cheaper by the Charter," *Newsweek,* Vol. 86, 18 August 1975, page 63.

Jax-Fax: The Standard Reference Directory of Air Charter and Group Tour Availability, Jet Airtransport Exchange, Inc. (JAX), JAX Building, 9 Webbs Hill Road, Stamford, Connecticut 06903 (monthly—charter schedules).

OTC SERENDIPITY

OTC's (one-stop tour charters) are an excellent charter buy during the summer. These include air fare, ground transportation, and accommodations. Reservations must be made four to six weeks in advance. The local sales offices for such charter carriers as Capitol International, Overseas National, Saturn, Trans International, and World can arrange OTC's for you.

For further information:

Vacation Charter Flights for Everyone, National Air Carrier Association, Suite 710, 1730 M Street, N.W., Washington, D.C. 20036.

FORTNIGHT FARES

For that long-awaited, two-week European vacation, the two-week basic tour package is far and away the best deal offered by the conventional airlines. Special low rates are in effect from November through March (excluding Christmastime).

For example, a tour package including bargain accommodations, Continental breakfast, and a "two dinners for the price of one" deal costs $509—the exact same price as the straight round-trip fare. At other times of year, the tour package costs around $50 more than the straight air fare, which is still far cheaper than arranging separate accommodations.

Planning to take in some shows in Europe? For an extra $10 or $15, you can purchase five show tickets as part of the package.

PLAN AHEAD DEDUCTION

If you are able to plan a coast-to-coast (U.S.) or transatlantic air trip and buy your ticket two months in advance, you are in for a remarkable mark-down in fare. Traveling this way on Monday through Thursday round trip from Los Angeles to New York City, for example, will give you a solid 40 percent discount off the regular day coach fare, and close to 60 percent off the regular first-class fare! The discount on transatlantic flights amounts to almost 50 percent.

Note: Your trip must last between 22 and 45 days. There is a cancellation charge of $50 or 10 percent of your ticket, whichever is highest.

For further information:

"Fly Later, Pay Less," William Mead, *Money,* May 1975, pages 68–70.

EXCURSIONS ABROAD

If you can't plan your trip abroad two months in advance, but plan to stay for from 22 to 45 days, it's still possible to save more than 35 percent over the regular round-trip transatlantic air fare. How? Under the excursion plan.

On transpacific flights where your vacation lasts one to four months, you'll save a whopping 45 percent of the normal fare. You can make your reservations any time, and there is no cancellation charge.

Round trip from New York to London saves you well over $200 using this plan. Round trip from Los Angeles to Paris saves $400!

For further information:

"Bewildering Air Fares—What You Should Know," *U.S. News and World Report*, Vol. 78, 28 April 1975, pages 30–31.

DIRECTIONAL FARES

Extra low-cost excursion air fares, which cannot be advertised or sold in the United States, can be purchased only in the country where the flight originates. London, Singapore, and Bangkok are noted for such "directional fare" bargains. Details can be had from travel agencies in these cities.

For further information:

Whole World Handbook: A Student Guide to Work, Study, and Travel Abroad, Council on International Educational Exchange, 777 United Nations Plaza, New York, New York 10017 (orders to Simon & Schuster), 1974.

HALF PRICE HOPS

You can slash 50 percent off the cost of air fare from London to Paris (or vice versa) by taking one of Danair/Skyways' low-cost daily flights between these cities. Fares include bus transportation from Victoria Station (London) to Lydd Airport, a flight to Beauvais Airport (France), and a bus from the French airport to Paris. The fare: $31 (adults); $24 (children 2 to 10 years); $5 (children under 2).

For further information:

Danair/Skyways, Bilbao House, 36/38 New Broad Street, London EC2M INH, England.

BARGAINS FOR BOOKWORMS

A discount of 50 percent or more is available to the full-time student with a Student Identity Card on flights between European, Mediterranean, and Asian countries. For example, student flights from Madrid to London cost just $54 (a $151 savings over regular flights). The trip from Rome to Singapore costs just $304—a savings of $939 over regular flights.

For further information:

The 1976 Student Travel Catalog, Council on International Educational Exchange. Student Travel Services, 777 United Nations Plaza, New York, New York 10017, 1976. Arrangements for flights are also made through the Student Travel Services.

MAMMOTH MARKDOWNS

The full-time student can travel between European and African cities at an incredible 75 percent discount over regular fares! For example, the flight from Rome to Dar Es Salaam, Tanzania, costs $230 (you save $326); and Madrid to Monrovia, Liberia, costs just $133 (you save $253).

A Student Identity Card (see travel introduction) is a must.

For further information:

The 1976 Student Travel Catalog, Council on International Educational Exchange. Student Travel Services, 777 United Nations Plaza, New York, New York 10017.

MIDDLE EAST MELANGE

Some rock-bottom fares on Europe-Middle East flights are offered by Middle East Airlines. For example, you can take a daily flight from Rome to Beirut, Cairo, or Amman, for just $97, compared to $254 on most airlines.

The discount rate is available only for youths 12 through 25 years old; full-time students; and teachers with groups of ten or more students.

For further information:

Middle East Airlines, North American Headquarters, Suite 1606, 680 Fifth Avenue, New York, New York 10019.

STOPOVER SHREWDNESS

Should you be planning a *lot* of air travel with much stopping over for sightseeing in various countries, by all means look into the unlimited stopover tickets offered on long trips by all international airlines. Provided you don't double back on your tracks, these regular fare round-trip tickets offer stopovers anyplace along the way to your farthest destination, and on your way back from that destination, at no extra fee.

For example, the round-trip fare from the West Coast to Bangkok is $1,235 for a two- to three-week excursion. Since no stopovers are allowed, you must pay extra for any side trips you wish to make. By paying only $200 more on your round-trip ticket, you can stopover, going and coming, in Tokyo, Taipei, Manila, and Singapore—an enormous savings over the cost of individual side trips.

For further information:

Air Travel Bargains: How to Get the Lowest Fares on all Airlines World Wide and USA, From First Class to Charter, Jim Woodman, Jr., Miami, Florida, Air Travel Bargains World Wide Guidebook (orders to Simon & Schuster), 1974.

YEN FOR YOUTHS

If you're between the ages of 12 and 21, the airlines will give you a discount of $200 to $300 on transatlantic air fare. Return trip tickets are good for a year. The catch: You can't make reservations more than seven days prior to departure, so your plans must be flexible.

If you're under 22 and live near Canada or Mexico, taking Air Canada or Mexicana Airlines to Europe will save you $80 over the cost of student fares for New York-European trips offered by U.S. airlines. For youths leaving from such cities as Detroit, Buffalo, and Nogales, these extra low-cost flights are well worth considering.

For further information:

Air Canada, Suite 1100, 1888 Century Park East, Los Angeles, California 90067.

Mexicana Airlines, Suite 600, 851 Burlway Road, Burlingame, California 94010.

FAIRER FARES

Anyone associated with the academic field—full- or part-time students, staff, or teachers—can take advantage of special discount fares for scheduled airlines flying from the United States to Asia or Latin America.

For example, you can fly round trip from Miami to Bogota, Colombia, for $216, a $118 savings over the regular fare. Your ticket is good for 150 days. Another bargain: New York to Delhi, India, for $725 on a 120-day ticket (saves $1,023).

For further information:

Student Travel Services, 777 United Nations Plaza, New York, New York 10017. (Ask for information on "Scheduled flights from the United States to Latin America," or "Scheduled and charter flights from the United States to Asia.")

ICELANDIC—THE INDIVIDUALIST

The reason why the fares of the vast majority of airlines are precisely identical is this: Fares are fixed by the International Air Transport Association (IATA), a federal organization to whose dictates almost all airlines subscribe. The best-known airline to deviate from these fares is the IATA nonmember Icelandic Loftleidir.

Icelandic offers a transatlantic excursion fare for stays of up to 14 days which will save you more than $200 round trip over the rates of other airlines. They also offer discounts on other fares. Their advance purchase excursion fare, for example, is discounted about 5 percent over all other airlines. Cheap thrills, but no frills!

For further information:

Icelandic Loftleidir, 630 Fifth Avenue, New York, New York 10020.

GOVERNMENT GIMMICKS

Other IATA-ignoring fares have been ordered by the governments of Afghanistan, India, Ceylon, and Pakistan on flights to these countries. For instance, you can fly *round trip* from New York to Afghanistan for $150 less than the normal one-way fare!

For further information:

Whole World Handbook: A Student Guide to Work, Study, and Travel Abroad, Council on International Educational Exchange, 777 United Nations Plaza, New York, New York 10017 (orders to Simon & Schuster), 1974.

U.S. EXCURSIONS

Planning a round trip by air within the United States for 7 to 30 days? If you're going more than 1,500 miles round trip, you can purchase an excursion ticket for a discount of 25 percent off the regular fare—or as much as 30 percent if you travel at night. The savings for a Los Angeles–New York round trip amounts to about $100 a person.

Warning: You can't get this discount during "blackout periods" around Christmas, Easter, Thanksgiving, and other holidays.

For further information:

"Air Travel Can Still Be a Bargain," *Changing Times*, Vol. 29, March 1975, pages 6–9.

A SLEW OF STOPOVERS

For just $373, you can fly round trip from Los Angeles to New York, Washington, D.C., or Boston with *unlimited* stopovers and a short Puerto Rican vacation thrown into the bargain. How?

Puerto Rico is the key. A stopover there classifies your trip as international, thereby entitling you to the unlimited domestic stops.

For further information:

"Air-fare Savings," W. G. Moore, Jr., *Money*, July 1975, page 76.

NIGHT FLIGHT

Even on short notice for a quick round trip, you can often save 20 percent on your air fare within the United States by traveling between 9 P.M. and 2 A.M. The airlines save by not serving meals and by filling seats in off-hours. You can save around $70 on a Los Angeles–New York City round trip. Pretty good deal for a minor disruption of your biological clock!

For further information:

"Fare of Flying," Harry Steinberg, *Holiday*, Vol. 56, November 1975, pages 24–25.

ALLEGHENY GAINS

If you're planning on a tour of the northeastern United States, by all means take advantage of Allegheny Airlines' special package deal, which allows you to travel to any of 82 airports serving 150 cities in the northeast for only $129 (7-day pass); $152 (14 days); or $182 (21 days). Children under 12 travel at half price.

You must buy your ticket a week before leaving, stay away three days before returning home, and return either on a weekend or before noon on weekdays.

We know of one enterprising young man who used this special pass to travel 22,000 miles in 16 days, at a savings of $2,800 in standard fares!

For further information:

Allegheny Airlines, Executive Offices, Washington National Airport, Washington, D.C. 20001.

NO FRILLS FARES

Bowing to the inroads of inflation on the American way of thought, some airlines now offer no-frills flights between certain cities. On these flights, no meals are served, nor are any of the extras offered with which massive advertising campaigns for regular flights beguile our guilelessness. If you want entertainment in flight, better bring a good book, a pack of cards, or a jigsaw puzzle.

The reward for this pioneering spirit? A walloping third off your regular air fare. The practice currently applies between Miami and San Francisco, Los Angeles or New York, but popularity should see its expansion in the near future.

For further information:

"No Frills Flights," H. W. Shane, *Travel,* Vol. 143, May 1975, page 8.

CHEAPER BY THE DOZEN

The airlines are so anxious to have your whole family enjoy a trip that they offer substantial discounts for children.

Within the U.S.: Children under the age of 2 travel free. Children 2 through 11 get a discount of up to 35 percent off their parents' fares, depending on the plan the parents are traveling under. Wives pay the same as husbands.

Outside the U.S.: Family plans are available for East Coast to Puerto Rico or the Virgin Islands, and for West Coast to Samoa trips. The first adult pays full fare. The second immediate family member (adult or child) pays half price. The third and all succeeding family members pay only a quarter of the regular fare. Children under 2, as always, get the best deal—10 percent of the regular fare when accompanied by an adult.

For further information:

"Bewildering Air Fares—What You Should Know," *U.S. News and World Report,* Vol. 78, 28 April 1975, pages 30–31.

CARIBBEAN EXCURSIONS

Twenty-one-day excursion fares to the Caribbean offer outstanding opportunities to economize on a tropical vacation. For exam-

ple, Eastern Airlines offers a 40 percent discount on their weekend excursion fare from Miami to Jamaica, and a whopping 50 percent discount for excursion travel from Tuesday through Friday. For a couple, the savings in cold hard cash is close to $200.

For further information:

Eastern Airlines, Marketing Department, Miami International Airport, Miami, Florida 33148.

Air Jamaica Limited, 545 Fifth Avenue, New York, New York 10022.

FLYING SOUTH AMERICA

Planning on extensive sightseeing in Venezuela? A 17-day unlimited travel ticket is available for $120 through Avensa (a U.S. airline) or Linea Aeropostal Venezolana (a Venezuelan airline). These airlines will fly you to any of 51 Venezuelan airports. In Colombia, Avianca Airlines offers 30 days' unlimited travel at $95 (ten cities). In Argentina, 30 days of travel cost $129 through Argentine Airlines.

For further information:

Avensa, 7 West 57th Street, New York, New York 10019.

Linea Aeropostal Venezelana, Centro Capriles Plaza Venezuela, Caracas, Venezuela.

Avianca Airlines, 6 West 49th Street, New York, New York 10020.

Argentine Airlines, 9 Rockefeller Plaza, New York, New York 10020.

WRITE YOUR OWN TICKET

Are you a writer, reporter, or artist? If so, you are indeed fortunate. The governments of Brazil and Argentina have a policy of providing free air fare to their country for those who will give them favorable publicity in the form of newspaper or magazine articles, books, posters, or other promotional material.

To get details, write the Brazilian Embassy, 3006 Massachusetts Avenue, N.W., Washington, D.C. 20008, or the Argentinian Embassy, 1600 New Hampshire Avenue, N.W., Washington, D.C. 20009, on your letterhead, explaining the nature of your work.

Bargains by Sea

FREIGHTER FACTS

If you have more time than money, let us recommend crossing the ocean—any ocean—by freighter. Bargain prices, a relaxing ride (in smooth seas), and congenial shipmates are the fine points of this type of transportation. On a long trip, you can save as much as *half* the cost of passenger ship fare by taking a freighter instead.

For further information:

Klevens' Freighter Travel Letter, 6500 Kelvin Avenue, Canoga Park, California 91306 (monthly publication).

Glaessel Newsletter of Freighter Sailings, Glaessel Shipping Corp., 44 Whitehall Street, New York, New York 10004 (monthly publication.)

Freighter Travel News, Freighter Club of America, P.O. Box 504, Newport, Oregon 97365 (monthly publication).

Trav-L-Tips Freighter Bulletin, Bestseller Book Exchange, 40–21 Bell Boulevard, Bayside, New York 11361.

Siemer & Hand Ltd. Travel, Security Pacific Building, One Embarcadero Center, San Francisco, California 94111 (West Coast freighter departures).

SWITCH-A-ROO

Because the cost of living is higher in America than in most countries, freighter fares directly from the United States to a given destination are often higher than the combined rate of sailing first from a U.S. port to a European port, and then on to the desired point. For example: On the price of a freighter cruise from New York to Hong Kong via the Cape of Good Hope, you can cut travel costs in half (you save about $1,000) by changing freighters in Hamburg. Good cause to arrange for a European freighter switch-a-roo!

For further information:

Travel Routes Around the World: All the World's Passenger-Carrying Freighters, Fredric Tyarks et al. Greenlawn, New York, Harian, 1975.

EXCURSE YOURSELF!

If you expect to spend no more than 35 days in Europe and can arrange to travel eastbound between August 1 and May 31, or westbound between mid-September and mid-July, you'll qualify for a 15 percent excursion fare reduction on freighter travel. You need not return by the same line, and you can disembark at one European port and return from another port. The discount amounts to about $150 on the typical transatlantic round trip by freighter.

For further information:

Today's Outstanding Buys in Freighter Travel, Norman Ford and Margaret Drouet. Greenlawn, New York, Harian, 1975.

TOURING TIPS

Planning to take a freighter cruise to Europe, and then sightsee in several countries? Stretch those travel dollars by finding a freighter that normally calls at ports of the various countries in which you're interested. In most cases, you'll find it far less expensive to see these countries by ship than to embark upon a do-it-yourself tour.

For example, one Polish freighter's first European port of call after New York is Le Havre, France. It then calls at Rotterdam, Netherlands; Hamburg, Germany; and Gdynia, Poland. The cost to ride to the end of the line is only $20 more than getting off in Le Havre. It would be well nigh impossible to tour these countries on your own for such a paltry sum!

For further information:

Today's Outstanding Buys in Freighter Travel, Norman Ford and Margaret Drouet. Greenlawn, New York, Harian, 1975.

WINTER WISDOM

Chop 14 to 17 percent off the price of summer transatlantic sailing by traveling in the winter season. For transatlantic liner companies, the winter season lasts from mid-September to the end of March, eastbound; and from the beginning of November to mid-May, westbound.

For transatlantic freighter companies, winter season starts from the first of August and continues throughout May, eastbound; and from mid-September to mid-July, westbound.

For further information:

Harman's Official Guide to Cruise Ships, Jeanne Harman and Harry Harman. New York, Simon & Schuster, 1971.

FAMILY AFFAIRS

Here are a few special seafaring savings that apply to family members: All passenger liners and those freighters that allow children offer half fare for children under 12 and free passage for children less than a year old. In addition, if your spouse is crossing the Atlantic as a *bona fide* business or political convention delegate at anytime except during the summer season, you can accompany him or her at half price. This applies to the sea portion of your trip, whether you make the round trip by sea, or fly one way and sail the other.

For further information:

Ford's International Cruise Guide, Winter 1975–76, Merrian Clark. Woodland Hills, California, Merrian Clark, 1975.

TRAMPING ABOUT

If regular freighter fares—cheap though they be—are still too rich for your blood, you can save $100 to $200 round trip if you travel by *tramp* freighter. Whereas a regular freighter works on a set schedule between various points, a tramp does not. Picking up cargo and passengers where and when they can, these independents are happy to collect any fares that come their way.

Your main problem will be finding one that goes where you want to when you want to go there. The most obvious thing to do is to go to a major port and ask around.

Greek tramps are especially likely possibilities. Movements of a number of Dutch, German, and other European tramps leaving from Montreal, the East Coast, and the Gulf Coast have been consolidated by Bowerman Shipping Ltd., 7 Dock Square, Warrenpoint, Northern Ireland. Contact them for information.

STEAMSHIP SWITCH

Through the cooperation of a number of passenger ship lines (including some freighter services as well), an interchange system has been arranged to allow the voyager to switch over between member lines, and even many major airlines, for round trips in the area of northern Europe, Africa, Australia, and Japan. Stopovers are unlimited.

You get a 10 percent discount on sea fare and a 5 to 10 percent discount on air travel and some bus lines for round trips through these areas.

For further information:

P & O Lines, 155 Post Street, San Francisco, California 94108.

GROUP SCOOP

If you are able to get together a group of 15 adults—members of your club or church, for instance—for a cruise, and are willing to avoid traveling in the peak (summer) season, you can all get a 15 percent fare reduction.

That's almost $200 for the typical transatlantic tourist-class round trip by passenger liner. You may even go one way by air, and still get the group rate for the ocean portion of your trip.

A group of 15 or more students (ages 16 to 28) who are traveling together to school sometime other than during the peak season are entitled to the same discount.

For further information:

Guide to the Cruise Vacation: A Practical, Helpful and Interesting Analysis of the Cruise as a Vacation with Facts and Figures on Cruise Ships and Ports of Call, Steven Stern. Hicksville, New York, Exposition Press, 1974.

Student Rates on Transatlantic Ship Sailings, Student Travel Services, 777 United Nations Plaza, New York, New York 10017.

THE WELL ROUNDED VOYAGE

By planning your round-trip transatlantic sea voyages in the off-season (eastbound, August through May; westbound, mid-September to mid-July), you may be able to latch onto a mellow 5 to 10 percent discount. For example, the Marchessini Line offers its lowest-priced round-trip fare at $57 less than two equivalent one-way tickets. You need not take the same line on your return trip, and you can even *fly* back from Europe and still get the round-trip discount on the sea portion of your journey.

In other than transatlantic travel, this discount generally applies to 14- to 200-day trips any time of year, and can save you several hundred dollars. For example, for the least expensive Orient Overseas Line fare from Los Angeles to Hong Kong, a round-trip ticket saves you $233 over two one-way tickets.

For further information:

Travel Routes Around the World, Fredric Tyarks, et al. Greenlawn, New York, Harian (orders to Grosset & Dunlap), 1973.

TOUR LURE

If the idea of a guided tour in Europe appeals to you, consider a European passenger liner cruise with a tour attached. You must prepay a specified amount of land-tour costs; in exchange, you get 15 percent off the one-way ocean fare—about $80. You must go along with an escorted tour of 15 or more adults and be willing to travel some time other than peak season. You can go one way by sea and one way by air, and still get the discount on your sea fare.

For further information:

Cruises and Tours Everywhere, 250 West 57th Street, New York, New York 10019 (monthly periodical).

CRUISING CAPER

You can spend your two-week vacation cruising the Bahamas on a yacht for $200 or $300, meals included. This combination form of transportation, lodging, and meals will cost you far less than the typical hotel vacation. And what a change of pace!

Cruises to the Bahamas leave from Florida; to the Mexican Coast from the U.S. West Coast; and to the Maine coastline from Penobscot Bay.

For specifics, see display and classified ads in *Yachting, Sea, Boating*, and *Motor Boating and Sailing*.

MEDITERRANEAN NAVIGATION

Students can cross the Mediterranean at a savings of 40 percent by using Hellenic Mediterranean Lines, 555 Fifth Avenue, New York, New York 10017. For example, Hellenic will take you from Venice to Piraeus for just $36, and from Piraeus to Haifa for $84.

You can also cross the Adriatic Sea for a measly $19 on the Brindisi–Patras car ferry. Write for "Student Rates on Mediterranean Ship Sailings," Student Travel Services, 777 United Nations Plaza, New York, New York 10017.

CANOEING CANAPÉS

For $5 a day, two people can spend a week canoeing and fishing in the wilderness lakes between northern Minnesota and southern Ontario. The $5 covers the cost of renting a canoe and fishing gear. If you also rent camping gear but buy your own freeze-dried foods, a team of two can make it on $7 or $8 a day.

The area, called Boundary Waters Canoe Area in the United States and Quetico Provincial Park in Canada, has been specifically set aside for canoeists—and is a virtual paradise for those wishing to get away from it all.

For further information:

Chamber of Commerce, Ely, Minnesota 55731 (maps and lists of canoeing outfitters).

Superior National Forest, Forest Supervisor, P.O. Box 338, Duluth, Minnesota 55801 (maps and brochure).

District Forester, Department of Lands and Forests, Fort Frances, Ontario (information on Quetico Provincial Park).

Bargains by Land

A RAILROADING ROUNDELAY

Almost everyone has heard about the Eurailpass, which allows unlimited railway travel in thirteen countries of Europe for a lump sum. This pass, which must be purchased in the United States from a travel agent or a European Railway Office, represents a great bargain for those who plan on extensive travel—and European trains are an experience in themselves.

If you're planning to travel extensively in only one country, however, consider such one-country unlimited travel passes as BritRail Pass and the Swiss Holiday Pass. The British pass is also good for some bus lines,

boats, and ferries; the Swiss pass can be used for travel by lake steamer and postal motorcoach as well as by train. As with the Eurailpass, you *must* purchase your Swiss Holiday Pass and BritRail Pass in the United States. Switzerland also offers a half-fare pass, purchasable at the border, for a specific itinerary.

Other countries likewise offer rail passes at reduced rates. For example, an unlimited-travel Austrailpass, at $94 to $295 for 2 weeks to 3 months, is available from Thomas Cook travel agents in North America, Europe, South Africa, Japan, and from New Zealand railways. An unlimited railroad pass to six South American countries for $60 (1 month), $90 (2 months), or $110 (3 months) can be bought from the Association Latina Americana de Ferrocarriles, Paracas 50, Buenos Aires, Argentina. A Canrailpass (Canadian National Railways) allows one month's travel between October 1 and April 30 for $119 (purchasable in United States only).

For further information:

Eurailpass, P.O. Box 90, Bohemia, New York 11716.

BritRail Travel International, Inc., 270 Madison Avenue, New York, New York 10016.

Swiss Federal Railways, 608 Fifth Avenue, New York, New York 10020.

"Around Europe on a Rail Pass," Tom Grimm, *Los Angeles Times*, 7 March 1976, Part VII, page 4 (Ireland, Finland, Australia).

AMTRAK FACTS

Your family can travel at a considerable discount on the network of train lines Amtrak has woven across America. To get this discount, you must begin traveling on some day *other* than a Friday or Sunday. The lowdown: Wives, as well as children 12 to 21, travel at three-quarters fare; children 2 to 11 at three-eighths fare; and kiddies under two squeeze in for free.

Amtrak also offers unlimited travel for 14, 21, or 30 days at $150, $200, and $250, with family discounts available as above. Groups of 15 or more adults can obtain discounts of one eighth to one fourth, but must contact an Amtrak sales office in advance for approval.

For further information:

Amtrak, Marketing Department, 955 L'Enfant Plaza North, S.W., Washington, D.C. 20024.

GROUP RAILROADING

Railroading with a group can get you discounts on a number of European railroads. Swiss Federal Railways and Austrian Railways, for example, offer a 20 percent discount to groups of ten or more. French National Railways offers a solid 30 percent discount to such groups. Here, families can also participate in savings. The first two persons in a family making a round trip or circular tour pay full fare. The rest pay a fourth, and children aged 4 to 10 pay only one eighth of the regular fare!

For further information:

Swiss Federal Railways, 608 Fifth Avenue, New York, New York 10020.

Austrian Travel Agency, 101 Park Avenue, New York, New York 10017.

French National Railways, 610 Fifth Avenue, New York, New York 10020.

YOUTHFUL TRAINING

If you're a student aged 14 to 25, and plan on some heavy European traveling, get yourself a Student-Railpass. For just $195, this moderately priced pass, available through travel agents, entitles you to two months of second-class railroading in thirteen European countries.

A Youth Pass is likewise available for Great Britain. Costing $50 to $120 for one week's to one month's travel, this pass may be obtained through a travel agent of BritRail Travel International, 270 Madison Avenue, New York, New York 10016. Both the Student-Railpass and the Youth Pass must be purchased before leaving the United States.

In Ireland, a combination train/bus ticket gives students 8 days of riding for $24, 15 days for $36, and 30 days for $48. A similar setup is available for nonstudents. Write to CIEE, P.O. Box 1975, Boston, Massachusetts 02125; or the Irish Tourist Board, 590 Fifth Avenue, New York, New York 10036.

For further information:

Official Student Guide to Europe 1970–71, New York, Essandess Specials (orders to Simon & Schuster), 1970.

THE SENIOR RAILROADER

The senior citizen traveling in Switzerland can take advantage of an unbelievable travel bargain. A $28 senior pass is available which allows a whole year of travel within the country at half price. It also entitles women over 62 and men over 65 to reductions in hotel rates during the off-season.

In Austria, women over 60 and men over 65 can purchase an ID at any rail station, allowing them a 50 percent discount on rail travel. And in France, women over 60 and men over 65 may inexpensively purchase a Carte Vermeil. This entitles them to a 30 percent discount on railway fares anywhere in the country.

Other countries offering senior citizen rail discounts include Canada, Germany, Denmark, Norway, Sweden, and Spain.

For further information:

Swiss National Tourist Office, 608 Fifth Avenue, New York, New York 10020.

Austrian Travel Sales Organization, Inc., 545 Fifth Avenue, New York, New York 10017.

French National Railroads, 610 Fifth Avenue, New York, New York 10020.

"Around Europe on a Rail Pass," Tom

Grimm, *Los Angeles Times*, 7 March 1976, Part VII, page 4.

STUDENTS IN INDIA

Foreign students can get a 50 percent discount on third-class train travel anywhere in India. Using this rugged, dirt-cheap method, for example, the fare from Calcutta to Bombay is a mere $4. Or, students can pay full third-class fare and travel second-class, or pay second-class fare and travel first-class.

You will need an International Student Identity Card ($2) from the Council on International Educational Exchange, 777 United Nations Plaza, New York, New York 10017, as well as an official letter from your school identifying you as a student. The letter has to be verified by the U.S. Consulate in Delhi, Bombay, or Katmandu.

BUS BARGAINS

If you plan to do a lot of bus traveling within the United States and Canada on your vacation, look into the one-week ($76), two-week ($125), one-month ($175), and two-month ($250) passes offered by Continental Trailways and Greyhound.

To give you an idea of the savings involved, a round-trip ticket from New York to San Diego costs close to $260. If you plan to make the trip in a month, a vacation pass will cost you about $85 less. And you may stop over wherever you wish along the way at no extra cost.

For further information:

Continental Trailways, 1500 Jackson Street, Dallas, Texas 75201.

Greyhound Bus Lines, 111 West Clarendon Avenue, Phoenix, Arizona 85013.

BLIND BENEFITS

The blind can apply to The American Foundation for the Blind, 15 West 16th Street, New York, New York 10011, for a travel identification card. This card entitles both them and a friend or guide to travel on the interstate bus systems, Greyhound and Continental Trailways, for the normal one-person fare.

Through this foundation, the blind can also get coupons that will entitle them and a guide to a 25 percent fare discount on the Amtrak rail system.

AUSTRALIAN ANOMALIES

Hundreds of dollars' worth of land transportation savings await you in Australia. For $176, you can obtain a 30-day unlimited-mileage express bus pass from the Ansett-Pioneer motorcoach line. Ansett-Pioneer also offers a two-week sightseeing pass for major cities and resorts at $57. And on the Australian island of Tasmania, you can rent a car from any of a dozen firms for $1.25 a day. Of course, there are no roads in Tasmania. . . .

For further information:

Holmes Associates, P.O. Box 126, Ross, California 94957.

BITING THE BIG APPLE

On weekends and holidays from 10 A.M. to 6 P.M., $1.25 will buy you a ticket to Manhattan's Culture Bus Loop I Tour. This entitles you to a tour of twenty-two points of interest ranging from Grant's Tomb to Times Square, from Central Park to the Empire State Building, as well as a 44-page illustrated tour guidebook. You can stop to examine the attractions, then board a later bus on the line. Taking advantage of this bargain saves you $10 to $15 over the cost of the more conventional bus tours.

A similar tour of Brooklyn and downtown Manhattan, Culture Bus Loop II ($1.25) takes in thirty-two stops including Greenwich Village, the United Nations, and the World Trade Center. Buses run every twenty minutes from 9 A.M. to 6 P.M. on weekends and holidays.

For further information:

Metropolitan Transportation Authority, Marketing Division, 1700 Broadway, New

158   A TORRENT OF TRAVEL TIPS

York, New York 10019. Ask for the Culture Bus Loop I (or II) Tour details.

WEEKENDERS

Many auto rental agencies offer a weekend or three-day rental plan at a substantial savings over the day-by-day rental rate. For example, through Hertz Rent A Car you can rent a medium-sized car for a 200-mile trip out of San Diego lasting from Friday afternoon through Monday afternoon for $16 less than the weekday rate with similar mileage. These deals differ from agency to agency, but most offer some weekend discount plan.

For further information:

"Car Rentals: Getting the Best Deal," Douglas Lidster, *Better Homes & Gardens*, Vol. 54, January 1976, page 26.

EUROPEAN AUTO SHARING

Driving in Europe? Passengers to share driving and gas can be found in Paris through PROVOYA, 219 bis, Boulevard Saint Germain, Paris 7e, France (tel. 544-12-92).

If you need transportation from Paris to any point in Europe, call PROVOYA for a lift ($2 registration fee).

RENTAL RUDIMENTS

While renting a car in Europe is far from being the cheapest way to travel, you may have decided that this method is the most pleasurable for you. Rental costs vary greatly from city to city. The least expensive European cities in which to rent a car are Amsterdam, Munich, Frankfurt, and Copenhagen.

For further information:

"Inexpensive Auto Rentals for Do-it-yourself Travel," *Europe on $10 a Day, 1975–76 Edition*, Arthur Frommer. New York, Arthur Frommer, Inc., 1975.

AUTO ACADEMIA

Students, staff, and faculty at high schools, colleges, and universities can rent, lease, or buy a car in Europe at special academic discounts. Typical rental rates: $98 for one week; $468 for six weeks. One outfit even throws in a two-man tent with every car rental.

Also, Fiats, Volkswagens, and Volvos are for sale overseas at discounts of up to $125 for the academic community.

For further information:

Student Car Plan, Car Plan Headquarters, Suite 2560, 420 Lexington Avenue, New York, New York 10017.

CAR CAPERS

One of the cheapest ways to get around overseas, and one of the most convenient, is to buy a used car from a dealer when you arrive, and then resell it to him just before you leave. We've known people who have worked this plan successfully in countries as diverse as Great Britain and New Zealand. No doubt it will work in any country where the used-car dealer abides.

Depending on your bargaining power, you can save about 50 percent over renting or leasing a car abroad in the conventional way. Make sure that your auto has been approved for the use to which you wish to put it, and that you have adequate insurance. Of course, you'll want to have a written "buy back" agreement from the dealer before any money changes hands.

For further information:

How to Buy and Sell a Used Car in Europe, Gil Friedman. San Francisco, Yara Press, 1972.

INDIAN ADVENTURES

Travel the streets of Indian cities at *half* the usual taxi prices and with twice the local color by using a motordriven rickshaw! Or, hire a bicycle rickshaw for half again as much. Or, rent your own bicycle in any major city at just 25¢ a day!

For further information:

Whole World Handbook: A Student Guide to Work, Study, and Travel Abroad, Council on

International Educational Exchange, 777 United Nations Plaza, New York, New York 10017 (orders to Simon & Schuster), 1974.

BICYCLING THE WORLD

Planning a trip to Europe? Consider renting a bike there, where cycling is a major form of transportation, or taking your own bike along. In fact, you can enjoy this combination pastime, transportation mode, and physical fitness program just about anywhere in the world. A multitude of organizations exist for the pleasure of your participation.

International Bicycle Touring Society, c/o Dr. Clifford Graves, 846 Prospect Street, La Jolla, California 92037, helps set up long bike trips on a worldwide scale for experienced bicyclists. The Bicycle Touring League of America, Roland Geist, 260 West 26th Avenue, New York, New York 10001, can give you a wealth of touring information. *Le Cycliste*, 18, rue du Commandeur, Paris 14e, France; can provide you with the latest bicycling news of that country.

HITCH WITH A SWITCH

While the outstretched thumb is without a doubt the cheapest form of transportation around, an undeniable drawback to this time-honored method is the fact that freeway hitchhiking is illegal in most states. The next best thing to hitching is to get together with someone who has a car, or to share your car with several other people for that cross-country trek. Check the bulletin boards of local colleges and universities, and watch newspaper classifieds.

If there are any share-a-ride agencies in your area (the student union at a local college may put you onto one), take advantage of their services. Agencies that match drivers with riders for a small fee include Share-the-Gas, 924 Presidential Street, Brooklyn, New York 11231; New York Ride Center, 159 West 33rd Street, New York, New York 10001; Peoples' Transit Inc., P.O. Box 8393, Port-

land, Oregon 97207, tel. (800) 547-0933; and Travelers Aid Society, with offices in most United States cities.

For further information:

Vagabonding in America, Ed Buryn. Berkeley, California, Bookworks, 1973.

POLISH UP YOUR ACT

You can travel throughout Poland—a grand total of 1,116 miles—for $2.75! All you need is a special auto-stop booklet from ALMATUR, 9 Ordynacka Street, 00-364 Warsaw, Poland. You dispense coupons from the booklet to drivers who pick you up. They send the coupons to a special lottery, with a chance to win big prizes. With this impetus, you can get a ride faster than you can catch a bus in Poland, and the price can't be beat!

Sightseeing, Shopping, and Serendipity

If you find yourself caught in a foreign country minus vital supplies—anything from shower caps to ski clothes—don't buy from that tourist shop at your hotel where the salespeople speak perfect English. Hie yourself down to the bargain basement of the large department store, where local people jostle for cut-rate prices. Not only will you save valuable traveling dollars, but you'll add one more experience to your world-roaming "repertoire." And don't be afraid to haggle over prices—in most foreign countries, it's expected of you!

One more word to the wary: Nothing can be more disheartening than that unexpected confrontation with the customs man over the treasures you're trundling home. Avoid unnecessary duties by boning up on customs regulations and restrictions in the booklet *Know Before You Go* (232D), Consumer Information, Public Documents Distribution Center, Pueblo, Colorado 81009 (1974—55¢).

TOUTABLE TRAVEL CLUBS

If you're doing, or would dearly like to do a lot of traveling, check out one of the many travel clubs around. These offer unbeatable travel deals and tour packages that will save you hundreds of dollars per trip!

For example, an $8 membership fee to the $10-a-Day Travel Club will buy you two low-cost-travel guides to countries of your choice, $100 worth of New York attraction coupons, and numerous reductions on lodging, restaurant, auto-rental, and tourist-service prices in the United States and abroad. You'll also get the club's quarterly newsletter, which lists club members who will put you up all over the world, as well as members who would like to share a trip and so cut costs.

Another bargain bringer is Pat and Buddy's Travel Club, offering combination tour-charter trips, as well as a monthly newsletter. The membership fee is $25 (singles) or $35 (families).

For further information:

$10-a-Day Travel Club, Inc., 70 Fifth Avenue, New York, New York 10011.

How to Fly Major Airlines at the Lowest Possible Cost. Pat and Buddy's Travel Club, Suite Eight, 387 Park Avenue South, New York, New York 10016 (free).

Other travel clubs are listed in the travel section of the *Encyclopedia of Associations*, Vol. 1, Margaret Fisk, ed., Detroit, Gale Research Company, 1975 (at your library).

TRAVEL TIMING

For almost every destination, air fares and/or hotel rates are cheaper during the "off-season." But there are just about as many "off-seasons" as there are destinations. In Mexico, the Caribbean, the Bahamas, Arizona, and the California deserts, for example, you can travel cut-rate from May through early December.

In Canada, Europe, Japan, North Africa, and Alaska, you will get lower rates on air fare and accommodations any time *except* June through August. Then there are the individualist areas such as Las Vegas (off-season February to April); Florida (off-season May to mid-June, plus September to mid-December); Bermuda (mid-November to mid-March); and Argentina (April to June, and mid-September to mid-December).

Finally, areas where rates remain constant year-round include Hong Kong, most of the United States, coastal California (except resort areas); and Brazil (except during Mardi Gras).

For further information:

Better Times, Frances Cerra, ed., New York, Doubleday Dolphin, 1975.

LOW-PRICED LUGGAGE

One way or another, many pieces of luggage are dented or otherwise damaged by airlines enroute to your destination. It is the airlines' responsibility to replace such items, which leaves them with a lot of damaged luggage on their hands.

Call airlines in your area and ask who they sell these damaged goods to. You can get such luggage, after it has been repaired, at outlets named by the airlines for a mere 25 percent of the original retail price.

For further information:

The Traveler's Guide to Luggage, How to Choose It and Use It. The Traveler's Guide to Luggage, 300 East 44th Street, New York, New York 10017 (send 25¢ plus a self-addressed, stamped, long envelope).

MAP MISCELLANY

Yes, indeed! A *free* full-color atlas of the world can be yours! Write to Hammond, Inc., 515 Valley, Maplewood, New Jersey 07040, for your copy.

GUIDEBOOK GUILDERS

No need to plunk down $5 to $25 for travel guidebooks when you roam the United

States and its possessions. A wealth of information—booklets, maps, brochures, photographs, and posters—is available free from state divisions of tourism or travel and city chambers of commerce across the land.

For a list of state travel information sources, see "Facts for Tourists on Each and Every State," *Changing Times*, July, 1975, pages 41–42. For chamber of commerce addresses, see *World Wide Chamber of Commerce Directory*, Loveland, Colorado, Johnson (annual), at your library.

Other sources of free travel information include oil company headquarters (maps, routes, lodging, restaurants); airlines, railroads, ship and ferry lines, bus lines (travel brochures), and travel agents.

For further information:

"Fifteen Fabulous Maps Free for the Asking," *Moneysworth*, 20 January 1975, page 10.

JUNGLE JOURNEY

For a truly unique adventure at rock-bottom prices, consider a horseback trek through the jungles of Chiapas, the southernmost of Mexico's states. At $2 a day for a horse, and $4 a day for a guide with his horse, both of which can be hired in San Cristobal Las Casas, the state capital, you will be paying a mere one-tenth of U.S. prices for such a trek.

For further information:

"Travel Through the Jungle on Horseback," Jean-Louis Etienne and Sondi Field, *The Great Escape: A Source Book of Delights and Pleasures for the Mind and Body*, Min Yee, ed. New York, Bantam, 1974.

CURRENCY CAPERS

When traveling, you'll get a higher exchange rate on your dollars at banks and foreign exchange offices—rather than at hotels, restaurants, and shops. Retail establishments must give the lower rate in order to protect themselves against sudden unfavorable currency fluctuations.

Another tip: Before leaving on your trip, buy small denomination travelers' checks so that you can convert foreign currency a little at a time. This way you will not be stuck with large amounts of currency from one country (which will cost extra to convert a second time) when you cross over to another or when you return home.

For further information:

"Exchanging Your Travel Checks," Joel Sleed, *Los Angeles Times*, 7 December 1975, Part X, page 11.

MARKDOWN FOR MINORS

For Canadian visitors under 21, it is well worth the $3 membership fee to join the Swing-Air Club formed by Air Canada and Canadian National Railways.

Membership bargains include a 20 percent standby discount on Air Canada, as well as reductions for many other Canadian airlines; discounts of 10 to 20 percent on Canadian National Railways, depending on the day of week; and discounts of 50 percent on most hotels run by Canadian National, and other hotels as well.

For further information:

Air Canada's Swing-Air Club, 1 Place Ville Marie, Montreal 113, Quebec, Canada.

MOBILE LAUNDROMAT

You probably won't believe this no-cost clothes-laundering technique until you try it, but ranchers of the western United States have been using it successfully for decades. If you plan on a fair amount of driving in a dirt-road or bumpy-road area, such as in many foreign countries or the rural United States, place your dirty clothes in a milk can or other large container, add soap and hot water, cover securely, and place in your vehicle.

We used this method on a two-month trip across the United States last year. Not only did it save us $10 in laundromat charges, but our clothes came out sparkling clean!

For further information:

"Hand Washers," Norman Soloman, *The Updated Last Whole Earth Catalog: Access to Tools,* Pam Cokeley, ed. *The Whole Earth Catalog,* Box 428, Sausalito, California 94965, May 1974, page 201.

BUDGET BREAKFASTS

If rolls and coffee, the traditional Continental breakfast, are not served free with your European lodging, order them at a bar or sidewalk café. According to Arthur Frommer, author of *Europe on $10 a Day,* you'll save two-thirds on your breakfast check by eating here, rather than at a full-fledged restaurant.

MENU MADNESS

In European restaurants, you'll profit greatly by asking the waiter for a fixed-price menu, which is considerably cheaper than à la carte and which often will not be presented unless it is specifically requested. Second, check the fine print on your menu for an overlarge cover charge.

In Europe, as opposed to the United States, it's the custom for restaurants to display their menu near the outside entrance to their establishment. Avoid embarrassment —and a gouging—by checking menu prices of such establishments *before* entering. Be especially aware of those restaurants that *don't* display their menus on the outside.

BARGAINS IN BRITAIN

Stateside tailored menswear will cost you an arm and a leg—which will make that suit hang at a rather awkward angle. If you expect to spend several weeks in London, have a tailor whip up a suit for you at half the U.S. prices. Or, if you haven't much time, shop at such purveyors of fine ready-made menswear as Burton's Tailoring, 114 Regent Street.

For well-made women's woolen sweaters at half the prices of the land of the free, try the sales rack of such department stores at Marks and Spencer, on Oxford Street.

For those of you with scholarly inclina-

tions, books can be bought at similar discounts at Foyle's, Charing Cross Road.

For further information:

Fodor's Europe, 1976, Eugene Fodor, ed. New York, David McKay, 1976.

DUTCH DELIGHTS

Shopping in Amsterdam? Fine art reproductions and quality posters can be had for $5 and under at Kunsthandel Verkerke, Leidsestraat 12; at Stedelijk Museum, Paulus Potterstraat 13; and at the Ryksmuseum, Stadhouderskade 13.

For about the same price, you can get authentic wooden shoes at A.W.G. Otten, 102 Albert Cuypstraat. Our last suggestion: Pick up some hand-painted tiles at Kunsthandel Rembrandt, 61 Rokin, for only a few dollars each.

For further information:

Fodor's Holland, 1976, Eugene Fodor, ed. New York, David McKay, 1976.

TAX FREE TREATS

The tax-free international airport shops of Europe are truly a shopper's delight. The biggest and best of these is the free shopping center at the Schippol International Airport in Amsterdam, where a veritable sea of tax-free merchandise temptingly beckons the bargain-hunting tourist.

Liquor is cheaper here than anywhere else in Europe—less than half the price charged stateside. Dutch cigars and fine perfumes are other excellent buys.

For further information:

"Bargains Fly at Airport Emporiums, Percy Rowes, *Moneysworth,* 17 February 1975, page 7.

WATCH YOUR DOLLARS!

In all Switzerland, Lucerne is by far the cheapest place to buy the fine watches for which this country is famous. Many small shops there offer superior timepieces at a 40 percent discount off U.S. prices.

You should find the watchsellers at Birnhaum's, Pilatusstrasse 34, to be friendly faces in a sea of strangers. In addition to offering low prices, they are an excellent free source of tourist information, and will even make dinner reservations and hold letters for you!

SAVIN' IN COPENHAGEN

This is the place to go for designer-quality yard goods at half the price they would cost in the U.S.—that is, if you were fortunate enough to find such lovely material domestically.

Such large department stores as Anva's, which is near the railroad station, sell a wide array of ultramodern merchandise—teakwood candlesticks and salad bowls, ceramics, and stainless steel. Such style just isn't available in the U.S. unless it has been imported—and at what prices!

For further information:

Scandinavia on $10 a Day, 1973–74 Edition, Stanley Haggart and Darwin Porter. New York, Arthur Frommer, Inc., 1973.

FLORENTINE FINERY

Florence is the place to buy leather and ladies' wear. Where to get the best bargains in town? At the open-air stalls and carts that line the street near the Mercato Centrale.

You can get beautiful ladies' gloves, leather wallets, cigarette cases, notebooks, and change purses for under $5. Women's silk blouses, mohair sweaters, and leather briefcases and suitcases go for less than $10 apiece. And don't pay more than 75 percent of the asking price, tops.

For further information:

Street Markets: London, Paris, Rome, Florence, Madrid, Carol Cohen. New York, Grosset & Dunlap, 1973.

PRICES IN PARIS

It's easy to lose your shirt in Paris. Like to know where you can buy one instead—for less than $5? Try the Prisunic, a bargain dime store on the Champs Elyseés. For fine but moderately priced copies of the women's dresses that make Paris famous, try such department stores as the Galeries Lafayettes.

Looking for art reproductions at one third to one half of U.S. prices? Try the museum store at the Louvre, and the Museum of Modern Art.

It is said that some of the best and most trustworthy buys (be careful—imitations are plentiful) in fine perfumes can be had at Paul's, 210, rue de Rivoli, and at other high-class perfume houses.

For further information:

Fielding's Selective Shopping Guide to Europe 1976, Temple Fielding and Nancy Fielding. West Caldwell, New Jersey, Fielding (orders to William Morrow), 1975.

ROMAN RELICS

For the full flavor of Rome, and the opportunity of latching onto some rare bargains in secondhand goods, visit one of the many flea markets of the Eternal City. On Sunday mornings, you can try the fantabulous flea market at Porta di Portese, in the Trastevere section. Everything from antiques to used toothbrushes are sold there!

On weekdays, try the flea market at the Piazza di Fontanella Borghese, selling reproductions, posters, and etchings. In either case, the pigeon that pays more than half the asking price deserves to get rooked!

For further information:

The Blue Guides: Rome and Environs, Stuart Rossiter, ed. Chicago, Rand McNally, 1971.

MOMENTOS OF MADRID

Some of your best buys in Madrid are leather goods. Leather shoes for under $10 can be purchased at Los Guerrilleros, on the Puerta del Sol. Leather-backed gloves for a few dollars; saffron, a unique gift idea and a spice which would cost ten times as much in the United States; and the famous Spanish toilet soap Maja Jabon (at half U.S. prices) can be bought in such discount centers as the Oportunidades, which is the bargain basement of the Galerias Preciados.

For further information:

Spain on $5 and $10 a Day, 1974–75, Stanley Haggart and Darwin Porter. New York, Arthur Frommer, Inc., 1974.

13

CHEAP SLEEP: MOTELS AND MONASTERIES

Ye gads! At $20 to $30 a night, it takes a Rockefeller to afford a motel room. Then again, the big R's probably own 'em, so they don't have to pay the fee.

If the high cost of lodging is thwarting your dreams of travel, take heart. With the following information, you'll be footloose and fancy-free without giving accommodation costs a second thought. Many thousands of comfortable beds in cut-rate motels, hotels, farmhouses, truck stops, rustic cabins, student dormitories, country inns, private homes—and even monasteries—in the United States and abroad can be yours free for the asking or at a small fraction of the normal rate. It's just a matter of knowing where to find them!

For details on accommodations for specific countries, check the introduction to the previous chapter, "A Torrent of Travel Tips," for references and tourist-office addresses. Also read *Directory of Low-Cost Accommodations*, Commission on Voluntary Service and Action, 475 Riverside Drive, New York, New York 10027, and *Where to Stay USA (from 50¢ to $10 a Night)*, Council on International Educational Exchange, Student Travel Services, 777 United Nations Plaza, New York, New York 10017.

Here

CRASH CASH

You don't need cash to spend the night at any of hundreds of crash pads scattered across the United States. At most, the donation 50¢ to $1.00 is optional. Others are just plain free! Accommodations may consist of a mattress on the floor, or just a place to lay your sleeping bag, but the atmosphere is congenial and the price unbeatable.

For a copy of *Crashing in North America*, a directory of cooperatives that will put you up, write the North American Student Cooperative Organization, 1500 Gilbert Court, Ann Arbor, Michigan 48105.

Or, check with the local Hotline switchboard, or Information Referral Service. Two good Hotline directories: *National Directory of Hotline Switchboards and Related Services*, Ken Beiter, ed., The Exchange, 311 Cedar Avenue South, Minneapolis, Minnesota 55404, 1973; and *Western Regional Directory for Hotlines and Other Related Services in the Western United States*, L. Almeda Decell, ed., The Current, P.O. Box 2526, Huntington Beach, California 92647, 1974.

BATH BEDS

The cheapest possible places to spend the night including the option to exercise, steam, and sauna are the baths found in every large- or medium-sized city. But in the midwest, you can purchase a stay of from 12 to 24 hours in the baths, with private room, for just $3.

See your Yellow Pages under "Baths" or "Health clubs."

TRUCKIN' TALE

Save a third on the cost of conventional motels by spending your nights at truck stops. While truckers get first bid at the facilities, a call ahead will let you know if any rooms are available. Such stops often serve good, inexpensive food as well.

For further information:

24-Hour Full-Service Auto-Truck Stops, Reymont Associates, 29-T Reymont Avenue, Rye, New York 10580 (lists over 500 stops, $2.50).

DOUBLE THE PLEASURE

Spend two nights for the price of one in any of over 200 nationally known hotels or motels. Your $11.00 membership fee to R.E.C.C.O. Official Travel Club, P.O. Box 15384, Fort Lauderdale, Florida 33318, entitles you to this discount at such well-known motel chains as Holiday Inns, Ramada Inns,

Best Western, and Travelodges for a full year following your subscription.

SENIOR HOLIDAYS

If you're over 55 and wish to stay at any of a thousand Holiday Inns around the world at a 10 percent discount, harken to this. Joining the National Council of Senior Citizens, Inc., 1511 K Street, N.W., Washington, D.C. 20005, entitles you to this rate reduction. Costs $5 for a couple to join, less for a single.

Every Holiday Inn has a directory of motels that offer the discount, provided you show your National Council of Senior Citizens membership card upon registering.

STUDENT SERENDIPITY

Students planning to visit one of the three U.S. biggies—New York, Los Angeles, or San Francisco—can plan on comfortable accommodations with other congenial students for $8 or less a night.

The Council on International Educational Exchange New York Student Center, Room 2273, Hotel McAlpin, Broadway and 34th Street, New York, New York 10001, will provide you with lodging in a three- or four-bedded room at $7.50 per person, or in a twin-bedded room at $8.50. If you're traveling alone, they will place you with others.

In Los Angeles, the Los Angeles Student Center, Northrop University Residence Halls, 733 South Hindry Avenue, Inglewood, California 90301, offers lodging from June 30 to September 1 in twin-bedded suites with shared baths at $5 per person a night, or $6 with American breakfast.

And in Baghdad-by-the-bay, the San Francisco Student Center, Hotel Stratford, 242 Powell Street, San Francisco, California 94102, will rent you a single for $8, or a double or triple for $6 per person.

MOTEL MARKDOWN

The economy motel chains, generally charging $10 or less per night, single, will save you over half the price of most of the well-known family motel chains. By eliminating such luxuries as color TV, overpriced entertainment and eating facilities, and excess motel staff—but retaining clean, modern, and comfortable accommodations—such chains are able to offer their customers these down-to-earth prices.

Three nationwide economy chains are Days Inns of America, Inc., 2751 Buford Highway, Northeast, Atlanta, Georgia 30324; Imperial 400 National, Inc., 375 Sylvan Avenue, Englewood Cliffs, New Jersey 07632; and Motel 6, 1888 Century Park East, Los Angeles, California 90067. Write them for free national directories or brochures.

For addresses of regional economy chains, see "More and More Budget Motels," *Changing Times*, June 1975, pages 13–14. Also see *The 1975 National Directory of Budget Motels*, New York, Pilot ($2.50).

DOMESTIC DOLLAR DRAIN DODGE

Generally speaking, vacationing in the United States costs one fourth to one third more than vacationing abroad. Much of this increase can be blamed on the high cost of accommodations in our country.

If you're planning a vacation in the U.S., you should be aware that bargain accommodations whose prices rival those of European pensions *do* exist in this country. For example, you can rent a housekeeping cottage on Cape North, Maine, close to fishing, ocean swimming, and mountain climbing, for $7 or $8 a day. A room in Acoma, New Mexico —the oldest town in America, picturesque but lacking in plumbing, and inhabited by Keresan Indians—can be had for $2 or $3 a day. Or, bask in the summer sun of Maui, Hawaii, beside your $3-a-day cottage in Waianapanapa State Park. There are many more such bargains.

For further information:

Off-the-Beaten-Path: America's Own Bargain Paradises, Norman Ford. Greenlawn, New York, Harian, 1973.

GUEST HOUSE GUSTO

Old-fashioned guest houses or tourist homes, offering inexpensive lodging and warm hospitality, are sprinkled throughout the United States and Canada. In the French Quarter of New Orleans, for instance, you can stay at the Hedgewood Hotel, 2427 St. Charles, for $12.50 double. And in Williamsburg, accommodations are available at The Cedars for $10 a night, double. Write them at 616 Jamestown Road, Williamsburg, Virginia 23185.

How to find more inexpensive accommodations? For the Washington, D.C., area, write to Holiday Hosts, P.O. Box 1108, Langley Park, Maryland 20787 ($10 single for lodging and breakfast in private homes). If you're thinking of vacationing in Cape May, write to Victorian Accommodations of Cape May, Cape May, New Jersey 08204. For a folder on tourist lodges in Montreal, write to the Municipal Tourist Bureau of Montreal, P.O. Box 123, Station H, Montreal 107, Quebec, Canada.

HOTELS AHOY

On several treks across the United States, when we were tired of camping out but couldn't see shucking out twenty bucks on one of those slick, impersonal freeway motels, we discovered that priceless gem, the small-town hotel. Since these are mostly located in the center of town, you'll have to drive a bit off the freeway to get there. But heavens to Murgatroyd, what rates!

For $5 or $6 a night, double, these typically offer an old-fashioned, high-ceilinged room with wood floor, private sink, and comfortable bed. The bathroom is down the hall, as in Europe. Essentially, however, you have a private bath, because all the travelers who shared the freeway with you are spending the night in those high-priced roadside motels!

For further information:

Hotel and Motel Red Book 1975. American Hotel Association Directory Corporation, 888 Seventh Avenue, New York, New York 10019, 1975 (at your library—gives locations of motels and their rates).

INEXPENSIVE INDEPENDENTS

One hundred thirty-five independent U.S. hotels and motels, charging an average of under $10, single (some cost as little as $7), have joined a Ma and Pa association involving twelve states: Colorado, Nevada, Texas, New Mexico, Wisconsin, Iowa, Minnesota, North Dakota, South Dakota, Nebraska, Montana, and Wyoming. For a free directory to these money-savers, write: Ma and Pa Motel Directory Service, 703 Mount Rushmore Road, Custer, South Dakota 57730.

For further information:

America on $8 a Night, Ellen and Robert Christopher, Christopher's Travel Discoveries, P.O. Box 47, Milford, Connecticut 06460 ($4.95).

FARMS FOR THE FRUGAL

Low-cost vacations and a revitalizing change from the harried pace of city or suburban living can be had on one of the many American farms that regularly take in vacationing families. For example, at Summit Guest Ranch in Gore Range, Colorado, Mrs. Bulah Walls will set you up in a rustic log cabin at $50 a week, all meals included, or at $30 a week without meals. Can't beat the scenery: 10,000 acres untouched by automobiles, streams for fishing, ghost towns and mines to explore, and horse trails galore. Or, at $60 a week, all meals included, visit the ponies, calves, sheep, pigs, chickens, ducks, and bunnies on John and Marguerite Morgan's Century Farm in rural Pennsylvania.

Other such farm-resorts may be located by contacting travel services, chambers of commerce, and county agents or conservation districts in farm areas.

For further information:

Farm, Ranch, and Countryside Vacations, Patricia Dickerman, editor. New York, Farm and Ranch Vacations (orders to Berkshire Traveller), 1974.

DIRT CHEAP

Nothing beats the freeway view from a motel window like that forest panorama and smell of woodland soil from your open tent flap. And nothing beats the financial savings —which amount to around 90 percent! A few things to consider when planning to pitch your tent at one of 2,000 federal campsites: While the scenery is often spectacular, the more popular campgrounds are full to overflowing in the summer months. In spring and fall, however, these campgrounds can be paradise on earth.

If you require, not breathtaking scenery, but a convenient plot of ground on which to spend the night enroute, take advantage of one of the 200 inexpensive, often uncrowded, state parks across the United States. In the winter these are often free. Occasionally county parks also allow camping.

Other cut-rate camping possibilities include mobile home parks and private campgrounds. While these are generally rather expensive for what they offer in the way of esthetics and privacy, bathroom, shower, and often laundry facilities are provided.

For further informatoin:

Directory of Federal Recreation Entrance, Admission, and User Fee Areas, U.S. Bureau of Outdoor Recreation, Box 7763, Washington, D.C. 20004.

For state campgrounds, contact the Department of Parks for the state you're interested in.

California Campgrounds and Trailer Parks, 1975, Ed Peterson, ed. Chicago, Rand McNally, 1975. Also see Midwestern, Northeastern, and Southeastern campground and trailer park guides by this editor.

CUT-RATE CAMPING

If you're planning to vacation in any of the national parks, you may save considerably by purchasing a Golden Eagle Passport for $10 at the park gate. This allows free entrance from January of one year to January of the next. (If you buy this permit in November, you will not save much unless you plan to do some extensive park-entering before the end of the year.)

If you're over 62, get yourself a free Golden Age Passport at a National Park gate. This will entitle you to free entry to any national park, and to camping in national forests at half price.

For further information:

Camping in the National Park System (228D) and *Guide to the National Parks* (231D), Consumer Information, Public Documents Distribution Center, Pueblo, Colorado 81009, 1975 (65¢) and 1974 (35¢).

ALASKAN ABODES

At $5 per party (the whole family!), you can reserve any of 150 Alaskan wilderness cabins for the night. Located in Tongass National Forest (southeast Alaska) and Chugach National Forest (south-central Alaska), many on the shores of trout-filled lakes and streams, these hideaways can be reserved through the U.S. Forest Service, Regional Forester's Office, Juneau, Alaska 99801.

SHOWER CENTS

To our way of thinking, one of the worst aspects of camping out across the U.S. is the lack of bathing facilities. Sooner or later there comes a time when sponge baths are an unacceptable substitute for a good hot 20-minute shower. This is the moment when the thriftiest traveler is most likely to succumb to the motel-hotel temptation.

Last summer, we virtually showered our way across the country by stopping at trailer courts and private campgrounds and requesting permission to use their showers. The cost was usually only 25¢ or 50¢ per shower, with many generous managers just letting us use the facilities gratis.

For further information:

California Campgrounds and Trailer Parks, 1975, Ed Peterson, ed. Chicago, Rand McNally, 1975. Or, see Midwestern, Northeastern, and Southeastern campground and trailer park guides by this editor.

There

BUDGET BOOK

If you are in any way involved in the educational community—even if you're only taking an adult class in pottery—and plan on traveling in Europe, get yourself a copy of the *Budget Accommodation System Directory*, International Student Travel Conference, Student Travel Services, 77 United Nations Plaza, New York, New York 10017 ($2.50).

Presenting this directory at the door of listed hotels in major European cities before 1 P.M. will guarantee you a room at an average of $6 per night, double—more than a 50 percent discount over their usual rates!

EUROPEAN FRIENDS

Need a place to stay or friends to show you around in Europe or Britain? For $2.50, airmail, get a copy of *The Complete European and British Address Network* from BIT, 146 Great Western Road, London W11, England (telephone 01-229-8219). This organization caters to the younger, less conservative set.

PENSION PENCHANTS

One of the most spectacular money-saving institutions in the area of accommodations for the European traveler is the pension (*pensao* in Portugal; and in Britain, the "bed and breakfast house"). Like many of the less expensive hotels, the pension offers a room with bath down the hall. It generally offers breakfast as well, but showers sometimes cost extra. Many of these pensions cost less than $5 a day.

A cross between the hotel and the pension, the "hotel-pension" offers rooms by the week at a discount, and often includes breakfast. You won't get such lodgings through a travel agent; the room rates are too low to support his commission!

For further information:

Sav-on-Hotels across Europe, 1975, Traveltips, P.O. Box, 11061, Oakland, California 94611 ($2.25).

Passport to Inexpensive European Hotels, Passport Publications, Box 24684, Los Angeles, California 90024 ($1).

HOSTELING

If you're planning an unmotorized vacation "under your own steam"—hiking, biking, horsing, boating, skiing—gain the right to use 4,400 low-priced accommodations around the world (130 of these are in the U.S.) by becoming a member of the American Youth Hostels. Accommodations abroad cost 75¢ to $2 a night. Fees for all but the most luxurious U.S. hostels are $1.50 to $3.50 a night. Membership costs $5 a year for those under 18, and $11 for those 18 and over.

To join this organization, send your name, address, phone number and, if you're under 18, your birth date, to your local AYH chapter, or to American Youth Hostels, National Campus, Delaplane, Virginia 22025.

For further information:

International Youth Hostel Handbook, volumes 1 and 2. International Youth Hostel Federation, Midland Bank Chambers, Howardsgate, Welwyn Garden City, Hertfordshire, England.

PAN AM'S PLAN

Through their Eurotelpass, Pan American World Airways will guarantee you European accommodations, with private bath and continental breakfast, for only $14 a day, double.

Eurodrivepass, Pan Am's companion plan, will get you the use of an auto with *unlimited mileage* for $93 a week.

For further information:

Pan Am, Tour Information, Pan Am Building, 200 Park Avenue, New York, New York 10017. Ask for "Europa" brochure.

CHEAP CHALETS

Does a vacation amidst the mountain wilds of Banff National Park, Alberta, Canada, strike your fancy? You can stay at the Alpine Club of Canada's Clubhouse in Canmore, just outside this area, or in their huts or shelters throughout this spectacular region, for just $1 a night ($3 for nonmembers).

For further information, write to Evelyn Moorhouse, Club Manager, P.O. Box 1026, Banff, Alberta, Canada.

CARIBBEAN CRAFTINESS

Scattered throughout the beguiling isles of the Caribbean are scores of hotels that cater specifically to the penny-pinching patron, the frugal traveler, the tight-fisted tourist.

You won't find these low-priced lodgings through your travel agent because, with their low rates, they can't afford to pay the travel agent's high commission. But you can obtain a list of them by writing to the Caribbean Tourism Association, 20 East 46th Street, New York, New York 10017.

SUNNY SAN ANDRES

Want to vacation on a Caribbean island where even the tourists speak Spanish and prices for accommodations are a mere fraction of those in the much-frequented northern Caribbean isles? Try San Andres, off the coast of Nicaragua.

Prices for lodgings run as low as $5 a day, breakfast included, or $8 a day with three meals and an ocean view. Compare this with $60 a day on other more popular islands!

For further information:

Colombian Government Tourist Office, 140 East 57th Street, New York, New York 10022.

CAMPING À LA CARIBE

One way to beat those $50-a-day Caribbean motel costs is to make reservations at the lovely campgrounds in the Virgin Islands, Puerto Rico, or Jamaica.

Campsites are available in Virgin Islands National Park at $2 a day. For $7.50, two persons can rent a tent with cots, linen, and cooking gear; for $14, you can rent a cottage with same. Make reservations early with Cinnamon Bay Camp, P.O. Box 120, Cruz Bay, St. John, U.S. Virgin Islands 00830.

In Puerto Rico, the Monto deo Estado area of Maricao State Forest (near Mayaguez) offers 24 cabanas, each with sleeping accommodations for 6, at $12 a night. (Linens and kitchen gear cost extra.) Playgrounds, forest paths, and a swimming pool are included in this bargain. Write Parks and Recreation Administration, Box 3207, San Juan, Puerto Rico 00904.

In Jamaica, you can rent an elevated tent or palm-thatched cabin at $98 a week, double (winter rates), at a beachfront campground near Annotto Bay. Write Strawberry Fields, Robin's Bay, Jamaica.

FOREIGN FARMING

Whether you wish to vacation in Great Britain, Ireland, or one of the Scandinavian countries, it's possible to enjoy the rustic atmosphere and local color of farm living at rock-bottom prices.

The cost is only about $5 per person per day out of season, and only a few dollars more in season. In Great Britain, this price often includes meals. And in Norway, it often includes two meals a day, with saunas twice a week thrown in for good measure.

For further information:

Guide to Inexpensive Holiday Accommodations, British Tourist Authority, 680 Fifth Avenue, New York, New York 10019.

Patricia A. Tunison, Irish Tourist Board, 590 Fifth Avenue, New York, New York 10036.

Scandinavian National Tourist Office, 75 Rockefeller Plaza, New York, New York 10020.

CHEAP LIVING IN EXPENSIVE COUNTRIES

You don't have to ruin your budget on accommodations in Great Britain and the Scandinavian countries. Instead, try out such low-cost accommodations as country inns, cottages, boardinghouses, private homes, camps, hostels, and Y's.

If you want to concentrate on London, request the *Guide to Inexpensive Accommodations in London*. Many of its listings offer rooms which cost about $6 per person, double. Does the thought of spending a week in the home of a Londoner at $35, including breakfast, appeal to you? Write two months in advance to the Private Accommodation Bureau, London Tourist Board, 4 Grosvenor Gardens, Victoria, London SW 1, England, for pertinent addresses.

Norway offers similar bargains at cottages and boardinghouses. In Sweden, the Land of Lakes, you can stay in one of 200 family-sized rooms called Vandrarhem, with kitchen facilities available, for up to five nights in each location. Such rooms cost about $3 per person a night. Write to the Svenska Tourist-foreningen Fack, S 103 80, Stockholm, Sweden, for reservations.

For further information:

Guide to Inexpensive Holiday Accommodations, British Tourist Authority, 680 Fifth Avenue, New York, New York 10019.

Scandinavian National Tourist Office, 75 Rockefeller Plaza, New York, New York 10020.

BEDS GALORE!

The London Tourist Board has gotten together with Christian Action to offer camping facilities and schools converted into hostels to youthful travelers during the summer. About 2,500 beds with shower facilities are offered in London for around $3 a night! Details can be had from the London Tourist Board, 4 Grosvenor Gardens, Victoria, London, SWI, England.

About 2,000 similar beds are available to students for a few dollars a night in Copenhagen. Make reservations in person at Use-It, 13 Rådhusstraede, Copenhagen, Denmark.

For further information:

Let's Go: The Budget Guide to Europe, 1975–76, Paul Rowe, ed. New York, Dutton, 1975.

LIVING IN LONDON

In London—where housing is in short supply—find semi-permanent living quarters through an "estate agent" who handles rentals for landlords on a no-fee basis to the tenant.

Otherwise, unless you luck out and find your own housing through newspaper ads, you'll pay an accommodation bureau up to a week's rent for their services.

For further information:

How to Double Your Travel Funds, Charles and Carolyn Planck. Millbrae, California, Celestial Arts Publishing, 1973.

MONASTIC MELANGE

If you need an astoundingly cheap place to rest and recuperate from riotous vacation living, and you happen to be in Italy, just knock on the door of a monastery (if you're a man) or a convent (a woman). For men, a room will cost no more than $3 per day, meals included. Some monasteries even offer free accommodations. For women, rooms including meals cost $2 to $5 per day. Life is tranquil and austere, and you won't need reservations to be welcomed there.

For the name of the nearest sanctuary, ask at any church. Some of the better-known retreats include Santa Rosalia (near Palermo); San Francesco di Paola (near Cosenae); Sacro Monte di Orta (near Novara); Santa Maria del Monte (near Varese); Madonna dei Miracoli (near Chieti); Santa Rita (near Perugia);

Madonna di Montallegro (near Genoa); Sanctuary of San Francesco (near Rieti); and Santa Margherita da Cortona (near Arezzo).

PARADORES AND ALBERGUES??

In English, that's country hotels and wayside inns. They're operated by the Spanish Tourist Department. Because all lodging prices in Spain are government-controlled, you'll find accommodations in many of these modern, often colorful, lodgings for $6 to $8 per day.

For further information:

Spanish National Tourist Office, 122 East 42nd Street, New York, New York 10036.

DUTCH TREAT

Could up to $200 in free lodgings and entertainment persuade you to enjoy an off-season vacation in Holland? This windfall is called "A Stay on the House in Holland" and has been set up for tourists courtesy of the Netherlands National Tourist Office, 681 Market Street, San Francisco, California 94105.

Bargains include two-for-the-price-of-one dinners; discounts on rental cars; a free hotel room for one night; free tours and boat excursions; free admission to museums, concerts, and nightclubs; free drinks and snacks; and your own going-away present.

Specials offered by other European countries include Sweden's seven-night Stockholm package ($130 double, including nightclub and sightseeing extras) and Belgium's Bonus Day benefits (up to $260 in discounts). Write to the Scandinavian National Tourist Offices, 3600 Wilshire Boulevard, Los Angeles, California 90010 (Sweden) and the Official Belgian Tourist Office, 720 Fifth Avenue, New York, New York 10019 (ask for "Europe Begins in Belgium with a Bonus").

CONTINENTAL CAMPING

The European, who has less money to spend on a vacation than the average American tourist, long ago settled on camping as a delightfully cheap way to stretch his vacation dollars. Campsites are often scenic and the companionship of fellow campers congenial. For the more than 10,000 camps in Europe, prices average less than $1 a day per person!

For further information:

Rand McNally Guide to European Campgrounds, Rand McNally Editors. Chicago, Rand McNally, 1975.

YUGOSLAVIAN SUGGESTIONS

Talk about bargain accommodations! With the help of Yugoslavian municipal tourist bureaus, you can arrange to rent a room in a private home for only $1 or so a day. For a little more, you can eat with your hosts.

If this fascinatingly close contact with foreign home life does not appeal to you or is not available during your visit, you will find most formal accommodations are cheaper by up to one fifth in the winter. A discount is offered for a stay of three days or more as well.

For further information:

Yugoslav State Tourist Office, 509 Madison Avenue, New York, New York 10022.

PACIFIC PARADISE

For those who wish to get away from it all, true bargain accommodations are still available in the Fiji Islands. Cut-rate prices range from $1.45 per person per night at the government rest houses on Taveuni and Vanua Levu to $3.60 at such establishments as the Waimanu Hotel, Marks Street, Suva, Vita Levu; and Korotoga Beach Cottages, Sigatoka, Coral Coast, Vita Levu.

For further information:

Fiji Visitor's Bureau, P.O. Box 92, Suva, Fiji Islands.

NIGHTS IN NEPAL

No need to hire a host of Sherpa guides and porters to trek through the Himalayas. It is amply possible to journey through the primitive but well-marked byways of Nepal, stomping grounds of the abominable snowman, with a light backpack. Costs as little as *$1 a day!*

Rustic way stations have sprouted up along the 60-mile-long trail from Pokhara to Jomoson, offering bed and board for 35¢ a night. In Katmandu, hashish haven for travelers young and old, tiny rooms can be had on the street called Johche Tole for 50¢ or 70¢ a night.

For further information:

Nepal on $2 a Day, Prahash Raj. Council on International Educational Exchange, 777 United Nations Plaza, New York, New York 10017 ($2).

THAILAND TIP

For air-conditioned rooms in a hotel featuring a swimming pool, room service, and clean sheets, try the Malaysia Hotel in the heart of Bangkok. The price for a double is just $3!

For further information:

Whole World Handbook: A Student Guide to Work, Study, and Travel Abroad. Council on International Educational Exchange, 777 United Nations Plaza, New York, New York 10017 (orders to Simon & Schuster), 1974.

JAPANESE JEWELS

Where can you stay in Japan, land of sky-high prices, at $1.50 per day for food and lodging? At a Buddhist temple! While accommodations are often austere, the scenery at these often isolated sanctuaries can be spectacular. For nonreligious but still beautiful surroundings, try such national park and resort area vacation villages as Azuma-Taishaku at $6 per day with two meals.

If you prefer accommodations in the midst of it all, try the Y's, which charge $3.30 per night without meals. Or, stay at a national lodging house, run by the government, at $4.50 per day with two meals.

For further information:

Japan National Tourist Organization, 624 South Grand Avenue, Los Angeles, California 90017.

MINCING WITH MINSHUKU

Although lodging in Japan is generally very expensive, relatively cheap accommodations can be had at *minshuku,* private homes with good food and clean rooms. As these are often out of the way, either a taxi or a guide is frequently provided as a service to guests.

By the way, two of the cheapest lodges (not *minshuku*) in all of Tokyo are Daiichi Sagamiya in Shinjuku and Asia Center in Akasaka, both offering rooms at $4.50 for a single.

For further information:

Tokyo Minshuku Center, 2–13 Yurakucho, Chiyoda-ku, Tokyo.

Japan National Tourist Organization, U.S. Offices, 45 Rockefeller Plaza, New York, New York 10020 (request information on low-cost lodgings).

BEDDING DOWN UNDER

For the conscientious budgeter, the motor camps of New Zealand and the caravan parks of Australia are a lively way to relieve purse strain and enjoy the companionship of travelers from many lands.

The booklet *Outdoor Guide* lists New Zealand cabins ranging in price from a few dollars to five dollars for a night for two. You must bring your own sleeping bag and sheets, but cooking, toilet, and often laundry facilities are provided. For Australia, the booklet *Camping and Caravaning Directory* lists many small housetrailers available for overnight camping at just a few dollars a night. Showers and toilets are shared, but often private cooking facilities are available in the trailers. To get these booklets, you must join the Automobile Association of the country in which you are interested.

For further information:

Automobile Association, NRMA, 131 Clarence Street, Sydney, Australia.

Automobile Association, North Island, 33 Wyndham, Auckland, New Zealand.

Automobile Association, South Island, 21 Hereford, Christ Church, New Zealand.

Everywhere

LOADS OF LODGING

Free food and lodging anywhere in the world? By subscribing to the *Travelers' Directory*, 6224 Baynton Street, Philadelphia, Pennsylvania 19144, you can have just that. The 500 or so people listed in the directory will put you up, feed you, and sometimes even give you a massage or share a sauna. Listings include the United States and Canada, the Caribbean, Central and South America, Eurasia, Africa, Australia, and Oceania.

What's the catch? Simply that in addition to subscribing to the directory ($8 per year) you must agree to be *listed* in it. This means that you must be willing to offer similar hospitality to other *Travelers' Directory* subscribers. However, you may use your own discretion as to who you assist and to what degree—whether a night's lodging, a snack, or just advice.

FREE HOMES AWAY FROM HOME

For a rent-free vacation, temporarily exchange your home with that of someone in the vacation area of your choice. For $15 or less, you can receive and/or have your name and address put on a list of people who would like to trade homes with you at vacation time.

For further information:

Holiday Home Exchange Bureau, Inc., P.O. Box 555, Grants, New Mexico 87020.

Elliott's Worldwide Home Exchange Directory, P.O. Box 2383, Castro Valley, California 94546.

Vacation Exchange Club, 350 Broadway, New York, New York 10013.

Your Personal Invitation, 1089 Second Avenue, New York, New York 10022.

The Gracious Host Club, 1301 West 36th Street, San Pedro, California 90731.

GLOBAL DOUGH

Free accommodations worldwide, as well as a wealth of low-cost travel suggestions, can be yours through the Globetrotters Club, BCM/Roving, London WCIV 6XX, England. The $4 annual membership fee entitles you to the *Globetrotters Directory* (free lodging with members, and advice) and *The Globe,* a newsletter loaded with money-saving travel tips.

VACATION HOME CO-OPS?

Buy yourself a vacation home together with ten or twenty other families. Each family will spend its vacation—one week to a month or more—in the home at a cost of $1,000 to $10,000 down, plus maintenance costs, depending on the area and season during which their vacation is scheduled. This plan puts the vacation home—typically $30,000 on up—within the reach of everyone.

There are about sixty cooperative resorts in the United States and the Caribbean today, and their number is growing by leaps and bounds. For a list of such resorts, send a stamped, self-addressed envelope to Jon DeHaan, 5638 Professional Circle, Indianapolis, Indiana 46241. He can also send you information on a time-sharing resort trading plan, called Resort Condominiums International. This is a plan of his own devising to allow families who own cooperative vacation homes to switch off with families who own such homes in other areas.

CHEAP SLEEP

All over the world, students can obtain extra-cheap accommodations in college residence halls and special student hotels. The average price of a night's lodging is just

$4.50, and curfews or household chores are seldom imposed. Get yourself a Student Identity Card ($2.50) from Student Travel Services (see introduction to this chapter for address) to prove your student status.

For details on these cheap lodgings, as well as on student-discounted restaurants, write International Student Travel Conference, Student Travel Services, 777 United Nations Plaza, New York, New York 10017 (*Student Hostels and Restaurants*, $1).

COLLEGE CAPERS

You don't have to be a student to take advantage of the inexpensive accommodations of-fered by hundreds of colleges and universities in the U.S. and abroad.

If the thought of a stay in Yugoslavia at less than 50¢ a night, in expensive Paris and New York at $2.50 and $5.00 respectively, appeals to you, get yourself a copy of *Mort's Guide to Low-Cost Vacations and Lodgings on College Campuses*, Mort Barish and Michaela Mole, Princeton, New Jersey, CMG Publishing, 1975.

An added attraction: Access to campus sports facilities, libraries, cultural events, and, of course—the opposite sex!

FROM BEACHBALLS
TO BOATS: REASONABLE
RECREATION

An infinite number of recreational pleasures can be had at little or no cost. At half the normal price, you can purchase a kit for making anything from a sleeping bag to a hangglider or a trimaran. For the less ambitious, similar discounts on camping gear, ski equipment, and scuba gear can be had through cut-rate mail-order firms and sporting goods outlets.

Many sports require little or no outlay for special equipment. Such, for example, are spelunking, hot-springing, barrel staving, and grunting (fishing) for worms (a "sport within a sport"). And the number of free festivals, fairs, and sightseeing tours available to everyone, here and abroad, staggers the imagination of the fun-loving "budgeteer."

Whether you count your riches in quarters or C-notes, this chapter will, indeed, stretch your fun dollar(s) joyously out of proportion.

Hiking, Biking, Camping

CAREFREE CYCLING

Nothing beats bicycling for a low-cost down-to-earth vacation, whether it's for a weekend or a week. There are hundreds of scenic paths laid out specially for bikers in the U.S., not to mention thousands of charming country roads. You certainly won't be alone. For scattered throughout the width and breadth of this country are literally thousands of biking organizations—containing hundreds of thousands of members—offering information, activities, and companionship in this sport.

The Amateur Bicycle League of America, 101 Maiden Lane, New York, New York 10038, with a membership of 5,000, supervises U.S. amateur bicycle competitions. The American Cycling Union, 192 Alexander Street, Newark, New Jersey 07106, is geared toward the recreational or competition cy-cler. The League of American Wheelmen, 5118 Foster Avenue, Chicago, Illinois 60630, sponsors bike rodeos, century runs, and cycle trains. This club also sponsors an annual Winter Rendezvous in Homestead, Florida, in March. American Youth Hostels, Inc., National Campus, Delaplane, Virginia 22025, sponsors low-cost bike vacations.

Up-to-date news and cycling tips can be had from such magazines as *Bicycling!* H. M. Leete and Company, 256 Sutter Street, San Francisco, California 94108; *The Two Wheel Trip*, 440 Pacific Avenue, San Francisco, California 94133; and *Bike World*, 95 Main Street, Los Altos, California 94022.

For maps of 100 bike rides in the U.S., try the *North American Bike Atlas*, Warren Asa, Delaplane, Virginia, American Youth Hostels, Inc., 1973.

BIKE BAG BONANZA

Save up to 50 percent on the cost of a bike bag in which to tote your books, beachballs, or other belongings. Get a colorful, sew-it-yourself nylon kit from Frostline Kits, 452 Burbank Street, Broomfield, Colorado 80020.

At $5.50 to $16.00, kits include precut material, zippers, straps, thread—the works!

RACK RACKET

Don't plunk down $45 for a new bicycle parking rack. Instead, salvage an old metal-frame bed headboard from the dump or a second-hand store. Set the legs in cement in the ground, and stand back to admire your fancy bike rack!

For further information:

Heloise's Work and Money Savers, Heloise Cruse. New York, Pocket Books, 1971.

FOOTWORK AND FRIENDS

At organizations like YM- and YWCAs, American Youth Hostels, and the Sierra Club, you will find a vast panorama of low-cost, or no-cost, hiking activities.

These groups include congenial individuals, young and old, whose main interest is in getting back to nature for anywhere from a few hours to a few weeks. See the White Pages of your telephone book for local branches of the above organizations, or write the National Campers and Hikers Association, 7172 Transit Road, Buffalo, New York 14221, for the name of a local group. This association also publishes *Tent & Trailer Bulletin* (quarterly).

For further information:

National Council of the YMCA, 291 Broadway, New York, New York 10007.

YWCA of the U.S.A., 600 Lexington Avenue, New York, New York 10022.

American Youth Hostels, Inc., National Campus, Delaplane, Virginia 22025.

The Sierra Club, 1050 Mills Tower, San Francisco, California 94104.

BOOT BOOTY

Need hiking boots? We've discovered two sources of unbelievably low-priced jungle boots:

Mercantile Sales, 1141 South 7th Street, St. Louis, Missouri 63104 (heavily insulated, olive-colored uppers, black-cleated soles, #2005—$3.85).

Golden Gate Surplus, 524 West Main Street, Alhambra, California 91801 ($10.95 for U.S. Army jungle boots—still about $20 cheaper than retail store prices).

UP WITH DOWN

If the light weight (two to three pounds), compactness, and excellent insulating qualities of the down sleeping bag appeal to you, these four mail-order houses will get you top-quality bags at a savings of up to $50 over down bags sold in most retail stores:

Fairydown, Arthur Ellis and Company, Private Bag, Dunedin, New Zealand ($50–$71, free information).

Antarctic Products, P.O. Box 223, Nelson, New Zealand ($56, free catalog).

Appalachian Designs, 200 Pioneer Building, Chattanooga, Tennessee 37402 ($76, free information).

Recreational Equipment, Inc., 1525 Eleventh Avenue, Seattle, Washington 98122 ($58–$108, $1 membership fee).

DOWN WITH DOWN

While down sleeping bags have been basic equipment for serious campers for years, foam bags are more comfortable and durable, need no ground pad, keep you warm in temperatures as low as 10° F. even when wet, weigh only five pounds, and cost about a third less than down bags (about $50, compared to $75).

For further information:

Trail Tech, 108–02 Otis Avenue, Corona, New York 11368.

WORLD'S BIGGEST BAGGIE

If you need a sleeping bag for occasional camping trips, you can't get a better buy for the money than the durable, nonflammable moisture-resistant paper sleeping bags put out by Paperpak. For $5.95, you can get a lightweight bag good for two to three weeks of camping in temperatures down to 30° F.

For further information:

Paperpak, 1941 White Avenue, La Verne, California 91750.

BOY SCOUT BONUS

You don't have to be a Boy Scout to save 25 to 50 percent on the sturdy line of camping equipment put out by this organization (tents, $18; packs, $6.50; compasses, $3.50). Write to the Supply Division, Boy Scouts of America, North Brunswick, New Jersey 08902, for a free catalog of supplies carried by Boy Scout Equipment Distributors. For names of distributors in your area, contact your Regional Boy Scout Supply Division.

Another source of good, cheap camping gear is Recreational Equipment Inc., 1525 Eleventh Avenue, Seattle, Washington

98122. For a $1 membership fee, this non-profit cooperative mail-order house will offer you prices well below those of discount retail stores and lower than most mail-order houses as well.

YOUNG AND OLD

Not many people know that the Salvation Army sponsors dirt-cheap day camps for children and moderately priced residence camps for senior citizens. A local chapter can give you more information, or write The Salvation Army, National Headquarters, 120 West 14th Street, New York, New York 10011.

Camping for children and families, payable on a sliding scale, is also available through The Volunteers of America, 340 West 85th Street, New York, New York 10024.

For further information:

The Guide to Summer Camps and Summer Schools 1975–76. Boston, Porter Sargent, 1975.

SPECIAL SUMMER CAMPS

If your child is blind, crippled, diabetic, or afflicted with a neuromuscular disease, there's a good chance he or she can attend a summer camp at a low cost or for free.

Parents of blind children should contact the local Lion's Club or Lion's International, 22nd Street, Oak Brook, Illinois 60521.

The Salvation Army sponsors low-cost camps for handicapped children. Call a local office or write The Salvation Army, National Headquarters, 120 West 14th Street, New York, New York 10011.

Parents of crippled children should apply to a local office of The National Easter Seal Society for Crippled Children and Adults, or to their headquarters at 2023 West Ogden Avenue, Chicago, Illinois 60612.

For diabetic children, contact The American Diabetes Association, 1 West 48th Street, New York, New York 10020, or a local office of same.

Children with neuromuscular diseases should be recommended by the family doctor

to the local office of The Muscular Dystrophy Association of America, Inc., or to their headquarters at 810 Seventh Avenue, New York, New York 10019, for their summer camp program.

For further information:

Directory of Agencies Serving the Visually Handicapped in the United States. New York, American Foundation for the Blind, 1975.

The Guide to Summer Camps and Summer Schools 1975–76, Boston, Porter Sargent, 1975.

Water Wampum

WORM WISDOM

Why pay $1 a dozen for fishing worms? You can find your own with a minimum of effort by using a four-foot hickory or sweet gum stake, an old piece of flat iron such as a car leaf spring, and the time-honored technique of "grunting" (also called twiddling, scrubbing, or fiddling). Simply drive the stake into the ground and rub the top of it hard with the flat iron. The ground will begin to vibrate, sending bucketfuls of annoyed worms squirming out of their holes. Believe it or not, this works!

For further information:

"Worm Grunting, or, Fishing Worms Cost a Dollar a Dozen at the Bait Store, But You Can Make Them Come to You," Charles Kuralt, *The Great Escape: A Source Book of Delights and Pleasures for the Mind and Body,"* Min Yee, ed. New York, Bantam, 1974, page 13.

SAILING STEAL

What a daysailer! At 200 pounds, 20 by 4½ feet, Windy's aluminum mast carries 130 square feet of Dacron sail. She can hit 15 knots, and accommodates 4 in her cockpit. What's more, the kit for a complete boat costs only $695—a savings of $3,000 over a ready-built model. Order from Freedom Sailcraft, Box 404, Grandview, Missouri 64030.

DO-IT-YOURSELF DEPTH-FINDER

Build a digital-readout depth-finder for your boat at $100 less than ready-built! The device, which reads depths of 2½ to 200 feet, can be assembled by mere amateurs, using simple tools, in two evenings of work. It's available from retail outlets of the Heath Company, Benton Harbor, Michigan 49022, at $159.95 FOD Benton Harbor.

For further information:

"A Depth-Finder You Can Build From a Kit," *Mechanix Illustrated*, August 1975, page 58.

PONTOON DOUBLOONS

For under $450, a savings of $1,500 over the retail equivalent, you can make a handsome, electric-powered pontoon boat in only one day. You'll need Styrofoam pontoons, a sheet of plywood, two electric trolling motors, and miscellaneous plywood.

For plans, see "Build This Raft Boat for Under $450—*with* Power," Michael McDougall, *Popular Mechanics*, January 1976, pages 96–97.

DIVING DOLLARS

You can explore a new world under the water without spending $500 or more on scuba gear. Just get yourself a new version of the old-fashioned diving helmet from Aqua Bell Corp., Box 221, Winsor, Wisconsin 53598 ($49.95). The helmet comes equipped with a 35-foot air hose and can be used with a hand pump or compressor. Pumps costing $10.95 to $109.95 are also available from the above company.

AQUA FISH FUN

Build yourself a popular one-person sailboard during your spare time by using plywood, fiber glass, and sunfish mast,

boom, and sail. Materials cost $360, compared to $750 ready-built. Order Plan B–8–75 ($5) from *Mechanix Illustrated* Plans Service, Fawcett Building, Greenwich, Connecticut 06830, or read "Build Our AquaFish," Bob Whittier, *Mechanix Illustrated*, August 1975, pages 40–42.

TRAILER TRIP

For $215, a savings of $45 over ready-made models, you can have a lightweight trailer capable of carrying boats up to 14 feet in length and weighing up to 250 pounds. Although the unit comes in kit form, it can be assembled in minutes. Order from Trailex, Inc., 60 Industrial Park Drive, Canfield, Ohio 44406.

CATAMARAN PLANS

At a total cost of $300 ($700 less than retail) for Styrofoam, plywood, and fiber glass mast, sail, and rigging, you can build your own 14-foot, unsinkable catamaran, aptly called the "Thrifty Cat." The price can only be beat by the ease of construction! Order Plan B–8–74 ($5) from *Mechanix Illustrated* Plans Service, Fawcett Building, Greenwich, Connecticut 06830.

FLY CASE COSTS

Don't spend $5 or more on a fancy fly case when you can make your own alluring 100–fly model from scraps! You'll need a small cigar case, glue, rivets, a few scraps of sheet aluminum and fleece, and the instructions found in "Budget Fly Case," *Mechanix Illustrated*, September 1975, page 85.

KAYAK KASH

The perfect lightweight small boat that will keep dry through thick and thin is the kayak. While the designers of this unique and practical craft, the early Eskimos, used animal hide as material, the modern variety utilizes a canvas hull.

You can get a do-it-yourself kayak kit for

about $275 less than a ready-made model from Dedham Kayaks, Inc., P.O. Box 281, Millis, Massachusetts 02504. They charge a mere $36.25 for a 9-foot kayak with paddle; $53.75 for a 15-footer with paddle.

CANOE CRAFT

If you prefer to stick with the traditional canoe for your water travel, you can make your own rugged, durable fiber glass model at a savings of up to $250 over a ready-made canoe by purchasing a canoe kit from Riverside Fiberglass Canoe Company, P.O. Box 5595, Riverside, California 92507. The kit costs just $39.95 (12-foot) to $59.95 (18-foot).

SCOTTISH SCHOONER

A build-it-yourself 15½-foot runabout that accommodates 6 adults, with room for gear, can be yours for $300, including motor. That's $3,000 less than ready-made! Order Plan B–8–71, Scottish Schooner ($5), from *Mechanix Illustrated* Plans Service, Greenwich, Connecticut 06830.

A YAWL IN THE FALL

Although it's possible to get a good deal on a used boat in the winter and early spring, the biggest bargains are to be found in the fall. Furthermore, in the fall you can see the boat in it's most unglamorous state—examine it after it's received a summer of use. By the time winter or spring rolls around, the boat may have been repainted or repaired, concealing weaknesses and raising the price.

If you're shopping for a new boat, you'll find that dealers are anxious to make way for the new line in the fall and will offer up to a 20-percent discount at this time of year.

The same line of reasoning applies to having new sails made up for your sailboat. During the off-season, you get the advantage of more careful workmanship (sailmakers are less harried), plus a discount of 10 percent or more.

For further information:

BUC's 1976 Used Boat Directory. BUC International, Fort Lauderdale, Florida, 1975.

BUC New Boat Directory. BUC International, Fort Lauderdale, Florida, 1975.

See also classified ads in *Soundings*, Box 210, Wethersfield, Connecticut 06109 (northeastern U.S.) and *Yachtsman*, Box 819, Rio Vista, California 94571 (West Coast).

A CONCRETE FACT

Half as expensive as traditional boats, a ferrocement boat can be built in your own backyard. The hull is constructed from a mixture of sand and cement plastered over a wire framework. This method is not only cheaper than conventional boat building, but the techniques involved are simpler and very few special tools are needed.

For further information:

Concrete Boatbuilding: Its Technique and Its Future, Gainor Jackson and W. Morley Sutherland. John de Graff, Inc., 34 Oak Street, Tuckahoe, New York 10707.

$30 BOAT

You can build a one-man dinghy out of a single sheet of plywood for a mere $30! For complete instructions and large-scale plan, send $5 to *Mechanix Illustrated* Plans Service, Fawcett Building, Greenwich, Connecticut 06830. Ask for Plan B–3–74.

SLOOP SCOOP

A molded fiber glass sailboat that sleeps five can be yours for just $4,000 ($8,000 less than retail) through the Tradewinds kit offered by Luger, 3800 W. Highway 13, Burnsville, Minnesota 55337.

Once you've purchased and built it, live loose by anchoring out, rather than paying fancy docking fees.

SINKING SENSATION

Considering the mortality rate of fish-line sinkers (weights), it takes a blamed fool to fork out $1 for a set at a sporting-goods store. Instead, make your own from leftover toothpaste tubes. Simply cut the tubes to whatever length you wish and crimp around the line or hook shank. For added weight, insert bolts or nuts inside the tube before securing it to the line. If you don't brush your teeth, if you don't have any teeth, or if you use baking soda as a dentifrice, try using old bolts as sinkers.

For further information:

Heloise's Work and Money Savers, Heloise Cruse. New York, Pocket Books, 1971.

TRIMARAN, MAN!

Build your own 18-foot trimaran, which can be folded down from an 11' 7" beam to a 6' 6" beam in order to fit on a trailer, for just $600. Made of a fir hull, a plywood body, and fiber glass, Dynel, or Vectra exterior, this craft will take about 350 hours of work to complete.

For previous plans of the Cross 18, send $3 to Norman Cross, 4326 Ashton, San Diego, California 92110. Full-size frame patterns cost $37.50.

All Sorts of Sports

HANG IT ALL!

Hang gliding, the closest thing to Icarus in this day and age, can be a poor man's sport as well as a rich man's. You don't have to put out $500 or more for a ready-to-assemble one-man kite kit. Instead, send $5 to Eipper-Formance, Inc., 1840 Oak Avenue, Torance, California 90501, for a set of plans. Then scavenge up your own materials and make yourself a glider in jig time for as little as $100.

You'll need 1½ inch (diameter) aluminum tubing from your neighborhood junkyard or industrial supply shop; aircraft control cable from the latter or from an aircraft service facility; and either sailcloth or 6-mil-thick

polyethylene from a nautical supply house. A kiddie swing can sub as your glider seat, and, with a few bolts, a hacksaw, and a borrowed electric drill, you're in business!

For further information:

Hang Gliding Handbook, George Sopiss. Blue Ridge Summit, Pennsylvania, TAB Books, 1975.

SPELUNKING

Speleological expeditions need not cost you a fortune, as they do at such well-publicized places as Carlsbad Caverns, Luray Caverns, and other nationally recognized attractions. Write to The National Speleological Society, Cave Avenue, Huntsville, Alabama 35810, for the location of lesser known, often more interesting caves scattered throughout the United States. Many of these caves can be explored free, with permission of the owners. Naturally, you'll want to take an experienced spelunker along with you in order not to lose yourself!

For further information:

Amateur's Guide to Caves and Caving, David McClurg. Harrisburg, Pennsylvania, Stackpole, 1973.

JOIN THE CLUB

Taran Enterprises, 3401 N.W. 36th Street, Miami, Florida 33142, markets a special removable shaft and four interchangeable golf clubs, three of them with double functions: driver-brassie, combo driving iron-midiron, combo mashie-niblick, and combo chipperputter. The cost, about $25 less than conventional equivalents, includes a ball and tee carrying case.

BALL HAUL

For the tennis enthusiast, the cost of new tennis balls, at $2.60 for a package of three, really piles up. Avoid this unnecessary expense by rejuvenating your own!

Sagging tennis balls can be repressurized by using the Tennipump, a device which punctures duds, replaces pressure, and seals for renewed life. At $31.95 including sealant for 400 balls, you will save $300 in the cost of tennis balls over the years. Order from Explore, Inc., Box 20534, Charlotte, North Carolina 28282.

SKI SENSE

If the idea of skiing through the snowy countryside appeals to you, but the thought of putting out $400 for ski equipment and $200 a weekend for lifts and lodging in a ski resort turns you off, here's a great idea: cross-country skiing.

Equipment for this low-key sport can be had for $50: skis with cable bindings, bought off-season for $30; ski poles for $7; a pair of heavy hiking boots ($10) subbing for tour boots; wax and scrapers for your skis at $3. A double layer of heavy clothes will keep you warm.

For further information:

The Complete Guide to Cross-Country Skiing and Touring, Art Tokle and Martin Luray. New York, Holt, Rinehart and Winston, 1973.

STAVING OFF COSTS

Ever heard of barrel staving? This sport, which started as a joke, has attracted enthusiasts from across the nation. Instead of skis, barrel staves are varnished and strapped onto the feet. Needless to say, this cuts down drastically on your outlay for skiing equipment! Purchase staves from a cooper (barrel maker); straps from a surplus store or auto supply shop. Or, secure the staves with strips of used inner tube.

For further information:

"Barrel Staving in Vermont," Mike Michaelson, *The Great Escape: A Source Book of Delights and Pleasures for the Mind and Body*, Min Yee, ed. New York, Bantam, 1974, page 137.

SKI BOOT SENSE

No need to pay sky-high prices for your kids' boots as they outgrow them every year. Find yourself one of those priceless ski shops that offer a trade-in allowance on children's ski boots. In San Diego, for instance, Summit Sports offers you 50 percent off the price of each pair of boots purchased at their store when accompanied by a trade-in.

SPORTS FOR A SONG

Have a hankering to learn mountaineering, rock climbing, scuba diving, or white water canoeing? No doubt you've already discovered how expensive commercial instruction in such sports is. Don't give up the idea for lack of funds. Check with your local clubs as well as such nonprofit organizations as the Sierra Club, Red Cross, and American Youth Hostels, through which low-cost or even *free* instruction is often available. In San Diego, for example, the Red Cross offers sailing, rowing, and canoeing lessons, with emphasis on water safety. You pay only a few dollars for materials. The Sierra Club offers a two-month course in backpacking and mountaineering for a paltry $15.

For further information:

Sierra Club, 1050 Mills Tower, San Francisco, California 94104.

American National Red Cross, 17th and D Streets, N.W., Washington, D.C. 20006.

American Youth Hostels, National Campus, Delaplane, Virginia 22025.

BILLIARD BAN NOTES

That pool table for which you yearn can be had for $400 less than store-bought prices. At $260, the pool-table kit offered by Banner Billiards Manufacturing Company, Inc., Department 9, 4208 Commerce Avenue, Fairfield, Alabama 35064, features Philippine mahogany frame and a shale-aggregate playing surface. Assembly takes only a few hours.

LOAD UP THE SAVINGS

For those of you who use a lot of ammunition—say in skeetshooting or hunting—the best way to save those ammo bucks is to join a skeetshooting or hunting club with its own loading tools. You will save several dollars on each box of shells made this way. Or, check with sporting goods stores. In our town, one of these stores allows customers to use loading facilities in order to promote their sales of cases and primers.

If no free facilities are available, consider buying your own loading setup. These range in price from $50 on up. But you'll chalk up a 90 percent savings doing your own loading and using recycled cases. Kits and materials are available at your local sporting goods store.

For further information:

ABC's of Reloading, Dean Grennell. Chicago, Follett, 1974.

PENURIOUS PILOTING

Slash a sizeable hunk off the cost of obtaining your private pilot's license by taking lessons at a college- or university-affiliated flying club.

At San Diego State University, for example, an extension course will qualify you for the written pilot's exam for $60, a savings of $50 over commercial rates.

DON'T BE A POOR SPORT

Evenings and weekends are prime time for the bowling alleys, as with many sports facilities. If you schedule your sporting fun during their off-hours, you can often obtain a discount of about 30 percent on use costs. For such outdoor sports as golf, prime time is weekend daylight hours. Beat the crowds and golf for less during the week. If you're a heavy golfer, get yourself a monthly pass—you'll save about two-thirds on greens fees just golfing three days a week.

If you're working nine to five, get yourself a copy of our book *1001 Ways to Be Your Own Boss* (Englewood Cliffs, New Jersey, Prentice-Hall, 1976), and get out of that shtick. Meantime, take a morning off in midweek for golf, and make up your work on Saturday morning.

15

CHEAP THRILLS

The best in hobbies, amusements, and good times needn't cost you a cent. The most intriguing hobbies allow you to make something—whether a camera, musical instrument, telescope, or whatever—literally out of nothing. Other hobbies can be pursued at little expense by using do-it-yourself equipment kits, plans, and instructions.

In this chapter, we'll put you onto a host of such ideas, as well as providing valuable information on discount sources of ready-made equipment with which to pursue your favorite hobby.

For more information, read *The Great Escape: A Source Book of Delights and Pleasures for the Mind and Body*, Min Yee, ed. New York, Bantam, 1974.

Hobby Hoarding

POTTERING ABOUT

Make your own potter's wheel with a little patience, a few simple tools, and some miscellaneous wood scraps, pipe, and a steel ball or a thrust bearing. The cost? Only $15 or less, compared to $200 or more retail.

For instructions, see *Making Do: Basic Things for Simple Living*, Arthur Hill. New York, Ballantine, 1972.

RADIO RUSE

A crystal detector radio receiver can be built from scraps of lumber, wire, a few screws, and empty bottles (insulators), plus an inexpensive detector crystal and headphone set from a radio supply shop. For details, read John Rowland's *Cache Lake Country*, New York, Norton, 1959.

DANDY CANDLES

Slash two thirds off retail candle prices by making your own. Request instruction booklet #C26, *Candlemaking*, from The Beadcraft Club, P.O. Box 5754, Augusta, Georgia 30906 (enclose 25¢ for postage).

WAXING ELOQUENT

How much you save in your candle-making endeavors depends on where you buy your supplies. For savings of up to 50 percent or more on dye, candle scent, wicks, and molds (compared to prices of other candle suppliers), write to Celebration! Candle Supplies, P.O. Box 28, Pentwater, Michigan 49448 (catalog—25¢).

For bulk candle wax at a third of hobby shop prices, order wax that melts at 143° to 148° F. from any large oil refinery. Request addresses from your local oil company, or see the *Thomas Register of American Manufacturers*, Vol. 4 (at your library) under "Oils: Fuel, Gas, etc."

SOCK IT TO 'EM!

Why pay $10 or more for children's toys when you can make everything from toad beanbags to alligator puppets from cast-off socks? For easy-to-follow instructions, read Helen Sattler's *Sock Craft: Toys, Gifts, and Other Things to Make*, New York, Lothrop, Lee and Shepard, 1972.

MARBLE MARVELS

If your kids seem to be losing their marbles, and if you have access to even a small stream of water, make some more for them—at no cost!

Just below a small drop in stream level, drill a hole in a rock. Place a roundish pebble in the hole. Now position a hollow stem or length of narrow pipe so that water runs from the stream through the pipe and falls a few inches into the hole. The action of the water will tumble the stone smooth in a week or so. Repeat for as many marbles as needed.

For further information:

"Mother's Newspaper Column," *The Mother Earth News*, No. 37, January 1976, pages 57–60.

TOYS FOR TOTS

Stanley Tools, Advertising Services Department, P.O. Box 1800, New Britain, Connecticut 06050, offers inexpensive toy-making plans. By following their simple instructions, you'll save 75 percent over the price of store-bought toys, and your creations will last forever. Plans for a Three-Way Hobby Horse cost just 25¢. Or, send $1.25 for the booklet *18 Toy and Workshop Patterns*. These projects are easy enough for even a beginning wood-worker.

Rainy-day entertainment for your children that will cost nothing but a few scraps of plastic wrap, scrap Styrofoam, wire, and a little time are a turkey, a reindeer, a butterfly mobile, and a lovely doll. For free instructions on constructing these toys, as well as for making plastic-wrap centerpieces and Christmas tree ornaments, request *Craft Magic: Creating with Saran Wrap, Handi-Wrap, Ziploc Bags* from The Dow Chemical Company, Consumer Products Department, P.O. Box 68511, Indianapolis, Indiana 46268.

CLAY PLAY

Inexpensive, nontoxic modeling clay for the kiddies can be made from ingredients you probably already have on hand: cornstarch and baking soda.

Mix two parts cornstarch, four parts baking soda, and three parts water. Add a little food coloring and stir over medium heat until the mixture assumes a claylike consistency. Products made of this "clay" will keep indefinitely if coated with shellac.

For inexpensive flour, salt, sawdust, and plaster of Paris homemade clay recipes, request Instruction Sheet #C20, *Homemade Craft "Clays"* from The Beadcraft Club, P.O. Box 5754, Augusta, Georgia 30906 (enclose 25¢ for postage); and *Artistic Projects with Salt* from Morton International, Inc., 110 North Wacker Drive, Chicago, Illinois 60606 (free).

PHREE PHILATELIC PHRIPPERY

For the neophyte philatelist (no, it's not illegal), the following gimcracks and gewgaws are available for the asking or for peanuts.

A free twenty-page booklet on philately is available from Consumer Information, Public Documents Distribution Center, Pueblo, Colorado 81009. Ask for *United States Postage Stamps and Postal Stationery* (236D), 1972. For a comprehensive, illustrated catalog of worldwide stamps, write to Bick-International, 6253 Hollywood Blvd., Los Angeles, California 90028, for their 88-page *Stamp Encyclopedia* (enclose 30¢ for postage).

You can get over 100 stamps with which to begin your collection by sending 30¢ (for postage) to Globus Stamp Company, 276 Park Avenue South, New York, New York 10010. Other free stamp sources: Kent Stamp Company, GPO Box 87, Brooklyn, New York 11201 (50 stamps); Jayto Stamp Company, P.O. Box 177, East Syracuse, New York 13057 (307 stamps—30¢ postage); Hudson Stamps, P.O. Box 497, Crugers, New York 10521 (51 stamps—13¢ postage); Douglas A. Decock, Route 1, Wadena, Minnesota 56482 (100 British Empire stamps—25¢ postage; or 125 worldwide stamps—13¢ postage); Continental Stamp Company, Box 94137, North Hollywood, California 91609 (100 stamps—13¢ postage); Jamestown Stamp, Jamestown, New York 14701 (110 German stamps); Bacon's Stamp Shoppe, Rolla, Missouri 65401 (100 stamps); Martin, Box 218, Tustin, California 92680 (100 stamps); and K & B, Box 70, Brooklyn, New York 11233 (100 stamps). All of the above will send you samples on approval, which you need not accept. The freebies are yours regardless.

SCOPE DOPE

The lightweight (four pounds) Bushnell Portascope Field Kit, including 8 x 30 binoculars that bring objects eight times closer and a 16-power field microscope (which uses the binocs as an eyepiece), a dissecting kit, neck strap, and carrying case, costs just $59.95. That's $140 cheaper than the binoculars and microscope alone would cost you. Order from Bushnell Optical Company, 2828 East Foothill Boulevard, Pasadena, California 91107.

For further information:

"Mimi," *Mechanix Illustrated*, May 1975, page 66.

TELESCOPE DOPE

Make your own telescope at virtually no cost by constructing it from pipes, wood and metal scraps, tin cans, bottle caps, cardboard tubes, and lenses from old magnifying glasses and eye spectacles. For details, get *All About Telescopes*, Sam Brown, Edmund Scientific Company, 555 Edscorp Building, Barrington, New Jersey 08007, 1967. Another good source of information is: *The Standard Handbook for Telescope Making*, N. E. Howard, New York, Thomas Y. Crowell, 1959.

SCRAP CRAFT

Unique, imaginative knickknacks, wall decorations, toys—even jewelry—can be made wholly of materials that cost you nothing. For instance, you can make colorful necklace beads of rolled paper; pebble animals and people that would cost $5 in a gift store; trees, turtles, and birds from pine cones, and nut and sea shells; string wound around discarded tin cans for one-of-a-kind pencil holders; or no-cost mosaics from broken flowerpots and tiles or bits of windshield glass.

Raw materials for these projects can be found in the woods, at the beach, in any trash pile or junkyard, and often, simply by talking to the manager of a retail store or factory. A printer might give you paper scraps. An upholsterer has odds and ends of cloth, foam rubber, and webbing. Tile shops and garden shops will provide you with mosaic makings. Just use your ingenuity to ferret out a host of free materials to fire your creative talents.

For further information:

Art from Scrap, Carl Reed and Joseph Orze. Worcester, Massachusetts, Davis Publications, 1960.

WHAT A GEM!

There's nothing like finding and grinding your own gems to cut the cost of expensive hand-wrought jewelry down to a tenth of store prices. To begin your lapidary lumberings, two instruction booklets are yours for the asking: *Lapidary Hobby Book,* Charles Rogers, AIDE, 1465 Neptune Avenue, Leucadia, California 92024 (enclose 30¢ for postage); and *So You Want to Cut Gem Stones,* Covington Engineering Corporation, 112 First Street, Redlands, California 92373 (free).

BEAD BREAD

Primitive tribes do it and so can you! Make your own beads for decorating everything from cats to cars at one tenth the cost of retail beads by using the free instruction guide from The Beadcraft Club, P.O. Box 5754, Augusta, Georgia 30906. (Send 15¢ for postage and request #C22, *Make Your Own Beads*.)

TAPE TIP

Reprocessed video tape, excellent for learning or duplicates, can be had at 75 percent off new retail prices from E. H. I. Corporation, 8983 Complex Drive, San Diego, California 92123. The cost is just $5.95 for a half-hour reel, compared to $21 for a new tape, and $12 for a reprocessed one, at one local sound equipment outlet.

FREE MONEY

About to begin a coin or paper money collection? You can receive five exotic bills (Japanese World War II, Chinese 1938, etc.) or five foreign coins (Yugoslavia, Peru, Colombia, Finland, Japan) free for the asking from Jolie, Box 50 FP, Brooklyn, New York 11224. Include 30¢ postage for either set.

FOR IMPOVERISHED PAINTERS

If you're a starving or near-starving artist, you'll appreciate the following tips on getting free materials. For watercolors, use beet juice for red, bluing for blue, and simmered onion skins for yellow; all other colors can be mixed from these. Obtain an oil-paint effect by using tobacco, sand, shredded cardboard or excelsior, or just about anything else, as thickeners.

For paintbrushes, use old nail polish or mascara brushes, toothbrushes, or cotton-covered wooden matches or cotton swabs. Such items as scrap wood, plaster board, hardboard, or even laminated plastic can be used as painting surfaces. And finally, kerosene, cleaning fluid, or plain old dish-washing detergent will many times serve as an effective brush cleaner.

For further information:

"Painting and Craft Tips," Chuck Kennedy, *The New Earth Catalog: Living Here and Now,* Scott French, ed. New York, Putnam/Berkley and Heller & Son, 1973, page 72.

MILLING ABOUT

Model builders, camera buffs, and electronic hobbyists can build their own milling table from scratch for one third of the retail price. The parts, which cost about $30, are available at hardware, plumbing supply, and hobby shops. Complete plans PL 1402 ($6.95) can be had from *Popular Mechanics* Plans Library, Department D5, Box 1014, Radio City, New York, New York 10019.

WOODWORKING WONDERS

You can save $100 or more on stationary woodworking power equipment if you're willing to make the wooden stands for the machines yourself.

Gillom Manufacturing Co., 1109 North 2nd Street, St. Charles, Missouri 63301, will mail you a bandsaw kit for $23.99; a lathe-grinder for $28.99; an eight-inch tilt-table saw for $18.99; and plans for the stands for $1. You must buy your own motors.

FRAGRANT GIFTS

Much-appreciated gifts can be made for nothing by picking and drying wild mint leaves. Fashion a scrap of silk into a pincushion and stuff it with the sweet-smelling leaves. It's far more aromatic than the $2 store-bought variety, and free!

Or, stuff a sachet with the mint leaves and place it in a bureau drawer or hang it among your clothes. You can even stack the leaves in old tea tins for gifts of homemade mint tea.

For further information:

Making Gifts from Oddments and Outdoor Materials, Betsy Creekmore. Great Neck, New York, Hearthside, 1970.

Foto Frugality

PINHOLE POTENTIAL

A burgeoning interest in photography on your part doesn't mean you *must* plunk down hundreds of dollars on camera equipment. In fact, you can make your own pinhole camera for nothing, just by using a Quaker Oats box, photosensitive paper, and a little experimentation.

For further information:

The Hole Thing, Jim Shull, care of Mount Angel College, Mount Angel, Oregon 97362 ($2).

KIRLIAN CUTBACK

Kirlian photography, the technique by which energy forces of animate and inanimate objects are captured on film, is a truly exciting new field. While a ready-to-assemble Kirlian electrophotography kit will cost you $50, you can make your own by using $10 worth of such scrounged parts as a 12-volt auto radio vibrator, lantern battery, auto ignition cell, a switch, and odds and ends of scrap wire, metal, wood, and felt.

For a diagram and instructions, see "Build a Kirlian Camera for Less Than $10," Mitchell Waite and Bruce Brower, *The Great Escape; A Source Book of Delights and Pleasures for the Mind and Body,* Min Yee, ed. New York, Bantam, 1974, page 22.

FILM FARE

For you photo phreaks, film can be had at one sixth of drugstore prices by investing in a bulk film loader (about $11) at any camera store, then purchasing your film in 100-foot rolls and loading it yourself. Saves you $1 per 36-exposure roll of tri-X film.

One large supplier of bulk film is Freestyle Sales Company, 1427 North Western Avenue, Hollywood, California 90027. See the ads in photography magazines for other outlets.

MAILORDER EQUIPMENT

Here's how to get up to 50 percent off list price on cameras, lenses, strobe lights, and other photographic equipment. First, decide what make and model of equipment you want by visiting local photo stores. Or pick up a copy of one of the many photo buyer's guides found in libraries, on newsstands, and in camera shops.

Then order your equipment through any of the cut-rate mail-order photo supply houses advertising regularly in such publications as *Popular Photography* or *Modern Photography*. Most of these firms offer a money-back guarantee if you are not satisfied, so your risk is minimized.

For further information:

Consumer Guide: Photographic Equipment Test Report, Editors of *Consumer Guide Magazine*. New York, New American Library, 1974.

HONG KONG CAMERAS

Got a yen for a $280 Canon FT–QL at just $118 (plus $15 import duty)? Similar bargains can be had on other 35-mm camera makes, 8-mm movie cameras and projectors, tuners, amplifiers, speakers, turntables, and tape recorders through various Hong Kong mail-order firms. U.S. customs will obliterate the trademark, but not those fantastic savings!

Some reputable suppliers: Far East Company, P.O. Box 6784, Kowloon, Hong Kong; Woods Photo Supplies, 60 Nathan Road, Kowloon, Hong Kong; and Universal Suppliers, P.O. Box 14803, General Post Office, Hong Kong.

ENLARGER CHARGE

Black-and-white photo buffs will save 88¢ per 8 by 10 enlargement by operating their own darkroom. Although you'll need chemicals and paper, an enlarger will represent by far your biggest initial outlay. But since such good quality home enlargers as the Federal E Master, the Spiratone LC–356, the Durst F30, and the Vivitar E32 can be had at any photo supply store for well under $100, your first hundred enlargements should pay for the enlarger and start you saving on those high commercial printing costs.

For further information:

"Good Enlargers for Under $100," Charles Self, *Mechanix Illustrated*, December 1974, pages 48, 50–51.

LONG LENS LOGISTICS

For just $35, you can make your own 762-mm lens which will bring a photographic image 15 times closer. This lens, which can be made to fit either a 35-mm or 2¼ camera, normally retails for $500 or more.

All you need is a single, coated achromatic lens, a length of plastic pipe, a few scraps of wood, and odds and ends from the hardware store. A macrophotography bellows, which will allow the image to be brought into focus, can be purchased at a photo supply store for $10 or so.

For plans, see "Build This 762-millimeter Lens for $35," Lane Sander, *Popular Mechanics*, May 1975, pages 86–87, 197.

FILM FRANCS

Cut your film costs in half by purchasing a half-frame camera. These make two exposures (instead of one) on every frame of the 35-mm film they use. Modern film quality is so good that even the larger half-frame prints have excellent clarity.

For further information:

The Consumer's Handbook. Editors of *The National Observer*, Princeton, New Jersey, Dow Jones, 1969.

CHEAP SLIDE COPIER

If you want to convert your photo slides to black-and-white or color negatives, or if you just want duplicates of your own color slides, you don't have to pay a photo lab an arm and a leg or purchase expensive equipment to do it yourself. For under $1, make yourself a slide-copy illuminator from cardboard scraps and a piece of diffusion plastic.

For plans, see "Slide-copy Illuminator for Less Than $1," James Abbott, *Popular Mechanics*, January 1976, page 69.

Music Magic

MUSICAL MAGIC

If you have a musical ear and no money to satisfy it, you'll be pleased to know that beautiful music can be made from everyday junk—flowerpots, cans, coconuts, bottles, cheese boxes, hoses, shells. . . . Children as well as the young at heart will enjoy *Make Your Own Musical Instruments*, Muriel Mandell and Robert Wood, New York, Sterling.

CHEAP NOTES

For discounts of 25 percent on many types of guitars—as well as on fiddles, banjos, harmonicas, autoharps, dulcimers, and recorders—send for a catalog from The Guitar's Friend, 1240 Brogan Road, Stockbridge, Michigan 49285. This firm also offers musical instruction books at a 10 percent discount.

WIND WONDERS

High-quality wind instruments can be yours with a minimum of labor for one third the price of store-bought models! How? By making them yourself, following the careful instructions in *The Amateur Wind Instrument Maker*, Trevor Robinson, Amherst, Massachusetts, University of Massachusetts Press, 1973. Included are plans for making flutes, trumpets, oboes, recorders, and many, many more instruments.

DULCIMER DUCATS

Enthusiasts of this old-time instrument that is shaped like a fiddle and played with light hammers can get around its usual $125 price tag in any of several ways. If you possess wood-acuity and supreme patience, the cheapest method is to make it yourself. For this, get *How to Make and Play the Dulcimer*, Chet Hines, Harrisburg, Pennsylvania, Stackpole, 1973; or *The Mountain Dulcimer: How to Make It and Play It*, Howard Mitchell, Fold-Legacy Records, Inc., Sharon, Connecticut 06069.

An $18 dulcimer kit, requiring substantially less time and skill, is available from Here Inc., 410 Cedar Avenue, Minneapolis, Minnesota 55404. And for good-quality, ready-made instruments at prices starting as low as $40, write to George Pickow, 7A Locust Avenue, Port Washington, New York 10050.

GUITAR GOLD

If you want a truly fine guitar, but cannot afford the $1,000 and up that is charged for handmade models, make your own! Patience, care, a nominal fee for tools and materials, and the painstaking instructions found in *Classic Guitar Construction*, Irving Sloane, New York, E. P. Dutton, 1966, are all you'll need. Another good book is Arthur Overholtzer's *Classic Guitar Making*, Lawrence A. Brock, 1929 Mangrove Avenue, Chico, California 95926, 1974.

TUNING IN

Avoid high fees charged by the professional piano tuner by learning to tune the instrument yourself. Write to Tuners Supply Company, 94 Wheatland Street, Somerville, Massachusetts 02145, for H. Staunton Woodman's *How to Tune a Piano* (Stock Number 288, $4) and for their *Basic Tuning Kit*

(Stock Number 5100, $20). This kit will allow you to place your piano in tune *with itself*, saving you $20, or to bring it to standard pitch—a big job which costs perhaps $40 if done by a professional.

BAGPIPE BADINAGE

At a quarter of United States prices, and half the price of a cheap Pakistani imitation, you can order an authentic full-size bagpipe ($84.52) from Hugh MacPherson Ltd., 17 West Maitland Street, Edinburgh 12, Scotland. These folks also feature a smaller indoor model for about $50.

HARP LARK

Quit pining over that $700 price tag on the harp of your dreams at your local music store and get yourself a folk harp kit from Robinson's Harp Shop, Mount Laguna, California 92048. At $95 to $350, the harp you make from this kit is less than half as expensive—and every bit as melodious—as the ready-made variety.

GET PICKY

Guitar picks, which cost 25¢ a set at a music supply shop, can be easily cut from an old plastic gallon milk bottle. This normally discarded material makes a firm but quiet pick that works *better* than many ready-made flat picks!

For further information:

Scrap Craft, Michael Dank. New York, Dover, 1969.

PIANO SURROGATES

Who wants a harpsichord or clavichord? Perhaps a music-lover trapped in a cramped, low-noise-level-required apartment building, or any gentle soul tuned in to the tranquil sounds of a more sensitive era.

You can make your own instrument for $150, a savings of several hundred dollars over the least expensive ready-made models,

from kits by J. Witcher, Ancient Instruments, 17715 La Rosa Lane, Fountain Valley, California 92708, or Zuckermann Harpsichords, Box 121, Stonington, Connecticut 06378. For kit discounts on one third to one half on a more serious and more expensive line of instruments, try E. O. Witt, Route 3, Three Rivers, Michigan 49093. And for top-notch kits ($700 to $900) equivalent to $4,000 ready-mades, contact Frank Hubbard, 185A Lyman Street, Waltham, Massachusetts 02154.

For further information:

Three Centuries of Harpsichord Making, Frank Hubbard. Cambridge, Massachusetts, Harvard University Press, 1965.

MUSICAL MONEY

Whether you're buying musical equipment for your rock group or for your child's first musical attempt, you'll find some fabulous bargains in the $1 catalog put out by Warehouse Music Sales, P.O. Box 16339, Fort Worth, Texas 76133.

Effects are also bargain-priced. For example, their linear power booster (used to triple amplifier acoustic output) is $10.50 compared to $21 at most retail outlets.

BUDGET BANJOS

For down-home, good-time music, build and learn to play a banjo. By constructing your own, you'll save a good two thirds of the $100 to $300 that one of these instruments would cost you in a music store.

Get complete instructions in G. W. Stamm's *How to Make a Banjo and a Banjo-Guitar*, Stamm Industries, 905 Washington Street, Oregon, Illinois 61061.

CASH SLASH

At stores which offer major credit-card purchase plans, you can slash $50 or more off the cost of such major purchases as pianos and organs, furniture suites, and kitchen appliances by offering to pay cold cash for your purchase.

By granting you a 2 percent discount for cash, the store can avoid the 2.5 to 7 percent service charge made by credit-card firms.

For further information:

Get More for Your Money, Tom Philbin. New York, Fawcett World Library, 1975.

ELECTRIC ORGAN-IZER

You don't have to put out $3,000 or more for a fancy, store-bought electric organ. With no technical knowledge except for the ability to solder, you can build an electric organ from one of the kits ($500 to $1,850) offered by Schober Organ Corp., 43 West 61st Street, New York, New York 10023.

TV's, Books

WIDEST SCREEN IN TOWN

If you would like a 40-square-inch TV picture, but can't see spending $2,800 or more on a color TV that'll give you this size picture, harken to the following. You can modify your own solid-state TV to project this size image onto a screen for only $125. Here's how.

Turn your TV upside down. Get yourself a small plastic tub about the size of your TV screen and a Fresnel lens with a 10-inch diameter and a 10-inch positive focal length. This can be ordered through Fresnel Optics, Inc., 1389 Mount Read Boulevard, Rochester, New York 14606. Cut a hole in the bottom of the tub the size of the lens. Line the bucket with black paper and place the lens in the hole. Now put the tub over the TV screen. Your converted TV is ready to project onto a 40" by 40" Kodak Ektalite screen for Sunday movies with an authemtic flair.

For further information:

"Super-Screen TV Cheap!" Roger Field, *Science Digest*, Vol. 78, August, 1975, pages 80–81.

DON'T BE A BOOB TUBE RUBE

Costing up to $150 for purchase and installation, buying a new TV picture tube can indeed wreak havoc with your finances. Instead, tell your TV repairman (whom we assume is the lowest-priced in town) that, instead of a *new* picture tube, you want a rebuilt one. Although the glass in these has been recycled, the wiring is completely new.

Last year, we managed to get a rebuilt tube for our Zenith for $20. A new one would have cost at least three times that much.

For further information:

Get More for Your Money, Tom Philbin. Greenwich, Connecticut, Fawcett, 1975.

TV TROUBLES

Why pay a TV repairman exorbitant rates to do a job that you could probably do yourself? You'd be surprised, but the trouble with the vast majority of TV sets involves such elementary work as replacing a defective tube, repairing an electrical plug, or simply pushing a "reset" button on the back of the set.

For help in better understanding the basics, get the book *Make Your Own TV Repairs*, Art Margolis, New York, Arco, 1968.

LEFTOVER LOWDOWN

For book-lovers with a little patience, here is an excellent way to slash $8 to $10 off the cost of that deluxe hardcover book. Buy your books after they have been remaindered—marked down drastically as a publisher's close-out sale. Some stores—Central Book Store in Chicago is an example—deal only in "remaindered" books. Many chains—Pickwick, Doubleday, and Brentano's are a few—have a "remaindered" table where prices have plummeted.

If such deals are not available at bookstores in your area, write to the following for their mail-order remainder catalogs: Marboro Books, 205 Moonachie Road, Moonachie, New Jersey 07074; and Publisher's Central

Bureau, 33–20 Hunters Point Avenue, Long Island City, New York 11101.

BOOK BENEFITS

The avid reader will find the $20 yearly subscription fee to *Bookman's Weekly* or the *Antiquarian Bookman*, both at Box 1100, Newark, New Jersey 07101, worth its weight in gold. These publications list secondhand books wanted or for sale, often at one twentieth the original price.

Or, ask your local secondhand bookstore or library to locate your selections in the above catalogs for free.

For further information:

Secondhand Is Better, Suzanne Wymelenberg and Douglas Matthews. New York, Arbor House, 1975.

MAG BAG

Rock-bottom prices on magazines are offered by Publisher's Clearing House, Channel Drive, Port Washington, New York 11050. They offer an average 40 percent discount on their magazines.

The deal they give you is like a broken drum: You can't beat it.

FREE HOBBY MAGAZINES

Hobbyists and handicrafters can get a free sample copy of the following informative magazines just for the asking—with no obligation to subscribe:

Quilter's Newsletter, Leman Publications, Box 394, Wheat Ridge, Colorado 80033 (30¢ postage).

Jaybee's Handicraft Magazine, Claudine Moffatt, J. B. Printing, Box 39FT, Valley Park, Missouri 63011 (13¢ postage).

Show Me, 901 Brookvale, Manchester, Missouri 63088 (enclose a self-addressed, stamped envelope).

Little Magazine, Claudine, Box 39 FWS, Valley Park, Missouri 63088.

FREE LOVE

On the intriguing subjects of love, sex, and marriage, you need never again pay $5, $10, or more for how-to manuals and expert advice. A list of 1,000 books, pamphlets, and guides on these subjects, all free for the asking, has been compiled by that tireless tabulator, Mark Weiss. Subjects covered: "Teenage Pregnancy: Prevention and Treatment," "New Styles in Young Marriages" (living together), and many other topics. Sources of free films and filmstrips, as well as a comprehensive list of agencies involved in this field, are also included:

For further information:

1,000 Free Materials on Love, Sex and Marriage, Mark Weiss. Chatsworth, California, Books for Better Living, 1973.

Good Times

SPRING THING

A healthful, relaxing minivacation can be had for only a few dollars a day at any of numerous hot springs dotting the country. For example, a day's use of Tassajara Hot Springs, 40 miles south of Carmel Valley, California, on Zen Mountain Center property, costs just $2. In Oregon, you can spend a day at Lehman Hot Springs, 25 miles west of La Grande on Calmas Creek, for only $1.25. And in Idaho, Challis Hot Springs resort, 5 miles south of Challis, has a daily rate of just one thin dollar!

For a reprint of "Thermal Springs of the United States and Other Countries of the World," send $2 to *Place*, P.O. Box 515, Walnut Grove, California 95690. Ask for *Place*, Vol. 1, No. 2.

For further information:

"Warm Wallows in a Cold World," Susan Sands, *The Great Escape: A Source Book of Delights and Pleasures for the Mind and Body*,

Min Yee, ed. New York, Bantam, 1974, pages 44–45.

GUIDE GUILDERS

For discounts on such tourist attractions as steamship rides; sightseeing cruises; and wax museum, cave, and summer theater admissions, get a *Mobil Travel Guide* for the area you intend to visit. The price of $3.95 entitles you to ten times this amount in coupon savings! Contact your district office of the Mobil Oil Corporation (see your White Pages) for the address of a dealer who stocks them.

PLANT TOURS

Would you like to see money or champagne in the making, cows milked, paper milled, sugar or oil refined, bread or bricks baked —or any of a hundred and one other products in the process of transformation—all for free?

You don't have to be a visitor from abroad to get *Plant Visits for International Visitors to the United States* from the Superintendent of Documents, U.S. Government Printing Office, Washington, D.C. 20402 ($1). This booklet lists, by state and product, thousands of plants you can visit just for the asking.

FERRY FROLIC

Caught in the backwaters of progress, only a few of the ferries that once crisscrossed this nation's rivers and bays still ply their way peacefully back and forth. For a day's outing or a cross-country trip, go out of your way to take the ferry. At a dollar or two a car for such scenic water rides as those offered by the Westport and Arlington ferries on the Columbia River in Oregon, you won't find cheaper entertainment. Some ferries, such as the three on the Willamette River in Oregon, are free.

For further information:

"Slow Down on an Oregon Ferry," Ralph Friedman, *The Great Escape: A Source Book of Delights and Pleasures for the Mind and Body*, Min Yee, ed. New York, Bantam, 1974, page 85.

"Alaska by Ferry—with Your Car," *Sunset*, Volume 154, May 1975, page 33.

"Island-Hopping Off the Coast of New England," Mitchell Goodman, *Redbook*, Vol. 129, July 1967, pages 35–38.

"Salt-water Highways of Puget Sound: How to Use Them on Any Visit to Western Washington," *Sunset*, Vol. 135, August 1965, pages 42–51.

FESTIVAL FRANCS

Why pay $25 a throw to get your family into amusement centers and tourist attractions this vacation? Instead, plan your trip to coincide with the fascinating *free* festivals staged year-round by fun-loving Americans. Take in an iceworm festival or sled dog race in Alaska, a tobacco-spitting contest in Mississippi, a popcorn festival in Nebraska, or a hobo convention in Iowa!

Planning a vacation abroad? Enjoy the Festival of the Hungry Ghosts (Singapore), Bastille Day (France), or African Freedom Day (Zambia). In fact, with a little forethought, free entertainment can be yours *wherever* you go!

For further information:

Mort's Guide to Festivals, Feasts, Fairs, and Fiestas (U.S.A.—Canada—Mexico), Mort Barish and Michaela Mole. Princeton, New Jersey, CMG Publishing, 1974.

Chase's Calendar of Annual Events, William Chase. Flint, Michigan, Apple Tree Press (annual publication).

PARTY BARGAINS

For a fine low-cost children's party, look into group party rates at your local amusement park. At Disneyland, perhaps the most famous of all the amusement parks, groups of fifteen or more children between the ages of 3 and 11 are entitled to a total discount of $7 to $9, depending on the number of rides purchased.

At Belmont Amusement Park in San Diego, groups of from 8 to 20 children can get unlimited rides, plus cake, ice cream, and punch served in a "birthday house"—all for only $3.25 per child. The kids can ride themselves silly and your house will not be a disaster zone after the party. In addition, two chaperones are admitted free and each receives a free ride and refreshments.

For further information:

A Family Guide to Amusement Centers: From Disneyland to Jungle Habitat, Susan Hunter. New York, Walker & Company, 1975.

MOVIE MONEY

In our youth, two bits would getcha two full-length movies and several shorts in any theater in town. These days, you'll pay more than that for the popcorn!

The public libraries of many larger cities will loan out 16-mm feature films—as well as educational films—just for the asking. If your library has no films, there are many other low- or no-cost possible sources of supply, including motion picture film libraries, museums, airlines, railroad lines, foreign embassies, colleges, oil and utility companies, state game departments, and the members of local movie makers' clubs.

Get together with friends and neighbors and start your own home movie theater. If no one has a projector, rent one for about $15 a day. Not bad when split fifteen ways. See your Yellow Pages under "Motion picture equipment rentals."

THE CASE FOR THE KEG

Planning a rip-snorting, wingdanging hoopla of a party for your beer-drinking buddies? Why not buy yourself a full or half-keg of beer? A half-keg, equal to 8½ cases, will give you a whopping 40 percent off the cost of same.

Since keg beer goes bad in a few days, however, your friends will be happy to know that they'll have to consume all the beer during the party in order not to be wasteful.

DOMESTIC DALLYING

From the Wright brothers' airplane dangling from the ceiling of Washington, D.C.'s Smithsonian Institution to the Woodland Park Zoological Gardens in Seattle, Washington, this nation is full to bursting with the bounteous bustle of serendipitous sights to see. Before you spend your vacation dollars on costly transportation to foreign lands, check out the sundry free attractions across our nation.

For further information:

See America Free, Sallie Ann Robbins. New York, Hearthside Press, 1968.

Tripping in America: Off the Beaten Track, Bill Thomas. Radnor, Pennsylvania, Chilton, 1974.

STROBE STUNT

Here's a homemade strobe light that costs nothing, provided you already have an electric fan. Remove the protective wire and blades from the fan. In their place, attach a one- or two-foot-wide cardboard disc in which a 3- to 5-inch-wide hole has been cut near the rim. Place a lamp behind the fan and turn it on. Voilà! Instant strobe! Saves you the $33 cost of the ready-made kind.

SENIOR CENTER SERVICES

The 2,000 or so senior centers in the United States offer oldsters a wealth of recreational, educational, and socializing opportunities —free! Many offer free arts and crafts classes, free or low-cost hot lunches, free transportation, medical referral services, psychological counseling, plus valuable information on such topics as government benefits, living on a budget, and where to find employment or volunteer work.

Check your Yellow Pages for senior citizens' organizations.

For further information:

Senior Centers in the United States: A Directory, Institute for Interdisciplinary Studies, American Rehabilitation Foundation. Superintendent of Documents, U.S. Government Printing Office, Washington, D.C. 20402, 1970 ($2).

ROLL YOUR OWN

Make you own cigarettes at 14¢ a package—a savings of 50¢ over the vending-machine variety. For $2.25 ($2.45, king size), you can get a cigarette roller from Green River Tobacco Company, Inc., Box 1313, Owensboro, Kentucky 42301. For under $3, they will provide you with a starter kit consisting of 15 ounces of loose tobacco, cigarette papers, and filters. Tobacco samples are free on request.

TV TREATS

In Los Angeles and New York, you can spend $5 to see a movie or you can enjoy the best free in-person entertainment at TV variety and quiz shows. Always in need of an appreciative audience, TV studios welcome not only spectators, but quiz-show participants who often walk away with thousands of dollars' worth of prizes!

In the off-season, tickets for the less popular shows are available at the door. In the peak of the tourist season or for the more popular shows, make reservations as far in advance as possible.

For further information:

CBS, Inc., 7800 Beverly Boulevard, Los Angeles, California 90036, and 51 West 52nd Street, New York, New York 10019.

NBC, Ticket Division, 3000 W. Alameda Avenue, Burbank, California 91505, and 30 Rockefeller Plaza, New York, New York 10020.

ABC, 4151 Prospect, Los Angeles, California 90027, and 1330 Sixth Avenue, New York, New York 10009.

TAX FAX

Income taxes represent one of the grimmest areas of our lives. Grim because they are inevitable, unless we die—or move to some remote Pacific atoll. Grim because they take substantial bites from our paychecks. And grim because attempting to understand the many ramifications of present tax laws can rob us of many valuable hours. But the time is worth the effort. For once you learn the basics of this year's tax laws, you need only keep abreast of tax changes in succeeding years.

Comprehensive tax information is available in two free booklets put out by the Internal Revenue Service: *Your Federal Income Tax—For Individual (Publication 17)* and *Tax Guide for Small Business (Publication 334)*. Updated annually, these can be obtained free—as can other Internal Revenue Service publications referred to in this chapter—from your regional Internal Revenue Service office or by writing the Internal Revenue Service, 1111 Constitution Avenue, N.W., Washington, D.C. 20224. (Don't fall for the edition of Publication 17 available in bookstores—they charge $1.25 for the exact same information the Internal Revenue Service gives free.)

A word of warning: Although the Internal Revenue Service booklets are comprehensive and free, they obviously do not provide any information on tax loopholes or tax avoidance. Relative to this, your best bet is to refer to such annually updated publications as *J. K. Lasser's Your Income Tax*, J. K. Lasser Tax Institute, New York, Simon & Schuster; and Robert Holzman's *Take It Off!* New York, Thomas Y. Crowell.

You will find numerous rather enigmatic references to court cases and Internal Revenue Service rulings in the ensuing chapter. For specifics on each case, take the reference to any law library. Then ask the librarian to find you the appropriate text.

Income, Contributions, Casualties

ALL INCOME ISN'T

This may surprise you, but taxpayers pay out millions of income-tax dollars each year—on nontaxable income! Uncle Sam refunds these unnecessary payments when he spots them, but many go undetected.

Here's the lowdown on nontaxable income: The six broadest categories of such income—which almost everyone knows about—are Social Security payments, railroad retirement payments, unemployment compensation, welfare payments, and, in some cases, sick pay and workmen's compensation. However, there are less well-known cases of "non-income."

For example, if you work for the Civil Service and are retired with disability pay, this disability income is considered nontaxable sick pay until you reach the age of retirement. Other nontaxable income: gifts, life insurance benefits, inheritances, and in many cases, scholarships and grants.

For further information:

Taxable Income and Nontaxable Income, Publication 525, Internal Revenue Service.

A SINFUL SOLUTION

Two working single people living together as man and wife generally pay Uncle Sam less than two working married people would, whether the latter file jointly or separately. How much can you save by living in sin? Marrieds who earn $3,000 each pay $200 (jointly) more than singles earning the same. Marrieds earning $6,000 each pay all of $250 (jointly) more than singles with the same income.

Our advice, naturally: Get yourself an amicable do-it-yourself divorce or, if you haven't already tied the matrimonial knot, don't. If you don't cotton to the notion of a permanent common-law marriage, you can do as one Chicago couple did—divorce in December, combination Las Vegas remarriage and honeymoon in January.

For further information:

"Couples Divorcing to Avoid High Tax Rate," Loretta Larrabee, *Moneysworth*, 23 June 1975, pages 1, 15.

DISABILITY DUCATS

News flash! If you've been reporting disability pension payments as taxable income and did not reach retirement age before 1975, a tax refund on income of up to $5,200 a year for the last three years is due you. To claim the refund, file amended tax return Form 1040X. Henceforth, a new Treasury rule allows you to deduct up to $5,200 a year in disability pension payments as tax-free income until you reach retirement, or 65 years of age if your company has no mandatory retirement age.

For further information:

Pensions and Annuities, Publication 525, and *Pensions and Annuities (Civil Service Disability Retirees), Publication 575*, Internal Revenue Service.

RETIREMENT INCOME CREDIT

No matter what your age, if you receive a retirement income, you may be able to qualify for a 15 percent retirement income credit. Besides receiving retirement income, you must be a U.S. citizen or resident and have made over $600 earned income for each of ten years during your working life.

If you're under 62, you may be eligible for the credit if you had an earned income of under $2,424. Between 62 and 72, your earned income cannot exceed $2,974. And if you're 72 or older, you can earn a million dollars and still take the credit.

In any case, you cannot receive the credit if you've earned $1,524 or more in Social Security or railroad retirement benefits over the year.

For further information:

Retirement Income Credit, Publication 524, Internal Revenue Service.

JUGGLING THE BOOKS

If you're self-employed or have an amenable employer, you may be able to juggle yourself into a more favorable tax bracket by withholding receipt of some income or payment of some bills until next year. If you expect to make less money next year than this year, ask Mr. Jones to pay you for painting his house in January rather than December. That way, you'll be taxed for your work at the lower rate. Of course, if you expect to make *more* money next year, you might ask Mr. Jones to pay in advance as a favor to you.

On a small scale, many of us have had the frustrating experience of having earned just a dollar or two over one tax category in the tax table. For example, a person with an income of $9,050 might pay $10 more tax than the one who earned $9,049. A little book juggling (legal, or course) might put you in the lower category every time.

For further information:

J. K. Lasser's Your Income Tax, J. K. Lasser Institute, New York, Simon & Schuster (annual publication).

DEDUCTIBLE DALLYING

It is actually possible to deduct all your vacation expenses—everything from transportation, food, and accommodations to tips and laundry expenses—from your income tax as a contribution. How? By contributing your vacation time to working for a charitable organization abroad. This might be a nonprofit service project, a work camp, or a community development program.

To get the deduction, you must be well-qualified to perform the work, and must spend the majority of your time at the project. An archaeologist, for example, might spend his vacation helping excavate a pre-Colombian dig in Central America. A dentist could volunteer his services in a primitive village.

For further information:

Invest Yourself, Commission on Voluntary Service and Action, Room 665, 475 Riverside Drive, New York, New York 10027.

Income Tax Deduction for Contributions, Publication 526, Internal Revenue Service.

STUDENT LOOT

If you agree to allow a student 12th grade or lower to live with you, say, on a student exchange program, you can deduct up to $50 a month for expenses in maintaining the student. The child may be foreign or American, but you must have a *written* agreement with a *bona fide* charitable or educational organization to maintain the student.

For further information:

Internal Revenue Code, Section 170 (h).

CHARITABLE CONSIDERATION

Normally, the IRS limits the amount that you can deduct as charitable contributions each year to 50 percent of your income. What you may not know is that you can keep on deducting any amounts in excess of this for the next five years, provided your deductions don't exceed 50 percent of your income in any one year.

Warning: No carry-over is allowed for contributions to nonoperating private foundations to which a 20 percent ceiling rule applies.

For further information:

Income Tax Deduction for Contributions, Publication 526, Internal Revenue Service.

RIPOFF REBATE

Fraud, trickery, deceit! The homeowner bilked out of large sums by a swimming pool contractor; the taxpayer who lost a bundle for unsuccessful tax avoidance advice; the gullible victim of such confidence games as the "pigeon drop," the Murphy game, or the goldbrick trick—all may deduct the money lost as "theft" (a type of casualty loss) from their income tax.

Warning: Report such losses immediately to the police to back up your IRS claim. Otherwise, you must have a good reason for *not* reporting them in order to qualify for the claim.

For further information:

Evelyn Nell Norton, *Tax Court*, Vol. 40, page 500 (1963), affirmed, *Federal Reporter*, 2nd ed., Vol. 333, page 1005 (9th Federal Court of Appeals, 1964).

Perry A. Nichols et al., *Tax Court*, Vol. 43, page 842 (1965).

BIRTH CONTROL BONUS

The IRS will allow the cost of a vasectomy to be deducted as a "casualty loss" on the basis that it is performed to prevent an accident. The same, by extension, should apply to tubal ligation for a woman.

If your medical expenses this year have not been high enough to warrant taking the medical deduction, but your casualty losses have exceeded $100, you can nevertheless deduct the cost of such surgery as a casualty loss.

For further information:

Revenue Ruling 73–201, *Internal Revenue Bulletin*, 1973–1, page 24.

CASUALTY CALCULATIONS

What do sonic boom damage, vandalism, loss of a lawn due to misapplication of a weed killer, severe smog damage to housepaint, the loss of a diamond when a car door slammed against a ring, house damage because of subsoil shrinkage, and highway accidents all have in common? They're "casualty losses," deductible (except for the first $100 of loss) from your federal income tax —provided, of course, the loss was not covered under your insurance. The element of similarity in all these cases is the suddenness with which the loss occurred: If the loss is gradual, it is not a casualty loss.

To be sure that you can cash in on your casualty deduction, take clear photographs of the damage right after it occurs. Writing down details of the loss also helps support your case.

For further information:

Burrell E. Davis, *Tax Court*, Vol. 34, page 586 (1960).

Jack E. Farber et al., *Tax Court*, Vol. 57, page 714 (1972).

Revenue Ruling 71–560, 1971–2, *IRS Cumulative Bulletin*, page 126.

John P. White et al., *Tax Court*, Vol. 48, page 430 (1967).

Revenue Ruling 54–85, 1954–1, *IRS Cumulative Bulletin*, page 58.

Anderson vs. Commissioner, *Federal Reporter*, 2nd ed., Vol. 81, page 457 (10th Federal Court of Appeals, 1936).

Tax Information on Disasters, Casualty, Losses, and Thefts, Publication 547, Internal Revenue Service.

Medical

MEDICAL MÉLANGE

Did you know that the cost of liquor to alleviate back pains is deductible from your income tax as a medical expense? Provided, of course, that you can get your doctor soused enough to prescribe it!

Balding? You can deduct the cost of a wig, if you can get your doctor to state that lack of one would cause you mental upset.

Just as the blind can deduct the purchase and care cost of a seeing-eye dog as a medical expense, the deaf can deduct the expenses of a "hearing-ear" dog. These are dogs specially trained to alert their masters to burglars and phone calls in the home, and honking horns and other danger signals on the street.

Provided their services are legal, you can deduct the cost of many medical-care people other than physicians: Acupuncture specialists, psychologists, chiropractors, even Christian Science practitioners. Illegal medical care, however—such as an illegal abortion—cannot be deducted even if performed by a physician.

For further information:

Deduction for Medical and Dental Expenses, Publication 502, Internal Revenue Service.

TRANSPORTS OF PAIN

You've heard of transports of joy? You may experience these when you learn that Uncle Sam will allow you to deduct as medical expenses from your income tax what we call "transports of pain."

These include the cost of an ambulance, of course. They also include bus, taxi, train, and plane fares to and from places where you receive medical care, provided this was the principal purpose of your visit. If you drive your car to the doctor, you can deduct at a rate of seven cents a mile, plus parking fees and tolls; or actual expenses for gas, oil, and parking fees, if you prefer. You can deduct your own transportation expenses for accompanying a child, or those of a nurse whose presence is essential on the trip.

By the way, if you can get your doctor to advise you for health reasons to spend the winter in Florida or California, you can deduct the cost of transportation to and from!

For further information:

J. K. Lasser's Your Income Tax, J. K. Lasser Tax Institute, New York, Simon & Schuster (annual publication).

NOVEMBER MEMOIR

This November, add up all your medical expenses for the year and decide whether they will exceed the nondeductible amount indicated on your tax form. If so, schedule for the next few months all the major medical undertakings—that annual physical examination, the fitting of new eyeglasses or braces, dental work, perhaps a needed operation—you've been postponing. That way, you'll be able to deduct all these expenses on your income tax.

If your medical expenses have been low this year, put off all this work until January. Next year, heaven forbid, you may be eligible for the deduction.

For further information:

Deduction for Medical and Dental Expenses, Publication 502, Internal Revenue Service.

SCHOOLING SCOOP

If your child is mentally or physically handicapped, you can deduct part or all of the expense of special schooling for him or her. The cost of sending a blind child to a school to learn braille, for example, is wholly deductible. For a mentally disturbed child, the cost of a special boarding school over that of a regular boarding school may be deducted as a medical expense.

If your Johnny can't read and your doctor diagnoses his problem as "dyslexia"—a reading problem due to congenital brain damage that affects one out of ten American children—you can deduct the cost of a special tutor to teach him to read.

For further information:

J. K. Lasser's Your Income Tax, J. K. Lasser Tax Institute. New York, Simon & Schuster (annual publication).

MEDICAL MAZE

Here's a good way to reduce your family's outgo through income taxes if you furnish over half the support for one or more relatives. Instead of having them pay their own medical bills, hold back a portion of their support and pay these bills yourself.

If these folks have only a small income, chances are they won't be paying taxes anyway—whereas you can claim a sizeable deduction for laying out the money for these bills.

For further information:

Your Federal Income Tax—For Individuals, Publication 17, Internal Revenue Service.

LATIN LOOPHOLE

A tax-deductible Mexican vacation? You said it! You must get an American doctor to authorize the trip, which must include your annual physical examination *in Mexico.* This exam can be obtained at the Data Medica medical center in Mexico City. A "tourist-medical" seven-day vacation package is available, with the exam taking two and a half well-spent hours of your time.

For further information:

Roberto Fox, Data Medica, Paseo de las Palmas 745, Mezz., Mexico 10 D.F.

IMPROVEMENT INGENUITY

If you install on your property an elevator, ramps, air conditioner, air cleaner—even a stereo or swimming pool—on doctor's orders, you can deduct it in part or wholly as a medical expense from your income tax.

First, get an appraisal of the increase in value of your property due to the improvement. You may deduct the difference between the cost of the improvement and the increase in value.

By the bye, so long as it continues to be used for medical reasons, you can deduct all the maintenance costs on that swimming pool as well—the electricity used either by the filter or to warm a heated pool, chemicals to sanitize the water, even the cost of the water itself. And that's almost worth getting sick for!

For further information:

"How the Medical Deduction Helps," *Changing Times,* July 1975, page 8.

DONOR DEDUCTIONS

For kidney transplant operations, as for other types of medical treatment, your expenses for hospital care, the operation itself, and transportation to and from the hospital are deductible from your income tax. Realizing the financial hardships involved in this kind of operation, the IRS people have thrown in an extra kicker: If you, the kidney recipient, pay for the donor's transportation to and from the hospital and medical expenses while there, you may deduct these as medical expense from your own income tax!

For further information:

Deduction for Medical and Dental Expenses, Publication 502, Internal Revenue Service.

NURSING NUANCES

Nursing services need not be performed by an RN or LPN in order to be deductible from your income tax. The services of a paid companion, if recommended by a doctor as necessary to your health, can be deducted. However, if the companion also does household chores, you may only deduct that part of the salary which represents work a nurse would normally perform.

For further information:

Take It Off! Robert Holzman. New York, Thomas Y. Crowell (annual publication).

Work

INSTANT RELIGION

Under the right circumstances, it's possible to claim and receive as a deduction your entire living expenses for federal income-tax purposes. Send $2 to the Reverend Kirby J. Hensley, Universal Life Church, 1766 Poland Road, Modesto, California 95351, for an ecclesiastical diploma. For the next year, you must send him quarterly reports of services you hold every week. When the year is up, you must certify to the Reverend that you have a congregation of three or more people as well as a treasurer and secretary. He'll send you a church charter for which you must pay $2 a month.

In order to meet IRS requirements for this exemption, you must take a vow of poverty. This is done by transferring all your assets, cash and otherwise, to your "church." Henceforth, for yourself and your family, rent or house payments, repairs and mainte-

nance, furniture, utilities—even a "retreat" for yourself and your "congregation"—will be deductible under exemption number 501C3.

Two other churches from which you can obtain a mail-order ordination: Mother Earth Church, 469 Pacific, Monterey, California 93940; and the Church of Gospel Ministry, 486 Skyhill Court, Chula Vista, California 92010.

For further information:

"Artful New Tax Dodge," Parker Hodges, *Moneysworth*, 14 April 1975, page 1.

CHILD CARE COSTS

As a result of the Tax Reduction Act of 1975, if you and your spouse earn up to $35,000 jointly, you can now deduct from your income tax up to $4,800 in child-care costs —including such household-related expenses as property taxes, mortgage interest, repairs, rent, utilities, property insurance, food eaten on the premises, and wages for a housekeeper, cook, or maid—incurred because of your being employed, If the family income is between $35,000 and $44,600, part of the costs are still deductible.

For a family of four with an adjusted gross income of $15,000 and costs of $4,800, this means a tax savings of over $1,200!

For further information:

Child Care and Disabled Dependent Care, Publication 503, Internal Revenue Service.

SUCCOR FOR JOBSEEKERS

Possibly out of commiseration for the increasing numbers of pavement-pounding job hunters in these times of tribulation—and possibly to shrink lines at unemployment compensation windows—the IRS has made some concessions to the jobless. Where previously you could only deduct expenses if you were hired by the firm to which you applied, now you can deduct certain job-hunting expenses regardless of your success in landing a job. Even if you *never* got hired, you can deduct employment agency fees, resume-writing services, and transportation expenses to and from your places of prospective employment.

However, you must be looking for work in the same field as your previous job, and there must not be a "substantial lack of continuity" between your old job and your present efforts at finding work.

For further information:

"Employee Expenses," *Your Federal Income Tax, For Individuals, Publication 17*, Internal Revenue Service.

"Tax News That Didn't Make Headlines," *Changing Times*, July 1975, pages 19–20.

LESSON LOOPHOLES

You can get a fully deductible education by proving to Uncle Sam that the skills acquired therein will improve your ability in your present job.

A free-lance photographer took flying lessons so that he could pilot himself to out-of-the-way news scenes. A university tutor enrolled in a doctorate program. A physician obtained psychiatric training. In all three instances, the cost of their education was deductible because these individuals were able to show that this training was necessary in order to help them in their current work.

For further information:

Alan Aaronson, *Tax Court Memo*, 1970–178, filed June 25, 1970 (Prentice-Hall or Commerce Clearing House).

Marlor vs. Commissioner, *Federal Reporter*, 2nd ed., Vol. 251, page 615 (2nd Federal Court of Appeals, 1958).

John S. Watson, *Tax Court*, Vol. 31, page 1014 (1959).

HOBBY HOPES

Turn a hobby into a business and deduct the cost of such pleasurable activities as gem cutting, stamp collecting, spare-time writing, and gentleman farming as business expenses. How?

The easiest way to convince the IRS that you are in business is to realize a profit from your hobby. Enter the fruits of your lapidarian labors in exhibits and sell a few; trade your stamps profitably; contract with a publisher to sell that book; or sell some of your crops at a roadside stand.

Even if you made no money on your "business," you can deduct your losses if you have engaged in the activity in a businesslike way and can give a good reason why you didn't make a profit.

For further information:

George F. Tyler, *Tax Court Memo*, Docket No. 5508, entered March 6, 1947 (Prentice-Hall or Commerce Clearing House).

Woodrow L. Wroblewski, *Tax Court Memo*, 1973–37, filed February 14, 1973 (Prentice-Hall or Commerce Clearing House).

L. A. Bolt, *Tax Court*, Vol. 50, page 1007 (1968).

Lucien H. Tyng et al., *Board of Tax Appeals*, Vol. 36, page 21 (1937), affirmed and reversed on other grounds, *Federal Reporter*, 2nd ed., Vol. 106, page 55 (2nd Federal Court of Appeals, 1939), reversed, *United States Reports*, Vol. 308, page 527 (1940), Internal Revenue Code Section 183 (b).

TOOLING ALONG

Do you use your car or truck to transport heavy tools to and from work? You can deduct your commuting costs *if* you can prove that you would have used public transportation instead if the tool problem didn't make this mode of travel impractical.

Even if you can't prove your willingness to "take the bus," you can deduct 50 percent of transportation costs (where heavy tools are needed for work) as a business expense.

For further information:

Tyne, Jr. vs. Commissioner, *Federal Reporter*, 2nd ed., Vol. 385, page 40 (7th Federal Court of Appeals, 1972).

SNAFU COUP

If you are accountable for cash receipts, one type of employee expense you may not have thought of deducting are those obnoxious reimbursements to your employer for cash shortages. For example, a salesman may deduct out-of-pocket expenses for shortages due to change-making mistakes, inventory losses, and unreimbursed customer refunds.

Speaking of mistakes, an insurance broker can deduct amounts paid out of his own pocket because he quoted an insurance rate to a customer at too low a rate.

For further information:

Marshall J. Hammons et al., *Tax Court Memorandum*, Docket No. 31518, entered November 24, 1953 (Prentice-Hall or Commerce Clearing House).

Boyle, Flagg and Seaman, Inc., *Tax Court*, Vol. 25, page 43 (1955).

GETTING PHYSICAL

When is a physical examination an employee expense? When it is required by your employer as a condition of your job. This means that the complete cost of such a physical exam can be deducted, without regard to the 3 percent medical limitation. However, additional expenses to treat medical problems revealed by the exam must be deducted as medical rather than business expenses.

For further information:

Revenue Ruling 58–382, 1958–2, *Internal Revenue Service Cumulative Bulletin*, page 59.

DWELLING DEDUCTIONS

If you are self-employed and use part of your home in your work, you're in for some substantial income-tax deductions. For example, if you rent a six-room house and use one of the rooms as an office or workshop, you may deduct, as a business expense, up to one sixth of your rent, insurance, utilities, and general maintenance costs, proportional to how much time the room is actually used for business. If you own your home, you are entitled to take depreciation on that part which is converted to business use.

For further information:

Tax Information on Operating a Business in Your Home, Publication 587, Internal Revenue Service.

OFFICE HOUR POWER

Even if you aren't self-employed, you are entitled to a work-space deduction for any off-hours office work you bring home, provided the expense is "appropriate and helpful" to your job.

If, for example, you live alone in a three-room apartment, one room of which you use as an office two hours a night after work, you can deduct $1/3$ of $2/8$, or $1/12$ of your rent and utilities as an employee expense ($1/3$ because you use one of three rooms; $2/8$ because you work two of the eight hours you are home). If the person in the example above had a family that also used the office as a den during the day, the deduction would be $1/3$ times $2/24$ (2 work hours out of a 24-hour day).

For further information:

Richard Keith Johnson, *Tax Court Memo*, 1972–192, filed September 5, 1972 (Prentice-Hall or Commerce Clearing House).

George W. Gino et al., *Tax Court*, Vol. 60, page 304 (1973).

HANDBALL COURTS AND HEARING AIDS

Can you actually deduct massage treatments, gym facilities, the cost of a physical trainer, or handball court rent? A motion-picture actor was allowed to do so on the grounds that all these expenses were necessary to keep him in tip-top acting condition. Another actor was allowed to deduct the cost of a hairpiece for professional use only. If a good appearance is essential to the conduct of your business, you too can deduct such expenses.

Here's an interesting one: A lawyer was allowed to deduct as a business expense the cost of a hearing aid. If hearing well is essential to your business, you may thus be able to deduct such a cost without the 3 percent limitation imposed on medical expenses.

For further information:

Charles Hutchison, *Board of Tax Appeals*, Vol. 13, page 1187 (1928).

Reginald Denny, *Board of Tax Appeals*, Vol. 33, page 738 (1935).

Paul Blanchard, Jr., *Tax Court*, Vol. 23, page 803 (1955).

CASH IN ON FASHION

For income-tax purposes, a "uniform," the cost of which is deductible as an employee expense, can be almost anything. A fashion coordinator, for instance, deducted the cost of avant-garde designer clothing she wore to business meetings. A musician or actor can deduct the cost of clothing for a performance, provided it is not suitable for normal street wear. The same goes for transportation employees—air, rail, or bus—provided their uniforms can't be readily converted to everyday use.

However, an advertising executive who tried to deduct his wife's mink stole was turned down when he couldn't prove this luxury was a necessary uniform for a successful executive's wife.

For further information:

Betsy L. Yeomans, *Tax Court*, Vol. 30, page 757 (1958).

Wilson J. Fisher, *Tax Court*, Vol. 23, page 218 (1954), affirmed on another issue, *Federal Reporter*, 2nd ed., Vol. 230, page 230 (7th Federal Court of Appeals, 1956).

Oswald "Ozzie" G. Nelson et al., *Tax Court Memo*, 1966–224, filed October 11, 1966 (Prentice-Hall or Commerce Clearing House).

Miscellaneous Deductions and Credits, Publication 529, Internal Revenue Service.

Paul E. Jackson et al., *Tax Court Memo*, 1954–235, filed December 27, 1954

(Prentice-Hall or Commerce Clearing House).

DOMESTIC DEDUCTION

Most everyone knows that Uncle Sam is generous with deductions for entertaining business associates at a restaurant or for cocktails. But did you know that you can invite a client or potential business ally to your home and deduct his share of a quiet evening barbecue or home-cooked meal?

To qualify, you need not even discuss business at the affair—as long as you and your guest have a business relationship. Be sure to keep adequate records of dates and guests, as well as a list of itemized expenses for the IRS.

For further information:

Travel, Entertainment and Gift Expenses, Publication 463, Internal Revenue Service.

WIFELY WINDFALLS

How about expenses for entertaining a customer's wife, or your own wife, along with your client? If there is a good reason for the customer's wife to come along—if, for example, the couple is from out of town and the wife would otherwise sit alone in a hotel room—her cost is deductible. If your wife joins the group to entertain the customer's wife, the cost for both wives is deductible.

For further information:

Revenue Ruling 63–144, 1963–2, *IRS Cumulative Bulletin*, page 129.

MEAL TICKET

You can also deduct part of the cost of your own meals while entertaining business customers. The deductible amount is the cost over and above the maximum amount you spend on your lunches when you are not entertaining for business purposes. For example, if you bring your own lunch to work every day at a maximum cost of $1, but spend $10 on your own lunch when entertaining for business, you can deduct $9 as a business expense.

For further information:

Richard A. Sutter, *Tax Court*, Vol. 21, page 170 (1953).

La Forge et al. vs. Commissioner, *Federal Reporter*, 2nd ed., Vol. 434, page 370 (2nd Federal Court of Appeals, 1970).

Max Plishner et al., *Tax Court Memo*, 1962–208, filed August 30, 1962 (Prentice-Hall or Commerce Clearing House).

COUNTRY CLUB COSTS

Part of your social, sporting, or athletic club fees can be deducted from your income tax if you can prove that you use the club more than half the time for business rather than pleasure. A handy way to prove this is to calculate the percentage of meals at the club which are related to business. If it's over 50 percent, you may deduct an equal percentage of the club membership fees and dues as a business expense.

For further information:

Regulations Section 1.274–2 (e) (3), *Title 26, Code of Federal Regulations*.

Revenue Ruling 63–144, 1963–2, *IRS Cumulative Bulletin*, page 129.

La Forge et al. vs. Commissioner, *Federal Reporter*, 2nd ed., Vol. 434, page 370 (2nd Federal Court of Appeals, 1970).

Johnson vs. United States, *Federal Supplement*, Vol. 45, page 377 (District Court, Southern District California, 1941).

S. Charles Lee, et al., *Tax Court Memo*, Docket numbers 5562–3, entered April 5, 1946 (Prentice-Hall or Commerce Clearing House).

CREDIT CAPER

If you're a business person, you're probably aware of the fact that the Internal Revenue Service allows you to depreciate, for tax purposes, the cost of your business equipment. But in addition to this deduction, you can subtract up to seven percent of the cost of business equipment acquired after 1974 as a direct credit against your income tax.

For equipment with a useful life of seven or more years, you deduct seven percent of the total cost; for five to seven years, seven percent of two thirds of the cost; and for three to five years, seven percent of one third of the cost. Besides applying to the usual items —typewriters, business automobiles, and so on—farmers may take a credit for livestock, stock water wells, and various improvements. File Form 3468.

For further information.

Tax Information on Investment Credit, Publication 572, Internal Revenue Service.

MAD ADS

The tax-savvy businessman can deduct as advertising expenses such far-out items as show horses, wolfhounds—even an African safari.

For example, a dairy company brought back stuffed critters from their African safari to place in the dairy museum. Free tickets to the museum were then distributed by milkmen. The tax courts considered this safari a *bona fide* advertising expense falling well within the scope of current tax laws regarding deductions. A restaurant owner entered his horses and wolfhounds in shows in the name of his restaurant, adorned with the colors of the business. Result: tax-deductible pets!

You too can deduct such outlandish costs as advertising expenses—the sky's the limit!

For further information:

Sanitary Farms Dairy, Inc., *Tax Court*, Vol. 25, page 463 (1955).

Rodgers Dairy Company et al., *Tax Court*, Vol 14, page 66 (1950).

PROMO INFO

You can deduct sums you pay to prevent "bad" advertising as well as to promote "good" advertising. For instance, an insurance agent paid his customers' claims for a dissolved insurance company out of his own pocket. This was an advertising cost because it promoted his business.

In addition, you can deduct any advertising expenses you pay for someone from whom you receive income. A landlord, for instance, might decide to advertise on behalf of a business tenant in hopes that this will build up the tenant's business, thus assuring the landlord of rental income.

For further information:

Edward J. Miller, *Board of Tax Appeals*, Vol. 37, page 830 (1938).

Hennepin Holding Company, *Board of Tax Appeals*, Vol. 23, page 119 (1931).

WIN-NINGS

If you hire a person from a Federal Work Incentive (WIN) Program, which is meant to thin the ranks of welfare recipients, you can deduct fully 20 percent of his or her wages for the first year of employment as a direct credit against your income tax. This could save you $1,000 or more in taxes for the year. File Form 4874.

For further information:

Work Incentive Program, Publication 535, Internal Revenue Service.

THE LION'S SHARE

Planning to take your spouse along on that upcoming business trip? As you may know, your expenses (but not your spouse's) are deductible from your income tax. But don't think that you can only deduct half your joint travel expenses. Instead, if you travel on the family plan, deduct for yourself the rate for one person, round trip. That will be considerably more than half the family plan amount.

The same goes for those motel bills for a "double." If a double costs you $16, don't deduct $8. Instead, deduct $12, the amount charge for a single room.

For further information:

Travel, Entertainment, and Gift Expenses, Publication 463, Internal Revenue Service.

SPOUSAL ASSISTANCE

If you can show the IRS that your spouse accompanied you on your business trips during the year for *business* purposes—and not merely for pleasure—his or her expenses, as well as your own, are fully deductible.

In one instance, a wife's expenses for a European trip were deductible because she entertained the husband's customers and their wives in her hotel room, and because her presence made it easy for the customers to invite the businessman to their homes. In another case, a businessman's wife assisted him on a European trip in gathering information on housing, recreational and school facilities, and other problem areas for the firm's foreign officers. In both cases, the wife's expenses were deductible.

For further information:

Warwick et al. vs. the United States, *Federal Supplement*, Vol. 236, page 761 (District Court, Eastern District Virginia, 1964).

Wilkins et al. vs. the United States, *Federal Supplement*, Vol. 348, page 1282 (District Court, Nebraska, 1972).

ILLEGAL BUSINESSES

Even though you may have been caught and convicted of running an illegal business (a numbers game, a bookie joint), it may soothe you to know that all is not lost. Operating expenses for such enterprises can be deducted on your income-tax return—just as they would be on any legitimate business —provided that the expenses themselves are not illegal.

For further information:

Louis Cohen, *Tax Court Memo*, Docket No. 63366, entered April 8, 1958 (Prentice-Hall or Commerce Clearing House).

Commissioner versus Sullivan et al., *United States Reports*, Vol. 356, page 27 (1958).

KICKBACK FAX

Can bribes and kickbacks be deducted as business expenses? In some instances, yes! With the exception of payoffs to officials of any government, such expenses can be deducted provided that they are not illegal in the geographical area in which they occurred. In fact, you can deduct such payments even if they *are* illegal, provided you have not been successfully prosecuted for the crime.

For example, a beer distributor in one state illegally gave away free samples. But state officials, although they knew of the violation, did not prosecute. The tax court reasoned that an unenforced law is not a "law" in the usual sense. Thus, the samples were deductible from the distributor's income tax.

For further information:

Sterling Distributors, Inc., versus Patterson, *Federal Supplement*, Vol. 236, page 479 (District Court, northern district Alabama, 1964).

Investments, Taxes, etc.

SHELTER SENSE

One tax shelter involves investing as a partner in any legitimate enterprise. For many years, as an example, motion-picture production companies have attracted risk capital from investors seeking to lower their tax base. The investor can deduct *all* of his partnership losses, as opposed to a *capital* loss, which is often only partially deductible, or else deductible only over several years rather than as a lump sum.

Recently, however, the Internal Revenue Service has tightened up its regulations regarding this type of tax avoidance, and therefore, before proceeding, it's best to consult a competent tax attorney.

For further information:

Tax Shelters and Tax Free Income for Everyone, William Drollinger. Orchard Lake, Michigan, Epic, 1975.

DIVIDEND DOLLARS

If you have sizeable savings, but no stocks as yet, cut down on taxes by transferring some of your savings to dividend-producing taxable domestic stocks. All your interest is taxable income, but the first $100 of dividend income is deductible! This is a tax savings of $25 for those in the 25 percent tax bracket! Before you make this move, ask your local Internal Revenue Service office if the stock you're considering buying qualifies for the deduction.

For further information:

How to Pick a Perfect Growth Stock, William Gemmell, New Rochelle, New York, Windsor Books (orders to Arlington House), 1975.

PROFIT FROM YOUR LOSSES

Do you own stock that has decreased in value since you purchased it? Even if you plan to hold onto the stock and wait for better times, you can cash in on the lower value of the shares for income-tax purposes. The technique involves selling stocks at the lower price, and rebuying the same stocks, within the legally required 31-day waiting period either before or after the sale.

The loss you incur on this "sale" of stocks is deductible from your income tax. If you owned the stock less than six months, the whole "loss" is deductible. For longer periods, half the amount is deductible as a capital loss. For a long-term "loss" of $1,000, $500 would be deductible, meaning a tax savings of $125 for those of you in the 25 percent bracket.

For further information:

"Moneywise: How to Profit from Stock Market Losses," Donald Saltz, *Moneysworth*. 20 January 1975, page 6.

TABLE THOSE TAXES

Here's a lulu of a loophole for the self-employed person. Under the Keogh Plan established by the federal government, each year you can place up to $7,500 a year or 15 percent of your income—whichever is less —in a savings account as a retirement fund. The income *and* the interest are tax-free until these monies are withdrawn, at which time taxes must be paid on both. After the age of 59½, you may withdraw the funds. Then you'll be taxed for them at a lower rate than in your high-earning years. Earlier withdrawal of these funds, however, involves a 10 percent tax penalty. Similar shelters apply to some state governments as well.

Check with the IRS and your state tax agency for details.

For further information:

Keogh Plans (Self-Employed Retirement Plans), Publications 560 and 566, Internal Revenue Service.

DEFERRED DOLLARS

For the employed person who's not covered by a retirement plan other than Social Security, here's a dandy: You can place up to $1,500 or 15 percent of your wages— whichever is less—in an individual retirement account for yourself each year. The income *and* interest are deductible on your federal income-tax form and on some state income-tax forms as well. Upon withdrawal, taxes are then paid on both.

This plan assumes, naturally, that you'll be in a lower tax bracket at retirement time (when you withdraw the funds), and thus end up paying less taxes.

Note: There is a 10 percent tax penalty for withdrawal before age 59½.

For further information:

Tax Information on Individual Retirement Savings Programs, Publication 590, Internal Revenue Service.

CHEAP LIVING

Want to know how a couple with an average income can save $500 a year in taxes? By purchasing a home, whether it be a house, condominium, or cooperative, you'll be able to deduct all mortgage interest and real estate taxes from your income tax. And you'll be your own landlord to boot!

For further information:

Tax Information on Deductions for Homeowners, Publication 530, and *Tax Information on Condominiums and Cooperative Apartments, Publication 588,* Internal Revenue Service.

HOUSE HAUL

A tax credit of 5 percent of the purchase price for a new home of which you are the first occupant or $2,000 (whichever is less) may be yours. The new dwelling must have been built or under construction before March 26, 1975. The seller must certify that you got the best deal offered for the house since February 28, 1975. File Form 5405.

For further information:

Tax Credit for the New Home Buyer, Publication 591, Internal Revenue Service.

TAXLESS SHELTER

Normally, a capital gains tax must be paid on property that you sell at a profit. However, it is possible to avoid paying such a tax indefinitely if you sell your principal residence (this can be a house, condominium, cooperative apartment, houseboat, or house trailer) and buy and occupy a more expensive new principal residence within one to two years before or after the sale date of the first home. (The length of time depends on when you sold your old home and whether your new home is a brand-new building.) This process can be repeated indefinitely until you cease to own a home.

Eventually, when you sell your last residence and don't buy a new one, you'll have to pay a capital gains tax on all the gains you've accumulated along the way. By that time, however, you should either be in a high enough income-tax bracket to afford it, or a low enough one that the tax blow will be lessened.

For further information:

Tax Information on Selling Your Home, Publication 524, Internal Revenue Service.

ELDERLY ADVANTAGE

If you're 65 years of age or older and have lived in your home for five of the last eight years, you can deduct from your taxable gross income part, and in some cases, all of the capital gain realized in the sale of your home.

For further information:

Tax Information on Selling Your Home, Publication 523, Internal Revenue Service.

LOSS COSTS

Selling your home at a loss—due to an unanticipated company transfer, for example —will hit you twice as hard because it is not deductible on your income tax. If you expect to sell at a loss, renting your home out for a little over six months after you move will allow you to deduct the loss as a rental property loss on Form 4797, Supplemental Schedule of Gains and Losses.

For further information:

Sale of Rental Property, Publication 544, Internal Revenue Service.

PREPAYMENT POTENTIAL

As you may know, interest paid on loans is deductible on your income-tax return. What you may not know is that you can prepay loans up to a year in advance and deduct these payments in the year you shelled them out. However, the IRS may disallow this prepayment if it causes "a material distortion of income" and greatly lowers your income tax.

For further information:

Income Tax Deduction for Interest Expense, Publication 545, Internal Revenue Service.

THE LEASED AMOUNT

Leasing anything from buildings to Buicks, from land to Land Rovers—instead of buying—involves a number of tax advantages for the self-employed. All the money you put out for leasing such things for business purposes is deductible from your income tax, but the money you spend for purchasing the same thing is often not readily deductible.

If, for example, a salesman or real estate broker needs a new car every year for his business, leasing would be a good bet. If the car is purchased, the government's schedule of depreciation for tax purposes and the fact that the trade-in money received on the purchase is considered a taxable capital gain will mean extra tax dollars.

The second important advantage of leasing: It frees the money you would have spent on a down payment for other purposes, one of which might be investment at a sizeable profit. Not only that, but the headaches of maintenance, if so specified, are the lessor's, not yours!

For further information:

Manage Your Money and Live Better: Get the Most from Your Dwindling Dollars, David Markstein. New York, McGraw-Hill, 1971.

ALIMONY MAZE

You may declare alimony payments as itemized deductions on your income tax, Schedule A, *provided* your spouse is not deducting them. To qualify, payments must be periodic, obligatory, required by a decree or written agreement, and not specified to be child support.

For further information:

Income Tax Deductions for Alimony Payments, Publication 504, Internal Revenue Service.

CREDIT COUNSEL

If you've invested in mutual funds or an investment company, list a credit on your income-tax return for a portion of the tax paid by the company on undistributed gains. See Form 2439, which you should receive from the company, for your deductible share of the tax. Attach this to Form 1040, and deduct as "Credit from a Regulated Investment Company."

For further information:

Mutual Funds, Publication 564, Internal Revenue Service.

TAKE STOCK

Using the investment credit above, farmers can play the "stock" market. If you expect the price of livestock to drop in the next half year, or if you want to take a vacation and earn tax dollars at the same time, sell all your livestock (other than horses). Six months or more after the sale, you are allowed to buy similar livestock, for the price of which you are entitled to the investment credit.

GAS GOLD

If you use a motorboat, power saw, lawn mower, or other nonroad equipment, you may deduct 2¢ per gallon for the fuel used in operating these devices. Also, you may claim 6¢ a gallon for lubricating oil used in nonhighway equipment. Farmers get a gas break too—4¢ a gallon for nonhighway farm equipment fuel. File Form 4136.

For further information:

Federal Fuel Tax Credit or Refund for Nonhighway and Transit Users, Publication 378, Internal Revenue Service.

TAX MATTERS

Money you pay in connection with the determination, refund, or adjustment of a tax—whether it be federal, state, or city income, property, gift, estate, or other tax—is fully deductible from your income tax.

Not only is your tax-return preparation fee deductible, but so is the cost of tax counsel or of contesting your tax liability. A trip to Washington involving an additional tax imposed on your business is likewise deductible.

In addition, fees paid for estate planning, to the extent that they involve tax planning, are deductible. However, you must make certain that the state-planning bill indicates what part of the fee involves tax planning.

For further information:

Regulations Section 1.212–1 (1), Title 26, *Code of Federal Regulations.*

O. D. 849, *IRS Cumulative Bulletin,* Vol. 4, page 123.

Sidney Merian's et al. *Tax Court,* Vol. 60, page 187 (1973).

FREE ADVICE

Before you pay a tax consultant good money for income-tax advice, make an appointment to talk with a supervisor (not a regular clerk) at your local Internal Revenue Service office. These experts in tax law will spend hours at a time answering questions and explaining the law to you. Best of all, their services are free.

Also check with your local chamber of commerce or adult education department for free or low-cost seminars and courses on tax law.

For further information:

"How to Act in December to Ease Tax Bite in April," Harry Anderson, *Los Angeles Times,* Part VIII, 14 December 1975, pages 1, 3.

ANTISOCIAL SECURITY

If you worked for more than one employer last year, and made more than $14,100, the chance is you paid too much Social Security tax. Check your W-2 forms to see if more than $824.85 in Social Security was withheld. If so, you can get a refund by noting the excess on line 64 of Form 1040.

For further information:

Instructions to Form 1040, Internal Revenue Service.

GIFT-GIVING

When it comes to inheritance taxes, Uncle Sam can turn into Uncle Scrooge. Stave off that dolesome day by distributing your estate over the years to your beneficiaries in the form of gifts.

You can give up to $3,000 a year to individuals and $6,000 a year to couples without paying gift taxes. In addition to this, a provision called the "extra lifetime exclusion" allows you to give a total of $30,000 to one person, or $60,000 to a couple, either in installments or as a lump sum.

For further information:

Federal Estate and Gift Taxes Explained, Including Estate Planning: 1975 Edition, Commerce Clearing House. New York, Commerce Clearing House, 1975.

ESTATE REBATE

The federal government allows a credit for some of the state inheritance, estate, or succession tax in computing your federal estate tax. This credit is only available for taxable estates over $40,000.

On an estate of $60,000, for example, you can take a credit of up to $160 against death taxes paid to a state. If your estate is valued at $100,000, the credit jumps to $560, while an $8,960 credit awaits the individual with a $1 million estate.

For further information:

Tax Facts for Older Americans, c/o NRTA–AARP, 1909 K Street, N.W., Washington, D.C. 20049 (free), pages 3–4.

TAX RELAXERS

For as long as you live and make money in the United States, you can't escape Uncle Sam's ubiquitous income-tax bite. But you *can* influence your state income tax, simply by picking up and moving from a state where rates can go as high as 15 percent or more for those in high brackets—such states as Delaware, New Jersey, New York, Minnesota, and Rhode Island—to states where there is *no* personal income tax. These generous states include Florida, Nevada, South Dakota, Texas, Washington, and Wyoming.

For further information:

Tax Facts for Older Americans, c/o NRTA–AARP, 1909 K Street, N.W., Washington, D.C. 20049.

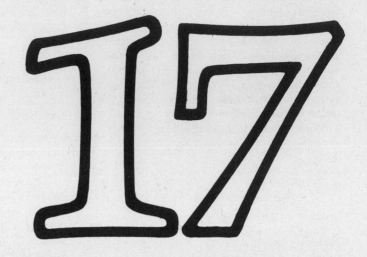

INSURANCE INSIGHTS
AND LEGAL LOGISTICS

In few areas of our lives are we placed more at the mercy of professionals than in the mind-boggling realms of insurance and law. Couched in obfuscatory phraseology and typed in miniscule print, insurance policies and legal documents cause more head scratching than a dandruff epidemic during a shampoo shortage. And to add insult to injury, while the head is being scratched, the wallet is being lightened!

What can you do to obtain top-rate insurance and legal aid for less? Get the basics by boning up on the subject. Your public library is an invaluable source of free knowledge in these fields. Once you possess an awareness of your real needs, then shop by phone for insurance rates and legal fees.

Next, cooly and in the privacy of your own home, take the time to compare your assortment of facts and figures. Armed with this knowledge, you'll then be able to make rational decisions, even when faced with the most glib-tongued insurance salesman or subtly domineering attorney.

Check into Medicare and free state health insurance; find out if your community offers no-charge legal aid services.

Regarding legal services, follow the lead of the many individuals who find they have neither the resources nor the desire to pay costly attorney fees: Obtain, fill out, and file your own legal forms. In most cases, only a modest filing fee is involved.

There are many, many ways to cut costs in these fields. Get started by referring to the two books listed below. In them, Herb Denenberg, former Pennsylvania insurance commissioner and a well-known consumer advocate, knowledgeably and lucidly explains these complicated fields.

The Shopper's Guidebook to Life Insurance, Health Insurance, Auto Insurance, Homeowner's Insurance, Doctors, Dentists, Lawyers, Pensions, Etc., Herbert Denenberg. Washington, D.C., Consumer News, 1974.

Getting Your Money's Worth: Guidelines About Insurance Policies, Health Protection, Pensions and Professional Services, Herbert Denenberg. Washington, D.C., Public Affairs Press, 1974.

Life Insurance

YOU CAN BANK ON IT

Do you live in New York, Massachusetts, or Connecticut? If so, you can buy a limited amount (up to $30,000 in New York, $41,000 in Massachusetts, and $5,000 in Connecticut) of Savings Bank Life Insurance for about half as much as prevailing company rates. The savings are due to the fact that no salesmen's commissions are involved.

Another localized life insurance bargain is available through a participating program, with coverages of up to $10,000, conducted by the Wisconsin State Commissioner of Insurance. If you live in or near Wisconsin, by all means check into it. Write to the Wisconsin State Insurance Fund, 201 East Washington Avenue, Madison, Wisconsin 53703, for details.

For further information:

The Great American Insurance Hoax, Richard Guarino and Richard Truto. Los Angeles, Nash, 1974.

COMING TO TERMS

In terms of dollar protection received for your money, term insurance gives you three to four times as much as other life insurance policies. While it is true that term premiums increase over the years, it is also quite likely that you will be better able to pay later in life. Moreover, you will never pay as much as for whole life coverage. For example, for a $100,000 policy, bought when you were 25 years old, you would pay well over $1,000 less annually at age 30 for a term premium. At age 45, you would still be paying several hundred dollars less a year.

However, make sure your policy is non-cancellable and guaranteed renewable so that you aren't left without a policy as you grow older or become a poorer risk. Also, obtain one of the convertible plans so you'll be free to convert this policy to a different—more appropriate—plan in the future.

For further information:

The Consumers Union Report on Life Insurance: A Guide to Planning and Buying the Protection You Need, Editors of *Consumer Reports*. New York, Grossman, 1973.

YOUR MONEY OR YOUR LIFE

Six out of the seven cheapest nonparticipating term life insurance policies are offered by the American branches of Canadian insurance firms. These six companies are: Dominion Life Assurance, National Life Assurance, Canada Life Insurance, Sun Life Assurance, North American Life Assurance, and Great West Life Assurance.

Naturally, any foreign-based insurance company doing business in this country must be licensed in the state in which it conducts business, so your investment is safe here. Why pay more?

For U.S. life insurance companies, there is an extremely wide range of rates. Some policies cost only a third as much as others. For a complete analysis of life insurance costs, see "Life Insurance: How Costs Compare Company by Company," *Changing Times*, June 1975, pages 15–17. Also, write to *Changing Times* Reprint Service, 1729 H Street, N.W., Washington, D.C. 20006, for their free survey of life insurance costs for 75 major companies.

DECREASING TERM INSURANCE

Decreasing term insurance offers the young family breadwinner the maximum amount of insurance at the lowest possible cost.

Usually, decreasing term is purchased to cover a home mortgage. The face value decreases annually (as does the outstanding balance on the mortgage) until it reaches zero, at which time the policy ceases to exist.

The advantage here is that, in his early working years, the policyholder has a substantial amount of coverage. Presumably, as he gets older, his assets will increase, thus compensating for the lower amount his beneficiary will receive in the event of his death.

For further information:

"Six-Figure Life Insurance for Three-Figure Premiums," Avery Comarov, *Money*, March 1975, pages 67–68, 70.

THE BARE MINIMUM

Depending upon the age of the insured and the type of insurance required, minimum-deposit life insurance may be even cheaper than term insurance. Here, funds from the dividends and loan value of the policy are automatically transferred by the company, at 5 or 6 percent interest, and applied to premium payments. Of course, the policy's face value is reduced by the amount borrowed, but interest paid is tax-deductible.

Savings to the insured using minimum deposit usually begin to outstrip term insurance savings seven to fourteen years after the policy is begun.

For further information:

"Life Insurance That Lends You the Premiums," Jeffrey Madrick, *Money*, October 1974, pages 79–80, 82, 84.

FAMILY FRUGALITY

You can save 20 percent on life insurance premiums by combining into one family policy coverages for various family members insured under individual policies. The more children there are in the family, the more you will save, as many family plans cost the same no matter how many children you have.

For example, at $385 a year, Metropolitan Life offers a whole-life family plan of $10,000 (30-year-old husband), $5,000 (28-year-old wife), and $2,000 for each child over 14 days. For a family with four children, this is a savings of about $72 a year over the cost of comparable individual policies.

Similar discounts apply to auto insurance for family cars—for a spouse or minor child insured under separate policies—provided you switch to a combination policy.

For further information:

Stop Wasting Your Insurance Dollars, David Goodwin. New York, Essandess Specials (orders to Simon & Schuster), 1969.

PREMIUM PRUDENCY

For savings of up to 15 percent on life insurance premiums, prepay a year in advance instead of by the month. Similar discounts are available for hospitalization and disability insurance.

THE RATE BREAK

Ask your agent at what points the standard rate for your life insurance changes to the cheaper, preferred rate. You may be able to increase your insurance $1,000 or so and benefit from the lower rate.

With Metropolitan Life, for example, the break occurs at $10,000 for women and $35,000 for men. A 30-year-old man can actually *save* $30 a year on a level 10-year term policy by insuring himself for $35,000 rather than $34,000!

For further information:

How to Pay Lots Less for Life Insurance . . . and Be Covered for as Much and as Long as You Want, Max Fogill. New York, Research and Education Association, 1971.

AGE SAGENESS

If your life insurance premiums would have been lower had you begun your policy within the last month or two, you can sometimes arrange to take advantage of that lower rate by asking your agent to backdate your new policy to an earlier date. You will be paying a few months' extra premium, but this will be far outweighed, not only by the decrease in premium but also by the substantially larger cash value as time goes on.

For instance, with one large company, you'll pay $150 less in premiums over the years and accumulate $1,000 more in cash value at age 65 by buying a $25,000 whole life policy at age 34 rather than at age 35.

For further information:

Life Insurance: A Consumer's Handbook, Joseph Belth. Bloomington, Indiana, Indiana University Press, 1973.

ANNUITY ACUITY

Thinking of buying an annuity to assure yourself of an income on retirement? Be sure to purchase a variable annuity, whose payments will increase with rising prices. Thus you will be assured that inflation won't make what today seems a generous retirement income less than adequate to meet even your basic needs when you retire.

For further information:

"Playing the Market: Variable Life Insurance," *Newsweek,* Vol. 81, 19 February 1973, pages 63–64.

Health and Disability

By far the most important consideration in purchasing health insurance is the percentage of the typical hospital bill your insurance pays, rather than the upper financial limits of the policy. It hardly matters whether the maximum policy amount is $20,000 or $200,000, for the chance that your hospital stay will cost more than $20,000 is indeed remote. But a plan that pays your full expenses for a 30-day hospital stay will put you several thousand dollars ahead of the plan that only pays half these charges.

Another tip: Forget about plans that cover only such limited circumstances as injury by accident, or catching such dread diseases as cancer, leukemia, or polio. The chance that the average person will need medical coverage for one of these is such a long shot that you are gambling needlessly with your money. Instead, plump for the broadest, most comprehensive health plan you can find. See that it covers such eventualities as accident, cancer, polio, mental illness, pregnancy, diagnostic tests, at-home nursing, and doctors' calls. While the cost of the policy will be greater, the likelihood is also far greater that, under the more comprehensive plan, you'll eventually be reimbursed for a large medical outlay.

There's a fair chance you can qualify for *free* medical insurance under the national Medicare program if you are sixty-five or older; if you've received Social Security disability benefits for at least two consecutive years; or if a member of your family needs a kidney machine or transplant, provided either you or your spouse is covered under Social Security. For more information, contact your local Social Security Administration office or write for *A Brief Explanation of Medicare*, Department of Health, Education and Welfare Publication Number (SSA) 75–10043, U.S. Department of Health, Education and Welfare, Social Security Administration, 6401 Security Boulevard, Baltimore, Maryland 21235, January 1975.

If you don't qualify for Medicare, check with the free state health insurance programs, such as Medicaid and Medical. In California, for example, not only does Medical cover the indigent, but average-income families caught without medical insurance after an auto accident or serious illness can let Medical foot the bill, either in whole or in part. Medicare recipients may find that Medical will plug the gaps in their Medicare coverage. For more information, check with your county welfare department.

INTENT ON PREVENTION?

If you live in an area where a health maintenance organization operates, find out if you're eligible to be a member. While plans offered by such outfits cost about the same as conventional health insurance, they provide far more benefits and preventive health care.

For example, the Kaiser Foundation Plan, available on the West Coast and in Hawaii, offers outpatient medical care ranging from examining eyes to treating chicken pox. You pay $2 for a visit to one of their specialists, and get prescriptions filled economically at their pharmacy as well. All this in addition to the normal hospital coverage!

Other such plans are offered by the Health Insurance Plan of Greater New York; the Group Health Association of Washington, D.C.; the Community Health Association of Detroit; the Group Health Cooperative of Puget Sound and the Group Dental Cooperative of Puget Sound; and the Roos-Loos Medical Group of Los Angeles.

For further information:

Office of Research and Statistics, Social Security Administration, U.S. Department of Health, Education and Welfare, Washington, D.C. 20201. (Ask for group practice prepayment plan information.)

THEIR LOSS—YOUR GAIN

When shopping for health insurance, one excellent way to measure potential benefits versus premiums is to determine the loss ratio of the companies in which you're interested. The loss ratio is the amount of money an insurance company pays out compared to the amount it takes in. Blue Cross and Blue Shield, for example, often have loss ratios of more than 90 percent. In other words, they are returning as benefits more than 90¢ out of every premium dollar to the policyholder.

To learn the loss ratio of the companies you're interested in, check at your library for *Best's Insurance Reports Life-Health 1975*, Oldwick, New Jersey, A. M. Best Company, 1975. Loss ratios for United States and Canadian accident and health policies are listed in that book under "Accident and Health Statistics," at the end of entries on each company.

MEDICARE MISCELLANY

If you're on Medicare, you'll not only be concerned with the benefits of this plan, but with what it *doesn't* pay as well. Both part A and part B of Medicare have deductibles, or sums you must pay before the plan starts footing the bill. Also, you must pay 20 percent of your doctor bills, and part of your hospital bill for every day over a 60-day stay. An excellent inexpensive coverage called "65-Special" or "Companion Care," available through Blue Cross–Blue Shield to plug these gaps, is well worth the small monthly fee.

In California, for example, you can eliminate hospital charges completely for only $5 a month. Combined hospital, doctor, and drug costs can be done away with for $18.50 a month. Plans vary from state to state, so contact your local Blue Cross–Blue Shield office for more information.

Supplemental Medicare coverage is also available through the National Council of Senior Citizens, 1511 K Street, N.W., Washington, D.C. 20005.

For further information:

Your Medicare Handbook, U.S. Department of Health, Education and Welfare, Social Security Administration, 6401 Security Boulevard, Baltimore, Maryland 21235, or write to your local Social Security Administration.

BLOOD MONEY

Does your health plan cover blood transfusions? If not, eliminate such costs in the future by donating blood in advance to the American Association of Blood Banks. A family member who donates a pint of his blood insures that he or any member of his family will be supplied with an unlimited amount of blood for a year at no charge. A single person who donates the same amount is insured for two years.

For further information:

The American Association of Blood Banks, 270 Masonic Avenue, San Francisco, California 94118. Or contact the local chapter of the American Red Cross.

ACADEMIC INSURANCE

For traveling students and teachers, a special low-priced discount insurance plan is available. Five dollars insures you for $10,000 major medical, $5,000 death and dismemberment, and baggage protection for the duration of your trip. An extra $2.50 covers you for the cost of emergency air fare home in the event of accident, illness, or death.

For further information:

Frank B. Hall & Company, Benefit Consulting Division, 261 Madison Avenue, New York, New York 10016.

DISABILITY AGILITY

Find out what your employer offers in the way of salary payment while you are ill. If you have accumulated several months of sick leave over years of service (one of our government employee friends accumulated seven months before he retired), you can save money on disability income insurance by including a one- to six-month waiting period in your policy. During this waiting period, your sick leave would act as income insurance.

For further information:

The Consumer's Guide to Insurance Buying, Vladimir Chernik, Los Angeles, Sherbourne Press, 1970.

GOVERNMENT INSURANCE

If you have a disability that prevents you from working, you may be eligible for Social Security payments—even though you are under 65. However, the disability must be serious: loss of a limb, or a progressive disease such as cancer, multiple sclerosis, or severe mental illness.

Unlike workman's compensation, this disability need not have occurred on the job. You must have worked under Social Security for from one and a half to five years (the amount depends on your age) with a certain period preceding the disability. For example: A disabled person who averaged $6,000 yearly before the disability can receive a payment of over $200 a month. Well worth looking into!

For further information:

Your Social Security Rights and Responsibilities: Disability Benefits, Department of Health, Education and Welfare Publication Number (SSA) 74–10153, U.S. Department of Health, Education, and Welfare, Social Security Administration, Baltimore, Maryland 21235, March 1974.

THE DISABLED CHILD

Many people think that disability insurance payments under Social Security apply only to workers who have paid into a disability insurance fund before becoming disabled. This is far from true. A child, unmarried when the benefits began, who has been disabled before the age of 18 to such an extent that he or she is unable to earn a living, can receive, in some cases, disability payments amounting to $200 a month. These benefits last until either the child recovers from the disability or dies.

In order to qualify, the child must have a parent receiving Social Security old age or disability payments, or the parent must have acquired the right to survivors' benefits by working under Social Security for a number of years.

For further information:

Your Social Security Rights and Responsibilities: Disability Benefits, Department of Health, Education and Welfare Publication Number (SSA) 74–10153, U.S. Department of Health, Education and Welfare, Social Security Administration, Baltimore, Maryland 21235, March 1974.

DEPENDENT BENEFITS

If you are getting disability insurance through Social Security, your children under age 18, as well as unmarried schoolchildren under 21, are also eligible for payments. If you have no eligible children, your wife or husband qualifies for payments after the age of 62.

For example, a disabled worker with a spouse over 62 years old who averaged $6,000 yearly before the disability will receive close to $100 more—and a worker with a dependent spouse and child will receive close to $200 more—than a single disabled worker would each month.

For further information:

Your Social Security Rights and Responsibilities: Disability Benefits, Department of Health, Education and Welfare Publication Number (SSA) 74–10153, U.S. Department of Health, Education and Welfare, Social Security Administration, Baltimore, Maryland 21235, March 1974.

COMPLIMENTS OF THE CLUB

Group hospitalization and life insurance are always cheaper than an individual plan. How can a self-employed or unemployed person take advantage of this group discount? You may already unwittingly belong to a group that entitles you to a discount. Some health plans, for example, offer a 10 to 15 percent discount to sole proprietors. If you belong to a professional association, such as a builders' and contractors' organization or a realtors' association, you may be able to obtain discount health or life insurance, particularly if you are older. Fraternal associations, credit unions, even the art guild, the local camera club, or the garden club, may be your tickets to lower insurance premiums.

In our area, one chamber of commerce offers its members (who may join as a business or as an individual) a group hospitalization plan. The difference in price between this group plan and the usual individual plan (less the $12 cost of the individual membership in the chamber means an annual savings of $75!

For a list of prepaid group health plans, write the Group Health Association, 1321 Fourteenth Street, N.W., Washington, D.C. 20005.

Auto, Homeowner's

SPECIAL DISCOUNTS

Auto insurance premiums are nothing to sneeze at these days. Therefore, you'll want to take advantage of some of the sizeable customer discounts being offered by many insurance companies.

State Farm, for example, offers discounts of 15 to 25 percent for those who have a history of relatively accident-free driving, students under 25 years of age who maintain a B-average in school, and drivers of farm vehicles.

Allstate offers a 15 percent liability discount for compact cars and a 10 percent liability medical discount for cars equipped with safety airbags. Other companies offer similar reductions for cars with factory-installed collapsible bumpers, safety belts, and headrests.

For further information:
"Ways to Save on Your Car Insurance," *Changing Times*, Vol. 27, October 1973, page 4.

SUSPENSE ACCOUNT

If your car will not be used for a month or more due to repairs, that long-awaited European vacation, or any other reason, have all insurance coverages except fire and theft suspended for that length of time. The prorated premium for the interval will be refunded to you, and barring the possibility of a truck or airplane crashing into your garage during this period, you'll save a pretty penny.

For example, if you go on an extended three-month round-the-world holiday, you'll save $30 in premiums—even on an older car.

TOBACCO TRADE-OFF

Kicking the tobacco habit can improve not only your health but your insurance premiums as well. Careful shopping will get you discounts of up to 25 percent on auto insurance, homeowner's, disability income, and life insurance.

For example, the lower incidence of accidents among nonsmokers has convinced Farmers Insurance Group to offer a 20 to 25 percent auto insurance discount to nonsmokers over the age of 21 living in the West and Midwest.

On homeowner's policies, Hanover Insurance gives a 5 percent discount to non-smoking households due to the decreased fire hazard.

For disability income insurance, Madison Life and Guardian Life discount their policies by 10 percent to nonsmokers; State Mutual Life and General Life of Wisconsin offer up to 5 and 10 percent, respectively.

In the life insurance field, Wisconsin National offers a nonsmokers' discount of 8 percent; American Agency Life and Kentucky Central offer 6 percent; American National and Executive Life of California, 5 percent; and Gulf Life and State Mutual, 3 percent. Other life insurance companies offer variable discounts depending on the age of the policyholder.

For further information:

"Insurance Breaks for Nonsmokers," *Changing Times*, December 1974, page 36.

LIABILITY LOWDOWN

If you're carrying the minimum auto liability coverage required by law, you are underinsured. A fact that many insurance agents neglect to relate is that you can get your liability limits raised mightily, enough to cover even the most money-hungry plaintiff, for only a moderate sum.

For example, if you're an average policyholder, you can increase your liability limits of $15,000 per person for injury, and $30,000 for all injuries per accident to $100,000/$300,000 for only an additional $3 or so per month!

For further information:

"Can You Cut Your Automobile Insurance Costs?" William Apple, *Consumer Bulletin*, Vol. 56, May 1973, pages 13–14.

HOMEOWNER'S HUSBANDRY

What's a homeowner's policy? It's one overall insurance policy that covers damage to your house by fire, theft, and other catastrophes, damage to furniture, clothes, and other belongings, and comprehensive personal liability (to cover suits for injury on your property).

One homeowner's policy can save you 20 to 30 percent over, and will cover you more thoroughly than, separate fire, personal, and comprehensive policies. Unlike these other plans, a homeowner's policy will insure some of your property away from home, will pay for your temporary lodging if you lose your home to fire, and will pay the full replacement cost of destroyed property (rather than merely the depreciated value of same).

For further information:

The Shopper's Guidebook to Life Insurance, Health Insurance, Auto Insurance, Homeowner's Insurance, Doctors, Dentists, Lawyers, Pensions, Etc., Herbert Denenberg. Washington, D.C., Consumer News, 1974.

Legal Fees

FREE LEGALIZIN'

If you can't afford a lawyer, you can get free or low-cost legal assistance from any member of the National Legal Aid and Defender Association. Such legal aid societies are found in just about every medium- and large-sized community across the land.

For instance, the San Diego Legal Aid Society deals with consumer protection problems; auto accidents; unemployment, welfare, and social security appeals; landlord-tenant disputes; divorces, separations, and annulments; and such situations involving juveniles as adoptions, guardianships, and arrests.

For further information:

Directory of Legal Aid and Defender Services, National Legal Aid and Defender Association, 1155 East 60th Street, Chicago, Illinois 60637 (annual publication).

LAWYERS ON THE LINE

In California, 500 lawyers have gotten together and formed Group Legal Services, Inc. You pay $25, which entitles you to call any of them with simple legal problems or questions for a whole year. For more involved problems, you must visit the lawyers in person, but will receive a 25 percent discount from them.

If you live in California, contact Group Legal Services, Inc., 1100 Glendon Avenue, Westwood, California 90024; or a similar organization, California Credit Union League, 2322 South Garey Avenue, Pomona, California 91801. Elsewhere in the country, check the legal listings of the *People's Yellow Pages*, Scott French, New Rochelle, New York, Richard Heller & Son, 1974, for help in tracking down a similar group.

CUT-RATE CLINICS

Operating on the same high-volume, low-cost principle as Group Legal Services, but without charging a membership fee, legal clinics located in Los Angeles, Phoenix, Washington, D.C., and Denver now offer a discount of up to 50 percent over regular lawyers' fees. Shared office space, streamlined procedures, and use of paralegal assistants reduces clinic costs.

These clinics function best in such relatively uncomplicated areas as bankruptcy, wills, uncontested divorce, adoption, disability claims, house purchase or sale, probate landlord-tenant disputes, social security and personal injury claims, and felony preliminary hearings. For $10 or $15, such clinics will teach you to be your own lawyer for traffic court or small claims court.

In Los Angeles, contact the Legal Clinic of Meyers and Jacoby, 2385 South La Brea, Inglewood, California 90301, or 6511 Van Nuys Boulevard, Van Nuys, California 91401. Other clinics include Legal Clinic of Bates and O'Steen, 617 North 3rd Street, Phoenix, Arizona 85004; Law Office of Washington (LOW), 1 Thomas Circle, N.W., Washington, D.C. 20005; and the Denver Legal Clinic of Sarney, Trattler and Waitkus, 738 Pearl, Denver, Colorado 80203.

BEATING THE BARRISTER BLUES

Just as most of us carry medical and hospitalization insurance to protect us against increasingly higher health-care fees, many individuals now carry "legal insurance" to avoid potentially backbreaking attorneys' fees.

Costing a modest $20 to $35 annually for up to $15,000 worth of benefits, this coverage is available through Lloyd's of London. If they're not listed in your telephone book, write in care of Le Boeuf, Lamb, Leiby and MacRae, 140 Broadway, New York, New York 10005.

CONTINGENCY CONSCIOUSNESS

Many individuals hesitate to engage a lawyer for a lawsuit—which they believe they can win—because of the attorney's high fees.

A sizeable number of lawyers, however, work on a contingency fee rather than on a flat rate. Here, the attorney is paid a percentage of the judgment awarded if he wins the case, and nothing if he loses. Such arrangements are often made in negligence cases —such as in auto accident suits for personal injuries.

Due to the risky nature of the enterprise, contingent fees are often quite high— sometimes as much as 60 percent. Here are two ways you can cut down on these fees: Ask that the lawyer's percentage of the take be cut in half if—as is often true of negligence

cases—litigation is settled quickly out of court. Also ask that the contingent fee be deducted *after* expenses rather than off the top. This can save you several hundred dollars in a small suit of $10,000 or so.

For further information:

The Shopper's Guidebook to Life insurance, Health Insurance, Auto Insurance, Homeowner's Insurance, Doctors, Dentists, Lawyers, Pensions, Etc., Herbert Denenberg. Washington, D.C., Consumer News, 1974.

A LAWYER FOR LESS

Through the Lawyer Referral Service set up by the American Bar Association, you can obtain inexpensively a half hour's worth of legal advice from a lawyer who is a member of the bar. The cost of this service, which is available in communities throughout the country, varies from $3 to $15.

See your White Pages under "Lawyer Referral Service of (your town)" or "Bar Association of (your town)."

DIVORCE DIVIDENDS

Getting an uncontested divorce in a case where there are no children involved need not mean the usual $300 in lawyers' fees for each party. Instead, get yourself a copy of *How to Get a Divorce Without a Lawyer for Under Fifty Dollars,* Ted Nicholas, Wilmington, Delaware, Enterprise Publishing, 1975, and oversee your own divorce. Or, go to one of the many cut-rate divorce bureaus, staffed by laymen, which charge only $50 to $65 for their services.

In California, the Wave Project operates in twenty-eight cities for $65. Similar services are offered by the California Divorce Council, 2525 Van Ness Avenue, San Francisco, California 94109, and 3921 Wilshire, Los Angeles, California 90010; and by Divorce Yourself, 695 Bonesteel Street, Rochester, California 14616. For names of similar services in your area, see your Yellow Pages under "Divorce assistance."

A CASE FOR CONSUMERS

If you have a complaint against a firm whom you believe may be violating the consumer affairs laws overseen by the Federal Trade Commission, don't run to a private attorney, check in hand. First, talk to a local office of the FTC about it. They may be willing to take over the litigation for you. Also, if the much-vaunted Federal Consumer Protection Agency has been set up by the time you read this, check with them for a much wider range of legal assistance in the consumer affairs field.

For further information:

Federal Trade Commission, Pennsylvania Avenue at Sixth Street, N.W., Washington, D.C. 20580.

LUDICROUS LEGALITY

Did you know there are laws in some states against such activities as sneezing in public, washing your car on Sunday, and—believe it or not—walking backwards?

If you fall victim to such archaic—or just plain asinine—laws, write to The Beadle Bumble Fund, c/o *The Richmond News–Leader*, Box 26971, Richmond, Virginia 23261. For victims of truly absurd laws anywhere in the United States, this fund will pay fines, court costs, and legal fees!

CORPORATE COST-CUTTING

Form your own corporation—*without* paying the usual $500 (and up) in attorneys' fees!

How? By merely paying a $20 filing fee, then following the word-for-word instructions in *Community Access Video*, H. Allen Frederiksen, 695 Thirtieth Avenue, Apt. E, Santa Cruz, California 95060 ($3). Instructions apply to all kinds of corporations, not just video.

LEGAL AID FOR LADIES

Women, who are traditionally underpaid (or, in the case of housewives, *un*paid) for performing work that would bore a horse, more often than not lack the financial resources to battle even a clear-cut violation of their rights.

If you're in such a predicament, don't despair! Monetary assistance for impending or in-progress female rights cases can be had from the National Organization for Women Legal Defense and Education Fund, 641 Lexington Avenue, New York, New York 10022.

POLITICAL PAYOFF

For all kinds of free legal services, but especially for help in defense against politically oriented charges, contact the National Lawyers Guild. Offices are located in Boston, Massachusetts; at 506 Monroe, Detroit, Michigan 48226; 853 Broadway, New York 10003; 712 Grand View, Los Angeles, California 90057; 558 Capp Street, San Francisco, California 94110; 930 F Street, N.W., Washington, D.C., 20004; and 1427 Walnut Street, Philadelphia, Pennsylvania 19102.

In Michigan, you may also contact Carl Bekofske, Attorney, 510 West Court Street, Flint, Michigan 48503, for help.

CRIMINAL CASES

About to be tried for a crime? You can obtain high-class representation even if you can't afford the fees charged by crack lawyers. Many of the 157 law schools in the United States have clinics which can provide you with up-to-date, sharp, *free* legal help.

Is your criminal case unusual or unique? The Plantations Legal Defense Services, 906 Reservoir Avenue, Cranston, Rhode Island 02910, will take on "interesting" criminal cases free of charge!

For further information:

"Appendix 1," *How to Get into Law School*, Rennard Strickland. New York, Hawthorn, 1974, pages 155–162 (list of law schools).

FOR PRISONERS AND PLAYBOYS

If that overwhelmingly conservative police establishment has nabbed you on a drug rap or censorship bust, or if your rights as a prisoner have been violated, contact The Playboy Foundation, 919 North Michigan Avenue, Chicago, Illinois 60611. This organization will often cover court costs for victims enmeshed in outmoded laws, which are a threat to their business.

Straights or gays who feel their sex life has been invaded should contact Marilyn Haft, American Civil Liberties Union Sexual Privacy Project, 22 East 40th Street, New York, New York 10016. Through her, you may be able to plead your cause cost-free.

BIG SAVINGS ON SMALL CLAIMS

For cases involving up to $1,000 in some states, you can save several hundred dollars in lawyers' fees—the cost of which would otherwise make many suits impractical—by filing your own claim in small claims court. The court clerk will show you how to fill out the form. Filing fees average $10.

For further information:

"Courts of First Resort," Champ Clark, *Money*, June 1973, pages 32–36.

RACIAL RECOURSE

Poverty need not be a barrier in seeking legal recourse for cases of racial discrimination. Whether the issue is voter rights, desegregation of schools, landlord-tenant disputes, or consumer issues, minority members will find an organization ready to take up their cause and foot the legal fees.

Blacks should contact their local NAACP, who will refer them to the national-level NAACP Legal Defense Fund. The Mexican-American Legal Defense and Educational Fund, 145 Ninth Street, San Francisco, California 94103, performs a similar function for Chicanos.

FUNDAMENTAL FREEDOMS

If you feel that your freedom of speech, movement, association, religion (pro or con), or privacy has been violated, legal recourse may well be yours without the expense of hiring a lawyer and footing court costs. Among organizations that will foot legal costs for group legal suits in these areas are the American Civil Liberties Union, 22 East 40th Street, New York, New York 10016; The Center for Constitutional Rights, 853 Broadway, New York, New York 10003; and The National Emergency Civil Liberties Committee, 25 East 26th Street, New York, New York 10010. Contact their headquarters or see the White Pages of your phone book for local offices.

POLLUTION PROBLEMS

Is that factory down the street spewing black smoke into your yard? Is a stripmining operation dumping tons of silt into nearby streams, without even bothering to plant saplings over the scars? Is that lumber mill dumping dangerous chemicals in a nearby lake and killing off all the fish? Legal recourse is yours through the Natural Resources Defense Council, 15 West 44th Street, New York, New York 10036.

This organization will handle, free of charge, cases involving the environment, pollution, or the adverse effect of environmental destruction on public health. The Sierra Club, 220 Bush Street, San Francisco, California 94104, handles similar issues, but you must work with the main office through their affiliates in your area.

NAME CHANGE KNOWLEDGE

Do you need to pay a lawyer up to $300 for a legal name change? No! Instead, visit your county court clerk and find out what forms, and how many of each, are needed for the change. Fill them out yourself, using papers already on file at the clerk's office as a sample.

You must have a valid reason for changing the name—i.e., no intent to defraud or deceive—and must petition a court, after which a court order provides the legal name change.

For further information:

"When to Take the Law into Your Own Hands," Don Sider, *Money*, March 1975, pages 59–60, 62, 64.

18

MISCELLANEOUS MISERLINESS FOR THE MULTITUDES

Now the problem arises of what to do with all that green stuff the preceding chapters have allowed you to save. In point of fact, how you handle your money means the difference between empty pockets and the pyrámiding of a few dollars into a substantial nest egg.

For the conservative investor, various types of banks offer a hedge against inflation. There are banks that offer interest on checking accounts; banks that offer 8¾ percent interest on the most meager savings. For the more imaginative investor, opportunites for much greater returns exist, along with the chance to save on initial investment in anything from common stocks to cartoon art. At the end of the road, it's possible to save thousands of dollars on funeral arrangements and estate taxes simply by planning ahead with care.

For more information, read: *Sylvia Porter's Money Book—How to Earn It, Spend It, Save It, Invest It, Borrow It and Use It to Better Your Life*, Sylvia Porter, Garden City, New York, Doubleday, 1975; *Better Times*, J. C. Suares et al., Garden City, New York, Doubleday, 1975; and *The Time-Life Book of Family Finance*, Carlton Smith et al., New York, Time-Life, 1969.

Salt It Away!

LAUGHING STOCK

For $15 a year, you can join the Museum of Cartoon Art, 384 Field Point Road, Greenwich, Connecticut 06830. Membership entitles you to a 20 percent discount on cartoon purchases, a free print, and other extras.

For a list of cartoon art for sale, write the Cartoon Museum, 561 Obispo Avenue, Orlando, Florida 32807.

For further information:

"Invest in Cartoon Art and Laugh All the Way to the Bank," Gus Turbeville. *Moneysworth*, 16 February 1976, pages 16–17.

PROSPECTING PELF

Do you own, or can you lease, property on which you'd like to explore for minerals? Uncle Sam will foot up to half of the exploration costs, provided you can put up the rest of the money. If gold (or any one of thirty-four other minerals) is discovered, he will take only 5 percent of your royalties. If you find nothing, you owe him nothing.

For further information:

Exploration Assistance. Office of Minerals Exploration, U.S. Department of the Interior, Washington, D.C. 20240.

BROKER BREAKS

If you don't need professional advice on when to buy and sell your stocks, you can save up to 50 percent on brokers' fees by dealing with a discount (third-market) broker. On a $1,000 order, for example, such no-frills brokers as Columbine Securities, Inc., 1820 Prudential Plaza, 1050 17th Street, Denver, Colorado 80202; and Rose and Company, Board of Trade Building, West Jackson Boulevard, Chicago, Illinois 60604, will save you 30 to 35 percent over the New York Stock Exchange trade rate (about $10). On trades of several thousand dollars, the percentage saved can be much higher.

One drawback: While discounts are available on about 1,500 issues, some third-market prices are the same as or more expensive than New York Stock Exchange prices, so stay on your toes.

For further information:

"Now the Small Investor Can Save on Brokers' Fees," *Changing Times*, September 1974, pages 17–20 (includes list of discount brokers).

TREASURED CASH

During periods of tight money, an excellent way to put sums of $10,000 or more to work gathering interest for short periods is to buy Treasury Bills (T-bills). These can yield as much as 7½ percent and can be had for three, six, nine, or twelve months. They're obtainable through your banker, or if you want to avoid his commission, by writing the Federal Reserve Bank of New York, Securities Department, 33 Liberty Street, New York, New York 10005, or one of its branches.

To find out which T-bills are available now and what they are yielding, check *The Wall Street Journal,* talk to your banker, or ask the Federal Reserve Bank to keep you up to date.

For further information:

"Making Big Money in Tiny Increments: U.S. Treasury Bills," *Business Week,* 23 June 1975, page 76.

MUTUAL FUNDS

What's a mutual fund? It's simply a corporation organized and operated solely for the purpose of investing the funds of its stockholders.

This type of investment is one of the surest ways, in a threatening world, of making your savings earn a profit at the least possible risk. If you had put $10,000 in the average mutual fund in 1950, and left it there for twenty years, you would be worth nigh onto $50,000 more than the bloke who placed his ten grand in a 5 percent savings account.

For further information:

Fundscope, Suite 700, 1900 Avenue of the Stars, Los Angeles, California 90067 (monthly magazine).

Investment Company Institute, 1775 K Street, N.W., Washington, D.C. 20006 (free list of mutual funds and addresses).

BUCKS FROM BONDS

If you have money to invest, consider investing in bonds. State, county, municipal, water district, and school district bonds are considered a relatively safe investment and will yield up to 6 percent interest, paid every 6 months as it accumulates, for terms up to 8 years or so. If you place this interest in a savings account, the compounded interest will amount to as much as eight percent.

Furthermore, the interest is totally tax-free due to the fact that bond money is invested in such community-strenghtening projects as building schools, improving utilities, and expanding public transportation facilities. As a result of this tax break, a person making $25,000 a year makes the equivalent of 10 percent taxable interest with a 6 percent tax-free bond.

Bonds can be purchased through a commercial bank or stockbroker. You'll be charged up to $25 per bond purchased, so save on the service charge by getting large denomination bonds.

For further information:

Too Good for the Rich Alone: The Complete Guide to Tax-Exempt Bonds for the Middle-Income Investor, James Reilly. Englewood Cliffs, New Jersey, Prentice-Hall, 1975.

ART SMARTS

As an excellent long-term investment and a chic addition to your home, buying original art is not an activity that should be left exclusively to the well-to-do. Buy your own limited-edition prints for just $15 from Associated American Artists, 663 Fifth Avenue, New York, New York 10022 (brochure—50¢).

Or, join Fine Arts (a division of the Book-of-the-Month Club) for $10. For this fee, you will receive an original print, a print-collector's guide, and the right to purchase their limited-edition prints, mostly at under $60 including frame.

Collector's Guild, 185 Madison Avenue, New York, New York 10016, charges only $50–$60 for fine framed lithographs, less for woodcuts and etchings. The membership fee is $15.

For further information:

"Buying Art at Prices that Aren't 'Off the Wall,' " Parker Hodges, *Moneysworth,* 8 December 1975, page 15.

LAND SAKES!

If you're a farmer, the federal government will actually *pay* you for improving your land! The Agricultural Stabilization and Conservation Service, for example, will foot the bill for half the cost of such improvements as planting land to prevent erosion, building ponds, and other projects that will increase the value of your property.

Do you own land in Appalachia? Uncle Sam will pay you as much as 80 percent of the cost of improving your land to prevent erosion. Your project must be approved through your state member of the Appalachian Regional Commission, whose address can be obtained from the Appalachian Regional Commission, 1666 Connecticut Avenue, Washington, D.C. 20235.

In the Great Plains area, the government will pay up to $2,500 a year to farms and ranches with erosion problems for such good conservation practices as planting grass, contour strip-cropping, planting trees, building dams and water runoff areas, and revamping irrigation systems. Needless to say, these cut-rate improvements will increase your crop yield and land values at the same time.

For further information:

Agricultural Stabilization and Conservation Service, 14th Street and Independence Avenue, S.W., Washington, D.C. 20250.

For more information on the Great Plains Conservation Program, contact a Department of Agriculture county office in the Great Plains.

Bank on It

A FOREIGN IDEA

The overseas branches of American banks offer considerably higher interest than their domestic branches. For instance, Bank of America, 29 Davies Street, London, England, offers savings certificates at 8½ percent compared to 7½ percent offered through their American-based branches.

Get the names and addresses of foreign branches of American banks by checking the *Polk World Bank Directory* (North American and International editions), Nashville, Tennessee, R. L. Polk and Company (semiannual publication) at your library.

NOW POWER

Now you can not only save the $36 or so a year most banks charge for checking account services, but you can actually draw interest on the money in your checking account. How? Through the negotiable order of withdrawal (NOW) banks of Massachusetts and New Hampshire. Two NOW banks paying 5 percent on checking balances and accepting out-of-state, bank-by-mail accounts are Home Savings Bank, 69 Tremont Street, Boston, Massachusetts 02108; and Citizens Bank and Trust Company, Park Ridge, Chicago, Illinois 60666.

For a list of 100 NOW savings banks, write the Savings Bank Association of Massachusetts, 50 Congress Street, Boston, Massachusetts 02109. Not all of the banks listed will accept out-of-state accounts, so you must write and ask them individually.

CHECK THIS!

Both Barclays Bank and Perera Company, Inc., offer free travelers' checks—a savings of $1 per $100 worth of checks—even to noncustomers!

However, if these firms don't do business in your community, you can still save $48 per $5,000 in travelers' checks by timing your purchase to take in Bank of America's and First National City's annual May travelers' check sales—up to $5,000 in checks for $2.

For further information:

Barclays Bank International, Ltd., 200 Park Avenue, New York, New York 10017 (branches in New York—including Kennedy International Airport—Chicago, and California).

Perera Company, Inc., Foreign Exchange, 29 Broadway, New York, New York 10006.

DOUBLE DEALING

You can earn twice as much interest on your "day of deposit to day of withdrawal" savings account. The technique is to transfer "imaginary" funds almost equal to your savings amount (for example, you might transfer $1,999 if your savings amount is $2,000) from your checking account to your savings account. These funds are "imaginary" because you'll have no money in your checking account (except the minimum amount needed to keep the account open).

Suppose the bank takes three days to clear the transfer. On the third day, in order for the check not to bounce, you'll withdraw $1,999 of your original savings from the savings account for deposit in your checking account. Meanwhile, you'll have collected three days of interest on the funds.

However—and now things get *really* complicated—immediately after depositing the $1,999, you'll write *another* check for the same amount to be deposited in your savings account. Thus you'll constantly be receiving interest on $3,999, even though you, in reality, only have savings totaling $2,000.

This technique requires precise forestudy and timing, as well as nerves of steel (steal??). Before attempting it, read carefully "Top Secret Money Key No. 46," *Martin Meyer's Moneybook*, Martin Meyer, Chatsworth, California, Books for Better Living (orders to Simon & Schuster), 1972, pages 188–197.

BOOKKEEPING BARGAIN

If your savings account sees a fair amount of deposit and withdrawal activity, you can earn much more interest simply by depositing your money in a bank whose bookkeeping system *favors* savings account activity.

Banks have deviously devised many complex bookkeeping systems relative to savings accounts. The most favorable to the customer, however, is the "day of deposit to day of withdrawal" method, which can earn as much as twice the interest for an active account as does the least favorable type. Only 10 percent of all banks use this system, however, and they are almost always located in large cities. If you live in a small community and your bank does not use this method, you can save considerably by transferring your savings account to a bank-by-mail "day of deposit to day of withdrawal" metropolitan bank.

CHUCKING CHECK COSTS

Here's a trick to eliminate check-writing costs if you have several checking accounts —business and personal, for example—in one bank. If your bank offers free checks for accounts with balances over a couple hundred dollars, as many do, speak to an officer at the bank about combining balances, as well as check charges, from the two accounts every month.

Often the combined balance will be enough to eliminate check charges for good.

For further information:

Martin Meyer's Moneybook, Martin Meyer. Chatsworth, California, Books for Better Living (orders to Simon & Schuster), 1972.

THE GREAT SAVINGS AND LOAN GIVEAWAY

Many savings and loan associations, in order to attract the "big money," offer membership in "statesmen's clubs" for those opening savings accounts of $2,500 to $5,000 or more. By virtue of membership in one of these clubs, one becomes entitled to a veritable bonanza of free and discounted products and services.

For example, at Home Federal Savings, a California savings and loan association, your $2,500 will entitle you to the following *free* services: conference space, the use of adding machines and copiers, safe-deposit box, notary public services, a checking account, five money orders a month, one thousand travelers' checks a year, and last but not least, coffee and refreshments in any of their statesmen's lounges.

You'll also be entitled to a 10 to 15 percent discount on California motel rates, merchandise, recreational facilities, and travel tours.

For further information:

"A New Kind of Club for Savers," *Changing Times*, February 1974, page 50.

MONEY ORDER ARDOR

Unbeknownst to you, free money orders and checks galore may be at hand. Many bank savings accounts allow withdrawals in the form of checks or money orders. Thus, you can pay your bills with money-order "withdrawals" made out either in your name (with "pay to the order of . . ." on the back) or in the name of the appropriate company or individual.

A quick check with the savings banks listed in the phone book will allow you to save that $30-a-year checking fee. Make sure you pick a savings bank that levies no penalty for withdrawals in excess of a few a month.

SAVINGS ACCOUNT SHENANIGANS

This ruse allows you to draw 10 percent interest on a 5 percent savings account for thirteen days out of each calendar quarter. Open two savings accounts: one that earns interest from day of deposit to day of withdrawal; and one regular account which pays interest only on funds which remain till the end of each quarter. The regular account *must* offer grace days (usually ten) at the beginning of the quarter—so that money deposited by the tenth earns from the first day of the quarter. It should offer bonus days—three days prior to the end of the quarter when your money can be withdrawn and still earn interest for the full quarter.

Place your funds in the regular savings account at the beginning of a quarter. When the first bonus day rolls around, withdraw your funds and place them in the "day of deposit to day of withdrawal" account until the tenth day of the following quarter. On this day (the last grace day of the regular account), redeposit the money in the original bank. Thus, you earn double interest for thirteen days.

For further information:

Martin Meyer's Moneybook, Martin Meyer. Chatsworth, California, Books for Better Living (orders to Simon & Schuster), 1972.

Credit

Does loan company lingo have you addled? It takes a mathematical genius to figure out the difference between add-on interest, discount and straight interest; to calculate monthly rates, penalties and points. So shop for a loan by requesting the total amount of interest you will pay over the loan period, which figures you can easily compare.

Shopping for a new car? If you're intending to finance an auto purchase through the dealer, you'll pay sky-high interest rates. For profiteering on auto loans comprises a goodly portion of the car dealer's income—at the consumer's expense! Before finalizing the deal, check the interest rates at your company or labor union's credit union. Next best bet is a bank—shop diligently for the one with the best interest rate.

The major sources of *mortgage* money are insurance companies, savings and loan associations, savings banks, commercial banks and mortgage companies. How do these compare in the interest they charge and in terms and mortgages offered?

Insurance companies are most likely to finance a very high-priced home at a low rate, but they require a high down payment. *Savings and loans* will finance very low-cost homes with low down payments, but at a high rate. *Commercial banks* will finance a high-priced home with extra low rates, but require a high down payment. *Savings banks* will mortgage a low-cost home at the second lowest rates, but they also require a high down payment. *Mortgage companies* will finance the purchase of a medium-priced home with the lowest available down payment, but they charge the highest rates.

The best method of getting the facts is by telephone: Call every lender in town for rates. Even a half a percent rate difference on a twenty-year, $10,000 mortgage will cost you over $700 in extra interest, so make your survey thorough!

SHORT-TERM SAVINGS

If you need cash for one to three months and are on good terms with your banker, you can save a bundle on interest charges by arranging for a short-term unsecured loan. Interest rates on these are about half as much as on longer-term personal loans.

For further information:

Of Interest: A Consumer's Basic Guide to the Cost of Borrowing Money, C. A. Farrell. Hicksville, New York, Exposition Press, 1975.

AN INTERESTING POLICY

Been paying into life insurance for some years now? Chances are you can borrow against the security of your investment in the insurance to date at rates as low as 4 percent. Check your policy to find out if it contains such provisions.

Be sure to repay this loan as quickly as possible after you take it out. Otherwise, the amount will be deducted from the face value of your policy should a claim be made.

For further information:

The Time-Life Book of Family Finance, Carlton Smith et al. New York, Time-Life, 1969.

BORROWING BRILLIANCE

If you need money but don't want to dent those savings which were accumulated with such difficulty, consider getting a passbook loan. You arrange with the bank to leave enough savings in your account to cover the loan until you pay it off. In exchange, they charge you only 9 percent annual interest on the loan instead of the current 16 percent charged on personal loans.

For further information:

Dollars and Sense. A Guide to Mastering Your Money, Art Watkins. New York, Quadrangle/The New York Times, 1973.

INSURED CREDIT

Usually a bank or other lender will include in your loan contract a charge for credit life insurance. That is, if you die before the loan is paid off, the balance of the unpaid loan is paid to the lender by the insurance company involved. These charges range from 0.5 percent to as much as 2 percent of the loan.

Examine your contract beforehand and decide whether you want to pay for the privilege of making your banker your beneficiary.

For further information:

J. K. Lasser's Managing Your Family Finances, J. K. Lasser Institute. Garden City, New York, Doubleday, 1968.

TWO PERCENT TRICK

If you need a short-term loan and have valuables, you might check with your venerable old pawn dealer as a source of some quick, cheap cash. In many states, pawnshop interest rates can run as low as two percent or less per month on money loaned on merchandise.

A few years ago, we had occasion to pawn a camera in a Washington, D.C., pawnshop. To our amazement, the interest rate was a very moderate one percent per month.

For further information:

Handling Your Money: All About Budgets and Credit and Investments and Taxes and How to Plug Your Personal Dollar Drain, Anthony Scaduto. New York, David McKay, 1970.

FREE FINANCING

Many credit-card plans are set up so that you need not pay their finance charge if you send them the total balance due within three weeks or so of the time you charge your items. BankAmericard, for example, levies no finance charge if you clear your account within 22 days of charging. For Master Charge, the time limit is 25 days. When large sums are paid off within these time limits, you will save $10 or $20 a month in finance charges.

For further information:

Twelve Ways to Earn Big Dollars with Your Credit Cards: How to Make Gold from Your Plastics. Earl Weinreb and Harold Prince. New York, Prince Communications, 1974.

LET US ASSUME

Shopping for an older home? By assuming the owner's mortgage rather than obtaining a new one, you will eliminate some paperwork in escrow and save valuable dollars in closing costs. Furthermore, an older mortgage will invariably carry a lower interest rate than the modern version.

Naturally, when assuming a mortgage, you'll have to reimburse the owner for the equity he has in the property.

VARIABLE RATE MORTGAGES

If you're planning to take out a home mortgage during a time when interest rates are high, there may just be a way to make the interest rate more favorable to you. Hard bargaining can get you a variable rate clause in the mortgage which allows the interest rate to come down on your mortgage as the market comes down. Many times the interest rate is tied to the prime rate (the interest rate charged by banks to their lowest-risk customers), with the interest rate on the loan running one percent higher than the prime rate.

You'll want to argue your way *out* of this clause, should you find it in a loan agreement during a low-interest market.

PREPAYMENT PLANNING

Making sure that you can prepay your mortgage without interest penalties can save you hundreds of dollars. Before you sign that mortgage, first be sure that no prepayment penalty clause is included. Second, make sure that the payment clause states a certain sum (say $300) *"or more"* is to be paid each month. (If those two words are omitted, the lender may refused to let you prepay.)

For further information:

The Complete Home Owner's Guide: From Mortgage to Maintenance, John Doyle. Englewood Cliffs, New Jersey, Reston (orders to Prentice-Hall), 1975.

Your Home: Building, Buying, Financing, L. Donald Meyers and Richard Demske. Englewood Cliffs, New Jersey, Reston (orders to Prentice-Hall), 1975.

MORTGAGE MANEUVERS

While it is generally true that a heavy down payment on a house will reduce your interest charges, there are times when it will be to your financial advantage to make as low a down payment as possible.

If a high down payment would force you to buy such costly items as a car, furniture, or home improvements at an interest rate higher than that of your mortgage, it is obviously cheaper to "borrow" on the mortgage and pay cash on the high-interest items.

THE FHA WAY

One of the cheapest ways to finance home improvements is to arrange for an FHA loan through a bank, finance company, savings and loan association, or other lender, before work is begun. FHA Title 203K loans can be had for sums from $2,500 to $10,000 at 9 percent interest plus a ½ percent insurance. Work done under this type of loan must be approved by the FHA before payment is granted. Thus, you are assured that the contractor will do good work on your property.

For further information:

Mortgage Insurance Information (203K), Central Office, Department of Housing and Urban Development, 451 Seventh Street, Washington, D.C. 20410.

TIME IS MONEY

Creditors at the door, on the phone, and in the mail? There *is* a legal way to obtain a breathing space of about three years in which to pay off the bills—without filing for straight bankruptcy. Under Chapter 13 of the Bankruptcy Act, the wage earner, and under Chapter 16, the businessperson, can apply for this extension of payment time.

Since this procedure will cost at least several hundred dollars in filing fees, attorney's fees, and so forth, it should only be used if your debts number in the thousands of dollars, and then only as a last resort. The advantage of the method lies, of course, in the fact that you not only get your creditors off your back for a while, but you avoid losing all your assets as you would if you simply filed for straight bankruptcy.

To initiate this action, you must petition the federal bankruptcy court. Check with your attorney or the Legal Aid Society for help in filing.

For further information:

How to Get Completely Out of Debt Through Chapter 13, Melvin Kaplan. Boston, Finan.

DROWNING IN DEBT?

Whatever you do, don't let the hounding of creditors drive you to a commercial debt adjuster. Many of these cannot be trusted with your money, and those who can will charge you 10 to 15 percent of your debt to ease your burden.

Many communities across the nation feature credit-counseling services, sponsored by banks and other lenders, which will help you budget your bills at no cost to you.

Your credit union may ease your debt burden with counseling and by consolidating several high-interest loans into one low-interest one.

For trustworthy debt help at a fee based on your ability to pay, go to one of the Family Service agencies which exist in most large communities. They will also tell you if help is available from other community organizations.

For further information:

What to Do When Your Bills Exceed Your Paycheck: Everything You Need to Know About Getting Out of Debt, Sidney Sherwin. Englewood Cliffs, New Jersey, Prentice-Hall, 1974.

1975 Directory of Member Agencies (family service), compiled by the FSAA Library. New York, Family Service Association of America, 1975 (at your library).

Wills and Funerals

FUNERAL FRUGALITY

Recent best-sellers have made everyone aware of the many devious schemes employed by the funeral industry. As a result, nonprofit memorial societies have been established across the nation to provide inexpensive funerals with dignity. Members must pay a small membership fee. The burial cost is about one third that of the traditional funeral home.

For further information:

Memorial Associations: What They Are and How They Are Organized, Continental Association of Funeral and Memorial Societies, 1828 L Street, N.W., Washington, D.C. 20036.

FAMILY GRAVEYARD

In our grandparents' time, when America was far more rural than urban, farm families buried their kin on the land they'd known and loved—in the family graveyard. These days, most folk are buried in an impersonal, expensive plot of ground invariably run by an unctuously money-hungry "memorial garden."

It may surprise you to know that burying your family on your own land is *not* illegal in many rural areas of the country. Furthermore, most people would prefer the "personal touch" of this act. Check with your local health department to find out if this is allowed where you live.

For further information:

Manual of Death Education and Simple Burial, Ernest Morgan. Burnsville, North Carolina, Celo Press, 1975.

CADAVER PALAVER

One way to eliminate burial costs and perform one last palpable service for the living at the same time is to donate your body to a medical school. As much as we would like to avoid the subject, it must be stated that these schools are in constant need of cadavers for educational purposes.

If your choose this eminently practical solution to the high cost of dying, discuss your decision with the medical school of your choice. They will help you make all the necessary arrangements.

CONSIDER CREMATION

If your preferences lie toward cremation, check out the simple cremation services offered by such societies as Telophase and Neptune (both West Coast) listed in your Yellow Pages under "Prearranged cremation services." These services cost one fourth as much as the simplest form of traditional burial, which runs well over $1,000. For example, Telophase offers a basic cremation service at $250 for members (plus a $15 membership fee) and $300 for nonmembers. The body is simply refrigerated, not embalmed, and is placed in a shroud rather than a casket.

CASKET COGENCY

When a body is to be cremated, the casket (not to mention the money spent for it) will also go up in smoke. So don't let some "sympathetic" mortician talk you into wasting a cool grand or two on a luxury casket. Instead, arrange to rent a suitable casket for viewing the remains, then have the body transferred to a corrugated-box casket before cremation.

This should cost less than a hundred dollars, by far the more sensible approach.

This service, however, is not available in all states, due to laws prohibiting the reuse of caskets.

BURIAL BENEFITS

If you qualify for social security payments, you're entitled to up to $255 toward your funeral expenses. If you're a veteran, not only you, but your spouse, minor children—and in some cases, unmarried adult children—are all entitled to free burial in a national cemetery.

Are you receiving public assistance? Check with your local Department of Public Welfare to see if you qualify for a burial allowance. (The amount varies from state to state.)

For further information:

The National Underwriter Company Social Security Manual. Cincinnati, The National Underwriter Company, 1975.

Federal Benefits for Veterans and Dependents, VA IS–1 Fact Sheet, 1 January 1975. Superintendent of Documents, U.S. Government Printing Office, Washington, D.C. 20402, stock number 051–0–00078–1, 75¢. Also available free from your local Veteran's Administration office.

1975 Public Welfare Directory, Perry Frank, ed. Washington, D.C., American Public Welfare Association, 1975 (lists welfare offices).

A FEW CRYPTIC REMARKS

Due to a combination of increasing population and decreasing land availability, a new type of "skyscraper" is beginning to dot the skylines of our large metropolitan areas: the high-rise mausoleum.

In the New York area, a crypt in such a structure sells for as little as one fourth of the cost of a traditional burial. In other regions, savings are smaller but still substantial—$500 or so for a double burial.

See your Yellow Pages under "Mausoleums."

A TRUSTY SOLUTION

If you're fortunate enough to be in a higher income-tax bracket, consider setting up a trust account for your beneficiaries in lower tax brackets. The income from the trust money is then taxed to your beneficiaries, who will pay less tax because of their lower brackets.

In addition, they will not pay an inheritance tax on the trust. And you will not pay a gift tax if you keep the trust contributions within the gift-tax limits.

For further information:

How to Make a Will, How to Use Trusts, P. J. T. Callahan and Oceana Editorial Staff. Dobbs Ferry, New York, Oceana Publications, 1975.

JOINT JOYS

The best way to avoid the expenses of probate court—which can amount to over $1,000 in court costs and executor, appraisal, and legal fees for a modest $10,000 estate—is for you and your beneficiary to become joint tenants. Under this arrangement, either party has full ownership and access to their joint assets in the event of the other's death.

Joint tenancy is accomplished very simply by stating on the certificate of ownership for your car, savings account, stocks, bonds, or other tangible assets the full name of each joint tenant, plus the words, "joint tenants with right of survivorship, and not as tenants in common."

Before you undertake this change, consult your local Legal Aid Society or your attorney for laws that apply in your locality.

For further information:

"When to Own Things Jointly," *Good Housekeeping*, Vol. 181, July 1975, page 150.

WILL WISDOM

If your estate is sizeable, and if you intend that your children as well as your spouse

benefit from it, don't will all of it to your spouse. If you do, the estate will be taxed once when it passes to the spouse, and again when the spouse dies and it passes on to the children.

The simple solution: Will half your estate to your spouse, and have half set up as a trust fund for the children with the spouse drawing on the income that develops, but not on the principal. This second method saves you about 75 percent in taxes—money that your heirs may someday need.

For further information:

You and Your Will: The Planning and Management of Your Estate, Paul Ashley. New York, McGraw-Hill, 1975.

How to Get Anything at Half Price

SURPLUS SHOWDOWN

Here's how to purchase the same surplus merchandise sold by army and navy stores at the prices for which *they* purchase it. Write to Property Disposal Service, Federal Center, Battle Creek, Michigan 49016, and request a bidder's application. Along with the application, they will send you a list of Defense Surplus Sales Offices which sell the merchandise wholesale.

For other bargains, check with surplus property disposal officers at nearby military bases for addresses of offices not on this list.

BIDDER BRAININESS

Your bidder's application (see previous entry), can get you everything from $9,000 worth of toggle switches for $57 to old buses for under $500. When you fill it out, be sure to include nearby locations and to specify every type of merchandise in which you are interested, then return it to the sender. Keep the sale catalogs they send you. When an item interests you, first check previous catalogs until you find a similar sale in the past. Next, send to Bidder's Service Company, Drawer 1790, Fort Stockton, Texas 79735, for an abstract of the prior sale ($2.50 each for first two, $5 each thereafter). This will tell you what bid won the last batch.

Now bid this amount for the merchandise currently offered. Even if your bid falls through, you can contact the person who bought the previous items and ask to buy a portion for a small markup.

For further information:

How to Buy Surplus Personal Property. Superintendent of Documents, U.S. Government Printing Office, Washington, D.C. 20402 (25¢).

GSA SURPLUS

Want an old post office van for $120 or $180? Or a post office motor scooter for $37.50 to $175? How about an old Forest Ranger horse or Job Corps kiln? These are just a few of the many surplus items available at fantastic bargains through another government agency: The General Services Administration. The agency's address is General Service Administration, Office of Property Management, Property Management and Disposal Service, Sales Branch, Washington, D.C. 20406.

Ask them for the address of the regional office nearest you. Then request a surplus personal property mailing list application from your regional office.

MAIL TALE

The dead-letter auctions sponsored yearly by post offices all over the country sell every conceivable type of merchandise from art objects to zithers. But these items are sold as is, so watch youself!

Customs houses often offer similar auctions of undeliverable goods from overseas—jewelry, perfume, handmade clothing, musical instruments—just about everything but dope! One of Vivo's friends picked up a year's supply of imported liquor at such an auction!

Check with your local post office and customs house for auction dates.

For further information:

U.S. Post Office, 475 L'Enfante Plaza West, S.W., Washington, D.C. 20260.

U.S. Customs Service, 2100 K Street, N.W., Washington, D.C. 20229.

OPTION TO BUY

In renting anything from a waterbed to a wheelchair, have it understood—in writing—that your rental payments can be applied to the purchase price of the item. A friend of ours in San Francisco rented a wheelchair for what was to be a short time, and she ended up paying three times the cost of a new one. Smart shopping (if this is possible while one is in pain) would have made the wheelchair hers after a year, allowing her to resell and recoup part of the investment when she recovered.

This kind of arrangement makes even more sense with a roomful of furniture, or a large item such as an organ or piano.

For further information:

The Consumer's Handbook: 100 Ways to Get More Value for Your Dollars. Editors of *The National Observer.* Princeton, New Jersey, Dow Jones, 1969.

COLLEGE CAPERS

One of the least expensive ways to purchase high-quality artwork is through the art department of a local college or university. Students will often settle for far less in price than the professional artist, yet the work of some students is better than that of many old-time professionals.

While you're at it, ask your college photographic or visual arts department for the names of students willing to take those family portraits you need at cut-rate prices. Check with the accounting department for help on your books, and secretarial students for part-time typing at a big discount. Planning to learn a foreign language? For heaven's sake, don't go to a commercial language school. Get yourself an inexpensive student tutor through the school's language department!

FREE ADVICE

Need firsthand advice on nutrition, new cars, nuts and bolts? Practical and technical information on these and a multitude of other subjects can be had for the asking from professionals at land-grant college extension services and county agricultural and home economics extension offices throughout the country.

Before you fork out for how-to books on any subject (except the book you're holding now, of course), check into the prodigious profusion of practical pamphlets available through these same extension services and through your state college.

For further information:

See the "Farm and home advisor" or "Agricultural extension service" listing under the White Pages listings for your county.

GREAT GIVEAWAYS

You can receive samples of soap, toothpaste, cigarettes—even cosmetics—by mail in exchange for telling manufacturers what you think of their products. Write to The Moneytree Club, Consumer Panel Department, 417 Water Street, Task Building, Kerrville, Texas 78028. Enclose a quarter for handling, and request a preference form.

After filling out and sending in the form, you'll start receiving regular shipments of free goods—no strings attached! Sort of like a year-round mail-order Santa Claus!